Globalisation and Natural Resources Law

To my boys. EMB

Globalisation and Natural Resources Law

Law

Challenges, Key Issues and Perspectives

Elena Merino Blanco

Senior Lecturer in Law, University of the West of England, UK

Jona Razzaque

Reader in Law, University of the West of England, UK

Edward Elgar

Cheltenham, UK • Northampton, MA, USA

Published by
Edward Elgar Publishing Limited
The Lypiatts
15 Lansdown Road
Cheltenham
Glos GL50 2JA
UK

Edward Elgar Publishing, Inc.
William Pratt House
9 Dewey Court
Northampton
Massachusetts 01060
USA

A catalogue record for this book
is available from the British Library

Library of Congress Control Number: 2009941151

ISBN   978 1 84844 249 8 (cased)
       978 1 84844 250 4 (paperback)

Typeset by Servis Filmsetting Ltd, Stockport, Cheshire
Printed and bound by MPG Books Group, UK

Contents

Boxes

Preface and acknowledgments

It is now twelve years since the first postgraduate course on 'Globalisation and Law' was taught on the LLM Programme at the Bristol Law School (UWE) and much has changed during this time. The design of the course emerged from ideas derived from international economic law, human rights, trade and the environment, natural resources, public international law and law and development courses studied and taught over the years. For the first couple of years the readings for the seminars were collected from a variety of disciplines, legal and non-legal, and the focus was on legal and institutional reform.

Now, the developments in human rights law, the attention devoted to multinational corporations, the economic upheavals that have challenged beliefs on unlimited economic growth through trade and investment liberalisation and the emergence of a consensus on the pressing urgency to solve global environmental problems and the finiteness of the earth's resources present a very diffident landscape for intellectual study and enquiry.

During our teaching of globalisation, international environmental law and natural resources law courses, we have had the opportunity to discuss at length the global nature of environmental issues and regulation and, crucially, the essential role that natural resources play in the process of economic globalisation. Time and again access, exploitation, management and control over natural resources appeared at the axis of the globalisation process. Globalisation, trade and natural resources law became so intertwined in our numerous conversations, our courses on globalisation, international trade and natural resources law respectively and our research that we decided to write a book on *Globalisation and Natural Resources Law* that would bring together the disperse and multiple theories, ideas and materials used for our courses.

While the rationale, underlying thesis and propositions are outlined in the introduction, we would like to use this short preface and acknowledgments page to thank a few people who have made this project possible and pleasurable.

In the first place, we would like to thank Professor Ed Cape and the Centre for Legal Research at the Bristol Law School (University of the West of England) for the support offered by way of funding a research sabbatical for both authors.

We would also like to thank our students who have taken courses on Globalisation and on Natural Resources Law as part of their LLM at the Bristol Law School. Their intellectual curiosity, commitment and enthusiasm for the courses have been, and continue to be, a constant source of inspiration.

Edward Elgar, Felicity Plester, Jenny Wilcox and Kate Pearce at EEP have made the often tortuous publishing process a pleasurable one. Their enthusiastic reception of our proposal, now almost two years ago, and the professional and friendly handling of the editorial phase are greatly appreciated. We also thank the reviewers for their insightful comments and suggestions that helped us to improve the mansucript.

Last, but certainly not least, we want to express wholehearted thanks to our families for their constant support, encouragement and inspiration and for making it possible to have the best of both worlds: a fulfilling career and a happy family life!

EMB and JR, Bristol 2011

Abbreviations

ABS	Access and benefit sharing
APEC	Asia-Pacific Economic Co-operation
ASEAN	Association of South East Asian Nations
BITs	Bilateral investment treaties
CBD	Convention on Biological Diversity
CDM	Clean development mechanism
CER	Certified emission reduction
CHM	Common heritage of Mankind
CITES	Convention on International Trade in Endangered Species of Wild Fauna & Flora
EC	European Community
ECHR	European Convention on Human Rights
ECtHR	European Court of Human Rights
ECE	Economic Commission for Europe (of the UN)
ECOSOC	Economic and Social Council (of the UN)
ECT	Energy Charter Treaty
EEC	European Economic Community
EIA	Environmental impact assessment
EIT	Economies in transition
ERU	Emission reduction units
ET	Emissions trading
EU	European Union
FAO	Food and Agriculture Organization (of the UN)
FCCC	UN Framework Convention on Climate Change
G-77	Group of 77 (developing countries)
GA	General Assembly (of the UN)
GATS	General Agreement on Trade in Services
GATT	General Agreement on Tariffs and Trade
GEF	Global environment facility
GHG	Greenhouse gases
IACHR	Inter-American Convention on Human Rights
IAEA	International Atomic Energy Agency
IBRD	International Bank for Reconstruction and Development (World Bank)
ICJ	International Court of Justice

ICSID	International Centre for the Settlement of Investment Disputes
IEA	International Energy Agency
IFC	International Finance Corporation
ILA	International Law Association
ILC	UN International Law Commission
ILM	International Legal Materials
ILO	International Labour Organization
IMF	International Monetary Fund
IPR	Intellectual property right
ITLOS	International Tribunal for the Law of the Sea
ITPGRFA	International Treaty on Plant Genetic Resources for Food and Agriculture
IUCN	International Union for Conservation of Nature and Natural Resources
JI	Joint implementation
LCA	Life cycle assessment
MAT	Mutually agreed terms
MDG	Millennium development goals
MEA	Multilateral environmental agreements
MERCOSUR	Mercado Común del Sur
MFN	Most favoured nation
MIGA	Multilateral Investment Guarantee Agency
NAFTA	North American Free Trade Agreement
NGOs	Non-governmental organisations
NIEO	New international economic order
OAU	Organization of African Unity
OECD	Organisation for Economic Co-operation and Development
OPEC	Organization of Petroleum Exporting Countries
PCA	Permanent Court of Arbitration
PCIJ	Permanent Court of International Justice
PIC	Prior informed consent
PIL	Public interest litigation
PPP	Polluter pays principle
PSNR	Permanent sovereignty over natural resources
PV	Photovoltaics
REN	Renewable energy network
SAAR	South Asian Association for Regional Cooperation
SEA	Strategic environmental assessment
TNCs	Transnational corporations
TRIMs	Trade-related investment measures

TRIPs	Trade-related intellectual property rights
TK	Traditional knowledge
UK	United Kingdom
UN	United Nations
UNCED	UN Conference on Environment and Development
UNCITRAL	UN Commission on International Trade Law
UNCLOS	UN Conference on the Law of the Sea
UNCTAD	UN Conference on Trade and Development
UNDP	UN Development Programme
UNEP	UN Environment Programme
UNESCO	UN Educational, Scientific and Cultural Organization
UNGA	UN General Assembly (also given as GA)
UNTS	UN Treaty Series
USA	United States of America
WCED	World Commission on Environment and Development
WEHAB	Water, Energy, Health, Agriculture and Biodiversity
WFD	Water Framework Directive (of the EU)
WIPO	World Intellectual Property Organization
WTO	World Trade Organization
WSSD	World Summit on Sustainable Development
WW II	World War II

Treaties

Introduction

The relationship between globalisation, natural resources and economic growth is undeniably complex. The process of globalisation, with its increased volume of world trade, transport and communications and the growing affluence it creates, depends on the Earth's resources for its very existence.

Globalisation opens up the natural resource market and promotes economic liberalisation. Consequently, globalisation has an important role in determining the way a state manages and implements laws and regulations to protect and preserve natural resources. While the global recession of 2008 has illustrated the intertwining nature of the global economy and the lack of sufficient and adequate institutions of governance to deal with global concerns, it has also highlighted that much of the economy rests upon unsustainable factors. For example, consumption patterns in developed and developing countries alike show a dependence on non-renewable resources such as coal, gas and oil. While the energy sector is one of the most profitable sectors advancing economic growth, it also adds to the growing greenhouse gas (GHG) emissions which in turn contribute to climate change.

There is a tension between the North and the South[1] regarding the ways to manage natural resources sustainably. Some resource rich developing countries push an unsustainable development path causing adverse environmental, socio-economic and related transboundary impacts. However, it is easier for the developed countries to call for a restricted approach to exploring natural resources when they have attained a certain level of economic development. The inability of the developed countries to reduce over-consumption of resources, regulate multinational enterprises causing destruction in the resource sector and control effectively their carbon footprints suggests a double standard. The distrust between the North and the South was evident during the negotiations of the Climate Change Convention and the Biodiversity Convention in 1992[2] and has remained

---

[1]   The term 'North' refers to the developed countries and 'South' refers to the developing or least developed countries of Asia, Africa and Latin America.
[2]   Drumbl, M.A. (2002), 'Poverty, Wealth and Obligation in International Environmental Law', 76 Tulane Law Review 843.

largely unaltered. This is exemplified in the failed efforts at Copenhagen to agree on a multilateral regime to curb carbon emissions which would be fair and acceptable to both developed and developing countries. In addition, developed countries have more political leverage to shape international agendas on natural resource management conducive to their needs, whereas most developing countries play a less active role. As developing countries such as China, India and Brazil take over the leading role of driving the world economy new tensions over traditional principles such as the scope of the right of permanent sovereignty over natural resources arise.

Free trade promoted by globalisation has a spill-over effect. Thus, problems occurring at the national level are no longer purely national – be it GHG from factories or financial meltdown at the banking sector. This requires initiatives at the global and regional scales. Many of the problems afflicting the world today, such as poverty, environmental pollution and economic crises, are increasingly transnational in nature and cannot be dealt with only at the national level. A combination of inclusive decisionmaking at the national level allowing public participation along with an effective international legal framework can lead to sustainable management of natural resources. Focusing only on a country specific management of resources can pose several problems including the over-emphasis of the sovereignty over natural resources and raises questions such as whether the state shares benefits arising from resource use with the resource holders, whether the state follows sustainable practices to manage natural resources and whether the state expropriates foreign investments with appropriate compensation. A global mechanism to protect natural resources provides guidance to states and, by providing cooperative approaches to managing natural resources, makes globalisation part of the solution.

In this book we argue that, along with an effective legal framework for economic activities, strong institutions of governance, rule of law and independent judicial institutions are important to managing natural resources. Sustainable resource management requires national mechanisms which facilitate inclusive multilayered governance complemented by an international legal framework where state and non-state actors adopt cooperative approaches to managing natural resources. Several points arise out of this proposition.

First, the role of law is crucial to integrating economic and natural resource governance within the context of globalisation.[3] Global legal

---

[3]   Discussed in chapters 1, 2 and 3.

frameworks promoting sustainable use, e.g. biodiversity conservation or the reduction of GHGs, limit the way natural resources are explored and managed at the domestic level. The formulation of sovereignty and ownership of natural resources needs to be appraised if global approaches are to work. While countries like China and India challenge the traditional division between developed and developing countries and their unprecedented growth has created a surge in demand for natural resources, it is important that their development does not lead to unsustainable use of natural resources. Some of the fast growing developing countries are formulating economic and environmental legal instruments to protect their natural resources (e.g. biodiversity laws in India) and investing in clean energy (e.g. wind farms in China). Along with these positive steps, there is an urgent need for a widely shared agreement and understanding of sustainable resource use.

Second, rights-based approaches, including the existence of a right to natural resources, can provide a tool of empowerment for the people and impose a duty on the government to utilise natural resources for the benefit of the entire population.[4] Moreover, adequate access to information, participation in the decision-making process and access to justice remain crucial for individuals. At the national level, there are tensions between the different levels of government (national, regional, local) and citizens over the control and management of natural resources. This tension is demonstrated in the confrontation between indigenous peoples and national governments over natural resource ownership, use and enjoyment. While permanent sovereignty equates to the exclusive right of states to extract or exploit natural resources and legislate in the resource sector, that does not always ensure the overall sustainable management of the resource sector. Both privatisation, e.g. water, and benefit-sharing agreements, e.g. biological resources, of natural resources largely depend on the strength of the contractual arrangement between the state and the non-state actors. Weak consultation and public participation mechanisms generally lead to poor management of natural resources. Governments as custodians or trustees of natural resources need to act for the common good of all the people in the country.

Third, transnational social and economic actors (e.g. multinational corporations, non-governmental organisations) have become forceful in the global context and play a crucial role in natural resource management, sometimes even more powerful than that of an individual state.[5] Weak

---

4   Discussed in chapters 3, 7 and 9.
5   Discussed in chapters 4 and 5.

regulation or exclusion from relevant governance institutions of non-state actors needs to be superseded by an inclusive system of participation and responsibility. Both state and non-state actors can and should work together.

Fourth, an open and competitive sustainable resource management needs to be supported by the regulatory and enforcement capacity of the state.[6] The recent economic and financial crisis and its aftermath have thrown a new perspective on the importance of strong regulatory mechanisms and institutions alongside market mechanisms. Yet, the development of these mechanisms and institutions on resource governance lags behind in relation to the development of the institutions of economic governance.[7] A renewed role for the state in the regulation of resources within and outside the realm of permanent sovereignty needs to be delineated.[8] In the context of shared natural resources, existing global, regional or bilateral arrangements do not always provide adequate protection. For resources within one state, over-emphasis of sovereignty over natural resources may provide weak protection to the resource holders. Examples from water, biodiversity or energy resources show that global or regional management can offer better protection than private management of natural resources.[9]

The discussion in this chapter shows that the concept of globalisation is intrinsically linked to resource management and that a shift from economic globalisation to sustainable globalisation is one of the consequences of the globalisation process itself. The changing pattern of resource management can be observed in the way resources are regulated nationally and at the transboundary level. International actors and institutions bring their own values and priorities into resource management, and legal instruments promote cooperative approaches allowing local people to play a more active role. This chapter also shows that international and regional laws restrict the absolute nature of sovereignty. Moreover, the rights of states to exercise permanent sovereignty over natural resources are limited by certain duties towards their own people. These duties have led some countries to opt for better conservation and regulatory practices, and efficient use of natural resources. Together, these external and internal dynamisms of sovereignty have contributed to the way globalisation influences natural resource management.

---

[6] Discussed in chapter 6.
[7] See chapters 1 and 4.
[8] Discussed in chapters 2 and 4.
[9] Discussed in chapters 7, 8 and 9.

1. RECENT TRENDS OF GLOBALISATION AND NATURAL RESOURCE MANAGEMENT

The present form of globalisation has a long history. To understand the meaning of contemporary globalisation requires us to look back. The 1944 Bretton Woods Agreement showed the true nature of pure economic globalisation between 1945 and 1970 with the development of a global finance mechanism through institutionalised entities such as the International Monetary Fund (IMF) and the World Bank. The effect of globalisation of mass production/consumption and investment was seen across boundaries. By the late 1960s, multilateral development aid increased in the developing countries as part of redistribution of wealth from the North to the South.[10] During the 1970s, the world went through economic turbulences in the form of a rise in oil price, export stagnation and increased national debts.[11] With the unequal bargaining power of the South in the world trading system (i.e. General Agreement on Tariffs and Trade – GATT), there was a recognition that a fundamental change was required at the global economic system.[12] At the same time, the UN agencies called for a 'New International Economic Order' (NIEO) which included proposals for South–South cooperation, transfer of technology, global regulation of multilateral corporations and increased multilateral aid.[13] Several UN declarations also reinforced states' right to regulate foreign commerce and investment and to permanent sovereignty over their natural resources.[14] NIEO drew resistance from the North, which was evident when the initiatives to control corporate bodies ended up as voluntary codes of conduct.[15]

The Washington Consensus shaped the global economic agenda during the late 1980s and 1990s. At the international level, the financial

---

[10] Kennedy, D. (2006), 'The "Rule of Law", Political Choices and Development Common Sense' in D.M. Trubek and A. Santos (eds), *The New Law and Economic Development: A Critical Appraisal*, Cambridge: Cambridge University Press, 115.

[11] Ibid. 111.

[12] Ibid. 114.

[13] General Assembly (1974), Declaration on the Establishment of a New International Economic Order, UN Doc A/RES/S-6/3201.

[14] For example, Permanent Sovereignty over Natural Resources, GA Res. 1803 (XVII), 17 U.N. GAOR Supp. (No.17) at 15, UN Doc. A/5217 (1962). GA Res. 2692 (XXV) 1970 on Permanent Sovereignty over Natural Resources of Developing Countries and Expansion of Domestic Sources of Accumulation for Economic Development. Programme of Action on the Establishment of a New International Economic Order and 3281 (XXIX) 1974 Charter of Economic Rights and Duties of States.

[15] Kennedy (2006), supra, 116.

institutions – the IMF, GATT and the World Bank – encouraged the developing countries to promote corporate law reform, establish more open and efficient financial markets, and support local enterprises. Their idea of neoliberalism (e.g. privatisation, market liberalisation) can be summarised in one word: reform. Implementation of neoliberal policies was one of the conditions attached to the IMF funds, and GATT's non-tariff barriers to trade had their implications on developing countries in the form of progressive elimination of national regulatory barriers to trade. Joseph Stiglitz, a staunch critic of 'Washington Consensus' summarised the impact of neoliberal policies on the developing countries:[16]

> . . . In many parts of the world, global institutions such as the International Monetary Fund and the World Bank came to be seen as instruments of postcolonial control. These institutions pushed market fundamentalism ('neoliberalism,' it was often called), a notion idealized by Americans as 'free and unfettered markets.' They pressed for financial-sector deregulation, privatization, and trade liberalization.

> The World Bank and the I.M.F. said they were doing all this for the benefit of the developing world. They were backed up by teams of free-market economists, many from that cathedral of free-market economics, the University of Chicago. In the end, the programs of 'the Chicago boys' didn't bring the promised results. Incomes stagnated. Where there was growth, the wealth went to those at the top. Economic crises in individual countries became ever more frequent – there have been more than a hundred severe ones in the past 30 years alone.

> Not surprisingly, people in developing countries became less and less convinced that Western help was motivated by altruism. They suspected that the free-market rhetoric – 'the Washington consensus,' as it is known in shorthand – was just a cover for the old commercial interests. Suspicions were reinforced by the West's own hypocrisy. Europe and America didn't open up their own markets to the agricultural produce of the Third World, which was often all these poor countries had to offer. They forced developing countries to eliminate subsidies aimed at creating new industries, even as they provided massive subsidies to their own farmers.

> Free-market ideology turned out to be an excuse for new forms of exploitation. 'Privatization' meant that foreigners could buy mines and oil fields in developing countries at low prices. It meant they could reap large profits from monopolies and quasi-monopolies, such as in telecommunications. 'Liberalization' meant that they could get high returns on their loans – and when loans went bad, the I.M.F. forced the socialization of the losses, meaning that the screws were put on entire populations to pay the banks back. It meant, too, that

---

[16]   Stiglitz, J. (2009), Wall Street's Toxic Message, *Vanity Fair*, July. Available at: www.vanityfair.com/politics/features/2009/07/third-world-debt200907 (accessed 15 January 2009).

foreign firms could wipe out nascent industries, suppressing the development of entrepreneurial talent. While capital flowed freely, labor did not – except in the case of the most talented individuals, who found good jobs in a global marketplace.

The disappointment with the economic as well as the political and social results of the neoliberal approach became apparent in the growing popular opposition to 'structural adjustment' policies across the South, and a widespread vulnerability in the North to globalisation. As faith in neoliberalism waned, states and non-state actors pushed the agenda of strengthening of national institutions and legal systems, procedural arrangements for decision-making and legal frameworks to accommodate a robust and active 'civil society'. There are growing signs of South–South cooperation, e.g. in the agenda setting for global trade talks targeting agricultural subsidies and non-tariff barriers, supporting one another in resisting the intellectual property rules within the WTO, and formulating adaptation funds under the Climate Change Convention. The unsustainable nature of contemporary globalisation has led to a fairness deficit and opened a space for new thinking about globalisation. The discussion below focuses on some of the trends which are explored further in the book. This discussion underscores several points: first, various international agreements (e.g. trade and environmental agreements) and institutions (e.g. UN, WTO) influence the shift of economic globalisation towards sustainability. Second, the sovereign rights of states over natural resources can be limited by international agreements. Third, states have a duty to share sovereign rights with their citizens in order to manage their natural resources efficiently. Fourth, empowering and involving people in the formulation and implementation of decisions on resource use can lead to sustainable resource governance.

1.1. From Economic Globalisation to Sustainable Globalisation

Economic globalisation, by removing trade barriers, liberalisation of world capital markets and rapid technological progress, has vastly accelerated the movement of people, commodities and capital. For developing countries, economic globalisation has provided opportunities as it expands the size of their markets for export and attracts foreign capital which aids development. The effects of globalisation are not the same on every country, and some countries suffer more than others because they lack adequate legal frameworks and financial capacity to minimise the negative effects of economic globalisation.

Economic globalisation, promoted by the Bretton Woods institutions and followed globally, came at a price: environmental degradation and social inequality. The imbalances of the global economy are 'ethically unacceptable and politically unsustainable' and '[t]he benefits of globalization have been unequally distributed, both within and between countries'.[17] The environmental and social dimensions of sustainability were the focus of the Brundtland Commission's[18] definition of sustainable development:

> Sustainable development is development that meets the needs of the present without compromising the ability of future generations to meet their own needs.[19]

This definition highlights that environmental degradation and inequality are interdependent obstacles to sustainability. Moreover, the principle of equity in the distribution of income and wealth and control of resources between generations must be extended to the distribution within each generation.[20] Sustainable globalisation means respecting the natural diversity of life on Earth and ensuring equity between present and future generations. Managing globalisation in a sustainable fashion has also been part of the ethos behind the commitments in the Millennium Development Goals (MDGs).[21]

These international instruments clearly show that the growth of the global market depends on the equitable distribution of wealth and sustainable exploration of natural resources. Some of the changes are already demonstrated in the governance practices:[22] strengthening of local

---

[17]   World Commission on the Social Dimension of Globalisation (2004), *A Fair Globalisation: Creating Opportunities for all*, Geneva: International Labour Organization, 3.

[18]   GA Res. 38/161 (1983) established the Commission to address growing concern about the accelerating deterioration of the human environment and natural resources and the consequences of that deterioration for economic and social development. See GA Res. 42/187, Report of the World Commission on Environment and Development (11 December 1987), Preamble, para. 1.

[19]   Report of the World Commission on Environment and Development: *Our Common Future*, chapter 2 (1987). Published as Annex to GA Doc. A/42/427 (Geneva, Switzerland).

[20]   Borghesi, S. and A. Vercelli (2003), 'Sustainable Globalisation', *Ecological Economics*, 44, 77–78.

[21]   Especially, MDG Goal 7 (ensure environmental sustainability), Target 1. Goal 8 (develop a global partnership for development), Target 2.

[22]   For national indicators of sustainable development see National Information, Division for Sustainable Development, UN Department of Economic and Social Affairs, available at: www.un.org/esa/dsd/dsd_aofw_ni/ni_index.shtml (accessed 15 January 2010).

governments in managing natural resources and involving people at the lowest level of decision-making processes, integration of sustainable development principles into national policy frameworks, and creation of new incentives for linking sustainability to growth. Multinational companies are adopting sustainable practices via internal and external actions,[23] and international institutions (e.g. The World Bank) have reformed strategies related to natural resources – this shift in attitude is crucial to secure a fair and sustainable globalisation.[24]

1.2. Calibrating Resource Sovereignty

The state, with its sovereignty over natural resources, remains central to the well-being of its citizens and is responsible for adopting legal policies which are conducive to greater economic integration and sustainable development. The sovereignty of a state is an integral part of its existence along with three other elements – a permanent population, a defined territory and government.[25] Sovereignty includes the power to impose authority over the population, freely use or dispose of territory under the jurisdiction (i.e. internal sovereignty), and no other state can intrude into the state's territory (i.e. external sovereignty).[26] Permanent sovereignty over natural resources is a legal concept and closely linked to political and economic aspects of sovereignty.[27] Sovereignty over natural resources also includes a bundle of rights – e.g. the right to possess, the right to use, and the right to manage.[28] With the exclusive control and use of the natural resources within the territory, the state has the right to profits gained from the resources, and to conserve, explore and exploit these resources.[29]

---

[23] IISD (2007), Sustainable business practices: IISD Checklist. Available at: www.bsdglobal.com/tools/principles_sbp.asp (accessed 15 January 2010).

[24] Zoellick, R.B. (2007), An Inclusive & Sustainable Globalization (10 October), Speech delivered at the National Press Club, Washington, DC, USA. Available at: http://beta.worldbank.org/node/3854 (accessed 15 January 2010).

[25] Shaw, M. (2008), *International Law*, Cambridge: Cambridge University Press, pp. 197–204.

[26] Cassese, A, (2001), *International Law*, Oxford: Oxford University Press, pp. 88–89.

[27] Schrijver (1997), supra, chapters 2 and 3.

[28] Barnes, R. (2009), *Property Rights and Natural Resources*, Oxford: Hart, pp. 228–230.

[29] Ibid.

To ensure that states respect the public goods[30] there are certain limitations imposed on their sovereignty over natural resources. First, 'permanent sovereignty over natural resources has to be exercised for national development and the well being of the people'.[31] With the wide discretion to interpret, states' exercise of this duty may not always be beneficial to the people or natural resources. Second, the duty of a state is to compensate foreign investors whose property has been expropriated and provide due legal process.[32] States should enter into foreign investment agreements in good faith and respect the 'sovereignty of peoples and nations over their natural wealth and resources'.[33] Third, the state has a duty to protect the interest of indigenous peoples. Fourth, the state has a duty to cooperate in respect of shared natural resources,[34] to notify and consult people in activities linked to resource use.[35]

The non-absolute form of sovereignty suggests that states, by accepting the authority of international law, entering into international agreements and agreeing to abide by the rules of international institutions, have imposed restrictions on their resource sovereignty. This positive limitation on sovereignty includes ratification of international treaties (e.g. UN Charter, human rights and environmental treaties) and membership of regional organisations (e.g. European Union, ASEAN, NAFTA) and international institutions (e.g. WTO). The European Union (EU) provides a unique example because the membership of this regional body limits the power of the Member States to adopt decisions in certain areas. This surrender of absolute sovereignty means the supremacy of the EU law.[36] The EU jurisprudence and legislation apply between the supranational level

---

[30]   Public goods are non-rivalrous (available for all to consume) and non-excludable (no one can be effectively excluded from using the good). Wijen, F., K. Zoetman and J. Pieters (eds) (2005), *A Handbook of Globalisation and Environmental Policy: National Government Intervention in a Global Arena*, Cheltenham: Edward Elgar, UK and Northampton, MA, USA, 89–91.

[31]   Para. 1 of GA Res. 1803 (XVII), 17 UN GAOR Supp. (no 17) 15, UN Doc. A/5217 (1962), Article 1(2) of the International Covenant on Civil and Political Rights, 1966, 999 U.N.T.S. 171. Schrijver (1997), supra, 168.

[32]   Ibid., 339–364. Several conditions have to be fulfilled by the state in order to exercise the right to expropriation or nationalisation. Any expropriation has to be for a public purpose and be non-discriminatory. The state has to pay compensation, follow due process and provide a right to appeal. See also the discussion in chapter 1 of this book.

[33]   Paragraphs 4 and 8 of GA Res. 1803 (XVII), 14 December 1962.

[34]   Discussed in chapter 2.

[35]   Discussed in chapter 3.

[36]   *Costa v. ENEL* (case 6/64) [1964] ECR 585.

and the Member States, and at the level of Union citizens.[37] However, the EU should only act where 'the objectives of the proposed action cannot be achieved sufficiently by the Member States' and 'by reason of the scale or effects of the proposed action', the EU could achieve better result.[38] Applying the principle of subsidiarity, the EU has the power to adopt measures to achieve its environmental objectives.[39] As nature does not have any boundary, there is a clear case for protecting habitats, migratory species or water at the regional level.[40]

Several acts of sovereign states may also limit sovereignty, e.g. by allowing market access to foreign investors (e.g. under BITs), sharing the benefits of genetic resources (e.g. Biodiversity Convention) or settling disputes (e.g. by use of ICSID, ITLOS). By accepting funds from international financial institutions, the states accept conditions which may have an adverse social and environmental impact (e.g. structural adjustment funds). Apart from these external restrictions, states may also limit their sovereignty by allowing human rights bodies to determine the quality of life of citizens and to ascertain the property and ownership rights of indigenous people, and implementing international standards for export products.

Sovereignty of states is closely linked to two issues: transboundary nature and ownership of natural resources. Management of transboundary resources requires the participation of states in the joint management of shared resources through treaties at the international, regional or bilateral level. The discussion on ownership of natural resources shows that government, as custodian or trustee of the natural resources, should manage natural resources.

---

[37] Kramer, L. (2006), 'The EU: A Regional Model?', in G. Winter (ed.), *Multilevel Governance of Global Environmental Change*, Cambridge: Cambridge University Press, 333.

[38] Article 5(3) of the Treaty of the European Union. Official Journal of the European Union, C115/13 (2008).

[39] Articles 191 and 192 of the Treaty on the Functioning of the European Union, Official Journal of the European Union, C115/49 (2008).

[40] There is also the issue of spill-over effect which suggests the need for community-based nature protection. Physical spill-over effect deals with the transboundary nature of global warming, water or air pollution. Economic spill-over effect deals with product and process standards affecting trade and competition, and psychic spill-over effect deals with concerns linked to the 'integrity of nature and the well-being of various living creatures'. Wils, W.P.J. (1994), 'Subsidiarity and EC Environmental policy: Taking People's Concerns Seriously', Journal of Environmental Law 6, 88–89.

1.2.1.   Transboundary natural resources

Natural resources can be under the sovereignty of a state like land for agricultural production, tropical forests, national rivers or gas and oil reserves.[41] The most challenging to regulate are those resources that are shared between states and are of relevance and importance to the whole of humanity, like biodiversity, oil and gas, marine resources, international watercourses.

While each state has permanent sovereignty over its natural resources, each state also has an obligation, under customary international law, not to cause transboundary environmental damage.[42] There is an obligation on the source state not to cause harm to other states and the source state is 'not permitted to use its territory for purposes injurious to the interests of other states'.[43] This is a limit on sovereignty itself in the sense that the state is required to respect the sovereignty of other states. This limitation is apparent from customary international law,[44] international conventions,[45] regional conventions[46] and bilateral agreements as well as non-binding

---

[41]   Even then there are some unresolved issues of resource ownership between minorities, groups or indigenous peoples at the national level. See the discussion in chapters 1, 2 and 9.

[42]   See the further discussion in chapter 3. Principle 21 of Stockholm Declaration, Principle 2 of the Rio Declaration. Perrez, F. (1996), 'The Relationship between Permanent Sovereignty and the Obligation Not to Cause Transboundary Environmental Damage', Environmental Law, 26, 1187.

[43]   Okowa, P.N. (2000), *State Responsibility for Transboundary Air Pollution in International Law*, Oxford: Oxford University Press, 65.

[44]   *River Oder Case* (1929) PCIJ Ser. A, No. 23 (equality of use and no preferential privilege of any riparian state). *Trail Smelter Case* (1941) 35 AJIL 686 (not to cause damage to the territory of another state). *Lac Lanoux Arbitration* (1957) 24 ILR 119 (duty on states to cooperate and negotiate to resolve potential problems). *Advisory Opinion on the Legality of the Threat or Use of Nuclear Weapons* [1996] ICJ Rep. 226, at 241, para. 29.

[45]   1972 UNESCO Convention concerning the protection of the World Cultural and Natural Heritage, U.K.T.S. 2 (1985) Cmnd. 9424. 1985 Convention for the Protection of Ozone Layer, U.K.T.S. 1 (1990) Cm 910. 1989 Convention on the Control of Transboundary Movements of Hazardous Wastes and their Disposal, 28 I.L.M. (1989) 657. 1995 UN Agreement relating to the Conservation and Management of Straddling Fish Stocks and Migratory Fish Stocks, 34 I.L.M. (1995) 1542. 1998 Convention on Prior Informed Consent Procedure for Certain Hazardous Chemicals and Pesticides in International Trade, 38 I.L.M. (1999) 1.

[46]   1983 Convention on the Long-Range Transboundary Air Pollution, U.K.T.S. 57 (1983).Cmd 9034. 1991 Convention on Environmental Impact Assessment in a Transboundary Context (Espoo Convention), 30 I.L.M. (1971) 902. 1992 Convention on the Transboundary Effects of Industrial Accidents, 31 I.L.M. (1992) 1333. 1992 Convention on the Protection and Use of Transboundary Watercourses and Lakes, B&B Doc. 345. 1998 Convention on Access to

instruments.[47] These instruments set out an obligation to inform and consult one another prior to undertaking any activity likely to cause transboundary harm. For some shared resources, such as non-navigational uses of international watercourses, absolute sovereignty may lead to denial of access to water of the riparian states. Thus, in the *Gabcikovo-Nagymaros* case,[48] the ICJ applied the concept of 'community of interest' instead of sovereignty. A similar approach is found in the UN Convention on Non-Navigational Watercourses which applies on equitable utilisation and cooperation principle.[49]

International law does not provide any forum with compulsory jurisdiction to bring a transboundary environmental dispute. There is an 'uncertainty of the law of state responsibility as regards environmental damage and absence of clarity concerning the remedies available to states and their scope'.[50] Using national law to remedy transboundary damage to natural resources may not be satisfactory for a number of reasons: lack of effective remedy, problem of jurisdiction, unequal access to remedies, and lack of enforcement mechanisms.[51]

1.2.2. Ownership of natural resources

While the limits of sovereignty are still being debated at the academic level,[52] it is difficult to find a balance between the sovereignty of the state

---

Information, Public Participation in Decision Making and Access to Justice in Environmental Matters, 38 I.L.M. (1999) 517.

[47] 1978 UNEP Draft Principles of Conduct on Shared Natural Resources. UN GA Res. 3129 (XXVIII) on 'Cooperation in the field on the environment concerning natural resources shared by two or more states' and 3281 (XXIX) on the Charter of Economic Rights and Duties of States. 1976 OECD Council recommendations on Transfrontier Pollution and the Implementation of a Regime of Equal Right of Access and Non-Discrimination in Relation to Transfrontier Pollution, OECD Doc. C (74) 224. ILA 1966 Helsinki Rules and 2004 Berlin Rules on water resources. ILC Articles on the Prevention of Transboundary Harm from Hazardous Activities (2001).

[48] *Gabcikovo-Nagymaros Project (Hungary v. Slovakia)*, Judgment of 25 September 1997 [1997] ICJ Rep. 7, at 56, para. 85.

[49] Convention on the Non-Navigational Uses of International Watercourses 36 I.L.M. (1997) 719 (not in force). McCaffrey, S. (2007), *The Law of International Watercourses*, Oxford: Oxford University Press.

[50] Birnie, P., A. Boyle and C. Redgwell (2009), *International Law and Environment*, Oxford: Oxford University Press, 303.

[51] Ibid. 304.

[52] Anghie, A. (2004), *Imperialism, Sovereignty and the Making of International Law*, Cambridge: Cambridge University Press. Jackson, R. (ed.) (1999), *Sovereignty at the Millennium*, Oxford: Blackwell.

and the ownership[53] of natural resources. GA Resolution 1803 (XVII) in 1962 declared, inter alia:

1. The right of peoples and nations to permanent sovereignty over their natural wealth and resources must be exercised in the interest of their *national development* and of the *well-being of the people* of the State concerned.
2. The exploration, development and disposition of such resources, as well as the import of the foreign capital required for these purposes, should be in conformity with the rules and conditions which the peoples and nations *freely consider* to be *necessary or desirable* with regard to the authorization, restriction or prohibition of such activities.[54]

UN Resolution 1803 creates a right of sovereignty of peoples and nations. It shows that internal sovereignty is shared between peoples and the state, and implies that peoples have some control over the management and development of natural resources and have a right to be consulted. Common Article 1 of the International Covenant on Civil and Political Rights and the International Covenant on Economic, Social and Cultural Rights provides:

2. All peoples may, for their own ends, freely dispose of their natural wealth and resources *without prejudice to* any obligations arising out of international economic co-operation, based upon the principle of mutual benefit, and international law. In no case may a people be deprived of its own means of subsistence.

These Covenants further add:

Nothing in the present Covenant shall be interpreted as impairing the inherent right of all peoples to enjoy and utilize fully and freely their natural wealth and resources.[55]

---

[53] Ownership provides exclusive right and control over property. It gives the right to possess, use and enjoy the benefits and dispose of the natural resource to the exclusion of others. Natural resources which are considered as public properties do not fall under this definition. This chapter does not deal with ownership of the global commons.

[54] The 1966 Res. 2158 (XXI) on 'Permanent Sovereignty over Natural Resources' does not mention 'peoples'. The emphasis is shifted to 'states'. Schrijver, N. (1997), *Sovereignty over Natural Resources: Balancing Rights and Duties*, Cambridge: Cambridge University Press, 387.

[55] Article 47 of the Covenant on Civil and Political Rights and Article 25 of the Covenant on Economic, Social and Cultural Rights. Also, Article 21 of the African Charter on Human and Peoples' Rights.

The UN Resolutions and Human Rights Covenants emphasise that peoples[56] are free to consider how they want to utilise their natural resources. They proclaim peoples' sovereignty over their natural resources, and include people who are under colonial rule[57] as well as the entire population of a state.[58] These international documents do not make any clear distinction between territorial sovereignty and the ownership of natural resources. At the domestic level, the issue of ownership is largely guided by the constitutional right to natural resources, and is a combination of private, community and state ownership often requiring balancing of competing claims.[59] States may hold ownership of many resources important to the national economy in the name of 'people'. Natural resources can be privately owned by individuals or companies, or they may be part of community ownership whereby people have the collective right to enjoy and utilise the natural resources.[60] Even where the natural resources are under private or community ownership, the state by virtue of territorial sovereignty retains the right to regulate the way individuals or community exercise their property rights, and people will have the right to be compensated if the resources are expropriated.[61]

For indigenous peoples, the right to own their property and natural resources is acknowledged in UN Declarations,[62] Conventions,[63] regional human rights instruments[64] and case law.[65] These documents positively

---

[56] 'Peoples' may include those who are under colonial occupation, indigenous people, or the whole of the population. Duruigbo, E. (2006), 'Permanent Sovereignty and Peoples' Ownership of Natural Resources in International Law', 38 George Washington International Law Review 52.

[57] Anghie (2004), supra, 217. Anghie discusses the issue of people who are under colonial rule.

[58] Duruigbo (2006), supra, 52.

[59] Haysom, N. and S. Kane (2009), Negotiating natural resources for peace: Ownership, control and wealth-sharing, Briefing Paper, Geneva: Henry Durant Centre for Humanitarian Dialogue, 8–12.

[60] Hancock, J. (2003), *Environmental Human Rights: Power, Ethics, and Law*, Aldershot: Ashgate, 138–139.

[61] Lammers, J.G. (1984), *Pollution of International Watercourses*, The Hague: Martinus Nijhoff, 390–392.

[62] Articles 3, 4, 26–28, 32 of the UN Declaration on the Rights of Indigenous Peoples (2007), adopted by GA Res. 61/295 (13 September 2007).

[63] Articles 7, 15, International Labour Organization Indigenous and Tribal Peoples Convention No. 169/1989.

[64] 1969 American Convention on Human Rights; African Charter on Human and Peoples' Rights, adopted June 27, 1981, OAU Doc. CAB/LEG/67/3 rev. 5, 21 I.L.M. (1982) 58.

[65] *Awas Tingni Mayagna (Sumo) Indigenous Community v. Nicaragua*, Judgment of 31 August 2001, Inter-Am. Ct H.R. (Ser. C) No. 79 (2001). *Maya*

recognise a broad range of human rights held by indigenous peoples, most notably the right to own property, the right of ownership of the lands they historically or traditionally use and occupy, the rights to self-determination and autonomy, the right to development, the right to be free from discrimination, and a host of other human rights. However, Article 46(1) of the UN Declaration states:[66]

> Nothing in this Declaration may be interpreted as implying for any State, people, group or person any right to engage in any activity or to perform any act contrary to the Charter of the United Nations or construed as authorizing or encouraging any action which would dismember or impair, totally or in part, the territorial integrity or political unity of sovereign and independent states.

According to Schrijver,

> States are under an obligation to exercise permanent sovereignty on behalf of and in the interests of their (indigenous) peoples. This implies that states are increasingly accountable, also at an international level, for the way they manage their natural wealth and resources, but also that for the time being (indigenous) peoples . . . are objects rather than subjects of international law.[67]

This leads to the conclusion that indigenous peoples will continue to be deprived of their resources through mineral extraction, environmental contamination, expropriation of land, bioprospecting, patents and other intellectual property rights. While it can be argued that governments are the custodians or trustees of the natural resources for the benefit of present and future generations, it is difficult to ensure that the governments are discharging their responsibilities in good faith.[68]

1.3.　Improved Resource Efficiency and Sustainable Development

Economic growth stemming from globalisation continues to put pressures on scarce resources, particularly energy sources, and on the environment.

---

indigenous community of the Toledo District v. Belize, Case 12.053, Report No. 40/04, Inter-Am. Ct H.R., OEA/Ser.L/V/II.122 Doc. 5 rev. 1 at 727 (2004). Decision regarding Communication 155/96 (*Social and Economic Rights Action Center/Center for Economic and Social Rights v. Nigeria*), Communication No. ACHPR/COMM/A044/1 (African Commission on Human and Peoples' Rights, 27 May 2002).

[66]　2007 UN Declaration on the Rights of Indigenous Peoples, UN Doc. A/Res/61/295 (2 October 2007).

[67]　Schrijver (1997), supra, 390.

[68]　Duruigbo (2006), supra, 67.

As emerging economies' and developing countries' energy needs grow, competition for scarce resources will intensify. To ensure that globalisation is sustainable, countries face the challenge of becoming more energy- and resource-efficient. An inadequate balance between the utilisation of natural capital, human capital and economic capital will be a move away from sustainable development with a huge cost to the environment, human well-being and ecosystems. With 60 per cent of the world's ecosystems degraded or exploited unsustainably, the Millennium Ecosystem Assessment concluded that over the past half-century 'humans have changed ecosystems more rapidly and extensively than in any comparable period of time in human history, largely to meet rapidly growing demands for food, fresh water, timber, fiber, and fuel'.[69]

Contemporary international legal development suggests that there is an obligation, albeit non-binding, on the state to regulate the resource sector to maintain its efficiency and productivity,[70] e.g. through life cycle assessment (LCA), exploitation and extraction through clean technology, better market instruments such as emission trading, eco-tax, and voluntary approaches. Resource efficiency is a global concern – it means reducing the environmental impact of the consumption (demand) and production (supply) of goods and services over their full life cycle.[71] Resource efficiency can contribute to poverty reduction through more cost-efficient products and processes, and help promote economic growth while ensuring environmental sustainability. Examples of various methods of resource efficiency from mining and the energy sector show that market-based instruments can help consumers to choose environment-friendly products leading to a better consumption pattern.[72]

---

[69] Ecosystem and Human Well-Being: Synthesis Report, Millennium Ecosystem Assessment (2005), 1.

[70] An analogy can be drawn from the human rights instruments, such as the International Covenants, International Criminal Court, which limit the internal sovereignty of states. See chapters 4 and 6 of this book.

[71] McMullen, C. and T. Hayden (eds) (2009), 'Resource Efficiency', UNEP Yearbook 2009: New Science and Development in Our Changing Environment (Nairobi: UNEP), chapter 5, 43–52. Available at: www.unep.org/geo/yearbook (accessed 15 January 2010).

[72] Discussed in chapter 2 of this book. Cleaner production strategies include using different and less environmentally damaging materials and using less material to achieve the same result to reduce the environmental impact of products. Better consumption strategies include using goods to the end of their life and reducing food waste.

The World Summit on Sustainable Development (2002)[73] stressed the need to attain the MDGs and the importance of decoupling economic growth from resource use:

> Encourage and promote the development of a 10-year framework of programmes in support of regional and national initiatives to accelerate the shift towards sustainable consumption and production to promote social and economic development within the carrying capacity of ecosystems by addressing and, where appropriate, *delinking economic growth and environmental degradation* through improving efficiency and sustainability in the use of resources and production processes and reducing resource degradation, pollution and waste. All countries should take action, with developed countries taking the lead, taking into account the development needs and capabilities of developing countries, through mobilization, from all sources, of financial and technical assistance and capacity-building for developing countries.[74]

The WSSD Johannesburg Plan of Implementation urged the international community to support regional and national initiatives to accelerate the shift towards sustainable consumption and production (SCP) – known as the Marrakech Process.[75] This Process is being supported by the scientific evidence provided by the International Panel for Sustainable Resource Management. This Panel aims at decoupling economic growth from resource use and from environmental degradation, and in particular developing a better understanding of the ways to increase resource-efficient economic growth.[76]

Resource efficiency maximises the use of goods and services from the natural resources and minimises the depletion of natural capital and any pollution associated with that resource use. Improved resource efficiency and sustained economic growth can play a crucial role in achieving the MDGs. International assessments, such as the Millennium Ecosystem Assessment,[77] the Global Environmental Outlook[78] and the

---

[73]   Chapter III on Changing unsustainable patterns of consumption and production, paras 14–23.

[74]   Para. 15, Johannesburg Plan of Implementation (2002).

[75]   To support Chapter III of the Johannesburg Plan of Implementation, the Marrakech Process was launched in 2003. It is a global informal multi-stakeholder expert process to accelerate the shift towards sustainable consumption and production patterns and to support the elaboration of a 10-year framework of programmes on SCP (10YFP).

[76]   Hosted by UNEP, the Panel was officially launched in November 2007.

[77]   Millennium Ecosystem Assessment (2005), *Ecosystems and Human Well-Being: Synthesis*, Washington, DC: Island Press, 95–97.

[78]   Section B (State and Trends of the Environment 1987–2007). UNEP (2007), *Global Environment Outlook 4: Environment for Development*, Malta: Progress Press.

4th Assessment Report of the Intergovernmental Panel on Climate Change,[79] make it increasingly evident that economic growth needs to decouple from the environmental impact of resource exploitation. These documents emphasise that sustainable use of resources involves sustainable production and consumption, and efficient use of resources contributes to growth. While the North is highly dependent on resources coming from the South, and some of the developing countries (e.g. Brazil, Russia, India, China) of the South are using natural resources at an accelerating pace, the environmental impact of such resource use is felt globally. Improved resource efficiency can reduce negative environmental impacts of resource exploitation, use and disposal, while at the same time securing adequate supplies of materials to sustain economic growth and reduce poverty.

There are several approaches to reducing environmental impacts from material extraction and use.[80] One approach is the 3R initiative which is linked to the 'reduce, reuse, recycle' of products. Japan provides a successful example of a 3R initiative[81] while China adopted the 'circular economy' approach.[82] Another approach is the Life Cycle Initiative which enables resource users to reduce a product's resource use and environmental emissions, while improving its socio-economic performance throughout the life cycle.[83] Better technology and innovation as well as managing selected materials (e.g. hazardous materials, recyclable metals) can reduce negative impacts from materials extraction and use.

One example of resource efficiency is found in the mining sector. Increasing global demand for materials associated with limited reserves

---

[79] Pachauri, R.K., A. Reisinger and the Core Writing Team (eds) (2007), *Climate Change 2007: Synthesis Report*. Contribution of Working Groups I, II and III to the Fourth Assessment Report of the Intergovernmental Panel on Climate Change, Geneva, Switzerland: IPCC, 61.

[80] Different approaches include: 3Rs (reducing, reusing, recycling waste), sound material-cycle society, circular economy, integrated or sustainable waste management, sustainable consumption and production, life cycle management and sustainable materials or resource management.

[81] 3R Initiative in Japan, available at: www.env.go.jp/recycle/3r/en/approach.html (accessed 15 January 2010).

[82] Circular economy is an economy which balances economic development with environmental and resources protection. It puts emphasis on the most efficient use and recycling of its resources and environmental protection. Circular Economy Promotion Law of the People's Republic of China, adopted June 2008, in force January 2009.

[83] Launched by the UNEP and the Society for Environmental Toxicology and Chemistry (SETAC), this initiative responds to the call for a life cycle economy in the Malmö Ministerial Declaration (UNEP, 2000).

and adverse social and environmental impacts necessitates the need to use resources efficiently. A number of tools such as the Kimberley Process Certification Scheme, the OECD Guidelines for Multinational Enterprises, and the Extractive Industries Transparency Initiatives are available to strengthen the governance of the mining sector in the host countries.[84] Following the 3R approach, it is possible to increase resource efficiency by reducing the consumption of material, reusing a product and recycling.[85] End-of-life regulation could increase the recycling rate and protect the environment. Recycling can also recover metals and materials from waste which would have ended in landfills.

In the energy sector, energy efficiency improvements and energy conservation are a high priority for many developing countries.[86] While high efficiency along with clean technology are needed to achieve a low emission development, most of the clean energy sources (e.g. wind, solar, geothermal) remain sidelined.[87] A number of measures are available to address energy efficiency: e.g. international emission trading is a market mechanism which allows developed countries to supplement domestic reduction. In addition, the Clean Development Mechanism provides an opportunity for developing countries to undertake emission reduction projects, with financial and technological assistance from developed countries. These market-based instruments are crucial for resource efficiency in the energy sector since a high level of GHG emissions are from the energy sector.

1.4. Inclusive and Participatory Governance of Natural Resources

The challenge for sustainable development is to ensure how best to conserve natural resources for future generations.[88] This largely depends on the governance mechanism of the natural resources. The governance structure needs to minimise the exploitation of natural resources, promote their sustainable use and consumption, and maximise long-term profits. In addition, an inclusive and participatory governance structure prioritises the well-being of the people by including them in the structures of

---

[84] See the further discussion in chapters 2, 5 and 6 of this book.
[85] Science and Technology for Sustainable Development, '3r' Action Plan and Progress on Implementation, G-8 Initiative, Sea Island, 2004.
[86] UNEP (2007), supra, 49.
[87] Ibid. See the discussion in chapter 8.
[88] Walde, T. (2004), 'Natural Resources and Sustainable Development', in N. Schrijver and B. Weiss (eds), *International Law and Sustainable Development*, The Hague: Kluwer, 119–152, 126.

participation and consultation.[89] The importance of inclusive governance is found in the definition of governance offered by international institutions.[90] For example, the UN Development Programme considers five basic dimensions of good governance: transparency, accountability, rule of law, efficiency and effectiveness, and *participation*.[91]

Natural resources have a global dimension, and encompass a shared sense of responsibility, but they also have a local dimension, and this local dimension is as important as the global. Globalisation with its expansion on communications technology and the worldwide sharing of information can offer opportunities for communities and activists to reach over national borders and unite peoples, organisations and institutions in a common cause and to make their voices heard. These opportunities have certainly been capitalised on by business, non-state actors and corporations to promote alternative regulations in the form of voluntary codes of conduct and self-regulation and by powerful think-tanks and NGOs in the developed countries which have acquired an increasingly active role in policy-making.

Participatory governance includes opportunity to participate in the decision-making process, ability to gather information and access to legal redress.[92] The conceptual development of participatory governance can be assessed from the opportunity for people to involve themselves in a decision-making process and the process itself which allows the people to participate in the decision-making.[93] While the final decision is important, the process through which the decision is achieved is also crucial. Issues related to natural resource management are often complex, with multiple conflicting and competing interests within and between communities.[94]

---

[89]   Hills, J., J. LeGrand and D. Piachaoud (eds) (2002), *Understanding Social Exclusion*, Oxford: Oxford University Press.

[90]   UN Economic and Social Council, Definition of basic concepts and terminologies in governance and public administration, E/C.16/2006/4 (5 January 2006). Swart, L. and E. Perry (eds) (2007), *Global Environmental Governance: Perspectives on the Current Debate*, New York: Center for UN Reform.

[91]   UNDP (1998), *Empowering People: A Guide to Participation*, a publication prepared by the International NGO Training and Research Centre (INTRAC) and UNDP, available at: www.fao.org/Participation/english_web_new/content_en/linked_Pages/UNDP_Guide_to_Participation.htm (accessed 15 January 2010).

[92]   See the further discussion in chapter 3. UN/ECE Convention on Access to Information, Public Participation in Decision-Making and Access to Justice in Environmental Matters (1998) (hereafter: Aarhus Convention).

[93]   Sen, A. (2002), *Rationality and Freedom*, Cambridge, MA: Harvard University Press, pp. 583–622.

[94]   Ebbesson, J. (1997), 'The Notion of Public Participation in International Environmental Law', Yearbook of International Environmental Law, 8, 59.

Public participation may provide a useful tool in assessing risks and evaluating how risks should be weighed against benefits.[95] The failure to consider efficiency, equity, effectiveness and legitimacy of the process could adversely affect the decision leading to an unsustainable outcome.[96]

Undoubtedly, international law plays a significant role in developing the concept of participation and internalising participatory processes in administrative decision-making and access to justice. The 1998 Aarhus Convention brought about one of the unique developments of procedural rights to protect the environment and natural resources.[97] The Convention adopts a right-based approach to information, participation and justice, makes reference to a substantive right to a healthy environment and allows people to enforce their procedural and substantive environmental rights in court. The Aarhus Convention plays a crucial role in developing laws which include rules on individual or community participation into the land-use planning procedures, plan and policy evaluation.

Since signing the Aarhus Convention,[98] the EU, for example, has adopted new legislation and undertaken necessary measures to apply the provisions of the Convention to its own institutions and bodies.[99] Another example of such inclusive approach is the EU Directive dealing with the deliberate release into the environment of genetically modified organisms (GMOs).[100] This Directive provides that Member States are under an obligation to consult the public on the proposed deliberate release of GMOs

---

[95]   Steele, J. (2001), 'Participation and Deliberation in Environmental Law: Exploring a Problem Solving Approach', Oxford Journal of Legal Studies, 21, 426–427.

[96]   Efficiency relates to economic sustainability, effectiveness to environmental sustainability, equity to social sustainability, and legitimacy to the viability of the transition itself. Adger, W.N., K. Brown, J. Fairbrass, A. Jordan, J. Paavola, S. Rosendo and G. Seyfang (2002), 'Governance for Sustainability: Towards a 'Thick' Understanding of Environmental Decision-Making', CSERGE Working Paper EDM 02-04, available at: www.uea.ac.uk/env/cserge/pub/wp/edm/edm_2002_04.pdf (accessed 15 January 2010).

[97]   Other regional conventions dealing with participation are the Convention on Environmental Impact Assessment in a Transboundary Context (Espoo, 1991) and the Protocol on Strategic Environmental Assessment (Kiev, 2003).

[98]   The EU approved the Convention in early 2005. See the list of parties and signatories to the Convention: www.unece.org/env/pp/ctreaty.htm (accessed 15 January 2010).

[99]   See the discussion in chapter 3.

[100]   Directive 2001/18/EC of the European Parliament and of the Council of 12 March 2001 on the deliberate release into the environment of genetically modified organisms and repealing Council Directive 90/220/EEC.

into the environment.[101] In doing so, Member States need to lay down arrangements for this consultation, including a reasonable time-period to give the public or groups the opportunity to express an opinion. Another example is the EU Water Framework Directive (WFD) where public participation plays a key role in the implementation of the Directive.[102] The WFD encourages active involvement of people in the implementation of the Directive with full access to information and requires written consultation in the river-basin management planning process.[103]

Environmental impact assessment (EIA) and public consultation at the project making level can lead to a sustainable decision concerning natural resource use. Largely influenced by the Stockholm Declaration (1972), many developing countries in Asia, Africa and Latin America went through a phase of legal reform for better resource management during the 1970s and 1980s.[104] Reforms in access to justice and access to information began slowly, if at all, in some countries. Globally, many countries have initiated EIA laws including the consultation procedure, but many of these laws lack enforcement and access mechanisms.[105]

For the developing countries, Principle 10 of the Rio Declaration (1992) plays a central role in formulating legal instruments (binding and non-binding) which allow citizen participation. Principle 10 asserts that sound resource governance and effective resource management policies depend on providing people with access to information, opportunities for participation, redress for environmental harm, and mechanisms to ensure that these rights are fulfilled. This need is reflected at the national level by legislation ensuring access to information including environmental information, EIA laws and public consultation accommodating communities' participation in the development projects. Public consultation, however,

---

[101]   Article 9.

[102]   Preambular para. 14 of the WFD states that '[t]he success of this Directive relies on . . . information, consultation and involvement of the public, including users'. Lee, M. (2009), 'Law and Governance of Water Protection Policy', in J. Scott (ed.), *Environmental Protection: European Law and Governance*, Oxford: Oxford University Press, 27–55.

[103]   Article 14, Annex VII. See also Articles 9 and 10 of Directive 2007/60/EC of the European Parliament and of the Council of 23 October 2007 on the assessment and management of flood risks. OJ L 288, 28 (2007).

[104]   Craig, D., N. Robinson and K. Kheng-Lian (eds) (2003), *Capacity Building for Environmental Law in the Asian and Pacific Region: Approaches and Resources*, Manila: Asian Development Bank, Volumes I and II.

[105]   Further discussed in chapter 3. Foti J., L. de Silva, H. McGray, L. Shaffer, J. Talbot and J. Werksman (2008), *Voice and Choice: Opening the Door to Environmental Democracy*, Washington, DC: World Resources Institute.

does come with its own risk package, as the identity and power of the consultees are crucial – consultation becomes fruitless if the 'stakeholder' does not represent the 'voice' of the local community.

In the developing countries, external actors such as international financial institutions, donor agencies and UN agencies play an important role in developing the concept of participation in these countries and in integrating participatory processes into the policies and regulations.[106] The development of the participation provisions in environmental decision-making is also influenced by the participation provisions found in multilateral environmental agreements.[107] Integration of international standards into national laws has also strengthened access rights.[108] In addition, NGOs in the developing countries play a very critical role in promoting 'people's empowerment' by supporting participation agendas at the law and policy-making level. Increasing use of participation in community-based natural resource management policy is found in forest, water and coastal resource management.

Some studies conducted in Asia show that community managed (bottom up) irrigation projects are working more efficiently than government managed (top down) projects.[109] Community managed forest projects (e.g. common property resource management) are also better managed when local communities are involved. For example, the Joint Forest Management Scheme in Madhya Pradesh (India) actively involves local people in forest management and ownership of the forest products.[110] A similar example is found in the Community Forestry Projects in Nepal.[111] A 'Community-Based Coastal Resource Management' project in the Philippines[112] addressed the problem of the marginalisation and exclusion

---

[106]   Braithwaite, J. and P. Drahos (2000), *Global Business Regulation*, Cambridge: Cambridge University Press.

[107]   For example, 1992 UN Framework Convention on Climate Change, 1992 Convention on Biological Diversity. See the discussion in chapters 3 and 9.

[108]   These can be quality standard (waste management), product standard (packaging, labelling), emission standard (air quality), technology or process standard (use of best available technology/techniques). Sands, P. (2003), *Principles of International Environmental Law*, Cambridge: Cambridge University Press, 155.

[109]   Ostrom, E. (2001), *The Drama of the Commons*, Washington, DC: National Academy Press. Ostrom, E. (1994), 'Constituting Social Capital and Collective Action', Journal of Theoretical Politics, 6, 527–562.

[110]   Durst, P.B., C. Brown, H.D. Tacio and M. Ishikawa (eds) (2005), *In Search of Excellence: Exemplary Forest Management in Asia and the Pacific*, Bangkok: FAO.

[111]   Ostrom (2001), supra.

[112]   L. van Mulekom (2008), 'Reflections on community based coastal resources management (CB-CRM) in the Philippines and South East Asia',

of small fishermen within the country's agriculture sector. Similarly, in Malaysia, the local people and local entrepreneurs worked together to manage a mangrove forest for community-based tourism purposes.[113] Evaluations have shown that this participatory approach to resource management has been much more successful than earlier top down approaches.[114]

2. MAPPING THE BOOK

The ubiquitous and complex processes surrounding globalisation have created an over-abundance of theories which attempt to address the various and interconnected challenges associated with globalisation. We do not aim to add to this already crowed academic space. Instead we are trying to find a common thread of arguments and analysis which establishes the relationship between globalisation and natural resources law.

The first part presents an overview of the main *theories* underlying the globalisation process (e.g. economic and sustainable globalisation) and *key concepts* (e.g. global public goods). These theories and concepts play a crucial role in the articulation of a legal framework for the regulation of globalisation, trade, access to and management of natural resources. This part highlights that the challenges of globalisation are many: e.g. inequitable access to natural resources, increasing poverty, the degradation of the environment, lack of public participation in decision-making, good governance. This part considers the legal framework, actors and institutions of globalisation within a political, economic and social context.

- *Chapter 1* examines the themes and challenges in the relationship between globalisation and natural resources which are later developed throughout the book. It outlines the different North–South perspectives on globalisation, access to natural resources, development and sustainability, and draws attention to the shared and unresolved problem of world poverty. The tensions arising out of the principle of permanent sovereignty over natural resources between developed and developing countries in the context of foreign

---

Oxfam. Available at: www.oxfam.org.uk/resources/downloads/FP2P/FP2P_Philippines_Fish_Coast_Resc_CS_ENGLISH.pdf (accessed 15 January 2010).

[113] UNESCAP/ADB (1995), *State of the Environment in Asia and the Pacific*, Bangkok: United Nations Economic and Social Commission for Asia and the Pacific, and Asian Development Bank and New York: United Nations.

[114] Durst et al. (2005), supra. Ostrom (2001), supra.

investment and expropriation of foreign property are considered in this chapter. Tensions around the scope of permanent sovereignty also arise internally and the claims of indigenous peoples to control over natural resources are outlined in this chapter. After considering the structures of global governance, it concludes that an unbalanced system of economic, and especially trade governance based on inequality, needs to be addressed and participatory organisations that balance trade and natural resource protection and management objectives need to be developed.

- *Chapter 2* considers the general principles underlying natural resource management, especially the principle of sustainable use and sustainable development. This chapter evaluates the different approaches to the management of resources (command and control, market-based instruments, voluntary and decentralised approaches) including the concept of 'ecosystem services'. It considers how natural resources management fits within multilateral trade agreements and whether the development of trade in ecosystem goods and services has an impact on human rights. The chapter ends with an overview of the relationship between natural resources and violent conflict.

- *Chapter 3* explores both the substantive and procedural aspects of decision-making in natural resource management. A brief discussion on the substantive rights to natural resources touches upon the issue of the use, enjoyment and management of natural resources. This chapter then examines access to natural resource decision-making. There are international and regional mechanisms to ensure people's involvement in the decision-making, and various aspects of public participation (e.g. consultation, information, access to court) are linked. It considers whether the participation of communities in the decision-making process effectively contributes to the objectives of sustainable resource management.

The second part of the book considers the *challenges* outlined in the first chapter and focuses on the conflicting needs of human beings over natural resources. These conflicts and challenges revolved round the main themes of inequality, lack of adequate governance institutions at the global level and the need to adopt new approaches for economic valuation and sustainable resource management. The three chapters in this part consider these challenges through the perspectives of the main state and non-state actors and their role in globalisation and natural resource governance. This part also considers the constraints to effective management posed by the limitations of compliance systems.

- *Chapter 4* introduces the actors and institutions that operate in the globalised world and focuses on state actors and international organisations. It examines how international institutions such as UN agencies, the IMF, the World Bank and the WTO play a role in both global governance and natural resource management alongside states. Regional organisations such as the EU are also briefly considered. Despite the globalisation process, states remain powerful actors. The state can, together with other actors, promote the national welfare and protect the general interest and well-being of citizens. The state can, through independent courts, guarantee the respect of human rights and justice. Its role is also fundamental in operating the intricate web of multilateral arrangements and intergovernmental regimes.
- *Chapter 5* focuses on the growing importance of non-state actors and their participation in global governance and natural resource management. Multinational corporations and civil society have emerged as important participants in global affairs and have developed collaborative networks in response to changes from the national to the supranational. Non-state actors share a growing sphere of power with traditional state actors and are crucial to the articulation of society's needs.
- *Chapter 6* looks at compliance and enforcement mechanisms, both nationally and globally, of natural resource management. It highlights the complex nature of the issues involved, and the problems and opportunities provided by globalisation for development, global justice and access to natural resources. Compliance of states with international norms is always hampered by the principle of state sovereignty, unless special arrangements such as those within the EU are in place whereby supranational institutions are endowed with some of the states' powers. Compliance at the national level is addressed to non-state actors, especially MNCs, but questions arise as to suitability of national laws for the regulation of transnational actors and the reliance on channels of national enforcement through an overview of litigation against MNCs in domestic courts.

The third part of the book deals with the *approaches* available to manage natural resources under international, regional and national legal systems. This part gives a thorough analysis of water (chapter 7), renewable energy (chapter 8) and biological resources (chapter 9). These three resources are chosen because of their enormous importance at the international level, the use of various legal approaches to manage the resource sectors and recent legal developments. These three chapters highlight both the increasing role of non-state actors (e.g. private actors, NGOs) as well as the growing power of international (e.g. WTO, World Bank) and regional (e.g. EU, Human Rights Courts) institutions.

- *Chapter 7* deals with renewable energy. Energy is directly linked with the key global challenges that the world faces – poverty alleviation, environmental sustainability and energy security. Fossil fuels are non-renewable energy sources which cause air pollution, environmental degradation and global warming. Therefore, renewable energy is set to play a substantial role to meet energy needs and improve access to energy. The chapter focuses on renewable energy sources such as wind, solar, hydro and thermal. It discusses the trends in energy consumption, the issue of energy security, the Energy Charter Treaty, renewable energy subsidies, and the link between climate change and renewable energy. Renewable energy sources play a key role in lowering future GHG emissions and in reducing the vulnerability of energy security. Developing countries (e.g. China, India) have taken several measures to improve energy security through the promotion of energy efficiency and renewable energy. In this globalised world, the trade regime at the international level (e.g. WTO) or at the regional level (e.g. Energy Charter Treaty in Europe) to guide renewable energy needs strengthening.

- *Chapter 8* outlines the approaches to water governance in human rights law, environmental law and trade law. Freshwater concerns are interlinked with health security, food security and environmental sustainability. The relevance of globalisation for water resources can be considered from two different perspectives: the first looks at water as a public good and the consequences of globalization on water resource management; the second considers water as an economic good. One of the impacts of globalisation is the influence that multinational corporations and international financial institutions (e.g. the World Bank, WTO) have on the domestic water sector and water related services. The chapter examines the effect of privatisation on marginalised communities and the issue of competing interests in relation to water use. It then examines regulatory mechanisms at the international and regional level dealing with sustainable water management. The chapter also explores water rights at the national level with judicial decisions outlining the scope of the right.

- *Chapter 9* discusses the role of globalisation in accessing and sharing biological resources. Biodiversity degradation is a global problem with global consequences. The process of economic globalisation further threatens the destruction of biological diversity, with the loss of crop and species variety and environmental pollution. The chapter concentrates on the Convention on Biological Diversity and the effect of globalisation on benefit sharing and traditional knowledge. It then considers the issues of intellectual property, traditional knowledge and human rights.

PART I

Theories, principles and key issues

1. Globalisation and natural resources: themes, challenges and dilemmas

1. INTRODUCTION

The process of globalisation with its increased volume of world trade, transport and communications and the growing affluence it creates (albeit not uniformly spread) depends for its very existence on the Earth's resources. Since the fifteenth century the need to expand the economic reach of countries and empires has been the motor behind the globalisation process. Historically the process has resulted in great economic disparity between cultures and nations in respect of access to natural resources, infrastructure and economic development. The causes of these disparities are various and complex, but the 'aggressive exploitation of resources by outside cultures'[1] is undoubtedly one of them. The so-called 'North' – the developed countries – has reaped the benefits of a long process which has been marked by the use of violence, political and economic coercion, while the 'South', 'Third World' or 'developing countries' have been left with a legacy of violence, broken social structures and uneven development.[2]

In this chapter we look at the main globalisation discourses and highlight the key issues in the relationship between globalisation and natural resources which are later developed throughout the book.

The first is inequality, largely promoted and maintained by the current economic system but rooted in a long process which begins with colonisation and a conflicting relationship between the North and the South. Inequality and poverty are also intrinsically and unavoidably intertwined, and we consider this problem in this chapter. Globalisation has had a complex effect on the distribution of wealth and prosperity. With China and India progressing at a pace which promises to close the gap between

---

[1]   Including colonisation and the slave trade. For a discussion see Goldin, I. and K.A. Reinert (2007), *Globalization for Development: Trade, Finance, Aid, Migration and Policy*. Washington, DC, Basingstoke and New York: World Bank and Palgrave MacMillan joint publication, p. 9.

[2]   Ibid.

developed and developing countries much of the consumption increase in those countries has helped promote growth in Africa and Latin America. The global crisis and the constriction in demand have put an end to this era of mild prosperity for the poorer regions. Inequality, it is arguable, itself contributes to economic crises since the money circulates among those with enough surplus to consume and goes, usually, to those who do not need it, while lack of income redistribution in the world reduces the possible cumulative effects of global demand, which could have an effect on economic prosperity.[3] Through the relationship between inequality, global governance and natural resource management we try to explore how inequality can be reduced in such a manner that would lead to poverty alleviation, sustainable natural resource use and economic growth. These challenges are outlined in this chapter and revisited throughout the book.

The second emerging issue is that of lack of global governance, which creates problems of instability and crises. Who makes decisions, how they are made, and with what information is at the heart of sustaining healthy growth and prosperity.[4] Decisions made by local and national governments, corporations and international financial institutions involve billions of dollars, affect natural resource use and have an impact on the lives of millions of people. This chapter considers the structures of global governance and comments upon the unbalanced system of economic governance imposed by developed countries on the one hand and the, by comparison, infant and fragmented system of global natural resource governance. The themes of participation in global governance are further developed in chapters 4 and 5 in the context of different global state and non-state actors.

The third emerging challenge in the relationship between globalisation and natural resources is whether globalisation structures and mechanisms have helped to protect and develop sustainable natural resource management systems or have, on the contrary, contributed to the destruction of natural capital. In a system driven by economic imperatives lack of valuation and pricing of natural resources and environmental goods creates dangerous opportunities for overuse with disastrous consequences. Yet, natural resources pose a serious problem of valuation as many of them are (global) public goods.

Inequality, global governance and the regulation and undervaluation

---

3 See Stiglitz, J. (2010), *Freefall: Free Markets and the Sinking of the Global Economy* (London: Allen Lane). Stiglitz suggest solutions which rest in increasing consumption by the poor or developing countries.
4 We discuss participation in chapter 3 of this book and consider governance also in chapters 4 and 5 in the contexts of the different actors involved.

of natural resources within the global framework are closely interrelated and solutions will need to address this intertwining and adopt a synergistic approach.

2. GLOBALISATION AND NATURAL RESOURCES: HISTORICAL AND PRESENT THEMES AND DISCOURSES

Theories and definitions of globalisation abound. One can find as many variations on the general themes as authors who have written about them. Globalisation, according to its various definitions appears to be a process of liberalisation of trade and investment, led by the West which has driven the internationalisation, de-territorialisation, and ultimately, universalisation of culture, politics and, above all, economic production and processes.[5] There are several recognisable historical stages in the ongoing process of globalisation which include colonisation, the slave trade, the spread of Christianity to newly conquered territories, the development of capitalism and industrialisation, advances in transportation and, lately, the communications and information technology revolution. They have all contributed to the building of wealth has usually resulted in the most notable phases of globalisation.[6]

Within the definitional abundance surrounding the concept of globalisation there is a relative absence of definitions which directly establish a relationship between globalisation and natural resources[7] despite the unavoidable dependence upon these for the globalisation process.[8]

---

[5] See Scholte, J. (2002), 'What Is Globalization? The Definitional Issue – Again', CSGR Working Paper No. 109/02 (December 2002) available at: www. warwick.ac.uk/fac/soc/csgr/research/.../2002/wp10902.pdf (accessed 15 November 2009). For further detail and a classification of the different definitions see Scholte, J.A. (2005), *Globalisation: A Critical Introduction*, Basingstoke: Palgrave Macmillan, chapter 3.

[6] Goldin and Reinert (2007), supra, p. 5.

[7] There are some excellent studies on globalisation and the environment even though their number is relatively low compared with studies on other aspects of globalisation. Among them are Wijen, F., K. Zoetman and J. Pieters (eds) (2005), *A Handbook of Globalization and Environmental Policy*, Cheltenham, UK and Northampton, MA, USA: Edward Elgar Publishing, and Speth, J.G. (ed.) (2003), *Worlds Apart: Globalisation and the Environment*, Washington, DC: Island Press.

[8] Thomas Pogge is an exception, as he establishes the dependence of developed countries on cheap and free access to the natural resources of developing

Globalisation has arguably been driven by a need to access and exploit natural resources as free trade and the expansion of foreign investment require increased amounts of both energy and raw materials. Developed countries have always relied on a ready access to natural resources to grow economically and expand politically and the existing international order has been designed to facilitate this access for their own benefit.[9] International law allows those governments which seize power in a country – even if it is by violent means and even if that government is undemocratic – to dispose of the resources of the country.[10] This situation is favourable for the North which can guarantee a supply of cheap materials and ignore the conditions under which the people of these other countries live.[11]

If the relationship between globalisation and natural resources has been relatively unexplored the relationship between globalisation and economic growth, on the other hand, has been analysed in depth with two divergent discourses dominating the debate. The first discourse maintains that economic globalisation through the integration of markets and the expansion of foreign investment will help both developed and developing countries to grow economically and achieve prosperity. Goods will be manufactured in places where this process is more effective – according to the principle of comparative advantage – and consumers in rich countries will have access to cheaper goods and services while producers in poor countries will have access to rich countries' markets. Migration will also allow workers to send money to their families and help promote local businesses in turn. This discourse has driven the national and international legislative agendas and has been reflected in the current governance model of the global system.[12] The promise of unfettered economic growth was to advance the economic prospects and well-being of the world population

---

countries. See Pogge, T. (2008), *World Poverty and Human Rights*, 2nd edn, Cambridge and Malden: Polity, esp. chapter 8.

[9]   Once the colonies became independent countries the system of free trade and investment secured access to the markets and resources of developing countries.

[10]   Due to a perverse interpretation of the principles of permanent sovereignty over natural resources, discussed below, and of non-intervention in the internal affairs of a state.

[11]   Good examples of this practice are the oil bought from the corrupt dictatorships of the Gulf countries or from Nigeria's dictators. See Pogge (2008), supra, for a spirited condemnation of the system.

[12]   Supporters of this discourse include Friedman, T.L. (2005), *The World is Flat: A Brief History of the Twenty-First Century*, New York: Farrar, Straus and Giroux; Wolf, M. (2004), *Why Globalisation Works*, New Haven: Yale University Press; Bhagwati, J. (2004), *In Defence of Globalisation*, New York: Oxford University Press.

and, especially, of the millions of the poor and destitute.[13] However the statistics show a very different story: GDP has increased in recent decades, but so has the number of the world's poor.[14] Moreover in order to participate in the process of globalisation access to technology is crucial and not all individuals and countries have the resources to be able to join in.[15]

The second discourse argues that globalisation has only created greater disparity in income and well-being between and within nations, and that some countries, the poorer countries, have become even poorer and suffered most of the negative externalities of the industrialist, trade-based model of economic development favoured by globalisation. In addition poor countries and poor people suffer the effects of over-consumption and affluence in the rich world and by the rich minorities of developing countries.[16] This view is reflected in the following section of the Report on Fair Globalisation by the World Commission on the Social Dimension of Globalisation:

> The current process of globalization is generating unbalanced outcomes, both between and within countries. Wealth is being created but too many countries and people are not sharing in its benefits. They also have little or no voice in shaping the process. . . . Even in economically successful countries some workers and communities have been adversely affected by globalization . . . [t]hese global imbalances are morally unacceptable and politically unsustainable.[17]

---

13 'Capital flows to developing countries had increased six-fold in six years, from 1990 to 1996. The establishment of the World Trade Organisation in 1995 . . . [w]as to bring the semblance of a rule of law to international commerce. Everyone was supposed to be a winner – those both in the developed and developing world. Globalization was to bring unprecedented prosperity to all'. Stiglitz, J. (2007), *Making Globalization Work*, London: Penguin, p. 13.

14 A look at the relationship between globalisation and poverty shows that in the three stages of the period of 'modern globalisation' poverty rose steadily. Goldin and Reinert (2007) at 21–22, although the authors point out that poverty also rose during the inter-war period when, technically speaking, the process of globalisation was driven to a halt due to the growth of trade protectionism.

15 Stiglitz (2007), supra, at 57.

16 De Souza Santos, B. and C.A. Rodriguez-Garavito (eds) (2005), *Law and Globalisation from Below. Towards a Cosmopolitan Legality*, Cambridge: Cambridge University Press; Chimni, B.S. (2003), *The Third World & International Legal Order: Law, Politics & Globalisation* (co-edited with A. Anghie, K. Mickelson and O. Okafor), The Hague: Kluwer Law International; Sachs, J. (2005), *The End of Poverty*, London: Penguin.

17 The World Commission on the Social Dimension of Globalisation (2004), *A Fair Globalisation: Creating Opportunities for All*, Geneva: ILO, available at: www.ilo.org/public/english/fairglobalization/report/index.htm (accessed 15 October 2009).

In fact globalisation to date has created growth in some areas and countries,[18] but in general the balance points to greater inequalities.[19] The reasons for these inequalities are various: an unequal system of international rules of trade, national policies, corruption, disease and bad governance. If in the early 1990s globalisation was greeted with enthusiasm, by the end of the decade discontent had grown as globalisation failed to deliver its promises of greater prosperity and equality. The 'anti-globalisation movement' became the visible expression of growing discontent and concern about the negative aspects of globalisation. The duplicity and double standards of economic rules and the poverty and destitution of the majority of the world population were exposed, while awareness about global environmental problems was raised through a cluster of media-followed protests at the main forums of global economic governance.[20] Protesters were united in their discontent with the dominant model of economic globalisation which ignored social, human and environmental concerns, but their disparate origins and ideologies prevented them from presenting a coherent or united programme of reform. In fact, although discontent against globalisation had united people across boundaries, countries and continents there was no agreement which could be reached about how to reform the current system. The South was of the opinion that the solution to the problems created by the process of globalisation revolved round a change in the international order which would eliminate unfair protection of certain markets in developed countries while allowing the protection of small and medium businesses in developing countries.[21]

---

[18]   The World Bank estimated in 2008 that accounting for the increased population between 1981 and 2005, the poverty rate has, however, fallen by about 25%. This masks major regional variations, and perhaps most glaringly the impact of China. China's poverty rate fell from 85% to 15.9%, or by over 600 million people and accounts for nearly all the world's reduction in poverty. Excluding China, poverty fell by only around 10%: http://econ.worldbank.org/external/default/main?pagePK=6416.

[19]   According to the UNDP more than 80 per cent of the world's population lives in countries where income differentials are widening: *2007 Human Development Report* (HDR), United Nations Development Programme, 27 November 2007, p. 25.

[20]   Seattle (1999, WTO Ministerial Conference), Melbourne (2000, at the World Economic Forum), Prague (2000, IMF, World Bank and G8 Summit); Genoa (2001, G8 meeting).

[21]   This was the consensus at the World Social Forum (WSF) in Mumbai, in 2004. The WSF is an open meeting for groups, individuals and civil society opposed to the dominance of the world by capital and neo-imperialism and seeking to build a society centred on the human person. See http://wsfindia.org/.

At the World Economic Forum (WEF)[22] at the same time, the financial global elite claimed that the developing world had to change further and liberalise more if it wanted to share in the prosperity brought by the global market.

The current dominant model of globalisation, often referred to as 'corporate globalisation', with its primary mission of enabling financial and investment markets to operate internationally, was criticised as plainly unsustainable and based on the aggressive exploitation of resources and peoples by a minority while failing to take into account the finiteness of the world resources.[23] But not every aspect of the globalisation process and the paradigms it generates and upon which it is in turn based has negative consequences. The expansion of the concept of sustainable development and the emergence of new ideas such as corporate social responsibility (CSR)[24] or socially responsible investment (SRI)[25] has enabled the emergence of a consensus on the limitations of continued growth and the need for an integration of sustainability models within the economic system.

3. INEQUALITY

3.1. Globalisation, Colonisation and Natural Resources

The North and the South have often been portrayed in international debates as two opposing parties engaged in Manichean politics with very little in common and disjunctive interests and perspectives on trade, globalisation and power. Developing countries trace globalisation back to the fifteenth and sixteenth centuries when the mercantilism which propelled colonisation and the European policies developed around the ideas of 'free trade' translated in the expansion of exports and the need for new

---

[22] The WEF is a an independent international organisation committed to improving the state of the world by engaging leaders in partnerships to shape global, regional and industry agendas. Created in 1971 it meets annually in Davos. Its motto is 'entrepreneurship in the global public interest'. See http://weforum.org/ and chapter 5, 'Civil Society', pp. 235–243.

[23] Diamond, J. (2005), *Collapse: How Societies Choose to Fail or Succeed*, New York: Viking. He argues that either cataclysm or a solution will take place in the not too distant future since the current path of exploitation of the Earth's resources without adequate management or replenishment is not sustainable.

[24] Developed in chapter 5 of this book, pp. 220–222.

[25] Developed also in chapter 5 of this book, pp. 231–235.

overseas markets.[26] Globalisation, for them, is not very different from colonisation: both globalisation and colonisation are processes led by the developed countries and shaped to suit their interests. In both cases the developed countries (formerly colonial powers) gained unfettered access to the natural resources of the developing world (or colonies), exploiting them for their sole economic advantage. The developed world has also been accused of supporting much of the oppression and corruption of the so-called Third World, directly and indirectly, because it is in its economic interests.[27]

It is difficult to refute the developing countries' perspective on globalisation and the problems it creates. Undeniably, developed countries gained access to the natural resources of developing countries, often by violent means, to fuel their industrial revolutions first and their affluent lifestyles later. Those initial violent means were substituted by political and economic coercion. The mixed legacy left over by colonialism left those in ex-colonial territories with one common feeling: that they had been cruelly exploited.[28] The political independence at the end of World War II left way for what has been called 'economic colonialism', where natural resources continued to be exploited for the benefit of the old colonial powers and the new institutions of global governance – IMF and World Bank – became the new instruments of post-colonial control.[29]

The North and the South have very different views, needs and priorities in respect of the process of globalisation, and especially with regard to natural resource use. The close relationship between natural resource use and economic growth makes debates about environmental protection or natural resource use a complex task of reconciling largely opposing positions. Usually rich in natural resources, with growing populations and lagging behind on the road to development and industrialisation the South's priorities lie in eliminating poverty and reducing a taxing international debt. The South zealously guards the principle of sovereignty over its natural resources[30] and is wary of engaging in environmental debates specified by the North which, in the South's view, seeks to continue its

---

[26] See Gupta, J. (2007), 'Globalisation, Environmental Challenges and North–South Issues' in Thai, Khi V., D. Rahm, and J.D. Coggburn, et al. (eds), *Handbook on Globalisation and the Environment*, Boca Raton: CRC Press, pp. 449–470 at 449.

[27] On this point see Pogge, (2008), supra, especially chapter 8 and Stiglitz (2007), supra, pp. 138–144.

[28] See, for an excellent discussion, Stiglitz (2010), supra, p. 220.

[29] Ibid.

[30] Discussed at pp. 67–73.

affluent lifestyle while blocking the South's right to develop. The South aspires to rapid industrialisation and considers it the answer to its poverty and underdevelopment problems. But economic development at its earlier stages has a high environmental cost attached and requires high energy consumption.[31] Developed and developing countries must consider the key question of how to encourage and allow a process of development without a high environmental cost. [32]

International environmental law has, in recent decades, made an incremental effort to devise regimes of protection and regulation which are inclusive, equitable and fair to all states.[33] Developing countries feel that it is the developed countries that must be responsible for the damage they have caused to the environment and for its consequences, suffered usually the most by developing countries despite their negligible contributions.[34] On the other hand rapidly industrialising developing countries, especially China,[35] India and Brazil, are increasing their use of natural resources and will become the next big polluters while their position as 'developing countries' shields them from commitments in international environmental regulation.[36] Principles like 'common but differentiated responsibilities'[37] try to reflect this reality but the scope of rights and duties of each party is

---

[31] It is estimated that the energy needs of developing countries will increase by 230% by 2050. Sierra, K. (2009), 'Energy Week Opening Plenary', Washington DC, Tuesday, 31 March. Available at: http://siteresources.worldbank.org/EXTENERGY2/resources./KathySierraEW2009OpeningSpeech.pdf? (accessed 15 January 2010).

[32] The International Energy Agency predicts that US$300bn per annum is required to meet the energy needs of developing countries up to 2030. The World Bank estimates the premium to achieve these developments cleanly may be as little as 10%. Ibid.

[33] See Birnie, P., A. Boyle and C. Redgwell (2009), *International Law and the Environment*, 3rd edn, Oxford: Oxford University Press, pp. 115–128. Examples are developed through the book: see especially chapter 2, pp. 93–104.

[34] The adverse consequences of climate change are perhaps the best example of these diverging perceptions. Other examples are desertification and the spreading of contagious disease which affects developing countries disproportionately because of their geographical location and their reduced capabilities of adaptation.

[35] China overtook the US in the dubious honour of being the biggest emitter of CO_2 in 2006. Rosenthal, E. (2008), 'China Increases Lead as Biggest Carbon Dioxide Emitter', New York Times, 14 June. Available at: www.nytimes.com/2008/06/14/world/asia/14china.html?ref=world (accessed 15 January 2010).

[36] China's lack of commitment to specific reduction targets in emissions of greenhouse gases was one of stumbling blocks in the Copenhagen summit in December 2009.

[37] The principle is discussed in chapter 2, pp. 101–104.

still contested, and while agreements remain elusive the number of those exposed to the negative consequences of natural resource scarcity and environmental ills increases.

3.2. Inequality and Poverty

That in a 'world of plenty millions live in the most abject poverty'[38] is both a tragedy and a contradiction. Developing countries share a disproportionate burden of global poverty as most poor people live in developing or less developed countries.[39] Although the process of colonisation and decolonisation is not the only reason for today's world poverty, undeniably most poor countries today are ex-colonies. Global poverty is also extensive in war-torn and post-conflict countries, many of which are ex-colonies the geographical boundaries of which in the granting of independence were inspired more by the politics of empire than the creation of new nation states. Many countries found themselves lacking a critical mass of resources or population, landlocked, or seething with irreconcilable ethnic division.[40] The newly independent countries also lacked the capacity to participate as equals or influence international negotiations and international law making, with world trade rules being one the clearest examples of the double standards and neocolonial domination imposed by rich countries upon the ex-colonies. Agriculture, the main occupation of developing countries' populations and one of their main exports, is made uncompetitive by the subsidies allowed to European and US farmers despite the WTO regime which seeks to eliminate subsidies in other areas of economic activity.[41] As a consequence most developing countries are unable to break free of the colonial economic model which depends largely on the export of natural resources. Control over domestic development strategies has also been interfered with by the conditions imposed by the International Financial Institutions (IFIs) to access grants and loans.[42]

Bad governance has drained economic growth through corruption and clientele politics, in many cases encouraged by developed countries.[43] Weak democratic structures pervert the allocation of resources, most apparent in

---

[38]   Stiglitz (2007), supra, Preface at xiii.
[39]   See in general the classic work by Harris, P. (1993), *Inside the Third World*, 2nd edn, London: Penguin.
[40]   Sachs, J. (2006), *The End of Poverty: Economic Possibilities for Our Time*, London: Penguin.
[41]   See chapter 4 of this book for a discussion of the WTO agricultural policy.
[42]   Discussed in chapter 4, pp. 185–196.
[43]   Goldin and Reinert (2007), supra, at 35.

African governments' failure to meet their own commitment to invest in agriculture, and the broader lack of institutional capacity and infrastructure hinders delivery of aid programmes and business investment alike. Except for investment in extractive industries low-income countries receive practically no inflows of foreign direct investment (FDI).[44] Economic globalisation was heralded as the answer to the task of addressing poverty and under-development, and as the vehicle whereby economic growth would expand worldwide and eventually be equitably re-distributed. Instead, poverty has steadily increased throughout the globalisation process.[45]

3.2.1. Poverty, human well-being and natural resources

There is a well-established two-way link between poverty and environmental degradation.[46] Poor people live in unhealthy environments with health risks arising from poor sanitation, lack of clean water, overcrowded and poorly ventilated living and working environments and air and industrial pollution.[47] A fifth of the disease burden in developing countries can be linked to environmental risk factors. For example there is a clear link between malaria and deteriorating ecosystems by deforestation,[48] while anthropogenic climate change also has a most profound and devastating effect on the poor.[49] The IPCC has indicated that 330 million people will be displaced by 2020 due to rising sea levels, while water shortages will affect two billion people. Of those affected by environmental disasters 98 per

---

44 Middle income countries are the net beneficiaries of liberalised exports and receive a much larger share of FDI. Ibid. at 37.

45 The World Bank announced in 2008 that more people are living in extreme poverty – defined as with an income of $1.25 – than ever before. In the poorest 20 countries human development indicators have failed significantly over the past decade. 'World Bank Find that Adjustment Places More in Steep Poverty', New York Times, 27 August 2008, p 7.

46 Shelton, D. (2009), 'Describing the Elephant: International Justice and Environmental Law', in Ebbesson, J. and P. Okowa (eds), *Environmental Law and Justice in Context*, New York: Cambridge University Press, pp. 55–76.

47 United Nations (2007), *World Population Report*, available at: www. unfpa.org/swp/2007/presskit/pdf/sowp2007_eng.pdf (accessed 15 November 2009).

48 Office of the High Commissioner for Human Rights (2008), *Claiming the Millennium Development Goals: A Human Rights Approach*, at 25 HR/PUB/08/3, sales no. E.08.XIV.6.

49 Intergovernmental Panel on Climate Change (IPPC) (2001), *Climate Change 2001: Impacts, Adaptation and Vulnerability*, A Report of Working Group II of the IPCC, Geneva.

cent are in the developing world.[50] Poverty contributes to environmental degradation due to the stress placed by the poor on already overexploited and fragile ecosystems.

> The environment is crucial to the four requirements of good development: increasing the asset base productivity; empowering poor people and marginalised communities; reducing and managing risks; and taking a long term perspective with regards to intra-and intergenerational equity . . . Long term development can only be achieved through sustainable management of various assets: financial, material, human. Social and natural. . . . . [S]ustainable development provides a framework for managing human and economic development, while ensuring a proper and optimal functioning over time of the natural environment.[51]

The relationship between poverty and the environment has been recognised by the UNDP–UNEP Poverty – Environment Initiative (PEI),[52] a joint programme between the United Nations Development Programme (UNDP) and the United Nations Environment Programme (UNEP) to provide financial and technical support to government decision-makers and a wide range of other stakeholders to manage the environment in a way which improves livelihoods and leads to sustainable growth. Created in 2005 it operates currently in seventeen countries and receives donor support from nine governments.[53] The UNPEI initiative is based on the premise that improved management of the environment and natural resources contributes directly to poverty reduction, more sustainable livelihoods and pro-poor growth. To fight poverty, to promote security and to preserve the ecosystems which poor people rely on for their livelihoods, we must place pro-poor economic growth and environmental sustainability at the heart of our economic policies, planning systems and institutions. Human well-being closely depends on healthy ecosystems, as these provide food, clean water, disease and climate regulation, spiritual fulfilment and aesthetic enjoyment. When a resource or service is relatively scarce, a small

---

[50]   Office of the High Commissioner for Human Rights (2008), *Claiming the Millennium Development Goals: A Human Rights Approach*, 25 HR/PUB/08/3, sales no. E.08.XIV.6.

[51]   The World Bank (2005), *Where is the Wealth of Nations? Measuring Capital for the 21st Century*, Washington, DC: The World Bank Publications, available at: www.siteresources.worldbank.org/INTEEI/214578 . . . /20748034/All.pdf (accessed 15 November 2009).

[52]   www.unepi.org.

[53]   Funded by the governments of Belgium, Denmark, Ireland, Norway, Spain, Sweden, the United Kingdom and the European Commission. Initially implemented in a core of nine countries, it is now to be expanded to other countries and regions: See http://unepi.org/about/index.asp (accessed 15 November 2009).

decrease may substantially decrease 'human well-being'.[54] Human well-being lies at the core of the human rights discourse and, arguably, access to natural resources and to the (ecosystem) services upon which human well-being depends should be considered a human rights issue.[55]

Recent attempts to reconcile human well-being and environmental protection are reflected in novel measurements which show the ecological efficiency with which human well-being is delivered around the world. The Happy Planet Index (HPI) from the New Economics Foundation is an innovative measure which combines environmental impact with well-being to measure the environmental efficiency with which, country by country, people live long and happy lives. The HPI strips the view of the economy back to its absolute basics: what we put in (resources), and what comes out (human lives of different length and happiness). The HPI shows that around the world high levels of resource consumption do not reliably produce high levels of well-being, and that it is possible to produce high well-being without excessive consumption of the Earth's resources. It also reveals that there are different routes to achieving comparable levels of well-being. The model followed by the West can provide widespread longevity and variable life satisfaction, but it does so only at a vast and ultimately counter-productive cost in terms of resource consumption.[56] Tools for pro-poor environmental protection and natural resource management are explored in chapter 2.[57]

3.3. Development

3.3.1. Defining development: human development and economic development

Since the end of World War II, development has included at least four related elements: peace and security, economic development, social development, and a system of good governance.[58] Together they contribute towards human well-being.

---

[54] Millennium Ecosystem Assessment, Ecosystems and Human Well-Being: Synthesis (2005) at 7, available at: http://millenniumassessment.org/documents/document.365.aspx.pdf (accessed 15 November 2009).

[55] Blanco, E. and J. Razzaque (2009), 'Ecosystem Services and Human Well-Being in a Globalized World: Assessing the Role of Law', *Human Rights Quarterly* 31.3 692–720 at 695–697.

[56] www.happyplanetindex.org.

[57] See pp. 86 et seq.

[58] Dernbach, J.C. (2002), 'Sustainable Development, Now More than Ever', Environmental Law Reporter, 32, No. 1.

Economic development constituted the focus of much of the development literature and efforts of the post-war period. Development was mostly associated with industrialisation and was traditionally measured in terms of gross domestic product (GDP) or GDP per capita.[59] Development and the environment were cast as residing in opposing poles of policy and practice, and environmental concerns were largely seen as an obstacle to rapid industrialisation and economic progress. The report of the Brundtland Commission, 'Our Common Future',[60] changed that perception. Not only did it link environment and development for any future development agenda, but it proposed that the environment is the foundation of development and that close synergies and relationships exist between both human and economic development and the environment.

Mounting evidence that increased economic growth did not amount to increased human well-being[61] and that the so called 'trickle down' power of market forces to spread economic benefits and end poverty did not take place, coupled with a wave of democratisation in the early 1990s and a resurgence of a rights-based approach to combating world poverty and human-centred development meant that in the 1990s the concept of human development was coined to vindicate a wider view of development beyond the narrow conception which measured development by economic indicators alone.[62]

In 1990 the United Nations Development Programme (UNDP) commissioned the Human Development Reports (UNHDR) and tried to measure development as a process which is centred on peoples freedom. An index – the Human Development Index (HDI) – is published annually which incorporates three indicators: health and longevity, education and

---

[59]   Gross Domestic Product (GDP) may or may not be associated with development. In East Asia, increased GDP meant less poverty only because governments had put in place policies to ensure that the benefits of increased economic growth were evenly shared. In other places, especially in Latin America, increases in GDP have meant more poverty as governments sold out national resources to foreign investors and speculators without any rules of taxation or social equality in place. See Stiglitz, supra, pp. 25–46.

[60]   World Commission on Environment and Development (1987), *Our Common Future*, Oxford: Oxford University Press.

[61]   Social ills (crime, weakening of social fabric, HIV/AIDS, pollution, etc.) were still spreading even in cases of strong and consistent economic growth.

[62]   Among the influential authors who were beyond this change in perspective perhaps the most famous is Prof. A. Sen. Sen, A. (1999), *Development as Freedom*, Oxford: Oxford University Press.

GDP per capita.[63] Human development was defined by the UNHDRs as a process of enlarging people's choices and enhancing human capabilities (the range of things people can be and do) and freedoms, enabling them to live a long and healthy life, have access to knowledge and a decent standard of living, and participate in the life of their community and decisions affecting their lives.[64]

3.3.2. The right to development

The relationship between economic development, human rights and human well-being found an uneasy articulation in the struggle for the proclamation of a 'right to development' within the United Nations.[65] The ex-colonies and newly independent countries had found that joining the existing international order, and especially the policies of the international financial institutions – IMF, World Bank and the trading regime created by the GATT – did not meet their needs or circumstances and started a long battle to establish a different economic order. This struggle crystallised in the approval of the Declaration on the Establishment of a New International Economic Order (NIEO).[66] One of the premises of this new economic order was to affirm the power of the newly independent states to pursue development policies without outside interference and the ability to exploit their natural resources and dictate the future of their populations according to internal principles and policies. Development was, in their view, a national undertaking, and as such no constraints in the form of human rights commitments or economic and vested interests of foreign investors should stand in its way.

With developing countries on the one hand urging the proclamation of a right to development firmly anchored in the principles of self-determination and permanent sovereignty over natural resources[67] and

---

[63] Together with the other three indices which are published: the GDI – Gender-Related Development Index which is the HDI adjusted for gender inequality, the GEM – Gender Empowerment Measure of gender equality in economic and political participation and decision making and the HPI – Human Poverty Index that measures the level of human poverty. See www.undp.org/statistics/indices/hpi.

[64] www.hdr.undp.org/en/humandev/.

[65] See Orford, A. (2001), 'Globalization and the Right to Development', in P. Alston (ed.) *People's Rights*, New York: Oxford University Press, 127.

[66] Declaration on the Establishment of a New Economic Order, adopted 1 May 1974, GA Res. 32011 (s VI) 6 (SPECIAL) UN GAOR 6th Spec. Supp. No. 1 at 3, UN Doc. A/9559 (1974) reprinted in 3 I.L.M. (1974) 715.

[67] Solomon, M. (2007), *Global Responsibility for Human Rights*, Oxford: Oxford University Press, at 112–133.

developed countries largely resisting it mostly on behalf of the commercial interests of the investors, development as a right was first proclaimed by the Organization of African Unity and included in the 1981 African Charter of Human and Peoples' Rights.[68] The UN General Assembly proclaimed development as a human right in its 1986 Declaration on the Right to Development (DRD).[69] It was later reaffirmed by the 1993 Vienna and 2000 Millennium Declarations.[70]

The much awaited declaration on the right to development left several questions unanswered. It remained unclear who was the subject of the right to development: individuals, states or both, as those in the developing world had long argued that development is a right of states *and* individuals and developing countries should be able to claim an entitlement to 'receive a fair share of what belongs to all'.[71] The final version of the declaration on the right to development dropped the reference to the rights of states and stated that only individuals and peoples are the holders of the right to development.[72] States can invoke the right externally or at the international stage on behalf of their people in order to encourage international and institutional arrangements conducive to the exercise of fundamental socio-economic rights.[73] At the same time it has been argued that the international community has an obligation to development cooperation within nation states which includes cooperation in areas of financial flows, debt restructuring, technology transfer, foreign aid and transfer of resources.[74]

---

[68]   African [Banjul] Charter on Human and Peoples' Rights, adopted 27 June 1981, OAU Doc. CAB/LEG/67/3 rev. 5, 21 I.L.M. (1982), 58 entered into force 21 October 1986: Article 22: '1. All peoples shall have the right to their economic, social and cultural development with due regard to their freedom and identity and in the equal enjoyment of the common heritage of mankind. 2. States shall have the duty, individually or collectively, to ensure the exercise of the right to development.'

[69]   Declaration on the Right to Development, adopted 4 December 1986, GA Res. A/RES/41/128.

[70]   Vienna Declaration and Programme of Action, A/CONF.157/23, 12 July 1993: cf. 10. 'The World Conference on Human Rights reaffirms the right to development, as established in the Declaration on the Right to Development, as a universal and inalienable right and an integral part of fundamental human rights'.

[71]   Particularly, Bedjadoui, M. (1991), 'The Right to Development', in M. Bedjadoui (ed.), *International Law: Achievements and Prospects*, Leiden: Martinus Nijhoff, 1177, at 1192.

[72]   Cf. Article 2 DRD: 'The human person is the central subject of development and should be the active participant and beneficiary of the right to development'.

[73]   See Rich, R. (1988), 'The Right to Development: A Right of Peoples?', in J. Crawford (ed.), *The Rights of Peoples*, New York: Oxford University Press, pp. 39–55.

[74]   Solomon, M. (2007), *Global Responsibility for Human Rights*, Oxford: Oxford University Press, at 112.

The right to development is better understood as a right to a process of development where all human rights – economic, social and cultural rights and civil and political rights – are realised. An improvement in the realisation of the Right to Development means that at least some rights should improve while no other rights are violated. Implementing the Right to Development would require implementation of a development policy for the economy as a whole. It would serve to harmonise policies for realising individual rights with a programme for economic growth which respects human rights standards. The DRD emphasises the indivisibility and interdependence of all aspects of the declaration itself.[75] There is also an umbilical link between poverty alleviation and the implementation of the right to development framework. This has been emphasised in the Second Report of the Independent Expert where he contends that '[f]rom the perspective of a rights-based approach to human development, the concept of poverty goes much beyond just income poverty . . . it is a gross violation of human rights. The eradication of poverty should be the first priority of a policy for realizing the right to development.'[76]

The right to development has been heavily contested at the international level. Developing countries claim that it imposes obligations on developed countries towards developing countries,[77] an assertion rejected by all developed countries. Despite these disagreements there is a core of elements to the right to development which are widely agreed.[78] These three elements are: first, the human person is at the centre of development;[79] second, the process of development should be respectful of all human rights and in particular of rights of participation at all levels; and, third, development should promote social justice and states have the primary responsibility at the national level to promote development and to enter into appropriate international policies and agreements for cooperation.[80]

In 1998 the Commission on Human Rights appointed an Independent

---

[75] Article 9(1) DRD: 'All aspects of the right to development set forth in the present Declaration are indivisible and interdependent and each of them should be considered in the context of the whole'.

[76] See *Second Report of the Independent Expert on the Right to Development*, UN Doc. E/CN.4/2000/WG.18/CPR.1.94, available at: www.hd-ca.org/pubs/5_1_Sitta.pdf.

[77] Bedjadoui (1999), supra, p. 1192.

[78] See for an overview on the status of the RTD, Piron, L.H. (2002), 'The right to development: a review of the current state of the debate for the Department of International Development', available at: www.odi.org.uk/resources/download/1562.pdf.

[79] Article 2 DRD.

[80] Solomon (2007), supra, at 128.

Expert on the Right to Development. This was followed by the creation of an open-ended Working Group on the Right to Development and, more recently, a UN Task Force on the Implementation of the Right to Development to assess compliance with the principles enumerated in the DRD. The Task Force has highlighted the links between the right to development and that the MDG8 requires a global partnership for development.[81] A human rights approach to economic growth and development seeks to integrate fairness into the process of wealth expansion and allocation of resources, while focusing on distributional aspects such as ensuring poverty reduction and a minimum quality of life for the whole population.[82] This emphasis on growth with equity could be interpreted as requiring 'equality of opportunity for all in basic access to resources, education, health services, food, housing, employment and the fair distribution of income . . . [and that] [a]ppropriate economic and social reforms should be accrued out with a view to eliminating all social injustice'.[83]

It has been argued that since most decisions about development policies take place collectively, and mostly through the international financial institutions (IFIs), countries taking part in decision-making in IFIs need to vote in a way which takes into account the effect that policies approved will have on the process of advancing development and human rights.[84]

3.3.3.   Right to development or right to sustainable development?

The integration of human rights considerations, fairness and equitable access to natural resources while ensuring that the environment upon which life depends is respected is epitomised in the impossibly complex yet ubiquitous principle of sustainable development.[85]

Environmental degradation is one specific manifestation of the diver-

---

[81]   Report of the High Level Task Force on the Implementation of the Right to Development (2nd session 2005), UN Doc. E/CN4/2005/WG18?TF/3, para. 82.

[82]   See Report of the Working Group on the Right to Development (2005), para. 46.

[83]   DRD Article 8(1). See discussion in Solomon (2007), supra, pp. 131–135.

[84]   There is case law of the European Court of Human Rights which establishes that the human rights responsibilities of states continue after the transfer of competences to international organisations. *Matthews v. United Kingdom* App. No. 24833/94, 18 February 1999 (28 EHRR 361), Grand Chamber Judgments of 18 1999, discussed in Solomon (2007), supra, at 137. Also in general Reinisch, A. (2005), 'The Changing International Legal Framework Dealing with Non-State Actors', in P. Alston (ed.), *Non-State Actors and Human Rights*, Oxford: Oxford University Press, 37.

[85]   The concept of sustainable development is discussed in some detail in the next chapter, pp. 93–97.

gence between economic growth and (human) development.[86] The concept of sustainable development is a response to this divergence and modifies the traditional development model by adding a fifth element, protection of the environment, to the classical four elements – of economic development, social development, peace and security, and a system of good governance. The World Commission on Environment and Development (WCED) recognised more than 20 years ago that the environment, economic and social issues are interlinked, and as such recommended that the three should be integrated into development decision-making.[87] Sustainable development is primarily the responsibility of national governments. Environmental and conservation laws provide a foundation for sustainable development; they do not reflect the range or depth of necessary actions, nor are they necessarily the most economically efficient means of achieving sustainable development. Sustainable development further places duties upon states which modify sovereignty and must be taken into account when legislation is passed both in economic development areas and in environmental protection. According to leading commentators, 'sustainable development implies not merely limits on economic activity in the interests of preserving or protecting the environment, but an approach to development which emphasises the fundamental importance of equity within the economic system'.[88] Noting the recent developments since the 1980s it is arguable that the right to development implies a right to sustainable development.[89]

3.3.4. The Millennium Development Goals

The turn of the century brought a sense of urgency to previous attempts to address poverty, environment and development challenges. World leaders committed to a world free from want where people would be free from '[t]he threat of living on a planet irredeemably spoilt by human activities, and whose resources would no longer be sufficient for their needs' in the Millennium Declaration[90] and agreed a set of time-bound targets – the

---

[86] Opschoor, J. (2005), 'Globalisation and Sustainable Policies in Developing Countries' in Wijen et al. (2005), supra, p. 279.

[87] See unep.geo4, 'Environment and Development', p. 4 available at: www.unep.org/.

[88] Birnie, Boyle and Redgwell (2009), supra, p. 55.

[89] For further discussion on this point see chapter 2, pp. 93–97. Also in general see Cordonnier-Segger, M.C. and A. Khalfan (2004), *Sustainable Development Law. Principles, Practices and Prospects*, Oxford and New York: Oxford University Press.

[90] United Nations Millennium Declaration, available at: www.un.org/millennium/declaration/.

Millennium Development Goals (MDGs)[91] – aimed at improving human well-being through the reduction of extreme poverty. In the words of United Nations Secretary-General Ban Ki-moon:[92]

> Eradicating extreme poverty continues to be one of the main challenges of our time, and is a major concern of the international community. Ending this scourge will require the combined efforts of all, governments, civil society organizations and the private sector, in the context of a stronger and more effective global partnership for development. The Millennium Development Goals set time bound targets, by which progress in reducing income poverty, hunger, disease, lack of adequate shelter and exclusion – while promoting gender equality, health, education and environmental sustainability – can be measured. They also embody basic human rights – the rights of each person on the planet to health, education, shelter and security. The Goals are ambitious but feasible and, together with the comprehensive United Nations development agenda, set the course for the world's efforts to alleviate extreme poverty by 2015.

The MDGs consist of an integrated normative framework for human development. All goals are inter-related and address the overall objective of reducing poverty. Environmental sustainability (Goal 7) is addressed through three specific targets: the integration of the principles of sustainable development into country policies and programmes and the reversion of the loss of environmental resources (Target 9); to halve the proportion of people without sustainable access to safe drinking water (Target 10); and to achieve an improvement in the lives of slum dwellers (Target 10).

The linkages between environmental sustainability (Goal 7) and the commitment to develop a global partnership for development have been the subject of recent attention by UNEP.[93]

Despite the substantial human and financial investment made in the last

---

[91]   The goals can be found at www.un.org/millenniumgoals/ (accessed 15 November 2009).

[92]   While advances have been made in some areas, most notably in the reduction of substances which deplete the ozone layer and in providing safe drinking water to rural communities, the world economic crises has slowed the already insufficient progress, and with only over five years to go it is clear that the targets fixed for 2015 will not be met. See United Nations (2009) Millennium Development Goals Report, Introduction, available at: www.un.org/millennium-goals/pdf/MDG_Report_2009_ENG.pdf (accessed 15 November 2009).

[93]   UNEP Geo 4 has established the links between the environment and the MDGs. *Claiming the Millennium Development Goals: A Human Rights Approach* (2008), UN Office of the High Commissioner for Human Rights. UN Doc. HR/PUB/08/3.

eight years, the developing world is still far from reaching the stated goals. Progress towards achieving the MDGs has been erratic and below expectations. The final recommendations[94] included action for the international community in three main areas: the international development aid system including debt relief,[95] trade reforms,[96] and investment in regional and global public goods.[97] Coordination of technical support round the goals was deemed key, and a call was made to multilateral and bilateral agencies involved in the aid system, governments, civil society, NGOs and business to unite in their efforts to fight poverty. The economic crisis of 2008–2009 has made it imperative that in the face of diminished worldwide economic growth efforts are directed to those most in need.[98]

Achieving the MDGs, reducing poverty, promoting sustainable development, and creating a system of natural resource management which allows developing countries to meet their needs without destroying their immediate environments are challenges which can be met only with collaboration from the whole international community and by a system of global governance which is fair, equitable, far-sighted and balanced between the economic and environmental interest, developed and developing countries' concerns and needs. We will turn to look at the system of global governance and see whether these conditions are currently in place.

4. GLOBAL GOVERNANCE

Globalisation has multiplied the links between peoples, nations, cultures and markets, and those links need not only 'regulation' but mostly inclusion within an overall structure of cohesive and coherent governance.

---

[94] Presented in a synthesis volume, *Investing in Development: A Practical Plan to Achieve the Millennium Development Goals* (2005), available at: www.millenniumproject.org/reports/index.htm (accessed 15 November 2009).

[95] Rich countries were asked to increase the aid to 0.7% of the gross domestic product and to cancel the external debt of the heavily indebted poor countries. The multilateral and bilateral agencies should organise their technical efforts around supporting countries to develop and implement MDG-based poverty reduction strategies. Ibid., 'Overview Report' (2005), available at: www.millenniumproject.org/reports/overviewEng33_55.pdf, at pp. 33–36.

[96] Ibid., at 45–46.

[97] Ibid., at 47.

[98] See United Nations (2009), Millennium Development Goals Report, pp. 4 and 5, available at: www.un.org/millenniumgoals/pdf/MDG_Report_2009_ENG.pdf (accessed 15 November 2009).

Lack of effective governance creates instability. Crises can be tracked down to the lack of governance in particular sectors.[99]

Most governance institutions were designed at the nation-state level and function relatively well within state boundaries. International institutions have evolved throughout the last half of the last century in an incremental effort to address the problems and issues that arise out of the world's inter-connectedness. Institutions designed to ensure peace and security after the devastation created by the two world wars were soon complemented by an array of various and inter-related bodies, organisations and secretariats with multifaceted or focused mandates, all of them within the overreaching aim of ensuring co-existence in the unavoidably interconnected world we inhabit.

As indicated in the introduction to this chapter we address govern-ance in this book with two different perspectives: we first consider what is governance and how it is articulated globally and whether in the area of natural resources there is an effective system of global natural resource management. We also address governance as a challenge through the prism of the different actors and the structures within which they operate.

4.1.   What is Governance?

Governance is a concept which has been much overused in recent years. At its most basic it relates to the 'rules and institutions that regulate the public realm in civil society',[100] or '[t]he sum of the many ways individuals and institutions, public and private, manage their common affairs . . . [a] continuing process through which conflicting or diverse interests may be accommodated and co-operative action may be taken'.[101]

The Commission on Global Governance[102] points out that governance

---

[99]   It has been argued that the recent global financial crisis has its root in the lack of effective governance of financial markets. See Stiglitz (2010), *supra*.

[100]   Nayyar, D. (ed.) (2002), *Governing Globalisation; Issues and Institutions*, New York: Oxford University Press, at 376.

[101]   Commission on Global Governance (1995), *Our Global Neighbourhood*, New York: Oxford University Press.

[102]   The Commission – an independent group of 28 public figures – was inspired by the belief that the end of the Cold War offered opportunities to build a more cooperative, safer and fairer world. It operated between 1992 and 2001 and published several reports including proposals for improving the world's govern-ance. The CGG was financed by United Nations, the European Union, national governments, large American corporations, and other organisations. See www.globalgovernancewatch.org/. . ./-commission-on-global-governance (accessed 15 November 2009).

is not just an aspect of intergovernmental relationships; it also includes formal institutions and regimes empowered to enforce compliance, as well as informal arrangements which people and institutions either have agreed to or perceive to be in their interest. Non-governmental organisations (NGOs), citizens' movements, multinational corporations, and the global capital markets all represent the interests and shape the lives of millions of people, and must therefore be included in an effective system of global governance.[103] At the global level there is a clear divergence between law and economic processes. Law creation and enforcement is still largely concentrated at the state or inter-state level, while economic processes function at a supranational or global level, creating what some authors have described as a 'regulatory fracture'. [104] States find it difficult – both in political and in practical terms – to apply their regulation to economic entities and actors which operate in a globalised context. Issues of economic necessity or jurisdictional power limit the effectiveness of national regulation.[105]

In the last few years theories and studies about new ways of governing the global economy through collaboration of non-state actors have proliferated. Names such as 'responsive regulation',[106] 'post-regulatory law',[107] 'collaborative governance',[108] or simply 'governance'[109] are now commonplace in the literature. Instruments such as corporate codes of conduct, industry guidelines or decentralised environmental regulation have arisen out of these collaborative efforts.[110] The shared premise of these theorists is that actors' interests can be engaged in deliberative and participatory processes once institutions are decentralised and democratised so as to involve all relevant 'stakeholders'.[111] This participatory liberal legalism is not without critics, who argue that important contradictions and conflicts between stakeholders' interests and needs are ignored in this model.

---

[103]   Non-state actors are discussed in chapter 5.
[104]   For a discussion see de Souza Santos and Rodriguez-Garavito (2004), supra, p. 7.
[105]   See chapter 5, pp. 276–283 for a discussion of the problems of national regulation of multinational corporations.
[106]   Ayes, I. and J. Braithwaite (1992), *Responsive Regulation: Transcending the Deregulation Debate*, New York: Oxford University Press.
[107]   Teubner, G. (1983), 'Substantive and Reflexive Elements in Modern Law', Law and Society Review, 17, 239.
[108]   Freemand, J. (1997), 'Collaborative Governance in the Administrative State', UCLA Law Review, 45, 1–98.
[109]   Nye, J.S. and J.D. Donahue (eds) (2000), *Governance in a Globalising World*, Washington DC: Brookings Institution Press.
[110]   For an explanation of all of these see chapter 2, pp. 111–116.
[111]   See chapter 3, 'Participatory rights', pp. 150–167.

Concerns are also expressed about the poor and all those excluded from social citizenship due to class, gender or ethnicity who in fact account for the majority of the world population and do not integrate into the neo-liberal participatory design.[112]

4.2.   Global Economic Governance: Trade, Foreign Direct Investment and Natural Resources

Throughout this book it is argued that lack of effective global governance is a problem in environmental and natural resources management. By contrast there is a rather sophisticated and efficient system of global economic governance described quite accurately as '[a] "new constitutionalism" represented by the WTO and other international institutions as a project of attempting to make transnational liberalism, and if possible liberal democratic capitalism, the sole model for future development'.[113] Economic governance has been driven and dominated by the Bretton Woods Institutions – the IMF, World Bank and, today, the WTO. It is built upon the so-called 'Washington consensus', a term coined to describe suggested market reforms in Latin America in the context of IMF lending.[114] The Washington consensus was based upon several pillars. First and foremost was the belief in the supremacy of markets which were considered to be both efficient and neutral in opposition to states and public intervention which was seen as mostly inefficient. This in turn created an urge to privatise all areas of social and economic activity which were under public control. Any country wishing to benefit from IMF or World Bank lending had to privatise, de-regulate and adjust its social spending accordingly, allowing dangerous and unfettered flows of speculative capital.[115]

But markets are not as efficient as their advocates would lead us to

---

[112]   de Souza Santos and Rodriguez-Garavito (2004), supra, p. 9.

[113]   Gill, S. (2003), *Power and Resistance in the New World Order*, Basingstoke: Palgrave Macmillan, p. 132.

[114]   Williamson, J. (1990), 'What Washington Means by Policy Reform', in J. Williamson (ed.), *Latin American Adjustment: How Much Has Happened?*, Washington DC: Institute for International Economics.

[115]   The latter had disastrous consequences. Latin America followed the Washington consensus, and opened capital markets to foreign speculative capital-collapse. China and Vietnam did not. East Asia, which has successfully controlled globalisation through careful government intervention and direction of the economy, was forced to open capital markets, and the financial crises which affected Indonesia, Thailand and the region in 1997 were met with a pathetic response of the IMF which would provide funds only to bail out Western interests and private financial and speculative capital but not to provide food subsidies

believe. Professor Stiglitz denounced the consequences of limited and imperfect information and imperfect competition of markets.[116] Markets, without government or public intervention, produce too many negative externalities – like pollution – which are un-priced, and not enough public goods – such as basic research – which are essential for a properly efficient system. Economic success requires getting the balance right between the government and the market. Globalisation, unfortunately, seems to have made the possibility of striking this balance harder by delegating important societal decisions which are essentially and fundamentally political to technocrats. Today the IMF and World Bank have reviewed their policies and acknowledged the importance of public participation, environmental protection and greater flexibility to take into account social concerns when designing economic and regulatory models.[117]

4.2.1.　The governance of world trade

The governance of world trade is highly advanced, with the WTO as the leading forum where a rules based system backed up by an expeditious and efficient system of dispute settlement enables global trade, providing participants with security and certainty.[118] The creation of the WTO in 1995 at the Uruguay Round of Negotiations with the signature of the Marrakech Agreements was greeted as the beginning of a new era of a rules based system of world trade which would bring prosperity for all. This prosperity, in turn, should reduce poverty in developing countries with a trickle-down effect to the poorest in society.[119] However it soon became clear that gains from liberalisation of trade were very unevenly

---

for the local population. It also imposed such an absurd and stringent list of conditions on recipient countries that it forced them further into financial collapse.

[116]　He won the Nobel Prize in economics for his work on 'Markets with information asymmetries' with George A. Akerlof and Michael Spence, and was fired as Chief Economist of the World Bank for his dissenting views from what he called 'market fundamentalism'. He revisits some of his original ideas in his latest book, *Freefall* (2010), supra.

[117]　See chapter 4, pp. 195–196.

[118]　See chapter 4 for a detailed study of the WTO and its role in globalisation governance and natural resource management.

[119]　After Marrakech the GATT Secretariat estimated that there would be minimum gains of $500 billion per year following trade liberalisation and the implementation of the Marrakech Agreement. Discussed in Safadi, R. and S. Laird (1996), 'The Uruguay Round Agreements: Impact on Developing Countries', World Development 24, p. 1223–1242. Other estimates put gains at $200 billion, with developing countries obtaining about a third of all total gains according to the OECD, *Assessing the Effects of the Uruguay Round*, Trade Policy Issues 2, Paris: OECD.

distributed. A few large export-oriented developing countries and developed countries reaped most of the benefits while the 48 least developed countries lost an estimated US$600 million a year as result of the Uruguay Round.[120] Several reasons were advanced to explain the disparity between the estimates and the reality. On the one hand some of the reforms which were suggested in the proposals and which would have provided the most significant gains for developing countries never took place. For example the Agreement on Textiles and Clothing was postponed in order to protect developed countries' interests. To add to this the costs of implementing the reforms in developing countries were completely ignored, and some of the reforms such as the tariff-rate quotas for agricultural goods did not amount to much of a market liberalisation on agricultural products.[121]

Agricultural products which were excluded from the GATT remained largely excluded from the WTO system although they constitute the largest output of developing countries. Subtle but effective trade barriers affecting those in developing countries the most have also remained in place.[122] But even if barriers were eliminated not everybody would have the same ability to access the market and benefit from free trade. For example in 2001 when Europe unilaterally opened up its markets to the poorest countries of the world hardly any goods came into Europe since poor countries lacked basic things such as the minimal infrastructure to bring their goods into the markets.[123] Lack of infrastructure is just one of the many obstacles which developing countries face coping with an all-liberalised, all-globalised trading environment.[124] Their restricted funds make it difficult to provide the necessary re-training and social security safety nets which are often necessary when changing or adapting the productive base of a country.

At the turn of the century a sense of collective responsibility for world poverty had gained momentum and culminated with the publication of the Millennium Development Goals (MDGs).[125] In 2001 the Doha

---

[120]   Stiglitz, J. and A. Charlton (2005), *Fair Trade for All: How Trade Can Promote Development*, New York: Oxford University Press, at 47.

[121]   Ibid.

[122]   These relate to issues such as product labelling and information which have been designed by developed countries and which constitute an economic burden to developing countries.

[123]   Stiglitz and Charlton (2005), supra, pp. 215–260.

[124]   One of the main problems reported in this meeting is the fact that small producers could not access credit since local banks had been overtaken by big multinational banking corporations. Stiglitz (2007), supra, at p. 7.

[125]   Discussed earlier in this chapter.

Ministerial Declaration[126] contained a commitment to development which followed that sense of collective responsibility. In its Article 2 it stated:

> International trade can play a major role in the promotion of economic development and the alleviation of poverty. We recognise the needs for all our peoples to benefit from the increased opportunities and welfare gains that the multilateral trading system generates. The majority of WTO members are developing countries. We seek to place their needs and interests at the heart of the World Programme adopted in this Declaration.

With this laudable intent in mind the work programme of Doha consisted of 21 subjects which would be subject either to future negotiations, analysis and monitoring or implementation. The subjects included ranged from agriculture, services, market access for non-agricultural products to trade related aspects of intellectual property rights and the relationship between trade and the environment.[127] Developed countries soon abandoned the good intentions which had accompanied the new millennium and pushed forward with the matters which were in their interest while delaying or frustrating negotiations on those areas which could make a real difference to developing countries.[128] After a turbulent itinerary[129] the Doha commitments are again at the negotiation table. Trade reforms are fundamental to development and to the achievement of the MDGs. The Monterrey Consensus[130] stated that a development friendly trade policy should focus

---

[126]　WT/MIN(01)/DEC/1, 20 November 2001. Ministerial declaration, adopted on 14 November 2001, available at: www.wto.org/english/thewto_e/minist_e/. . ./ mindecl_e.htm.

[127]　Paras 31–33. Developed in chapter 2, pp. 201–203.

[128]　See Stiglitz, J.E. (2004), 'A Development Friendly Prioritization of the Doha Round Agenda', The World Economy 28, 293–312 and Cardwell, M. and C. Rodgers (2006), 'Reforming the WTO Legal Order for Agricultural Trade: Issues for European Rural Policy in the Doha Round', International and Comparative Law Quarterly, 55, 805.

[129]　The Fifth Ministerial Conference (Cancun, 2003) ended without consensus on how to move the negotiations forward, and although the following year members adopted a framework for the negotiations on agriculture, NAMA & Services (the 'July Package'), which has served as a basis for the work since then on these topics, the original deadline to conclude the round in January 2005 was missed. In December 2005 the Hong Kong package enhanced commitment in agriculture and NAMA, while mapping out all other areas in the negotiations. Governments agreed to commit billions of dollars to an Aid for Trade package which would complement the Doha Round. In July 2006 talks were suspended and resumed in January 2007. Finally in July 2008 members met in Geneva to discuss the 'July 2008 package': establishment of Agriculture and NAMA modalities. Roadmap of all topics toward conclusion end 2008.

[130]　www.un.org/esa/ffd/monterrey/MonterreyConsensus.pdf.　Recently　the

on two overarching issues: improved market access and terms of trade for poor countries and improved supply-side competitiveness for low-income country exports through increased investments in infrastructure (roads, electricity, ports) and trade facilitation.

4.2.2. The regulation of foreign direct investment

Foreign direct investment (FDI) is closely linked to the demands of international trade. It has been described as one of the 'forces propelling globalisation'[131] and the increase in the flows of foreign investment one of its defining features.[132] Foreign direct investment is 'an investment made to acquire lasting interest in enterprises operating outside of the economy of the investor'.[133] The purpose of the investor (a foreign individual, entity or group) is to gain an effective voice in the management of the enterprise. There is always some degree of equity ownership (usually a minimum 10 per cent)[134] and it is almost always considered to be associated with an effective voice in the management of an enterprise. The unincorporated or incorporated enterprise – a branch or subsidiary, respectively, in which direct investment is made – is referred to as a 'direct investment enterprise'. The most important characteristic of FDI, which distinguishes it from foreign portfolio investment, is that it is undertaken with the intention of exercising control over an enterprise.[135]

As FDI is a measure of foreign ownership of productive assets, such as factories, mines and land, the protection of foreign investment has traditionally been a bone of contention between the North and the South. The South, although in desperate need of foreign investment, is wary of its implications and regards it as a new form of subtle colonisation and as having the potential to place restrictions on national policies. Policies such as import-substitution, nationalisation of key industries, and state

---

Follow-up International Conference on Financing for Development to Review the Implementation of the Monterrey Consensus (Doha, Qatar, 29 November–2 December 2008) resulted in the adoption by consensus of the 'Doha Declaration on Financing for Development'. See www.un.org/ffd/.

[131]   World Trade Organization Secretariat (1996), 'Trade and Foreign Direct Investment', World Trade and Arbitration Materials.

[132]   World Bank (2007), *Global Economic Prospects; Managing the Next Wave of Globalisation*, Washington DC: IBRD/World Bank, at 35.

[133]   IMF (1993), 'Balance of Payments Manual', 5th edn, Washington, DC, International Monetary Fund.

[134]   OECD (1996), 'Detailed Benchmark Definition of Foreign Direct Investment', 3rd edn, Paris, Organisation for Economic Co-operation and Development.

[135]   Ibid.

monopolies in sectors such as energy had the dual aim of improving and distributing economic development evenly between the local population and diminishing the influence and control of foreign powers.[136] Foreign investment was initially regulated by a mixed regime which relied on constitutional provisions,[137] domestic laws and even international instruments like the 1974 UN Charter of Economic Rights and Duties of States (CERDS). This regulation gave way to a more liberal regime which soon verged towards the liberalisation of foreign investment and centred on the protection of the investor, be it through an array of bilateral investment treaties (BITs) or regional agreements like NAFTA.[138]

BITs sought to provide a stable legal environment within which FDI would be encouraged.[139] A large number of BITs were signed in the 1990s[140] creating a quasi-constitutional regime of foreign direct investment. The terms of a BIT are reciprocal under public international law.[141] The global investment rules regime has been described as 'constitutional' in many ways, as its object is 'to place limits on the authority of government, isolating economic from political power and assigning to investment interests the highest possible protection'.[142] The main feature of the BITs is the protection of investors through two key rules of non-discrimination: the rule of 'national treatment' which entitles foreign investors to treatment no less favourable than domestic investors and the rule or principle of 'most favoured nation' which makes foreign investors of any given country entitled to the most favourable treatment granted to investors of any other country.[143] BITs also provide protection from expropriation and nationalisation – the so-called 'takings' rule, which prohibits both direct and indirect measures.[144] Further and crucially the

---

[136] For a good discussion see Schneiderman, D. (2008), *Constitutionalizing Economic Globalization: Investment Rules and Democracy's Promise*, Cambridge: Cambridge University Press, p. 27.

[137] Such as Mexico's Calvo's clause. Ibid., pp. 161–163.

[138] Discussed in chapter 4, pp. 205–206.

[139] See, generally, Gallagher, N. and L. Shore (2004), 'Bilateral Investment Treaties: Options and Drawbacks', International Arbitration Law Review 7(2), 49.

[140] According to UNCTAD more than 2573 BITs had been signed involving 175 countries, most of them during the 1990s. UNCTAD (2007), supra at 16.

[141] Lowenfeld, A.F. (2003), *International Economic Law*, New York and Oxford: Oxford University Press, at 474–484.

[142] Schneiderman, D. (2008), supra, at 4.

[143] For an overview of BITs see Dolzer, R. and C. Schreuer (2008), *Principles of International Investment Law*, Oxford: Oxford University Press.

[144] Including any measure which has an 'equivalent effect to' or is 'tantamount to' nationalisation or expropriation, Art. 4 of the 2005 BIT between China and Germany.

enforcement of investment disputes is left to the International Centre for the Settlement of Investment Disputes (ICSID), the UNCITRAL, the Court of International Arbitration of the International Chamber of Commerce in Paris, the Stockholm Chamber or the Cairo Regional Centre for International Commercial Arbitration.[145] All these are venues designed and suitable for commercial and private dispute settlement, and it has been argued that they may be unsuitable or ill-equipped to deal with the complex public law issues involved in investment disputes between foreign MNCs and states. Attempts to create a regulation of foreign investment at the global level, in a fashion similar to the regulation of international trade, failed with the rejection at several levels of the controversial Multilateral Agreement on Investment (MAI).[146]

The combination of the liberalisation of foreign investment and the system of free trade imposed by the WTO creates serious problems for developing countries and places limitations on their policy choices over natural resource management by including stabilisation clauses which reduce substantially the ability of host states to pass laws or modify the legislative environment for the benefit of local populations if it signifies a detriment to the investors' return, creating serious human rights risks[147] and the threat of international arbitration. Recently foreign investment has been directed towards land acquisition for food or non-food agricultural production, threatening the food supply and access to land of millions in already poor countries.

BITs could be modified and drafted in such a way as to include environmental and social concerns.[148] At present these take the form of 'best endeavour clauses' which do not impose any substantive obligations on the parties and require them only to apply their best endeavour 'to ensure that investment activity is undertaken in a manner sensitive to

---

[145]   The ICSID and investment disputes are discussed in chapter 6, 'Compliance', pp. 258–261.

[146]   At the international level the OECD initiative to create a Multilateral Agreement on Investment which would operate in parallel to the WTO in respect of trade on goods and services failed due to the heavily biased pro-investor rules of the proposed text. See chapter 5 for a discussion on the role of civil society and non-state actors in overturning the MAI.

[147]   See, for a detailed discussion of these risks, Shemberg, A. and J. Ruggie (2008), 'Stabilization Clauses and Human Rights', available at: www.business-humanrights.org/SpecialRepPortal/Home/. . ./2008 (accessed 15 November 2009).

[148]   Environmental and labour concerns were also included in the Preamble to the 1994 US Model BIT. See Articles 12 and 13 of the 2004 US Model BIT, available at: www.bilaterals.org/article.php3?id_article=137 (accessed 15 January 2010).

BOX 1.1. LAND ACQUISITIONS, FOOD SECURITY AND FOREIGN DIRECT INVESTMENT

Acquisition of large tracts of land in Africa, Asia and to a smaller degree Latin America by foreign states and corporations has recently been denounced by the international press and civil society organisations.[1] The food crisis of 2008 and the renewed interest in agriculture[2] have made both the investing states[3] and the host states focus their policies into this development. This is coupled with a desire to enhance food and energy security in investing states[4] and to obtain competitive returns for investing companies with the growth of carbon markets that make investments in afforestation, agrofuels or REDD related schemes an attractive option.[5]

Half of all cultivable land reserves are concentrated in seven countries: Angola, the Democratic Republic of Congo, Ghana, Sudan, Argentina, Bolivia and Colombia. Some of these countries are in receipt of food aid from the UN and other private donors and have large populations living below the poverty line with endangered food security. Yet if the current trend continues land in these countries will be used to grow food for the populations of the UAE and Gulf States, China, Saudi Arabia, Japan or South Korea, or biofuels or non-food commodities for the international markets. While host governments have been fast in creating a policy environment favourable and conducive to the transfer of land or land rights to foreign investors, an effective system of free prior informed consent (FPIC)[6] combined with adequate systems of redress and mitigation have not been so readily implemented.[7] Host states justify the leasing[8] of parts of their territory to foreign investors in terms of the benefits they claim will derive for the country in the form of technology, investments in irrigation and jobs for the local population. They also claim that some of the land they lease is 'available', 'idle' or 'waste' land, although research has shown that this classification does not reflect the status of the land since large tracks of the 'idle' land are used for shift cultivation, a practice common in African agriculture, or dry-season grazing.[9] These low productivity uses of land are in most cases vital for the local people in terms of food security and livelihood and the lease of land may irreversibly endanger them.

Yet, in a recent analysis of the 2008 food crisis UNCTAD Secretary-General Supachai Panitchpakdi pointed out that Africa, which was once a net food exporter but which has been a net food importer for the past 20 years or so, and is thus especially at risk.[10]

Notes:

1. See 'Fears for the world's poor countries as the rich grab land to grow food', The Guardian, Saturday, 4 July 2009. Also Smaller, C. and H. Mann (2009), 'A Thirst for Distant Lands. Foreign investment in agricultural land and water', IISD, available at: http://iisd.org/pdf/2009/thirst_for_distant_lands.pdf (accessed 15 November 2009).

2. See The World Bank (2008), *Agriculture for Development*, World Development Report which signals an increased interests from donors and investors into the until recently neglected sector, available at: http://siteresources.worldbank.org/INTWDR2008/. . ./WDROver2008-ENG.pdf (accessed 15 January 2010).

3. We shall use the term 'states' although we are aware that private entities are involved in this process, sometimes exclusively.

4. This is the case of the Gulf States which face a shortage of food production with increasingly large migrant populations. For other countries such as China other considerations may be at stake, for example to enhance the competitive edge of Chinese multinationals in food production.

5. Particularly as the financial crisis has made other investment alternatives less attractive and the price of land is very cheap in the countries involved.

6. In the case of indigenous peoples, often affected by land taking and the granting of state concessions to foreign companies without their consent Article 32 of the UNDRIP recognises that they have the right to say 'yes' or 'no' to development projects in their land. See chapter 3 for a discussion on indigenous peoples.

7. Often local people are insufficiently informed before consultations and their consent is obtained without the involvement of relevant stakeholders. For example, in Africa, only clan elders or chiefs are included into the process, while women who constitute the majority of rural households are traditionally excluded.

8. In most cases the investment takes the form of a long-term lease with periods ranging from 50 to 99 years. See Smaller and Mann (2009), supra, p. 135, Occasionally an outright sale take place.

9. Ibid., at 136.

10. UNCTAD Policy Brief (2008), 'Sustaining African Agriculture', available at: http://unctad.org/en/docs/presspb20086_eng.pdf (accessed 15 December 2009).

environmental concerns'.[149] Contracting parties have procedural rights to request consultations with the other party with a view to avoiding any

---

[149] Congyan, C. (2009), 'China–US BIT Negotiations and the Future of Investment Treaty Regime: a Grand Bilateral Bargain with Multilateral Implications' 12(2) Journal of International Economic Law 457, at 460.

FOR DISCUSSION

- Free foreign direct investment can conflict with human rights entitlements. How are these discrepancies resolved?
- Stabilisation clauses in particular present a serious threat not only to a country's legislative freedom but to a country's international human rights commitments.
- Given the human rights implications of certain FDI disputes is the ICSID the best forum for dispute resolution?[1]

Note:
1. See chapter 6, pp. 258–260 for a discussion on the ICSID and FDI dispute resolution.

---

derogation of environment and labour law.[150] These provisions, despite not imposing any obligation except a procedural one of consultation, have been rejected in all BITs signed by the US except the BIT with Uruguay of 2005.[151] BITs could also include compulsory mechanisms of participation and consultation of local communities which could be enforced within the existing ICSID and private arbitral mechanisms.[152] The existing enforcement system for investment disputes could easily be used not only as a forum where private investors seek to protect at all costs their forecast financial returns, but as a forum where legitimate social and environmental concerns and disputes arising in the conduct of an investment project could be expeditiously resolved.

5. NATURAL RESOURCE GOVERNANCE

5.1. Natural Resources: Definition and Types

Natural resources include all aspects of the environment which are not man-made and are of value to us (forests, oceans, fresh water, minerals, soil, and air).[153] These may be renewable if they have the potential to self-perpetuate, or non-renewable when self-perpetuation is not possible.

---

[150] See Articles 12 and 13 of the 2004 US Model BIT, available at: www.bilaterals.org/article.php3?id_article=137 (accessed 7 July 2009).
[151] Congyan (2009), supra, at 461.
[152] See chapter 4 'World Bank' and chapter 6 'The CAO'.
[153] Devlin, R.A. and R.Q. Grafton (1998), *Economic Rights and Environmental*

Certain natural resources are most directly related to human needs and human led economic production and are becoming scarce.[154] In some cases this scarcity is reaching critical levels[155] and whole populations or sectors within populations – especially the poor – face extreme vulnerability in the satisfaction of their basic needs. Natural resource management is, because of its influence on human well-being, closely related to human rights and ethics. Food, water and shelter are human rights entitlements which depend closely on adequate access to natural resources.[156]

Natural resources can be located within the boundaries of a state – for example oil found within the territorial sea or natural gas reserves found exclusively within territorial boundaries. Other natural resources, for example international watercourses, can be of a transboundary nature, making regulation subject to the agreement of several countries or to principles of international law.[157] Some natural resources, like the fish stocks in the High Seas or the mineral resources of deep seabed, are beyond the sovereignty of any state. Irrespective of their physical location natural resources have a global dimension: the Earth's climate, the oceans, the ice caps, biodiversity, oil and gas, all are of benefit to people beyond national boundaries and their use and misuse create externalities which are suffered beyond the frontiers of states and regulation. Compared with the governance of economic activity in the context both of trade and of foreign investment, natural resource governance is poorly developed and scattered across a variety of agencies and programmes within the UN with overlapping mandates, international treaties secretariats and national government initiatives.[158] Natural resources are under-regulated at the global level. This under-regulation is due to two main reasons. First, natural resources fall mostly under the territory and authority of national states. They constitute the bulk of the country's wealth and states are zealous guardians of the principle of permanent sovereignty over natural resources, particularly developing states which are reasonably and understandably weary of past exploitation by colonial powers. Secondly,

---

Wrongs: Property Rights for the Common Good, Cheltenham, UK, and Lyme, VT, USA: Edward Elgar Publishing, p. 68.

[154]   Scarcity is not correlative to renewability or non-renewability. There are renewable scarce resources, for example endangered species, and non-renewable non-scarce resources like some minerals. Ibid.

[155]   As is the case of freshwater resources in some areas of the planet, or the dwindling oil reserves.

[156]   We explore this idea in the next chapter.

[157]   The legal framework for these is discussed in the next chapter.

[158]   See chapter 4, pp. 176–184.

those natural resources which do not fall under the strict sovereignty of a state or which are of global relevance or importance are in most cases global public goods,[159] which makes their regulation and provision difficult. And yet it is of crucial importance that states abandon the national interest centred approach to natural resource governance and recognise the global dimension of all natural resource management and enjoyment. The words of Judge Weeramantry in respect of the new approach needed in international environmental law are also applicable to natural resource governance:

> We have entered an era . . . in which international law subserves not only the interests of individual States, but looks beyond them and their parochial concerns to the greater interests of humanity and planetary welfare . . . International environmental law will need to proceed beyond weighing . . . rights and obligations . . . within a closed compartment of individual State self-interest, unrelated to the global concerns of humanity as a whole.[160]

In the following two sections we explore both challenges: the tensions arising out of permanent sovereignty over natural resources and the special problem posed by public goods.

5.2. Permanent Sovereignty over Natural Resources

The heavily contested principle of permanent sovereignty arose out of the process of decolonisation closely related to another controversial principle of international law – the principle of self-determination[161] and also to the human rights codifications.[162] Sovereignty over natural resources involves both rights – to possess, use and manage and enjoy the profits arising out of the exploitation of those resources,[163] – and duties[164] imposed by international law.

The first UN General Assembly resolutions on permanent sovereignty[165] were adopted with the purpose of enhancing the economic development of

---

[159] Discussed in the next section.

[160] Dissenting opinion in the *Case Concerning the Gabcikovo-Nagymaros Project (Hungary v. Slovakia)* [1997] ICJ Rep 7, separate opinion of Vice-President Weeramantry, at C(c).

[161] Crawford, J. (2001), 'The Principle of Self-Determination in International Law', in P. Alston (ed.), *People's Rights*, Oxford: Oxford University Press, at 7.

[162] Schrijver (1997), supra, at 387.

[163] Barnes, R. (2009), *Property Rights and Natural Resources*, Oxford: Hart, p. 228.

[164] Discussed below in this section.

[165] Res. 523 (VI) of 12 January 1952 and 626 (VII) of 21 December 1952.

'underdeveloped' countries. In 1962, when Resolution 1803 (XVII)[166] was adopted, newly independent states were eager to end foreign ownership over their natural resources, and especially over oil, which was quickly becoming one the most valuable commodities in the world. The emphasis thus was on the newly independent countries' governments' power to decide the course of exploitation of the countries' resources, particularly in respect of ex-colonial powers. A wave of nationalisations of industries involved in natural resource exploitation followed. This implied several cases of expropriation of foreign owned property.[167]

The now widely accepted right of a state to expropriate, nationalise or more generally 'take property' from foreign investors is a recognised attribute of the principle of permanent sovereignty over natural resources.[168] Even before permanent sovereignty was articulated as a principle by the GA resolutions, international law recognised an inherent right of the state to expropriate foreign property in its own territory:

> Contemporary international law recognises the right of every state to nationalize foreign-owned property, even if a predecessor state or a previous government engaged itself by treaty or contract not to do so. This is a corollary of the principle of permanent sovereignty of a state over all its wealth, natural resources and economic activities and proclaimed in successive General Assembly resolutions[169]

Since natural resources constitute the basis for the economic development of developing countries it is essential that developing countries themselves are involved in the exploitation and management of natural resources in order to obtain the maximum benefit and invest this in national development.[170]

---

[166]   UN GA Res. 1803 XVII of 14 December 1962.

[167]   See for example the cases arising out of the nationalisation of oil exploitations in Libya: *Texaco v. Libya*, 53 ILR (1997) 389; *BP v. Libya*, 53 ILR (1977) 297. The nationalisations in Iran provide other examples of international dispute resolution in this area. The extensive case law of the Iran–US Claims Tribunal established by the Algiers Accords of 19 January 1981 to resolve claims by United States nationals for compensation for assets nationalised by the Iranian government, and claims by the governments against each other provides a valuable body of case law and interesting reflections on the subject. See, among others, Brower, C.N. and J.D. Brueschke (1998), *The Iran US Claims Tribunal*, The Hague: Kluwer International.

[168]   In general Schrijver, supra, at 285–315.

[169]   Jimenez de Arechaga, E. (1978), 'State responsibility for the nationalization of foreign owned property', New York University Journal of International Law and Politics 11, 179–195 at 179.

[170]   See GA Res. 2158 (XXI), 25 November 1966.

5.3. Tensions between Foreign Investors and Developing Countries in Natural Resources Control

The tension between the North and the South in the regulation of foreign investment played a crucial role in the debate on permanent sovereignty over natural resources. The need to access natural resources for economic growth has remained a constant driver of international policy throughout history. Colonisation, as has been discussed, procured ample and free access to the colonies' natural resources (timber, minerals, oil) to the colonial powers. The post-colonisation era was seen by those used to this unfettered access as problematic, and the old colonial powers looked at international regulation as an instrument which would ensure that access to natural resources remained unimpaired. Economic instruments and contractual arrangements needed to be used to ensure this access, duly supported by the regulatory frameworks of world trade and foreign direct investment. It was crucial that the ex-colonies allowed foreign direct investment, especially in the natural resource sector, and that commodities such as timber could be exported to developed countries with no restrictions.[171] In the colonial and post-colonial periods instruments such as concessions whereby a state would transfer some of its sovereign rights to a private person would be used as instruments of access to and exploitation of natural resources by individuals, companies and foreign countries.[172] Well known examples of this type of concession were those granted to the Dutch East India and West India Company and the British East India Company which enjoyed extensive rights granted by the local feudal rulers, or the Anglo-Persian Oil Company.

A body of rules to 'encourage' and protect foreign investors developed through the first half of the twentieth century. Foreign investors had a great degree of freedom in their establishment and, more importantly, export of profits while they were protected by their state of origin via diplomatic means[173] and the insistence on what was called the 'international minimum standard', a standard which included principles such as *pacta sunt servanda* or the respect of acquired rights and which focused on standards

---

171 The same cannot be said about the openness of the North to FDI. Even today the US rejects investments in several sectors which it considers critical. It did, for example reject attempts by China to buy Unocal, an energy company which operates mostly in Asia. See Stiglitz (2010), supra, at 231.

172 Schrijver (1997), supra, at 174.

173 Described as 'dollar diplomacy' by Jessup, P.C. (1949), *A Modern Law of Nations. An Introduction*, New York: Macmillan, at 96, cited in Schrijver (1997), supra, at 175.

round the conflictive issue of expropriation. However, following decolonisation several newly independent countries nationalised key industries and expropriation and the limits within which the 'taking', in its different forms, of foreign property could be exercised became the central point of international attention. Arbitral awards confirmed the right to nationalise property[174] which was regarded as an expression of a state's territorial sovereignty 'subject to the obligation of indemnification for premature termination of concession agreements'.[175] In the *Amoco Award*[176] it was acknowledged that 'nationalisation is a right fundamentally attributed to State sovereignty and commonly used as an important tool of economic policy by many countries, both developed and developing . . . and is a right which cannot easily be surrendered'. Further the ICC Guidelines,[177] the UN Draft Code of Conduct of Transnational Corporations,[178] the ILA Seoul Declaration[179] and the World Bank Guidelines on the Treatment of Foreign Investment,[180] all acknowledge the right to expropriate property subject to the need to do so according to 'applicable legal procedures'.[181]

With agreement on the legality of nationalisation or expropriation of property the debate tuned upon the conditions which made it legal and acceptable to foreign investors and the international community at large. Resolution 1803 (XVII) specified that:

> Nationalization, expropriation or requisitioning shall be based on grounds or reasons of public utility, security or the national interests which are recognised as overriding purely individual or private interest both domestic and foreign.[182]

The 'public interest', a translation from the 'public utility' wording of the resolution, as a requirement of legal expropriations is notoriously difficult to ascertain. Allegations that certain nationalisations were politically motivated and not in the 'public interest' failed in arbitral tribunals,[183] and

---

[174]   For example *Texaco v. Libya*, 17 I.L.M. (1978) 15 para. 59, confirmed in *Kuwait v. Aminoil*, 21 I.L.M. (1982) 1012.

[175]   By Mahmassani in *Liamco v. Libya*, 20 I.L.M. (1981) 120.

[176]   *Amoco Award* (1987) p. 243 para. 179.

[177]   Section V.3.iv.

[178]   Para. 55, UN Doc. E/1990/94.

[179]   Para. 5.5 of the ILA Seoul Declaration.

[180]   The 1992 World Bank Guidelines on the Treatment of Foreign Investment, see commentary in Subedi, S. (2008), *International Investment Law. Reconciling principle and policy*, Portland, USA and Oxford: Hart Publishing, pp. 34–37.

[181]   Section VI.1, World Bank Guidelines, September 1992.

[182]   Para. 4 of GA Res. 1803 (XVII), 14 December 1962.

[183]   This was the case in the *Liamco* arbitration. See Schrijver (1997), supra, at 291 for a discussion on this point.

it is widely recognised today that the nationalising state has a wide discretion to determine the 'public interests' of its citizens in respect of natural resources in its territory

The second and controversial issue in respect of nationalisation is that of compensation. From the international minimum standards (IMS) of the Hull doctrine[184] to the 'national standards of the Calvo clause, the question of what constitutes a 'fair' 'just' or 'appropriate compensation' – if any – has been debated in political terms, in the UN discussion in the context of the permanent sovereignty resolution, by academics and policy makers and by judges and arbitral tribunals at length.

Should compensation be 'full',[185] or should past 'excessive profits' above a 'reasonable rate of return'[186] be deducted from the amount of compensation paid? In a context where foreign investors had unilaterally overexploited national resources some countries were of the opinion that the retroactive excess profits should be taken into account when calculating compensation:[187]

> while international law undoubtedly sets forth an obligation to provide compensation for property taken, international law theory and practice do not support the conclusion that the 'prompt, adequate, and effective' standards represents the prevailing standard of compensation. Rather customary international law favours an 'appropriate' compensation standard . . . The gradual emergence of this rule aims at ensuring that the amount of compensation is determined in a flexible manner, that is, taking into account the specific circumstances of the case.[188]

Resolution 1803 (XVII) referred to an 'appropriate' compensation formula, and this was applied by the arbitral tribunals in the *Ebrahimi* Award just transcribed,[189] the *Texaco* and the *Amoco* Awards.

---

[184] The 'Hull rule' promoted by the US Department of State stated that 'expropriation of American private property must be non-discriminatory, for a public purpose and will receive prompt, adequate and effective compensation from the expropriating country'. Statement on Foreign Investment and Nationalization, 30 December 1975, 15 I.L.M. (1976) 186.

[185] As required by the 'Hull clause', above.

[186] This was discussed in the *Aminoil Award*, 21 I.L.M. (1982) at 1031–1033 paras 143–144 and has been applied by Chile (discussion in main text) and Libya.

[187] This was the view of Chile. See Chile's Decree No. 92 Concerning Excess Profits of Copper Companies of 28 September 1971, 14 I.L.M. (1975) 983 and Libya Law No. 42 of 11 June 1973, 13 I.L.M. (1974) 58–59. Discussed in Schrijver (1997), supra, at 295.

[188] *Ebrahimi v. Iran* (1994) Iran–US Claims Tribunal, 12 October 1994, The Hague, pp. 38–39, para. 88.

[189] Ibid.

I am inclined to be of the view that 'appropriate'; fair' and 'just' are virtually interchangeable notions so far as standards of compensation are concerned ... there is a wide choice of well-established methods of valuation applicable and appropriate under different circumstances.[190]

A further aspect to consider is that of lost profits or *lucrum cessans*. This request to include the *lucrum cessans* in the award for damages was rejected both by the tribunal in the *Amoco* case which specified that this compensation is only applicable in the case of unlawful takings[191] and, more recently, the tribunal under the ICSID arbitration in *Asian Agricultural Products v. The Republic of Sri Lanka*.[192]

Today the most widely shared view is that several factors need to be considered when assessing what constitutes appropriate compensation for nationalisation of property, especially if the nationalisation involves states' natural resources.[193] According to Brownlie, '[t]he principle of nationalization unsubordinated to a full-compensation rule may be supported by reference to principles of self-determination, independence, sovereignty, and equality'.[194]

In contrast to this so-called international standard, the national standard supported by colonial countries was manifested in the so-called Calvo doctrine.[195] The Calvo doctrine revolved round the abstention from interference by foreign governments in disputes arising over the treatment of aliens' property in an attempt to end the so-called 'gunboat diplomacy' that ruled foreign investment during that period and advocated the subjection of foreigners to the jurisdiction of the host state in such disputes and the equality of treatment between foreigners and nationals. It does recognise that expropriation needs to be met by fair compensation, but not because there is an international obligation; the obligations, it claims, arise from domestic law and constitutional provisions. The Calvo doctrine was naturally celebrated throughout Latin America and versions of it have been incorporated in Asian and African constitutions, but it has some legal holes. The most important is renouncing diplomatic protection by the foreign investor which is, in international law, a right of the state and not of the individual.[196]

---

[190]   Judge Lagergren, separate opinion, *INA Corporation v. Iran* (1985), reprinted in 8 Iran–USA Claims Tribunal Reports 385–389.
[191]   See Schrijver (1997), supra, at 295.
[192]   30 I.L.M. (1991) 577–627.
[193]   Schrijver (1997), supra, at 297, Dolzer (1985), supra, at 19.
[194]   Brownlie (1990), supra, at 535–536.
[195]   It was first outlined by the Argentinian jurist Carlos Calvo (1822–1906) See discussion in Schrijver, supra, at 178.
[196]   A point which was discussed by the American–Mexican General Claims

With interests so polarised and stakes so high due to the unavoidable dependence upon access to natural resources for the economic growth of both developed and developing countries discussions in the UN on the extent of the principle of permanent sovereignty over natural resources and the regulation and protection of foreign investments were protracted.

Control over oil resources has lain at the root of many tensions between resource owning and producing countries and the needs of those dependent upon those resources. The creation of the OPEC and its development over the last half century (see Box 1.2) illustrates this process and shows how strong cooperative networks can be created by countries with shared interests.

While foreign capital could play an important role in the host state's ability effectively and sustainably to exploit natural resource wealth, it is important that foreign companies act in a manner which ensures equitable benefit sharing. Regulations to achieve this aim have been, so far, unsuccessful.[197]

Towards the end of the century sources of foreign investment became scarce after the collapse of the Soviet Union and the power of capital exporting countries overtook the demands of capital importing countries. Through the development of BITs discussed in the previous section and an increasing body of arbitral awards delivered in the context of the ICSID[198] the principle of permanent sovereignty over resources has been constrained into stabilisation clauses and a pro-investment framework. On the other hand new challenges and tensions have refocused some of the debate towards the relationship between the state and its citizens or groups within a country and the exercise of permanent sovereignty over natural resources.

5.4 Indigenous Peoples

The principle of permanent sovereignty, although a key principle in historical terms, should not be understood as an absolute principle and should not, in the twenty-first century, be used as an excuse to avoid the inevitable cooperation that is required for the provision of global public goods and the conservation of natural resources. Crucially, permanent sovereignty in the age of globalisation cannot entail only rights, it should

---

Commission in the *North American Dredging Company of Texas Case* (1926) 4 RIAA 26–29.

[197] See discussion on regulation of MNCs in chapter 5, pp. 217–220.

[198] Discussed in chapter 6, pp. 258–261.

BOX 1.2.   THE OPEC: MANAGEMENT OF OIL
RESOURCES, PAST AND FUTURE
DIRECTIONS

'Against Western recognition of the need to assert control
over world oil stocks and proposals from International Cooperative Alliance, USA, to place Middle East oil under UN control
in 1947/1948 on 10th September 1960, the Organization of
Petroleum Exporting Countries (OPEC) was created in Baghdad,
Iraq. This organization was founded as a result of several meetings between high-level delegates from Iraq, Iran, Kuwait, Saudi
Arabia and Venezuela. These states argued that the oil price, at
that time around $2.0/bbl (and at times much lower due to auc-
tions), was unfair and should be adjusted. Further meetings led to
the creation of the OPEC organization. Later, other states joined
the organization: Qatar (1961), Indonesia and Libya (1962), UAE
(1967), Algeria (1969), and Nigeria (1971). Ecuador and Gabon
were members before they withdrew in 1992 and 1995 respectively. OPEC members hold 65–70% of the entire proven world
oil reserves and produce around 40% of the global oil production.

The organization members have two main issues to meet on:
pricing, as well as the production quota for each member, in order
to keep the market price stable. However, these states have different agendas and policies due to variations in their individual social
and political structures.

The creation of OPEC was necessary in order to balance oil
marketing between the major suppliers and demanders, and set
rules for pricing. Unfortunately, some of the rules for pricing were
not implemented. In the early 1970s some of the OPEC members
(Iraq, Algeria, and Libya) introduced their own political agenda into
OPEC meetings. It is believed that since then the oil market has
not followed the natural rules of supply and demand.

Historically, OPEC member countries, specifically those in the
Persian Gulf, dominated most of the power concerning oil policy.
Saudi Arabia, being the top crude oil producer in the world, always
possessed extreme control over policy decisions concerning price
and production. However, as relations between OPEC and non-
OPEC oil producing countries grew, policy power began to diversify, and non-OPEC members began to exert their voices and

increase their influence regarding major policy decisions. While the Persian Gulf formerly dominated world oil policy, in 1998, the power began to quickly shift to Latin America, as Venezuela and Mexico became the most important decision-making countries, followed by Saudi Arabia.

OPEC launched such a support network with the creation of the OPEC Fund for International Development, which is a multilateral development finance institution. Founded in 1976, OPEC began the fund with intentions to promote collaboration between OPEC countries and developing countries, and to help poor and low-income countries achieve social and economic advancement goals. OPEC gives the highest priority to the least developed countries with the highest needs. Thus far, over 110 countries have received assistance from the OPEC Fund. Recently, the OPEC Fund donated 43,000 metric tons of food to nine African countries, including Ethiopia, Zimbabwe, and Zambia.

Many major producers, whether OPEC members or not, have been in steady cooperation that has led to major impact for the oil industry as a whole, as can be seen through the two noteworthy examples; policy power distribution and response to crises. The fact that non-OPEC countries, such as Mexico, have the opportunity to have powerful voices in universal policy decisions, and share that power with OPEC countries, displays the strengthening, flexibility, and diversifying of oil country relationships. Furthermore, the dynamic of these relationships is apparent through the tendency of stronger countries to assume control during their periods of prosperity while paving the way for temporarily unstable or less thriving countries. The response to the Venezuelan crisis of 2002 is another example of the close cooperation between OPEC and non-OPEC oil producing countries.'

Source: Garza, C. and A. Gee (2004), 'The Global Oil Economy and the End of the Petroleum Era', EDGE, Winter.

also encompass duties. These duties are closely linked to the human rights codifications and to the principle of sustainability which permeate international environmental law and natural resource regulation.[199] In reality,

---

[199] Schrijver (1997), supra, at 387. See below for a full discussion on sustainability.

permanent sovereignty over natural resources should imply that resources found in the territory of a state belong to the population of that state and not to the government which only has a steward's role in respect of their exploitation and management, as well as to a duty to share the benefits arising out of such exploitation with the whole population.[200] The right to natural resources is a right of peoples[201] or communities to determine how their natural resources should be protected, managed and explored. Rights of peoples or collective rights are highly contested in the Western legal discourse[202] as the beneficiary is the group rather than its individual members, and sit uneasily with developed theories of individualism and human rights.

This includes the duty to respect the rights and interests of indigenous peoples[203] and not to compromise the rights of future generations.[204] It also includes a duty to have due care for the environment and to exercise permanent sovereignty in such a way as to prevent significant harm to the environment of other (neighbouring) states or of areas beyond national jurisdiction,[205] and to recognise the correlative rights of other states to transboundary resources and at least to consult with them as regards concurrent users with a view to arriving at equitable apportionments and use of these resources. Further, permanent sovereignty should be exercised in good faith and would include a duty to observe international agreements, to respect the rights of other states.[206]

Access to resources and land rights are a fundamental problem for indigenous peoples. Security of tenure in respect of land has been widely recognised as creating the necessary incentives for good land stewardship,

---

[200]   UN GA Res. 1803 (XVII) stresses that the rights belong to peoples and nations: '[t]he *right of peoples* and nations to permanent sovereignty over their natural wealth and resources must be exercised in the interest of their national development and of the wellbeing of the people of the State concerned'. Okowa, P. (2009), 'Environmental justice in situations of armed conflict', in J. Ebbesson and P. Okowa (eds), *Environmental Law and Justice in Context*, New York: Cambridge University Press, at 243.

[201]   Crawford, J. (1988), 'Rights of peoples: "Peoples" or "Governments"?' in J. Crawford (ed.), *The Rights of Peoples*, Oxford: Clarendon Press, 64.

[202]   Boyle, A. (2007), 'Human Rights or Environmental Rights – A Reassessment', Fordham Environmental Law Review 18, 471. See the discussion on this point in chapter 3, pp. 132, 149–150.

[203]   See chapter 5, pp. 245–248.

[204]   Epitomised by the principle of sustainable development discussed below.

[205]   Principle of good neighbourliness. See also Schrijver (1997), supra, at 391–392.

[206]   Including, according to some, an obligation to respect foreign investments, as represented by the 'taking rule', Ibid.

but systems of land tenure which favour individual property rights do not recognise and encompass that type of communitarian land ownership and the relationship (cultural, spiritual and productive) which indigenous peoples have with their land. Development policies, on the one hand, follow a pattern of Western development which favours industrialisation and agricultural policies alien to the grazing and hunting practices of most indigenous communities, while conservation projects, on the other hand, alienate and deprive indigenous peoples of choices in the management and enjoyment of their ecosystems.

The case of Awas Tingi[207] in the Inter-American Court of Human Rights signified a great advance in the recognition of community rights to land in the American continent. On 4 June 1998, the Inter-American Commission on Human Rights (hereinafter 'the Commission' or 'the Inter-American Commission') filed before the Court an application against the State of Nicaragua. The case in question had originated in petition No. 11,577, received at the Commission's Secretariat on 2 October 1995.

In its application, the Commission cited Articles 50 and 51 of the American Convention on Human Rights (hereinafter 'the American Convention' or 'the Convention') and Article 32 and subsequent Articles of the Rules of Procedure. The Commission presented this case for the Court to decide whether the state had violated Articles 1 (Obligation to Respect Rights), 2 (Domestic Legal Effects), 21 (Right to Property), and 25 (Right to Judicial Protection) of the Convention, in view of the fact that Nicaragua had not demarcated the communal lands of the Awas Tingi Community, nor had the state adopted effective measures to ensure the property rights of the Community to its ancestral lands and natural resources, and also because it granted a concession on community lands without the assent of the Community, and the state did not ensure an effective remedy in response to the Community's protests regarding its property rights.

The Commission also requested that the Court declare that the state had to establish a legal procedure to allow rapid demarcation and official recognition of the property rights of the Mayagna Community, as well as that it had to abstain from granting or considering the granting of any concessions to exploit natural resources on the lands used and occupied by Awas Tingni until the issue of land tenure affecting the community had been resolved.

The Court found that Nicaragua had violated Articles 1(1), 2, 21 and 25

---

[207] *The Mayagna (Sumo) Awas Tingi Community v. Nicaragua*, Judgment of 31 August 2001, Inter-Am. Ct H.R. (Ser. C) No. 79 (2001).

FOR DISCUSSION

- Why has *Awas Tingi* been described as a landmark case in the recognition of indigenous rights to land and territory?
- What have been the effects of the case in the struggle for rights of indigenous peoples?

---

of the American Convention, and in a landmark judgment ordered the state to recognise the communal property rights of the Mayagna Community and to start a process of land titling and demarcation which would ensure the respect of the community's rights. The case has been followed by work of the Inter-American Commission on several cases, including the protective measures in favour of the *Sarayaku* community in Ecuador.[208] Privatisation is one of the main dangers to indigenous land ownership. The granting of concessions and licences, or even the transfer of ownership, in forest and other indigenous territories to foreign companies is depriving indigenous communities of their land and means of subsistence. Although many countries have reformed their legal systems to take into account the collective nature of land rights of indigenous peoples,[209] this recognition is not always followed by effective implementation. For example in Bolivia where 60–80 per cent of the population are indigenous peoples and have filed claims for land amounting to 143,000 square miles, by the end of 2006 only a tenth of this area had been transferred and titled.[210]

On 13 September 2007 the United Nations General Assembly adopted the Declaration of Rights of Indigenous Peoples (UNDRIP) with 143 votes in favour, 11 abstentions and 4 votes against.[211] The countries which voted against (USA, Canada, Australia and New Zealand) all have large groups of indigenous peoples and ongoing disputes about natural resources and land. The Declaration states the right of indigenous peoples to their lands and territories and to a livelihood according to their traditional culture, emphasising the duties of states to consult and obtain an agreement from indigenous peoples in respect of any use of their lands, territories and natural resources.[212] In the case of indigenous peoples, often affected by

---

[208]   A/HRC/4/32/Add.2, paras 19–21.
[209]   Paraguay, Nicaragua, Argentina, Bolivia, Mexico.
[210]   Report of the Special Rapporteur on the situation of human rights and fundamental freedoms of indigenous peoples. Doc. A/HRC/4/32 of 27 February 2007.
[211]   UNDRIP: A/RES/61/295.
[212]   See Articles 8.1(b), 10, 20, 26, 28, 29 and 32.

land takings and the granting of state concessions to foreign companies without their consent, Article 32 of the UNDRIP recognises that they have the right to 'free, prior, informed consent' (FPIC), in other words to say 'yes' or 'no' to development projects in their land. This right had been at stake in the U'wa people's legal battle and the outcome of its interpretation by the government shows the difficulties that indigenous peoples face when engaging with the Western legal systems.

5.5. Natural Resources as Global Public Goods: Provision, Management and Finance

Global public goods are characterised by their non-rivalry and non-excludability on access, enjoyment and use.[213] This is true of many natural resources such as the climate, biodiversity, air quality, the atmosphere, and cooperative solutions for the allocation of costs and benefits are required. Providing global public goods requires a multifaceted approach which includes national and international initiatives with arrangements that have to be good specific. It is not the same to provide for 'clean air' as to preserve biodiversity. In some cases it may be necessary to increase spending from both the private and the public sectors in order to preserve such goods. In other cases, use or access may need to be reduced or limited in some way, and this could be achieved by using market-based instruments, for example by increasing the price of use by introducing carbon taxes, pollution will diminish and the consumption of 'carbon space' will be reduced.[214]

The Millennium Development Goals, poverty eradication, environmental conservation and sustainable natural resource management, cannot be achieved solely through country-level investments, debt relief and trade reform. National strategies need to link with one another and with international coordination mechanisms to provide regional and global public goods. Globalisation has made it possible to think of mechanisms which can contribute to the provision of global public goods beyond existing national mechanisms. A good example of these mechanisms is the creation of global funds. In the case of the Global Environmental

---

[213]   This is true of those so-called 'pure global public goods' and, to a greater or lesser degree, of all other 'impure public goods'. See Kaul, I. I. Grunberg and M.A. Stern (eds) (1999), *Global Public Goods: International Cooperation in the 21st Century*, New York, Oxford University Press, pp. 3–4.

[214]   See chapter 4 for a discussion of different types of regulatory instruments and approaches in natural resources management, and Kaul et al. (eds), supra, for different examples and approaches in the provision of global public goods.

Facility (GEF)[215] actors who undertake efforts to preserve biodiversity or participate in carbon sequestration projects can be compensated because of the service they provide to the global public good.[216] Financial assistance is crucial to attaining the purposes of provision of environmental goods and services, particularly if developing countries are to be included in the regime. This conclusion was quite unanimous after the 1992 Rio Conference on Environment and Development, even though the idea did not extend to the creation of a general fund for sustainable development which would have encompassed a variety of projects including green and renewable energy, forest and biodiversity conservation and green industrial technology.[217] Most post-UNCED treaties also include provisions on financial resources[218] or the provision of assistance through capacity building.[219] The creation of funds on treaty mechanisms was thought to have two advantages. On the one hand it would provide the much needed financial assistance to developing countries to enable them to comply with their treaty commitments. On the other it would allow developed states to insist upon more stringent standards for developing states, which would lead to better compliance and standards of environmental protection.[220]

But global environmental governance in respect of global public goods is not limited to the facilitation of payments to those providing the goods; it includes the creation of different schemes such as the management of scarce resources – those which are non-excludable but have rival consumption and are therefore at a higher risk of being over-consumed, such as fisheries[221] or a clean atmosphere.[222] In these cases regulatory provisions which may assign new property rights, such as tradable pollution permits[223] or fishing quotas, can be used to manage the resource. All of

---

[215]   The Global Environment Facility (GEF), established in 1991, helps developing countries fund projects and programmes which protect the global environment. See www.gefweb.org/ and chapter 2.

[216]   For a discussion on this see Conceicao, P. and T. Kaul (2005), 'Financing Global Public Goods', in Wijen et al. (eds) n. 7, at 99.

[217]   French, D. (2000), 'Developing States and International Environmental Law: The Importance of Differentiated Responsibilities', International & Comparative Law Quarterly, 49, 35–60.

[218]   Ibid. at 42.

[219]   For example Article 12 of the Kyoto Protocol.

[220]   French (2000), supra, at 53.

[221]   See Hey, E. (ed.) (1999), *Developments in International Fisheries Laws*, Kluwer International: The Hague.

[222]   In general on the management and protection of the atmosphere see Birnie, Boyle and Redgwell, supra, pp. 335–377.

[223]   These are discussed in chapter 2, pp. 108–109.

these measures and mechanisms necessitate the political commitment of nation states to participate in negotiations and the creation of new regulatory regimes both nationally and globally and to contribute financially to the financing of global governance. In order to facilitate the regulation and project implementation of these global public goods it has been suggested that a new global environmental agency (GEA) or mechanism (GEM) needs to be created. This GEA or GEM would be in charge of the implementation of a rules based system which could mirror the trade and investment regimes and could concentrate in areas such as the global commons that are under-regulated and over-exploited, and where externalities are high.[224] It could also play an active role in managing the transfer and use of technology to enable environmentally sound economic development by creating and managing an environmental fund and, above all, provide a forum for the resolution of disputes concerning environmental harm and compliance.

Other solutions for natural resource management are more radical. The creation of a Global Resource Dividend (GRD)[225] has been advocated, whereby states and their governments must share a small part of the value of any natural resources they sell. This payment is called a dividend because it is based on the notion that the global poor *own* a stake in all limited natural resources wherever these are situated. This stake does not challenge or interfere with the principle of sovereignty over natural resources as it confers no right to participate in decisions about whether or how natural resources are to be used. It only means that benefits from the Earth's resources must be partially shared with the world's poor. Pogge argues that affluent people appropriate and use the Earth's resources disproportionately without giving any compensation to the global poor.[226] Using the example of oil, he suggests that a $3 dividend per barrel would be enough to raise about 30 per cent of the total amount needed in a year ($300 billion) to lift 2,533 million human beings out of severe poverty.[227] The GRD could also be linked to environmental goals as it could be attached to the consumption of those resources which environmentally should be discouraged, be it because of high pollution or scarcity. As with any mechanism which puts a price on resources basic to human life care should be exercised in both its level, not to be too high to tax the end user

---

[224]   Conceicao and Kaul (2005), supra, at 99.
[225]   Pogge, T. (2001), 'Eradicating Systemic Poverty: Brief for a Global Resources Dividend', Journal of Human Development 2, 1, 59–77 further elaborated in *World Poverty and Human Rights*, chapter 8 p. 202.
[226]   Ibid., at 208.
[227]   Ibid., at 211.

disproportionably and its choice of resources – it should not be directed to consumption of resources which are used towards meeting basic needs.

A global fund to which contributions from mechanisms such as the discussed GRD or more conventional and existing systems such as those of the GEF managed by a global environmental agency and complemented with concerted action through treaty funds could contribute towards the financing of those resources which are currently over-used and under-financed.

6. CONCLUSION

The complex process of globalisation and its relationship with natural resources use and economic growth has been the focus of this chapter. The current dominant model of globalisation, often referred to as 'corporate globalisation', with its primary mission of enabling financial and investment markets to operate internationally, has been criticised as plainly unsustainable and based on the aggressive exploitation of resources and peoples by a minority while failing to take into account the finiteness of the world's resources.[228] But not every aspect of the globalisation process and the paradigms it generates and upon which it is in turn based has negative consequences. The expansion of the concept of sustainable development and the emergence of new ideas such as corporate social responsibility (CSR) or socially responsible investment (SRI) are themselves products of globalisation, which has enabled the emergence of a consensus on the limitations of continued growth and the need for an integration of sustainability models within the economic system.

In this chapter we highlighted the tensions that arise out of the needs of the global economy for access to and control over natural resources and the principle of permanent sovereignty. Two themes emerged from this tension: on the one hand national (permanent) sovereignty raises issues of control over natural resources, access and benefit sharing both internally and externally. The absolute sovereignty of the state is questioned both by its international (contractual) obligations in respect of economic actors via concessions, foreign investment licences or other arrangements and, internally, by groups with competing claims about use and exploitation of

---

[228]   Diamond, J. (2005), *Collapse: How Societies Choose to Fail or Succeed*, New York: Viking. He argues that either cataclysm or a solution will take place in the not too distant future since the current path of exploitation of the Earth's resources without adequate management or replenishment is not sustainable.

the resources, especially by indigenous peoples.[229] The second theme was the growing consensus that permanent sovereignty within a global natural resource governance framework needs to develop a nuanced approach which considers not only the interests of other states, individuals or groups recognised in international law, but also and crucially an approach which acknowledges the inter-relatedness of Earth's processes and the implications that unilateral actions – perfectly and legally acceptable under the umbrella of permanent sovereignty – can have and the indirect and long lasting effects in ecosystems well beyond national boundaries. Principles such as sustainable development and approaches such as the ecosystem approach attempt to crystallise and provide operative frameworks of action which acknowledge this interdependence.

While technology has been heralded as the saviour that will make possible both high levels of consumption and environmental protection, green technology has to date had a reduced impact in its geographical scope, with developed countries leading the way but not sharing the benefits of their innovation and research with developing countries.[230] It is estimated that the extra cost of facilitating greener technology to enable developing countries to increase their economic growth in a sustainable manner is only 10 per cent, yet developed countries have shown an extreme reluctance to help with the extra 10 per cent contribution, insisting on creating laws such as intellectual property or patenting laws which make access to this technology difficult or impossible for much of the world.

Those who see globalisation as a positive force in advancing environmental protection point out that the process has made possible the diffusion of environmental regimes which may be more stringent that those envisaged at the national level. While this may be true of countries with similar levels of economic development, for example intra-EU regulation has raised the general level of environmental protection of EU countries and between the EU and the US[231] it has not proved yet to be the case between regions or countries with different levels of development.

---

[229] The problem is outlined in the introduction and developed in chapters 5 (in general) and 9 in respect of the protection of traditional knowledge in the context of biological resources.

[230] See chapter 8, biodiversity and chapter 7 renewable energy.

[231] For example the Chicago emissions exchange market in the US was created by firms which do not wish to lose on competitiveness based on green performance in respect of their European counterparts due to the reluctance of the US administration to ratify the Kyoto Protocol. Henson, R. (2006), *Climate Change: The Symptoms. The Science. The Solutions*, London and New York: Rough Guides, Penguin Ltd p. 247. See chapter 2.

Multinationals could certainly export the higher standards of their home country to the countries where they operate but they often fail to meet even the lower standards of host countries, while lack of governance at the global level neutralises the positive opportunities brought about by the globalisation process.

It should be possible, in this world of plenty which we inhabit, to eradicate the abject poverty of millions of innocent people and to enjoy a peaceful and prosperous life based on technological innovation, the rule of law and the co-existence of different cultures in a global village. This proposition revolves round the ability of the global community to regulate access to, management and enjoyment of natural resources.

FURTHER READING

Birnie, P., A. Boyle and C. Redgwell (2009), *International Law and the Environment*, 3rd edn, Oxford: Oxford University Press.

Dolzer, R. and C. Schreuer (2008), *Principles of International Investment Law*, Oxford: Oxford University Press.

French, D. (2000), 'Developing States and International Environmental Law: The Importance of Differentiated Responsibilities', International & Comparative Law Quarterly, 49, 35–60.

Gupta, J. (2007), 'Globalisation, Environmental Challenges and North–South Issues', in Thai, Khi V. et al. (eds), *Handbook on Globalisation and the Environment*, Boca Raton: CRC Press.

Muchlinski, P. (2007), *Multinational Enterprises and the Law*, Oxford: Oxford University Press.

Sands, P. (2003), *Principles of International Environmental Law*, 2nd edn, Cambridge: Cambridge University Press.

Schneiderman, D. (2008), *Constitutionalizing Economic Globalization. Investment Rules and Democracy's Promise*, Cambridge: Cambridge Studies in Law and Society, Cambridge University Press.

Schrvijer, N. (1997), *Permanent Sovereignty Over Natural Resources*, Cambridge: Cambridge University Press.

Souza Santos, B. de and C.A. Rodriguez-Garavito (eds) (2005), *Law and Globalisation from Below. Towards a Cosmopolitan Legality*, Cambridge: Cambridge University Press.

Stiglitz, J. (2007), *Making Globalization Work*, London: Penguin.

Subedi, S. (2008), *International Investment Law. Reconciling Policy and Principle*, Portland, USA and Oxford: Hart Publishing, pp. 34–37.

Wijen, F., K. Zoetman and J. Pieters (eds) (2005), *A Handbook of Globalization and Environmental Policy*, Cheltenham, UK and Northampton, MA, USA: Edward Elgar Publishing.

2. Globalisation and natural resource management: principles and approaches

1. INTRODUCTION

Human beings depend on nature and its resources for the satisfaction of their most basic needs (food, water, air, shelter). This dependence makes the allocation of rights and entitlement to natural resources crucial for any society and the individuals inhabiting it.

In the previous chapter we outlined the tension arising out of the principle of permanent sovereignty over natural resources and the needs of the global economy exponentially highlighted by the increased networks of production and consumption promoted by the process of economic globalisation. Natural resources constitute in most cases the bulk of a country's wealth and their exploitation, management and distribution of benefits is closely interlinked with the politics of each country and with the groups in power in each society.

The dependence of humans upon nature is recognised by the 'ecosystem approach'[1] and the contribution which ecosystem services make towards the attainment of the Millennium Development Goals places them high on the development agenda.

> Everyone depends on the environment. It is the foundation of all development, and provides opportunities for people and society as a whole to achieve their hopes and aspirations. Current environmental degradation undermines natural assets, and negatively affects human well-being. It is clear that a deteriorating environment is an injustice to both current and future generations.[2]

---

[1] 'The ecosystem approach is a strategy for the integrated management of land, water and living resources that promotes conservation and sustainable use in an equitable way. It is based on the application of appropriate scientific methodologies focused on levels of biological organization which encompass the essential processes, functions and interactions among organisms and their environment. It recognizes that humans, with their cultural diversity, are an integral component of ecosystems.' See www.cbd.int/ecosystem/ (accessed 15 January 2010).

[2] 'An integrated approach to meeting the MDG targets should be focused

The increasing scarcity of natural resources has serious consequences for human well-being. Natural resources' scarcity is also at the heart of violent conflict[3] as human populations fight in the struggle to access resources to satisfy their most basic needs.[4]

Internally, different groups may struggle to control land, water, minerals, oil or gas and to manage these according to their culture, needs or preferences. This is particularly the case between indigenous peoples and the governments of states where their territories are situated.[5]

In the introduction to the previous chapter we identified together with inequality and weak governance a third problem in the relationship between globalisation and natural resource management – that of inadequate pricing and management of the natural resource base and the environment in general. In this chapter we consider the different types of natural resources and the general principles underlying natural resource management, including the concept of 'ecosystem services'. We suggest that a balance can be struck between the different interests of states and non-state actors and discuss whether better pricing and valuation of natural resources will promote increased sustainability without posing human rights questions of access for those less privileged. We finish with a brief overview of the problematic relationship between natural resource and conflict.

2. CLASSIFICATION OF NATURAL RESOURCES

Beyond a distinction between renewable and non-renewable natural resources[6] the main factor in the classification of natural resources is

---

on improved management of ecosystems and their capacity to sustainably deliver multiple types of ecosystem services.' Millennium Ecosystem Assessment (MA) (2005) 19.2.

[3] As it is, paradoxically, natural resource abundance, this is discussed in the final section of this chapter, 'Natural resources and conflict'.

[4] The situation in Darfur illustrates this well; droughts and land scarcity have fuelled the ongoing conflict. See also Collier, P. (2003), 'The Market for Civil War', Foreign Policy (May–June) where he argues that poverty and trade in natural resources are the real culprits of many civil wars, especially in Africa, and not historic ethnic conflicts as we are led to believe.

[5] See chapter 3 for an overview of the many conflicts between indigenous peoples and states over natural resources. Also United Nations Permanent Forum on Indigenous Peoples (2006), 'Indigenous peoples, land and natural resources'. For more information on the Sixth Session of the UN Permanent Forum on Indigenous Issues see www.un.org/esa/socdev/unpfii/en/session_sixth.html (accessed 15 November 2009).

[6] See chapter 1, p. 65.

their geographical location, as this determines the exercise of power by a state or by different states. Some natural resources are under the exclusive territory of a state and are subject to the principle of permanent sovereignty.[7] Others, like international watercourses, cross state boundaries and are subject to conventional regimes[8] or to general principles such as 'equitable and reasonable use' or those that deal with avoiding transboundary pollution.[9] Beyond these, three concepts have emerged to reflect those resources that are collective, global and transboundary in nature. These concepts are 'common areas', 'common heritage' and 'common concern'.

2.1. Shared Natural Resources

Geographical proximity or contiguity determines which resources are 'shared' between more than one state as they do not fall exclusively under the territory of a state. Examples of these are international watercourses, migratory species, forests, enclosed and semi-enclosed seas and regional air masses. UNEP has defined shared resources as 'an element of the natural environment used by man which constitutes a bio-geophysical unity, and it is located in the territory of two or more states'.[10]

The main challenge in the regulation of shared resources is to strike a balance between the interests of all parties concerned. This is more easily said than done as constant disputes over international watercourses have demonstrated.[11] For some states a general principle of not causing damage to the territory of other states, coupled with almost unlimited sovereignty to develop the resource according to national development policies, should

---

[7] In general see Schrijver, N. (1997), *Sovereignty over Natural Resources*, Cambridge: Cambridge University Press. See also the discussions on permanent sovereignty in the Introduction to this book and the previous chapter.

[8] For example the Convention on the Non-Navigational Uses of International Watercourses, 36 I.L.M. (1997) 719.

[9] *Trail Smelter Arbitration*, 33 AJIL (1939) 182 and 35 AJIL (1941) 684. *Nuclear Tests Case (Australia v. France)* [1974] ICJ Reports 253; Basel Convention on the Control of Transboundary Movements of Hazardous Wastes and their Disposal, 28 I.L.M. (1989) 657.

[10] UNEP/IG/12/2 (1978), para. 16.

[11] See *River Oder Case* (1929), PCIJ Ser. A, No. 23 (equality of use and no preferential privilege of any riparian state) and *Lac Lanouc Arbitration*, 24 ILR (1957) 101 (duty to consult other states). For a discussion of the tortuous process of agreement on the regulation of international watercourses see Birnie, P., A. Boyle and C. Redgwell (2009), *International Law and the Environment*, 3rd edn, Oxford: Oxford University Press, chapter 10, pp. 536–582.

suffice.[12] For others, equitable utilisation[13] requires a wider duty of cooperation based on information and prior consultation in order to ensure optimum use.[14] The ICJ has recently stressed in the *Pulp Mills* case the importance of the need to ensure environmental protection of shared natural resources while allowing for sustainable economic development, '[a]ccount must be taken of the need to safeguard the continued conservation of the river environment and the rights of economic development of the riparian states'.[15]

In 1978 UNEP published some 'Principles of Conduct in the Conservation and Harmonious Utilization of Natural Resources Shared by Two or More States'.[16] The principles' general and vague language which did not specify the existence of legal obligations and the reluctance of the General Assembly to endorse them suggest that the regulation of shared resources still remains controversial.

Beyond natural resources within the territory of a state three categories have emerged to regulate those resources beyond territorial jurisdiction or the exploitation of which has an importance well beyond the limits of national jurisidiction.

2.2. Common Areas

The term 'common areas' is used for those resources situated beyond the territorial jurisdiction of any state, for example the high seas and their fisheries,[17] Antarctica[18] or outer space.[19] These are the global commons.

---

[12]   *Trail Smelter Case*, 35 AJIL (1941) 686 (not to cause damage to the territory of another state).

[13]   Discussed below.

[14]   *Lac Lanoux Arbitration* 24 ILR (1957) 119 (duty on states to cooperate and negotiate to resolve potential problems). Also, in general Birnie, Boyle and Redgwell (2009), supra, at 192.

[15]   *Case Concerning Pulp Mills on the River Uruguay (Argentina v. Uruguay)*, Request for the Indication of Provisional Measures [2006] ICJ Judgment of 13 July 2006, para. 80.

[16]   17 I.L.M. (1978) 1091.

[17]   1958 Geneva Convention on the High Seas, 1982 UNCLOS. See Birnie, Boyle and Redgwell (2009), supra, pp. 194–195.

[18]   Regulated by a special regime 1991 Protocol to the Antarctic Treaty on Environmental Protection, 30 I.L.M. (1991) 1461. Although the parties to the Antarctic Treaty System of December 1959 have designed a comprehensive regime which has many of the features of a common heritage system it is not accepted that this is so.

[19]   Treaty on Principles Governing the Activities of States in the Exploration and Use of Outer Space, Including the Moon and Other Celestial Bodies (1967), or Outer Space Treaty.

As global commons they are subject to the 'no harm rule' which is an international obligation applicable *erga omnes*,[20] even though it may be difficult for individual states to take legal action against any one state the activities of which cause harm in the common areas.[21] Protection of common areas has sometimes been attempted by individual states by imposing unilateral trade measures. This was the argument advances by the US in the *Shrimp-Turtle* case,[22] although international courts and tribunals have repeatedly expressed a preference for consensual regulation in respect of common areas.

2.3. Common Heritage of Mankind

There are certain resources which, lying beyond the jurisdiction of any state (as before), are not open to all to enjoy but subject to a special regime due to the special factors affecting them. These are called the 'common heritage of mankind'. First, the regime of open access to all that characterises the 'global commons' embodies the danger of the so-called 'tragedy of the commons' which Hardin illustrated in his seminal work in 1969:[23] over-exploitation, free-riders and high externalities. Second, given the very different stage of development of states in respect of economic power or technological innovation it is fallacious to argue that all states have equal access to certain resources which would require a special degree of technological advancement or financial resources which would be well out of the reach of many states, particularly of developing states.[24]

With these considerations in mind, developing countries tried to ensure a regime of equitable exploitation and, unsurprisingly, received opposition from developed countries for which a system based on open access, such as the system applicable to 'common areas', would have been much more advantageous.[25] The 1970 UN GA Resolution which declared the seabed

---

[20] Obligations due towards the whole of the international community and which confer rights (of action) to each individual state.

[21] See *Nuclear Test Case (New Zealand v. France)*, Interim Measures [1973] ICJ Rep 135, although France's unilateral decision to withdraw nuclear testing in the South Pacific meant that the Court did not adjudicate on the merits.

[22] *US – Import Prohibition of Certain Shrimp and Shrimp Products*, 12 October 1998, 38 I.L.M. (1999).

[23] Hardin, G. (1968), 'The Tragedy of the Commons', *Science*, 162, 1243.

[24] Brunnee, J. (2007), 'Common Areas, Common Heritage, Common Concern', in D. Bodansky, J. Brunnee and E. Hey (eds), *Oxford Handbook of International Environmental Law*, Oxford: Oxford University Press, at 562.

[25] Ibid. For a fuller discussion see lrschan, B. and B.C. Brennan (1982), 'The

the common heritage of mankind was met with the abstention of 16 developed countries[26] and discussion on the exploitation of the seabed delayed the entry into force of UNCLOS.[27] Again the North and the South had very different views and priorities.[28]

The regulation of the deep seabed has several elements which constitute the basis for the regulation of resources subject to the principle of common heritage of mankind. In the first place the area is not subject to the jurisdiction of any state,[29] and all activities must be carried out for the benefit of mankind as whole.[30] The deep seabed is managed by an international authority which ensures equitable benefit sharing and environmental protection[31] and the area is be used exclusively for peaceful purposes.[32] The concept of common heritage of mankind has also been used in respect of the Moon[33] and soon gained currency in respect of other areas beyond national jurisdiction, the so-called 'global commons'. It was argued that the atmosphere should be regarded as common heritage,[34] or the whole environment,[35] even the Earth's biodiversity and genetic resources.[36] Developing countries opposed the idea that resources under their permanent sovereignty – such as biodiversity – would be subject to third parties' property rights, and as a consequence the concept of common concern was developed.

Common Heritage of Mankind Principle in International Law', Columbia Journal of Transnational Law, 21, 305.

[26]   Brunnee (2007), supra, at 562.

[27]   1982 United Nations Convention on the Law of the Sea (UNCLOS), 21 I.L.M. (1982) 1261, part XI.

[28]   See chapter 1 for an outline of the main issues.

[29]   It is a 'common' in the sense described before even though there are limitations on access and use: Article 137 UNCLOS.

[30]   Article 140 UNCLOS.

[31]   Articles 137 and 145 UNCLOS.

[32]   Article 146 UNCLOS. All discussed in Brunnee (2007), supra, at 562.

[33]   1979 Moon Treaty.

[34]   Westing, A.H. (1990) 'The Atmosphere as a Common Heritage of Humankind', Scientific World 34, 5–6, cited in Schrijver, N. (1997), *Permanent Sovereignty over Natural Resources*, Cambridge: Cambridge University Press, 388.

[35]   Verway, W.D. (1995), 'Protection of the Environment, in search of new legal perspectives', Leiden Journal 8, 7–40 at 37.

[36]   Article 1 of the International Undertaking on Plant Genetic Resources: 'plant genetic resources are the heritage of mankind and consequently should be available without restriction'. FAO Conference Res 8/83. Cited in Schrijver (1997), supra, at 389.

2.4. Common Concern

The concepts of common areas and common heritage, while useful in regulating natural resource access and management in areas beyond national jurisdiction, failed to provide an adequate solution for those resources which are not geographically bound and yet are of interest to the whole of humanity. A new concept – common concern – was coined. Both climate change[37] and biodiversity conservation[38] have been said to be the 'common concern' of humanity as all states derive benefits from protective action taken either unilaterally or collectively by other states. Many have referred to those resources as constituting 'global public goods'.[39] Some commentators have suggested that the whole 'global environment' is a common concern of humanity,[40] although in practice such a general statement only serves to inform policy and regulatory developments in respect of environmental assets.

Regulation of resources under common concern needs to take into account the fact that either the resource (i.e., biological diversity) or the action (mitigation actions to try to avert climate change) falls under the sovereignty of states and frictions may arise between the need to take the interests of other states (potentially all states) into account and the exercise of the right of permanent sovereignty over natural resources. There are examples of successful common concern regimes, like those of the protection of the ozone layer[41] and of areas of world cultural and natural heritage.[42] These regimes have successfully engaged the consent of the global community of states and have thrived in the context of cooperative regulation, compliance and enforcement. Unfortunately no such success has been

[37] Note that it is the change in the climate and its adverse effects on Earth which constitute the 'common concern', not the climate itself. Preamble, UNFCCC. Equally it is biodiversity conservation and not biological diversity as such.

[38] The 1992 CBD emphasises that biological diversity remains under the sovereignty of each state. See the preamble to the CBD: what constitutes the common concern of humanity is its conservation.

[39] See chapter 1, p. 67.

[40] Brunnee, at 564 cites the World Conservation Union (2004), Draft International Covenant on Environment and Development, 3rd edn Gland: IUCN, Article 3.

[41] 1987 Montreal Protocol on Substances that Deplete the Ozone Layer. See Mickelson, K. (2009), 'Competing Narratives of Justice in North–South Environmental Relations: the Case of Ozone Layer Depletion', in Ebbesson, J. and P. Okowa (eds), *Environmental Law and Justice in Context*, Cambridge: Cambridge University Press, pp. 297–315.

[42] Regulated by the 1972 Convention for the Protection of the World Cultural Heritage.

achieved in finding a globally acceptable regulation of climate change[43] or biodiversity.[44] Too many interests, and not least those of big corporations, are at stake in both cases and their economic power finds an easy reflection in the political attitudes of the developed countries in which they are based.

The concept of common concern should impose limits to the freedom of states' action in respect of the natural resources involved. How it does this is more difficult to define. On the one hand states should share the burden of cooperation and problem solving,[45] and this cooperation should be subject to the principle of common but differentiated responsibilities.[46] Further, and in order to ensure the legitimacy of any outcomes, the regulation of all these collective environmental concerns is best approached by treaty-based law making.

3.   PRINCIPLES OF NATURAL RESOURCE MANAGEMENT

While each state has permanent sovereignty over its natural resources, each state also has an obligation, under customary international law, not to cause transboundary environmental damage.[47] There is an obligation on the source state not to cause harm to other states and a state is 'not permitted to use its territory for purposes injurious to the interests of other states'.[48] Together with this general obligation the principles of sustainable development, sustainable use, reasonable use, a precautionary approach, the precautionary principle and the principle of common but differentiated responsibilities influence natural resource management at the international and national levels.

---

[43]   For a discussion on the failed talks in Copenhagen see chapter 8 and www. guardian.co.uk/environment/copenhagen.

[44]   The 1992 CBD has 193 parties (168 signatures) but has not been ratified by the United States.

[45]   Principle 7 Rio Declaration calls on states 'to cooperate in a spirit of global partnership to conserve, protect and restore the health and integrity of the Earth's ecosystems'.

[46]   Discussed in chapter 1. See also Principle 1 Rio Declaration, Preamble UNFCC.

[47]   Principle 21 of Stockholm Declaration, Principle 2 of the Rio Declaration. Perrez, F. (1996), 'The Relationship between Permanent Sovereignty and the Obligation Not to Cause Transboundary Environmental Damage', Environmental Law, 26, 1187.

[48]   Okowa, P.N. (2000), *State Responsibility for Transboundary Air Pollution in International Law*, Oxford: Oxford University Press, 65.

3.1. Sustainable Development and Natural Resource Management

The ubiquitous[49] principle of sustainable development (SD) is one of the central pillars which informs international environmental law and the law of natural resource management. Its origins can be tracked down to the late nineteenth century, to the *Pacific Fur Seals* arbitration[50] and, more recently, to the 1982 World Charter for Nature which called for 'all areas of the earth, both land and sea to be subject to conservation'.[51]

Sustainable development has been defined in many ways, all definitions requiring that we look at the world as a system which connects both time and space, but the most frequently quoted definition is from *Our Common Future*, also known as the Brundtland Report: '[s]ustainable development is development that meets the needs of the present without compromising the ability of future generations to meet their own needs'.[52] This definition contains two key concepts:

- the concept of *needs*, in particular the essential needs of the world's poor, to which overriding priority should be given; and
- the idea of *limitations* imposed by the state of technology and social organization on the environment's ability to meet present and future needs.

It was with the adoption of the instruments at Rio that sustainable development became the central and leading principle of environmental policy. As a normative concept sustainable development requires the integration

---

[49] The literature on SD is vast. See, among others, Cordonnier-Segger, M.C. and A. Khalfan (2004), *Sustainable Development Law: Principles, Practice and Prospects*, Oxford: Oxford University Press; Sands, (2003), *Principles of International Environmental Law*, Cambridge: Cambridge University Press, pp. 252–270; Boyle, A. and D. Freestone (1999), *International Law and Sustainable Development*, Oxford: Oxford University Press; French, D. (2005), *International Law and Policy of Sustainable Development*, Oxford: Oxford University Press, 10–34; Koskenniemi, M. (2009), 'The Politics of International Law – 20 Years Later', EJIL 20, 7, 10.

[50] *Pacific Sea Fur Seals Arbitration (United Kingdom v. United States)*, 15 August 1983.

[51] The WCN (23 I.L.M. (1983) 455) was elaborated under the auspices of the IUCN.

[52] World Commission on Environment and Development (WCED) (1987), 'Our Common Future', Annex to Doc. A\42\427, Development and International Co-operation: Environment; also as World Commission on Environment and Development (1987), *Our Common Future*, London and New York: Oxford University Press.

of three values: environmental, social and economic – known and referred to in the literature as 'the three pillars of SD'.[53] The frictions between the different pillars or values contained within the SD paradigm were manifest from the very beginning. In the discussion at the World Commission on SD which drafted the Brundtland Report of 1987 two particular positions seemed to dominate the discussion. On the one hand there was an imperious need to foster economic growth in order to meet the needs of a growing population and end, or at least alleviate, poverty. On the other hand the needs of future generations[54] had to be considered in this equation or in the policies that would outline the economic development which was deemed to be possible and 'sustainable'. Environmentalists and development advocates were confined, quite explicitly in the discussions of the Commission, to two camps from which they had to reach a compromise. The North and the South had, once again, very different views, needs and priorities. The extent of abject global poverty and the needs and expectations of developing countries quickly rose to the top of the agenda, while the idea that it was not the growth of developing countries alone, not even perhaps, substantially or significantly, which needed to be monitored and constrained but rather the pattern of growth and consumption in developed countries.

Sustainable development is an eminently flexible concept, and the many conceptions of justice – distributional, corrective – make it even less amenable to a crystallisation in a particular version which could be taken as the basis for a normative concept of international law.[55] It is arguable that it is its very flexibility which has afforded sustainable development the prominent and enduring role in global environmental policy since the 1980s. 'The continuing debate over the meaning of sustainability has ensured vibrancy and interest in a concept that might otherwise be marginalised if it were ossified through an artificial consensus advanced by a small club of nations. It also makes it open to multiple and changing interpretations . . . including international judicial bodies and arbitral tribunals'.[56] This does not mean that states cannot strive towards an agreement whereby sustainable development includes and is compatible with liberal

---

[53]   These were identified in the Johannesburg declaration, UN Report of the WSSD, UN Doc. A/CONF 199/20 (2002) Resolution 1, para. 5.

[54]   Brown-Weiss, E. (1989), *In Fairness to Future Generations*, Dobbs Ferry, NY: Transnational Publishers.

[55]   French, D. (2009), 'Global Justice and the (Ir)relevance of Indeterminacy', Chinese Journal of International Law 9, para. 43, 593–619.

[56]   Stephens, T. (2009), 'Sustainability Discourses in International Courts: What Place for Global Justice?', paper presented at the ILA Conference on SD in Sheffield, 26–27 August.

theories of justice but moves beyond them by recognising 'an accelerating ecological interdependence, historical inequality in past resource use, and 'the growth of limits'.[57]

Despite UNEP's Governing Council declaring that the formulation of sustainable development in the Brundtland Report 'does not imply in any way an encroachment upon national sovereignty',[58] sustainable development, it has been suggested, is a principle which limits state sovereignty on natural resource management.[59] Sustainable development should act as a restraint to the unfettered sovereignty of states in natural resource exploitation. Sustainable development could, at the global level, encompass a concept of stewardship whereby the power of states to exploit natural resources and ecosystems would be curtailed.[60] Individual countries have gone some way towards accepting this 'stewardship sovereignty': Brazil included the constitutional protection of rainforests in its 1988 constitution and Australia accepted that the World Heritage Convention could place limits on its power to exploit natural resources.[61]

There is no doubt that sustainable development is now part of the body of customary international law.[62] It has been referred to by international tribunals[63] as having both a procedural aspect – obliging the parties to look at the environmental consequences of their project[64] – and a substantive aspect.[65] In the *Shrimp/Turtle* dispute the Appellate Body of the WTO stated that 'the "objective" of sustainable development . . . has been accepted as a concept that integrates economic and social development and environmental policy'.[66]

While progress towards sustainable development has been made through meetings, agreements and changes in environmental governance, real change has been slow. Since 1987 population growth, increasing consumption and energy use, from both developed and developing countries, have placed increasing pressure on the state of the environment. The third conference

---

[57] Langhelle, O. (2000), 'Sustainable Development and Social Justice: Expanding the Rawlsian Framework of Global Justice', Environmental Values 9, 295–296. Cited in French (2009), supra, at 598.
[58] Annex II to UNEP GC Decisions 15/2, May 1989.
[59] See discussion below.
[60] Tarlock, D. (2007), 'Ecosystems', in Bodansky et al. (2007), supra, at 593.
[61] Ibid., at 594.
[62] Sands (2003), supra, at 254.
[63] See Sands' commentary on the *Gabčikovo-Nagymaros* case. Ibid., at 254–255.
[64] Ibid.
[65] In the case discussed this involved ensuring a 'sustainable' or appropriate volume of water flow. Ibid.
[66] 38 I.L.M. (1999) para 129.

of the UN on Environment and Development, the World Summit on Sustainable Development (WSSD) in Johannesburg, in 2002[67] adopted a Declaration on Sustainable Development and a Plan of Implementation.[68] Those documents reaffirm and refine existing polices and principles and try to strengthen the Commission on Sustainable Development.

The integration of environment and development is the main element of the concept of sustainable development from a legal point of view. It means that environmental considerations must be taken into account and integrated in economic development plans and project and the needs of economic development especially of the poorest countries) must be taken into account when agreeing on environmental policies and standards. The first proposition, that implying considering the environmental consequences of development plans, has been translated into requirements for environmental impact assessments and provision of information.[69] It is of particular relevance to the work of international institutions of global economic governance such as the WTO, the World Bank and its Agencies or regional Organisations such as the European Union. Since the late 1980s a change in policy at the core of these institutions has allowed the progressive introduction of environmental considerations into their policies, plans and actions. The European Community Treaty has been amended to include environmental considerations.[70] The World Bank has also developed policies which require environmental impact assessment for its activities and programmes[71] and has established its own environment department.[72] The WTO has adopted sustainable development as an objective in its Preamble and has confirmed through decision of the appellate body its importance in the integration of free trade and environmental considerations.[73]

---

[67] 'Johannesburg Plan of Implementation' Report of the World Summit on Sustainable Development, Johannesburg, South Africa, 4 September 2002, UN Doc. A/CONF.199/L.1., available at: http://un.org/esa/sustdev/documents/WSSD_P01_PDF/English/P01_Toc.htm (accessed 15 January 2010).

[68] UN Doc. A/Conf 199/20(2002), Resolution and Annex.

[69] These are developed in detail in chapter 3.

[70] See EC Commission Report (1999) 'Integrating Environmental Concerns and Sustainable Development into Community Policies' (SEC 1941) for an overview of these changes and the policy reasons supporting them.

[71] See chapter 4, pp. 189–191, for a discussion on these.

[72] The Environmentally and Socially Sustainable Development network (ESSD) later to be combined with Infrastructure (INF) networks into a new Sustainable Development network.

[73] See Preamble to the Marrakech Agreement and Decision of the Appellate Panel in the *Shrimp/Turtle* dispute discussed above.

Some commentators have proposed that sustainable development should be adopted as the key element of the overreaching framework for UN activities, with the ECOSOC overseeing system-wide coordination and integration of the different aspects of sustainable development.[74] Coordination among international institutions is key in implementing Agenda 21, WSSD outcomes, the sustainable development aspects of the Millennium Declaration, the Monterrey Consensus on Financing for Development and the WTO Doha Ministerial Declaration.[75]

3.2. Sustainable Use

Although there appears to be a customary obligation of sustainable use of natural resources which are beyond the jurisdiction of a state,[76] and treaty references can be found in respect of transboundary resources like international watercourses,[77] it is arguable whether that obligation can be predicated of natural resources which fall within the territories subject to state sovereignty.

Sustainable use was referred to in principle 8 of the Rio Declaration as the 'need to reduce and eliminate unsustainable patterns of production and consumption' and included in the Convention on Biological Diversity,[78] which defines sustainable use as '[u]se that . . . in any way and rate that does not lead to long-term decline of biological diversity'. The *Icelandic Fisheries* case[79] points to the existence of a customary obligation to cooperate in the sustainable use of common property, and a growing body of treaty law supports a general obligation of conservation and sustainable use.[80]

However it has been pointed out that 'only where specific international regimes have been developed, as in the management of fisheries and water resources, can it be said that the concept of sustainable use has acquired some normative content or could potentially be used to judge the permissibility of natural resource exploitations.'[81] In the absence of a specific

---

[74] Cordonnier-Segger, M.C. and A. Khalfan (2004), supra, at 43.
[75] Ibid.
[76] For examples of fisheries on the High Seas, see *Icelandic Fisheries* case [1974] ICJ Rep 1.
[77] The 1997 Convention on International Watercourses has several references to the 'sustainable utilisation of water'. See in Birnie, Boyle and Redgwell (2009), supra, chapter 10.
[78] Articles 2, 6, 8 and 10.
[79] [1974] ICJ Rep 3 and 175.
[80] Birnie, Boyle and Redgwell (2009), supra, at 200.
[81] Ibid.

treaty regime states have considerable discretion on to how to implement the principle.[82]

Tropical forests constitute a good example of this. Tropical forests fall under the sovereignty of national states and yet they are the subject of continuous international interests, and claims as they act as invaluable sources of biodiversity conservation and have a central role to play in controlling climate change both through their role as sinks and because of the large amounts of CO_2 released into the atmosphere following the cutting down of tropical forest. Yet they are, one could say, insurmountably difficult to regulate. Indeed only non-binding instruments have been adopted which address the regulation of tropical forests[83] and it is suggested that resort to other approaches such as those provided by MES may be more conducive to conservation and proper management.[84]

The concept of sustainable use has been used in respect of marine resources[85] and non-marine resources[86] with expressions such as 'the utilisation of natural resources must aim at satisfying the needs of man according to the carrying capacity of the environment'.[87] ASEAN was one of the first regional treaties to adopt a standard of 'sustainable utilisation of natural resources . . . with a view to attaining the goal of sustainable development'.[88]

Sustainable use is closely related to sustainable development and it is referred to in a multitude of international instruments with emphasis either on the sustainability of human activity, natural resource extraction or the relationship between both. The 1992 OSPAR Convention uses the term 'sustainable management of human activities',[89] the 1992 Biodiversity Convention defines 'sustainable use' as 'the use of components of biodiversity in a way and at a rate that does not lead to the long-term decline of biological diversity, thereby maintaining its potential to meet the needs and aspirations of present and future generations'.[90] The concept of

---

[82]   Ibid., at 201.

[83]   1992 Rio Non-Legally Binding Authoritative Statement of Principles for the Global Consensus on the Management, Conservation and Sustainable Development of all Types of Forests, 3 YbIEL (1992) 830; UN Non-Legally Binding Instrument on all Types of Forest, UN GA Res. 62/98 (2008).

[84]   See below.

[85]   1995 Straddling Stocks Agreement, Article 2; 1953 North Atlantic Fisheries Convention, Preamble and Article IV.

[86]   1968 African Nature Convention, Preamble.

[87]   Ibid.

[88]   Article 1(1). See discussion in Sands (2003), supra, at 258.

[89]   In the 1992 OSPAR Convention, Preamble.

[90]   Article 2.

sustainable use is also used in the 1992 Climate Change Convention,[91] the 2000 Biosafety Protocol[92] and a multitude of international agreements on marine resources where terminology such as 'rational',[93] 'wise',[94] 'sound',[95] 'proper'[96] or 'appropriate'[97] is used interchangeably with 'sustainable'.[98]

3.3. Reasonable Use and Equitable Utilisation

The notion that states must use common resources reasonably and must act in a way that does not interfere with the enjoyment of equal rights of access by other states has been used in the resolution of disputes over activities affecting common areas. Both the *Icelandic Fisheries* case[99] and the *Nuclear Tests* case[100] endorsed the idea that activities on the High Seas must be limited in order to allow for other states' exercise of their rights. Reasonable use is linked to equitable utilisation and it was so connected in the *Icelandic Fisheries* case. Equitable utilisation further is considered to be a rule of customary international law governing shared water resources.[101]

As a counterpart to 'equitable utilisation' and 'reasonable use', the doctrine of 'abuse of rights' can also be used in cases when it is necessary to balance the interests of different parties. Many commentators[102] opine that the doctrine is best used with restraint in order to encourage certainty

---

[91]   Article 3(4).

[92]   Article 1.

[93]   For migratory birds, 1940 Western Hemisphere Convention, Article VII; fisheries, 1978 Northwest Atlantic Fisheries Convention Article II(1); and 'all natural resources' 1978 Amazonian Treaty, Articles I and VII. Also principles 13 and 14 of the Stockholm Declaration.

[94]   Flora and fauna, 1968 African Conservation Convention, Article VII(1).

[95]   1985 Nairobi Convention, Article 4(1).

[96]   For fisheries 1949 Agreement for the General Fisheries Council of the Mediterranean, Preamble and Article IV(a); and forests, 1959 Agreement for the Latin American Forest Institute, Article III (1)(a).

[97]   1981 Lima Convention, Article 3(1).

[98]   The last part of this section and the references given to international treaties rely heavily on Sands (2003), supra, at 260–261.

[99]   *Icelandic Fisheries Cases (UK & Germany v. Iceland)* [1974] ICJ Rep 3 and 175.

[100]   *Nuclear Tests Case (Australia v. France)* [1974] ICJ Rep 253.

[101]   Article 6 1997 Convention on International Watercourses reflecting the principle of customary law.

[102]   Including Brownlie, I. (2003), *Principles of Public International Law*, 6th edn, Oxford, 490; Ago, R. (1970) *Yearbook of the International Law Commission, Vol. I*, 170 and Birnie, Boyle and Redgwell (2009), supra, at 204–205.

and stability, and only in those cases in which 'a state has failed to comply with a positive rule of international law thus enunciated'.[103]

3.4. The Precautionary Principle

It has been said that '[t]he precautionary principle may well be the most innovative, pervasive and significant new concept in environmental policy over the past quarter century. It may also be the most reckless arbitrary and ill-advised.'[104]

The precautionary approach, like the precautionary principle, reinforces the principle of sustainability,[105] especially the idea of inter-generational equity[106] which informs sustainable development. The precautionary approach, put simply, requires that all development decisions must be made with the aim of preserving options for future generations, and if there is uncertainty at the outcomes of a particular action or inaction would cause irreparable environmental damage then the action should either stop or action must be taken.[107] The precautionary principle, thus, in its most basic form states that uncertainty about the outcomes of a given action or process does not justify inaction 'where there are threats of serious or irreversible damage, lack of full scientific certainty shall not be used as a reason for postponing measures to prevent environmental degradation'.[108] In reality the application of the precautionary principle by national governments or international bodies like the EU has been tempered by diverse qualifications such as accounts for costs, countervailing risks and, in Europe, methods of regulatory impact assessment.[109] It has been argued that the precautionary principle requires the promoter of

---

[103]   Ago, supra, paras 25–35 cited in Birnie, Boyle and Redgwell, (2009), supra, p. 204.

[104]   Marchant, G.E. and K.L. Mossman (2004), *Arbitrary and Capricious: The Precautionary Principle in the EU Courts*, Washington DC: AEI Press, at 1. Cited by Wiener, J.B. (2007), 'Precaution', in *Oxford Handbook of International Environmental Law*, at 599.

[105]   Principle 13 Rio Declaration: 'A "precautionary approach" is to be applied'.

[106]   Famously formulated by Brown Weiss, E. (1989), *In Fairness to Future Generations: International Law, Common Patrimony and Intergenerational Equity*, Dobbs Ferry, NY: Transnational Publishers.

[107]   Tarlock, D. (2007), 'Ecosystems', in Bodansky et al. (eds), supra, at 595.

[108]   Formulation from the Rio Declaration, para. 15 and the Bergen Declaration (1990).

[109]   See Wiener J.B. (2007), 'Precaution', supra, in Bodansky et al. (eds), supra, at 610.

a potentially dangerous activity to prove that it would cause no harm,[110] but the most widely accepted view is that the party alleging the risk must prove, at least prima facie, the risk of irreparable environmental harm.[111]

In the context of natural resource management developing countries may have a very different attitude to environmental risk and precaution from that of developed, richer countries. Faced with the pressing demands of growing populations and widespread poverty their risk-analysis and related trade-offs would, in most cases, differ from those of developed countries. A good example of the difficulties in arriving at general or global approaches to precaution is the debate about GMO. Europe has rejected GMO in agricultural production. Most of Africa, where inefficient agriculture and hunger force millions into malnutrition and death every year has similarly rejected GMO in fear that if it were to accept GMOs then African countries' exports to the EU would be curtailed. Yet it has been argued that GMOs are part of the solution to the food crises and poverty in Africa.[112] Globalisation and the structures of consensus and governance it fosters could provide a platform where an open debate could be started to arrive at a middle ground which would unify attitudes to risk and prevention in environmental terms. In the meantime and until environmental governance develops and networks and forums for discussion are articulated, the precautionary approach remains a nationally or treaty bound, circumstantially ascribed principle.

3.5. Principle of Common but Differentiated Responsibilities

Climate change, the depletion of the ozone layer, the conservation of biodiversity and of freshwater resources, the depletion of fish stocks are all global problems which require cooperation from all states in finding global solutions. This task is not easy. Because of the close relationship between natural resource use and economic growth states have very different needs, priorities and vested interests. International environmental law has, in recent decades, made an incremental effort to devise regimes of protection and regulation which are inclusive, equitable and fair to all states. The debate round environmental protection has been crystallised

---

[110] Argentina's argument in the *Pulp Mills Case* (Provisional Measures) 2006. Discussed in Birnie et al. (2009), supra, 158.

[111] WTO: *EC Measures Concerning Beef and Beef Products* WT/DS26/AB/R (1998), paras 97–100.

[112] Collier, P. (2008), 'The Politics of Hunger', Foreign Affairs (Nov–Dec), available at: www.foreign affairs.com/articles/64607/paul-collier/the-politics-of-hunger (accessed 15 January 2010).

in a divide between developed and developing countries. On the one hand developed countries have created most, if not all, of the environmental problems that the world faces today. Their development path and their consumer societies are depleting the Earth's resources in a process which often started when they were colonial powers exploiting the natural resources of the colonies.

Developing countries are usually resource rich – to a greater or lesser degree – but face immediate problems such as poverty, hunger, disease and poor education. Having become independent from the colonial powers they found themselves in an unequal system of sovereign states with rules already drafted and devised to satisfy the interest of the old powers. Today they are looking at rapid industrialisation and economic development as an answer to their many internal poverty and underdevelopment related problems. They also feel that it is the developed countries that must be responsible for the damage they have already caused to the environment. This damage in most cases is suffered by developing countries despite their negligible contributions.[113]

This responsibility for historical damage was advanced by developing countries at the time of the discussion of the Declaration on the New International Economic Order (NIEO)[114] but found strong opposition by all developed countries and did not crystallise into any legal commitment.[115] The conviction of developing countries that developed countries were largely responsible for the environmental damage suffered in the planet to date was expressed in their proposed wording of Principle 7 of the Rio Declaration which placed an emphasis on historical contributions:

---

[113] This is especially the case in respect of climate change, with consequences such as desertification and the spreading of contagious disease which affects developing countries disproportionately because of their geographical location and their reduced capabilities of adaptation.

[114] 'Another argument used to justify preferential treatment for developing countries is that former colonial powers and some other industrialized states which benefited from colonial activities have a moral, if not a legal, duty to make reparations for past exploitation.' Vasciannie, S. (1990), *Land-locked and Geographically Disadvantaged States in the International Law of the Sea*, New York and Oxford: Oxford University Press, at 26, cited in French, D. (2000), 'Developing States and International Environmental Law: The Importance of Differentiated Responsibilities', International and Comparative Law Quarterly, 49, 35–60.

[115] The ICJ looked at the liability of trustee states for environmental damage to territories which they administered in *Certain Phosphate Lands in Nauru* [1992] ICJ Rep 240. However, the Court never discussed the substance of the case as Australia paid $107 million in full and final settlement.

The major cause of the continuing deterioration of the global environment is the unsustainable patterns of production and consumption, particularly in developed countries. In view of their main historical and current responsibility for global environmental degradation and their capability to address this common concern, developed countries shall provide adequate, new and additional financial resources and environmentally sound technologies on preferential and concessional terms to developing countries to enable them to achieve sustainable development.[116]

The final wording of Principle 7 eliminated any possible claim of developing countries against developed countries for past environmental harm. The international community's endorsement of differentiated responsibilities between developed and developing states was a means of achieving both global environmental protection and sustainable development:[117]

States shall cooperate in a spirit of global partnership to conserve, protect and restore the health and integrity of the Earth's ecosystems. In view of the different contributions to global environmental degradation, states have common but differentiated responsibilities. The developed countries acknowledge the responsibility that they bear in the international pursuit of sustainable development in view of the pressures their societies place on the global environment and of the technologies and financial resources they command.[118]

The principle of common but differentiated responsibilities was included in all the Rio documents: the UN Framework Convention on Climate Change, and the Convention on Biological Diversity, and the three non-binding documents, Agenda 21, the Rio Declaration and the Statement on Forests.

But once the principle had been stripped of the power to claim compensation for environmental damage many questioned whether it had any value beyond acknowledging 'the special leadership role of developed countries' due to their 'wealth, technical expertise and capabilities'.[119] Was

---

[116]   Wording proposed by the G-77, in French (2000), supra, at 36.

[117]   Ibid. For an excellent discussion see also Kiss, A. (1994), 'The Rio Declaration on Environment and Development', in L. Campiglio et al. (eds), *The Environment after Rio: International Law and Economics*, New York: Springer, 61.

[118]   The final version of Principle 7 eliminated any notion of responsibility for past environmental harm and of any rights that developing countries could have against developed countries for compensation. Principle 9 also alienated any obligation of technology transfer and left it open as a goodwill aim of commitment from developed states which may or may not happen.

[119]   Interpretative statement of the US to Principle 7 of the Rio Declaration '[t]hat Principle 7 does not 'imply recognition . . . of any international obligations . . . or any diminution in the responsibility of developing countries'.

it, as some wondered, 'simply an expedient means of ensuring the participation of developing states in what are primarily Northern concerns'?[120] Sands provides an answer to these questions by pointing to the diplomatic importance of the principle of 'common but differentiated responsibilities'. The commonality of obligations ensures the participation of all states in international environmental law while it is the differentiation within such obligations which makes international environmental law politically acceptable, in particular to developing countries.[121]

The principle also signified the emergence of a welcomed trend on the environment versus development debate: the recognition that different historical contributions, different present needs and different technological and economic capabilities need to be reflected in legal rules. This recognition can be articulated in different ways, for example by the setting of differential standards[122] permitting grace periods in implementation,[123] requiring flexibility in approach, and the provision of international assistance.[124]

4.　APPROACHES IN NATURAL RESOURCE MANAGEMENT

Natural resource management (NRM) is not a monolithic concept. It depends very much on the specific social, political and economic needs of each country. Differences in approach can be seen not only between natural resources rich countries and countries which are net consumers of natural resources but between countries belonging to either group due to the different political, social, historical and developmental needs. General approaches are thus invalid, as what works in one jurisdiction may not work in another.[125] Energy and natural resources regulation is heavily anchored and connected with the public interest and energy security. Consumer protection, social benefits and environmental concerns co-exist with the need to secure investors' protection.

---

[120] French (2000), supra, at 35.

[121] Sands, P. (1994), 'International Law in the Field of Sustainable Development', British Yearbook of International Law LXV, 344.

[122] As in Article 4 of the Climate Change Convention.

[123] Article 5 of the Montreal Protocol permitting grace periods.

[124] Convention on Biological Diversity, Article 6 allows accounting for the 'particular conditions and capabilities of the parties'.

[125] Barton, B., L. Barrera-Hernandez, A. Lucas and A. Ronne (2006), 'Conclusion', in B. Barton, L. Barrera-Hernandez, A. Lucas and A. Ronne (eds), *Regulating Energy and Natural Resources*, New York: Oxford University Press, p. 401.

The regulation of natural resources has evolved from the command and control models which emerged in the post-World War II period and revolved round forms of state ownership or state control of natural resources with strict regulation of private actors, towards a market-based instruments approach in the 1980s which saw a swift turn towards privatisation, de-regulation and liberalisation, particularly of the energy sector.[126] In the 1990s corporate capitalism and globalisation required new forms of regulation which in general favoured market instruments like emissions trading, and decentred forms of regulation in the form of industry compacts such as industry standards for environmental regulation (e.g. ISO14000-ISO 14001)[127] or corporate social responsibility (CSR) initiatives.[128] This period of market based reforms and self-regulation was followed by the electricity crisis in California[129] and the collapse of Enron in 2001,[130] which acted as a peremptory reminder that state regulation is necessary and that the consequences of self-regulation or lack of regulation are costly and difficult to address.

Today state regulation and market-based instruments are not seen as the two poles of an intractable dichotomy but as complementary tools to be used by governments and international institutions to ensure the sustainable, fair and efficient use of natural resources at the national, regional and international levels.

One of the main effects of globalisation with its variety of participants has been the 'de-centralisation' of regulation.[131] A multitude of actors besides the state are involved in the regulatory process.[132] Regulation has been defined as a 'sustained and focussed control exercised by a public agency over activities that are valued by a community'.[133]

---

[126] A good review of this period is provided by the special issue on 'Privatisation, Liberalism and De-regulation in the Energy Industry', (1996) Energy and Resources Law, 14, 1–113.

[127] See www.iso14000-iso14001-environmental-management.com/. Also the discussion below.

[128] Discussed in some detail in chapter 5, pp. 220–229.

[129] Sweeney, J.L. (2002), *The California Electricity*, Stanford, CA: Hoover Institution Press.

[130] See for the background to the fall of the energy giant www.specials.ft.com/enron/.

[131] Black, J. (2001), 'De-centering Regulation: Understanding the Role of Regulation and Self-Regulation in a "Post-Regulatory" World', Current Legal Problems, 54, 102. See also chapter 1, p. 55.

[132] See in general chapters 2 and 3, especially chapters 4 and 5.

[133] Selznick, P. (1985), 'Focussing Organizational Research on Regulation', in R. Noll (ed.), *Regulatory Policy and the Social Sciences*, Berkeley, CA:

Regulation often protects collective goals and aspirations, by rejecting the choices of private consumers in favour of public values. The protection of such aspirations and not the goal of economic efficiency has been said to be one of the functions of democracy,[134] and as such has often been identified with 'public interventions which affect the operation of markets through command and control'.[135] Today this command and control system is complemented by market-based instruments or substituted by delegation to other actors through the use of self-regulation.

There are several approaches to regulation in NRM. The main divisions identify command and control, market-based instruments, information based and de-centred approaches.[136] These categories should not be understood as mutually exclusive and, as we will see, overlap with one another in order to reach optimum resource utilisation.

4.1.   Command and Control Regulation

Command and control regulation specifies the required or prohibited conduct for each actor. Examples of command and control type regulation include prohibitions on the discharge of certain pollutants or wastes;[137] limitations on the amount of pollutants expelled or requirements for the adoption of certain technologies, design or practices which would ensure specified standards.[138]

Command and control regulation can emanate from states or international organisations. It is often mixed with some market-based instruments to elicit and encourage compliance, but the basis and essence of this approach is that state or international bodies with regulatory control establish both the regulatory parameters and the conditions and instruments that are to be used. In order to ensure compliance the general aim of prescriptive legal instruments is to create disincentives for the commission of an offence. These disincentives can be of different types with the use of subsidies and persuasion at one end of the spectrum, followed by taxes, fines, civil sanctions, criminal sanctions or revocation of licences at the other end.

University of California Press, quoted by B. Barton in 'The Theoretical Context of Regulation' in Barton et al., supra, at p. 12.

[134]   Ibid. at 18.

[135]   Prosser, T. (1997), *Law and the Regulators*, Oxford: Clarendon Press, at 4.

[136]   Stewart, R. (2007), 'Instrument Choice', in Bodansky et al., supra, at 148–150.

[137]   For example the 1972 Convention on the Prevention of Marine Pollution by Dumping of Wastes and Other Matter (London), 11 I.L.M. (1972) 1294.

[138]   Stewart (2007), supra, at 150.

In contrast to the general tendency towards de-regulation in other areas of the economy command and control is still the preferred method of regulation in natural resources management.[139] This may be related to the fact that natural resource governance has direct consequences for human well-being, and higher aims such as social justice can be achieved only by the state or public agencies coordinating the various and, at times, conflicting desires of individuals according to democratically agreed systems of values. Regulation today usually combines command and control techniques with economic incentives in order to maximise the benefits of both approaches.[140]

4.2. Market-based Legal Instruments

The idea of valuing the environment derives from the desire to avoid 'externalities', or adverse consequences which certain actions create. It is argued that the lack of a price on most environmental goods is the main reason for their overuse, depletion and unsustainable management.[141] Pricing environmental goods is a management tool which seeks to reflect the true cost of human activity (i.e. the atmospheric pollution created by a steel manufacturing company) and gives a more realistic view of the actual cost of goods and services, thus deterring free riders and encouraging changes in consumption patterns.

This approach addresses some of the problems of environmental and natural resource overuse but often assumes that *all* aspects of the environment can be valued economically. This has been heavily criticised from a variety of perspectives. On the one hand, environmentalists point out that economic valuation may devalue the 'cultural and spiritual meaning which the environment has for human society while ignoring altogether the rights of other species'.[142] This construction may also ignore cultural rights linked to rights to the environment especially in the case of indigenous

---

[139] Particularly after the failures of market-based approaches and de-regulation pointed out above.

[140] Stewart, R.B. (2008), 'Economic Incentives for Environmental Protection', in R.L. Revesz, P. Sands and R.B. Stewart, *Environmental Law, the Economy and Sustainable Development*, New York: Cambridge University Press, p. 171.

[141] Together with the fact that many environmental goods are 'public goods': see chapter 1, p. 67.

[142] Jacobs, M. (1994), 'The Limits to Neoclassicism', in M. Redcliff and T. Benron (eds), *Social Theory and the Global Environment*, London: Routledge, at 74, discussed in Dine, J. (2005), *Companies, International Trade and Human Rights*, Cambridge: Cambridge University Press, 241.

BOX 2.1.   THE CREATION OF TRADABLE RIGHTS TO EMIT GREENHOUSE GASES UNDER THE KYOTO PROTOCOL

With the aim of helping countries achive their targets on cutting emissions of greenhouse gases the Kyoto Protocol offers several 'market-based' mechanisms to achieve this at a lesser cost. Emissions trading under the 'Cap and Trade' system is one of them.

Annex I countries can buy 'permits' from any other Annex I country. This is called the 'cap and trade' system. Each nation is assigned the right to emit a certain amount of carbon dioxide. If this amount needs to be exceeded it needs to 'buy' emission permits from another country; if it has a surplus, it can sell its rights to emit.

The EU even before it had to start complying with its Kyoto obligation – in 2008 – created its own internal 'emissions trading scheme' (ETS) in 2005 which has been described as the 'most ambitious attempt yet to create an economic instrument to control climate change'.[1]

Despite many criticisms the scheme aimed at producing techno-logical innovation and cleaner industries while allocating to the producers, to a certain extent, the cost of pollution.

Note:
1. Helms, D. (2006) in R. Henson, *Climate Change: The Symptoms, the Science, the Solutions*, London: Penguin, at 284.

---

peoples.[143] Moreover, as Jacobs points out, 'the construction of markets, on the basis of "willingness to pay" cannot be divorced from the ability to pay which leads inevitably to inegalitarian outcomes'.[144] Transforming the environment or environmental goods and services into commodities also ignores important human rights entitlements linked to the access to food, water and shelter that are included in the right to life.[145]

Economic instruments and market-based alternatives can work well when there is an established market where transactions are already taking

---

[143] Ibid.
[144] Ibid., at 74.
[145] See the discussion below, pp. 118–119.

place as tradable property rights help to internalise externalities (i.e. the cost of pollution). Where there is no market or a commodity which can be immediately traded markets need to be created. The first step in the process of market creation is the allocation of property rights so that these can, at a later stage, be traded. As property rights, understood in the wider sense,[146] are essential to guaranteeing access to natural resources there may be human rights implications in the process which will require a large public-sector input.[147] In some cases the costs of exclusion, the difficulties with establishing geographical boundaries and the balance between community rights versus private property rights make this approach impractical.[148]

Market-based instruments are being promoted in the context of ecosystem services.[149] Supporters argue that they have an important role to play both in the sustainable management of ecosystem services and in the reduction of poverty.[150]

4.3. Incentives

4.3.1. Taxation

Taxes serve many purposes beyond the original one of raising funds to finance government spending. Taxation can be used for the redistribution of wealth, or to promote social, economic or environmental objectives. Currently most taxation is on human enterprise attaching, in some observers' view, an arbitrary penalty on employment. Other forms of taxation can help not only to raise government income but to persuade operators and citizens to engage in different consumption patterns. Some argue that shifting the burden from income to energy and CO_2 emissions from fossil fuels can for example be an effective way to control climate change. The money raised could be divided up among citizens or used to repay the national debt. A tax on carbon dioxide (CO_2) would give everyone an incentive to emit less of it. It would be simple, direct and transparent.[151]

---

[146] See in general Ostrom, E. and E. Schlager (1996), 'The Formation of Property Rights', in S. Hanna, C. Folke and K.-G. Maler, *Rights to Nature: Ecological, Economic, Cultural and Political Principles of Institutions for the Environment*, Washington DC: Island Press, pp. 127–1.

[147] See for example South Africa Water, creation of property rights prior to the introduction of PES.

[148] Fisheries constitute a good example of this.

[149] See the discussion below.

[150] See Stiglitz (2010), supra, at 186–187.

[151] See www.wbcsd.org/includes/getTarget.asp?type=DocDet&id=MzQ2MDc (accessed on 15 September 2009).

Finland was the first country to introduce a CO_2 tax in 1990 followed by Germany, Denmark, Sweden and the Netherlands.[152] The revenue from these taxes is used to reduce other distortionary taxes and charges. Sweden is also undertaking overall tax shift replacing taxes on income with taxes on energy, transport and pollution.[153]

4.3.2. Subsidies

Subsidies can take different forms. They can be direct payments by the state to an industry, sector or group of people, for example winter fuel subsidies for the elderly or water subsidies to agriculture, or can be indirect payments in the form of tax rebates, tax exemptions, preferential planning consent or even insurance cover provided by the government to energy operators regarded as 'too risky' for commercial insurers.[154] Subsidies were introduced in many cases with the aim of improving living standards for the poor or facilitating certain productive sectors such as agriculture,[155] consequently their elimination can be extraordinarily difficult in political terms. They may also be necessary to promote new forms of energy, for instance, renewable energy[156] or when investment in infrastructure is needed in order to exploit certain resources.

Despite their widespread use subsidies present some serious problems. The first of these problems is that they usually remain hidden, which makes it impossible to ascertain the true price for a certain type of activity de-incentivising competition. The price of energy is a good example of this. It is widely recognised that the use of fossil fuels is subsidised by governments in ways which often increase their consumption while there is also a growing consensus on the contribution of fossil fuels to global warming. The Kyoto Protocol specifically identifies elimination of national subsidies as one means of achieving greenhouse gas reductions. Subsidies for fossil fuels distort the prices charged for those fuels and create substantial economic distortions in the debate over the cost of Kyoto Protocol compliance.

Beyond price distortions other questions arise in respect of the use of

---

[152] Luebkeman, C. (2008), 'Drivers of Change: Energy', ARUP, p. 25.
[153] For a discussion of these so-called 'green taxes' see www.libdems.org.uk/environment/green-taxes-are-the-way-to-change-our-world.10733.html.
[154] Luebkeman (2008), supra, at 23.
[155] On agricultural subsidies see Diao, X., E. Diaz-Bonilla and S. Robinson (2003), *How Much Does It Hurt? The Impact of Agricultural Trade Policies on Developing Countries*, Washington, DC: International Food Policy Research Institute.
[156] See the discussion below and chapter 8.

subsidies. Doubts about whether subsidies are directed at the right people and, more importantly, whether subsidies encourage responsible natural resources management or land stewardship are common.[157] A good example of problems caused by subsidies is that subsidies to fisheries in developed countries have been blamed for over-exploitation of global fish stocks.[158]

Although general answers are not useful in this context the following case study illustrates the failures and problems created by the overuse of subsidies.

4.4. Decentred Regulation and Voluntary Approaches

In many parts of the world multiple actors such as communities, NGOs, international organisations and big corporations[159] play a major role in resource management and in the creation of norms to regulate natural resource use. Decentred regulation takes many forms, the most relevant being voluntary codes of conduct, stakeholders' guidelines and voluntary approaches to compliance.

Voluntary instruments are said to have the advantage of greater adaptability to the market and changing conditions as they are designed by business for business. They also have a global reach since their application is not constrained by the borders of a particular state. For example a code of conduct for a particular multinational or a particular sector of industry will apply in all countries where that company or companies in a particular sector have operations.[160] However voluntary instruments lack the accountability and enforcement mechanisms of prescriptive legal instruments. They rely on the voluntary compliance of particular companies, and critics point out that this compliance is at best erratic and at most self-interestedly targeted toward greater positive publicity. They also tend to be quite concentrated in scope and need to be accompanied by market incentives to be of any real persuasion and to act as deterrent to unsuitable actions.

The International Council on Human Rights Policy (ICHRP) in its review of the international legal obligations of companies has pointed out

---

[157] Salzman, J. (2006), 'A Field of Green: The Past and Present of Ecosystem Services', *Land Use Environmental Law*, 21, 133.

[158] Over 75% of global fish stocks are over-exploited – the resulting annual loss for the world economy is US$50 billion. Many small island states and poor coastal regions in developing countries depend on fisheries for their livelihood and food security.

[159] See MNCs' role in development, chapter 3.

[160] See Prakash Sethi, S. (2005), 'Voluntary Codes of Conduct for Multinational Corporations', *Journal of Business Ethics*, 59, 1–2. Also see chapter 5, pp. 220–222.

BOX 2.2.   SUBSIDIES FOR BIOFUELS

According to the proponents of biofuels, growing sugar cane and other agricultural products for the production of ethanol and bio-fuels would serve a twofold purpose: it would reduce dependence on carbon producing non-renewable energy sources such as oil and coal while acting as a carbon sink due to the increased cultivation which would trap carbon out of the atmosphere. Furthermore, it was argued, countries would cash in the prices for producing biofuels.

In the USA subsidies to biofuels have reached record levels but are a costly way of achieving public policy objectives.[1] Government subsidies to biofuels in the US have lately been promoted as a way simultaneously to address concerns relating to the environment, energy security, and rural development.[2] But the cost-effectiveness of achieving these goals under the current subsidy regime is low. The report finds, for example, that biofuels are an extremely high-cost means of reducing greenhouse gas emissions. It costs some $500 in federal and state subsidies to reduce one metric ton of CO_2-equivalent through the production and use of corn-based ethanol. 'That could purchase more than 30 metric tons of CO_2-equivalent offsets on the European Climate Exchange, or nearly 140 metric tons on the Chicago Climate Exchange.'[3] Moreover, the sheer levels of government support to biofuels appear out of proportion to the biofuels' ability to satisfy domestic transport fuel requirements with current forecasts that biofuels account for less than 5 per cent of total transport fuel use.

Notes:
1. The report provides the most comprehensive survey of subsidies to biofuels to date, cataloguing hundreds of government programmes which support virtually every stage of production and consumption relating to ethanol and biodiesel. ISSD Global Subsidies Initiative (2006), *Biofuels: At What Cost? – Government Support for Ethanol and Biodiesel in the United states*, available at: www.globalsubsidies.org/en/research/biofuel-subsidies.
2. The Report estimates that subsidies to biofuels are between $5.5 billion and $7.3 billion a year. Those figures are expected to grow significantly if current policies remain in place, as the bulk of biofuels subsidies are tied to output and output is increasing. Ibid.
3. Information from www.globalsubsidies.org/en/research/biofuel-subsidies-united-states.

FOR DISCUSSION

'The intentions of the Kyoto Protocol include phasing out subsidies in all greenhouse gas emitting sectors and the application of market instruments.'

- Discuss the potential advantages of this approach.
- Give examples of how this has been achieved.
- Do initiatives that subsidise biofuels contribute to the objectives of Kyoto?

Source: World Energy Council, *Energy for Tomorrow's World – Acting Now!*, available at: www.worldenergy.org.

---

that voluntary mechanisms alone are clearly not enough: 'even where voluntary approaches are working . . . anchoring these in a legal framework is likely to enhance its effectiveness. And where voluntary approaches are not effective, a legal framework provides powerful tools and incentives for improvement.'[161]

Often the best and most effective instruments are those which combine voluntary membership with some very strong incentives to support it – with mandatory compliance. An example of this is the Financial Action Task Force on Money Laundering,[162] an inter-governmental body which develops and promotes policies to combat money laundering and terrorist financing.

4.4.1. Voluntary certification schemes

Voluntary certification schemes are one of the most commonly used mechanisms of voluntary compliance. The best known of these are perhaps the Kimberley Process for conflict diamonds[163] and forest certification schemes which seek to curb illegal logging. The Forest Stewardship Council (FSC)[164] scheme incorporates legality requirements into its

---

[161] International Council on Human Rights Policy (2002), *Beyond Voluntarism: Human Rights and the Developing Obligations of Companies*, available at: www. ichrp.org/en/projects/107?theme=9 (accessed 15 January 2010).

[162] www.fatf-gafi.org (accessed 15 January 2010).

[163] www.kimberleyprocess.com/ (accessed 15 January 2010).

[164] The FSC is a non-governmental organisation of civil society groups, industry and forest certification organisations. See www.fsc.org/ (accessed 15 January 2010).

BOX 2.3.   THE KIMBERLEY PROCESS

'The Kimberley Process (KP) is a joint governments, industry and civil society initiative to stem the flow of conflict diamonds – rough diamonds used by rebel movements to finance wars against legitimate governments. The trade in these illicit stones has fuelled decades of devastating conflicts in countries such as Angola, Cote d'Ivoire, the Democratic Republic of the Congo and Sierra Leone.

The Kimberley Process Certification Scheme (KPCS) imposes extensive requirements on its members to enable them to certify shipments of rough diamonds as "conflict-free". As of November 2008, the KP has 49 members, representing 75 countries, with the European Community and its Member States counting as an individual participant': www.kimberleyprocess.com/.

'In May 2000, responding to a growing grassroots movement on "blood diamonds", governments and the diamond industry came together in the South African town of Kimberley to combat the trade in diamonds from conflict zones. The result of these negotiations was the Kimberley Process Certification Scheme, setting up an internationally recognized certification system for rough diamonds and establishing national import/export standards. In November 2002, 52 governments ratified and adopted the Kimberley Process Certification Scheme, which was fully implemented in August 2003.

The Kimberley Process was seriously flawed from the beginning. The Kimberley system of "voluntary self-regulation" on the part of the diamond industry has meant a significant lack of transparency and independent monitoring efforts. The World Diamond Council, initially established to represent the diamond industry at the Kimberley Process, has failed to coordinate effective industry monitoring. Governments, too, have been uninterested in monitoring and regulating the diamond trade. Some say the Kimberley Process amounted to little more than a public relations stunt for the diamond industry, and recent reports by Global Witness and other NGOs have found little evidence of genuine attempts to deliver on industry commitments'.

www.globalpolicy.org/security/issues/diamond/kimberlindex.htm.

FOR DISCUSSION

- Do you think the Kimberley Process has been effective in curbing trade in 'blood diamonds'?
- What steps are necessary to remedy the shortcomings of the Kimberley Process?

---

certification scheme of sustainable harvested timber. Products carrying the FSC label are independently certified to assure consumers that they come from forests which are managed to meet the social, economic and ecological needs of present and future generations. FSC is an independent, non-governmental, not-for-profit organisation established to promote the responsible management of the world's forests.

4.4.2. Stakeholder guidelines

Companies also may consider standards proposed by international, regional or local stakeholder groups. Several human rights organisations have engaged in dialogue with companies in recent years, and the output of some of these conversations has been proposed standards for business. A global example is Amnesty International's Human Rights Principles for Companies.[165] Amnesty's ten Principles are based on international standards and are designed 'to assist companies in developing their role in situations of human rights violations or the potential for such violations'. Human Rights Watch[166] and Global Witness,[167] amongst others, have developed country specific recommendations for oil companies operating in Nigeria and Angola, respectively, and a coalition of U.S.-based companies and NGOs, led by the International Labor Rights Fund[168] and Global Exchange,[169] have established draft principles for companies operating in China.

In the environmental field ISO 14000 is a series of international standards on environmental management developed after the Rio Summit on the Environment held in 1992. In order to unify the multiple national standards (BS 7750 being the first) which arose after the Rio Summit the

---

[165] http://amnesty.it/ailib/aipub/1998/ACT/A7000198.htm   (accessed   15 January 2010).

[166] http://hrw.org/ (accessed 15 January 2010).

[167] http://oneworld.org/globalwitness (accessed 15 January 2010).

[168] http://laborrights.org (accessed 15 January 2010).

[169] http://globalexchange.org (accessed 15 January 2010).

International Organization for Standardization (ISO) created a group to investigate how such standards might benefit business and industry. ISO 14001 is the cornerstone standard of the ISO 14000 series. It specifies a framework of control for an Environmental Management System against which an organisation can be certified by a third party.[170]

5.   ECOSYSTEM SERVICES

5.1.   Defining Ecosystem Services

Between 2001 and 2005 under the auspices of the United Nations a study, called The Millennium Ecosystem Assessment (MA), was carried out in order to assess the consequences of ecosystem change for human well-being and to establish the scientific basis for the actions needed to enhance the conservation and sustainable use of ecosystems and their contribution to human well-being.[171] The study crystallised a major shift in the conception of ecosystems and of ecosystem protection. Although it identified that 15 out of the 24 ecosystems studied were severely degraded and five more seriously endangered, it acknowledged the relationship of humans with the ecosystems they inhabit, and management rather than conservation became the focus of any subsequent effort addressing ecosystem protection.

The 'ecosystem approach'[172] consists of a strategy for the management of land, water and living resources in an integrated manner, thus promoting both conservation and sustainable use in an equitable way. It recognises that humans are a component of ecosystems and aims to apply the appropriate scientific methodologies to the management of live processes within ecosystems.

---

[170]   Other ISO 14000 Series Standards include: ISO 14004 providing guidance on the development and implementation of environmental management systems; ISO 14013/5 providing audit programme review and assessment material; ISO 14020+ labelling issues; ISO 14030+ providing guidance on performance targets and monitoring within an Environmental Management System; ISO 14040+ covering life cycle issues. See www.iso.org/iso/iso_14000_essentials.
[171]   Millennium Ecosystem Assessment (2005), 'Ecosystems and Human Well-being: Synthesis'. Preface, p. xiii, Available at www.millenniumassessment.org/documents/document.356.aspx.pdf.
[172]   Endorsed by the Conference of the Parties (COP) to the Convention on Biological Diversity (CBD) in 2000. It is the primary framework for action under the Convention website.

Humans are fully dependent on Earth's ecosystems and the services they provide, such as food, water, disease regulation, climate regulation, spiritual fulfillment, an aesthetic enjoyment . . . [b]ut also on the supply and quality of social capital, technology, and institutions.[173]

Social capital and institutions (especially legal institutions such as land tenure, human and constitutional rights) are of vital significance in the relationship between ecosystem, services and human well-being.

There is a conceptual debate on the difference between ecosystem goods and services. For some experts, ecosystem goods include timber products and non-timber forest products. Ecosystem services, on the other hand, refers to indirect ecosystem functions such as water purification, flood control, carbon sequestration, climate regulation, soil and nutrient cycling, groundwater recharge, sediment trapping, pollination by wild species, biodiversity, genetic libraries, pest control, recreation or aesthetics-associated tourism, and many more.[174] For others '[e]cosystem goods are generally tangible, material products that result from ecosystem processes, whereas ecosystem services are usually improvements in the condition of things of value'.[175] According to Heal et al., ecosystem services include 'the production of goods (such as seafood and timber), life support processes (such as pollination, flood control and water purification), and life-fulfilling conditions (such as beauty and serenity), as well as the conservation of options for the future (genetic diversity)'.[176] The MA does not attempt to make a clear distinction between goods and services and most of the provisioning ecosystem services can be termed 'ecosystem goods'. While goods extracted from the ecosystem are traded in markets, services provided by the ecosystem (e.g. fresh water, clean air) remain 'extra-market and largely unpriced'.[177] This creates the problem of having to value these ecosystem services (e.g. what would be the biological value? How would one assess the economic value?).[178] In most cases, assessing the economic value remains anthropocentric (i.e. how the human places

---

[173] Millennium Ecosystems Assessment (2005), *Synthesis Report*, Washington DC: Island Press, at 49.

[174] Robbins, A. (2005), 'Ecosystem Services Market' available at: www.cfr. washington.edu/nwef.documents/SciencePapers/tp12.pdf, at p. 1.

[175] Notman, E., et al. (2006), 'State of Knowledge: Ecosystem Services from Forests', available at: www.fs.fed.us/ecosystemservices/pdf/state-of-knowledge.pdf.

[176] Heal, G., et al. (2001), 'Protecting natural capital through ecosystem service districts', Stanford Environmental Law Journal, 20, 334 [cites Daily, G.C. et al. (2000), 'The Value of Nature and the Nature of Value', Science, 289, 395, 395–396].

[177] Ibid., at p. 2.

[178] Ibid., at pp. 2–3.

value on these non-market services). Moreover, definition and measurement of ecosystem goods may be easier than the definition and measurement of ecosystem services. For example, non-point water pollution with its different constituents and varying criteria can be difficult to measure.[179]

Definitional issues apart from ecosystem services are divided in the literature into several groups:[180] *provisioning services* which include water, food, timber, fibre; *regulating ecosystem services* are those which affect climate, floods, disease, wastes, and water quality; *cultural services* which provide recreational, aesthetic, and spiritual benefits and *supporting services* such as soil formation, photosynthesis, and nutrient cycling.[181] Fossil fuels are not mentioned as an ecosystem good nor does the literature, with the exception of Hodas, address ecosystem services that contribute to the formation of fossil fuels,[182] but to highlight the importance of ecosystem services to human life we can point out that more than 94 per cent of all society's usable energy is derived from ecosystem services.[183]

5.2.   Provisioning Ecosystem Services and Human Rights

Certain ecosystem services are closely related to human needs (food, shelter, fuel and water), and as such they are inter-related to the human rights instruments in the area. Although there is no direct reference to a 'right to ecosystem services in any human rights instrument', it is arguable that the rights to food, water and life in general include a right to healthy ecosystems.[184]

> However, the existence of human rights that include the availability of and access to fresh water, food, subsistence agriculture, and accommodation are linked to ecosystem services. Reference to these rights can be found in the 1948 Universal Declaration of Human Rights (UDHR), which states that everyone has the right to life, liberty, and security of person. The UDHR also states that everyone has the right to a standard of living adequate for the health

---

[179]   Notman et al. (2006), supra.
[180]   Lugo, E. (2008), 'Ecosystem services, the Millennium Ecosystem Assessment, and the conceptual difference between the benefits provided by ecosystems and the benefits provided by people', Journal of Land Use and Environmental Law, 23, 243, available at: http://works.bepress.com/ezequiel_lugo/1.
[181]   Ibid.
[182]   Hodas, D. (2007), 'Ecosystem Services of Fossil Fuels', Journal of Land Use and Environmental Law, 22(2), 605.
[183]   Ibid.
[184]   Blanco, E. and J. Razzaque (2009), 'Ecosystem Services and Human Well-Being in a Globalized World: Assessing the Role of Law', Human Rights Quarterly, 31, 692–720 at 697.

and well-being of himself and of his family, including having access to food, clothing, and housing.[185] The International Covenant on Economic, Social and Cultural Rights (ICESCR) and the Convention on the Rights of the Child (CRC) also establish the substantive right to food.[186] By ratifying these agreements, states agree to respect, protect, and fulfill the progressive realization of the rights therein contained.[187] For example, the 'right to adequate food is realized when every man, woman and child, alone or in community with others, have physical and economic access at all times to adequate food or means for its procurement'.[188]

This is of great importance as the human rights framework with its established mechanisms of reporting enforcement is much more developed than other compliance mechanisms at the environmental level and can therefore provide a useful tool for those struggling to gain access to basic natural resources for their survival.

5.3. Managing Ecosystem Services: Payments for Ecosystem Services

However promising, even attractive, the concept of ecosystem services is for the future of natural resource management there are several problems which have been identified with reference to the regulation of ecosystem services.[189] The first of these problems is the lack of knowledge about how ecosystems actually work.[190] The second problem is that most ecosystem

---

[185] Universal Declaration of Human Rights, adopted 10 December 1948, GA Res. 217A (III), UN GAOR, 3d Sess. (Resolutions, pt. 1), at 71, Article 25, UN Doc. A/810 (1948), reprinted in 43 AJL (Supp. 1949) 127. This list is not an all-inclusive list, and other elements, such as water, can be included. Gleick, P.H. (1998), 'The Human Right to Water', 1 Water Policy 487.

[186] International Covenant on Economic, Social and Cultural Rights (ICESCR), adopted 16 December 1966, GA Res. 2200 (XXI), UN GAOR, 21st Sess., Supp. No. 16, Articles 11.1, 2, UN Doc. A/6316 (1966), 993 U.N.T.S. 3 (entered into force 3 January 1976); Convention on the Rights of the Child, adopted 20 November 1989, GA Res. 44/25, UN GAOR, 44th Sess., Supp. No. 49, Article 24(2)(c), UN Doc. A/44/49 (1989) (entered into force 2 September 1990), reprinted in 28 I.L.M. (1989) 1448.

[187] 'States Parties to the ICESCR have the obligation to respect, promote and protect and to take appropriate steps to achieve progressively the full realization of the right to adequate food.' FAO, annex I, para. 17 (September 2004), available at: http://.fao.org/docrep/meeting/008/J3345e/j3345e01.htm#a1.

[188] *The Right to Adequate Food*, General Comment No. 12, UN ESCOR, Comm. on Econ., Soc. & Cult. Rts., 20th Sess., para. 6, UN Doc. E/C.12/1999/5 (1999).

[189] Salzman (2006), supra, at 133.

[190] Prof. Salzman gives the very graphic example of the failure of the Biosphere II experiments, ibid., at p. 3.

services are global public goods since they provide non-exclusive benefits of non-rival consumption.[191] Examples of these global public goods ecosystem services are pollination, flood control and climate stability. Natural capital, in general, is unrecognised by most people including those in charge of regulation. While markets can more easily place a price on ecosystem goods, the services upon which they depend for the production of those goods have, in most cases, no market value.[192] The lack of market value with the concomitant lack of a market creates further problems. Markets are important for knowledge investments and technology innovation. Private rights encourage both. Because ecosystem services such as water quality or flood control are not valued, there is no market for them and very little knowledge and understanding about how they work.[193]

As public goods the usual problems of lack of property rights over the resource or the service, uncertainty about who should receive the payments, overuse and free riders arise frequently.[194] While it is easy to find markets for ecosystem goods such as food, water or timber, as it is clear who own the goods and therefore who can sell them and at what price, the same cannot be said of ecosystem services. Think of water purification with no price mechanism which can easily be attached to it due to the complex ecological processes it involves. It cannot send a signal of its scarcity or degradation.

Markets, besides, need buyers and sellers. Buyers as the service beneficiaries need to be a discrete class, and that is not easy for all ecosystem services. Private rights were created for the water purification (an ecosystems service) provided by the Catskill mountain ecosystem. Since the 1990s, the Catskill Mountains which provide 90 per cent of the water to New York City, have been under a 'payments for ecosystems (PES) scheme to preserve drinking water quality. When it began, instead of investing US$6–8 billion in a water filtration plant, the city's authorities considered that investing in improving land use in the watershed was more cost-effective, requiring an investment of US$1.5 billion instead. Farms which opt to participate in the Watershed Agricultural Program receive technical assistance in designing a strategy for controlling potential sources of pollution on the farm, with New York City covering all costs associated with the implementation, and become eligible for other elements of the

---

[191]   Not all. See the classification above.
[192]   See Heal et al. (2002) supra, p. 340.
[193]   Salzman, J. (2005), 'A Field of Green? The Past and Present of Ecosystem Services', Journal of Land Use and Environmental Law, 21, 133, at 136.
[194]   See chapter 1, pp. 67–68.

compensation package for specific environmental services. In this case the state negotiated a settlement whereby existing private property rights were converted into a communal or collective right which was in turn bought by those individuals who valued the service.[195]

PES can have an infinite variety of forms. In public schemes (e.g. in Costa Rica, Mexico, China), the state acts on behalf of buyers by collecting taxes and grants and paying ecosystem service providers. Private schemes on the other hand tend to be more local and buyers pay directly to the service providers or a representative of them.[196] Public schemes are generally larger in scope and have the state providing legitimacy, which many private schemes struggle hard for. On the downside, public schemes can become overloaded, with side objectives catering to voters rather than supplying ecological services. They are less flexible vis-à-vis targeting of strategic ES sellers, and they tend to be less efficient in securing additional ES provision.[197] At the global level the Kyoto Protocol's Clean Development Mechanism (CDM), designed to promote sustainable development by creating a global system of payments for ecosystem services (PES) which funnel income to those in the developing world, generating environmental benefits, is a prime example of how PES work.

In the absence of government intervention it is unlikely that if a particular land use creates ecosystem benefits a market will spontaneously arise. Governments can play a crucial role in all robust service markets. In many cases they act as the only buyer in conditions of monopsony. A good example is provided by Costa Rica, the government of which was crucial in the introduction of PES. The scheme allows farmers to enter into binding contracts with the government for the provision of four services: carbon sequestration, water quality, biodiversity and aesthetic beauty and ecotourism.

---

[195] For more information visit the NYC Watershed Council website. See also Appleton, A.F. (2002), 'How New York City Used an Ecosystem Services Strategy Carried out Through an Urban–Rural Partnership to Preserve the Pristine Quality of Its Drinking Water and Save Billions of Dollars', A Paper for Forest Trends – Tokyo, November.

[196] See http://ecosystemmarketplace.org for a list of private projects.

[197] For example, Wunder, S. (2005), 'Payments for Environmental Services: Some Nuts and Bolts', Occasional paper no. 42, Bogor, Indonesia: Center for International Forestry Research (Cifor), available at: www.cifor.cgair.org/publications/pdf_files/OccPapers/OP-42.pdf.

BOX 2.4.   COSTA RICA: 'DEBT-FOR-NATURE' PROGRAMMES AND PES

In the 1980s Costa Rica had a deforestation rate of 71 per cent per year, and was one of the countries where deforestation was most studied. In 1983 Umaña, the first Minister for the Environment in Costa Rica, set to transform Costa Rica's national parks and forests from exploited lands to protected ones. To help fund the process, the ministry turned to a surprising source: Costa Rica's national debt. In a debt-for-nature swap, a creditor country exchanges the money it is owed for the debtor country's investment in conservation.

In Costa Rica, debt-for-nature programmes funnelled $100 million into protecting the country's natural resources – turning forests which would once have been harvested for lumber or removed to create grazing lands into expanded conservation areas. The conservation community, both in Costa Rica and internationally, provided crucial support for these programmes. In 1988, the Netherlands funded a $10 million project to encourage sustainable forestry practices, resulting in the planting of more than 12,000 hectares.

Costa Rica's earliest carbon incentives began nearly three decades ago. In 1979, the country offered tax cuts for people who planted trees. But the tax cut did not do enough to protect forests, as once you had taken the tax cut, you did not care what happened to the trees. In addition, many rural landowners did not pay income taxes, so there was little incentive for them to plant.

The Costa Rican government started to give the tax incentives, instead, in the form of a certificate. Those buying the certificates received bonds which could be traded and used to pay taxes – but the landowner had to plant trees before applying for a certificate. An associated programme helped farmers who could not afford to plant alone to get the tax benefits by linking up with a cooperative.

Now, Costa Rica's PES programme pays those who plant and protect forests for four services: carbon fixation, watershed protection, biodiversity conservation, and scenic beauty. 'Right now, the PES has 7,000 beneficiaries.'

The programme in Costa Rica has changed over time, trying to expand the number of its beneficiaries and continually increasing understanding of the services ecosystems provide. Along with direct payment programmes for ecosystem services, Costa Rica has several ways of creating economic value for its diverse natural resources, including a national 3.5 per cent fuel tax which pays for reforestation. Costa Rica's forests once covered more than 90 per cent of the landscape, but dwindled to less than a quarter of the country by the 1980s. Now, things are looking up. About 45 per cent of Costa Rica's mountains and valleys are now swathed in green.[1]

Note:
1. From Rodríguez, J. (ed.) (2005), 'The Environmental Services Program: A Success Story of Sustainable Development Implementation in Costa Rica. FONAFIFO, over a Decade of Action', San José: Rica National Forestry Fund (FONAFIFO), available at: http://ecosystemmarketplace.com.

FOR DISCUSSION

- What lessons can be learned from the Costa Rican experience with PES and complementary methods of ecosystem conservation?
  Payments for ecosystem services have been successfully implemented in Latin America and Asia but have failed to provide significant resources in Sub-Saharan Africa.
  - What are the problems that PES have encountered in Africa?
  - How can these be overcome?
- PES provide an invaluable opportunity to achieve sustainable development.
  - Should environmental concerns and priorities drive PES programmes or should PES be driven by poverty reduction and social gains strategies?

6. NATURAL RESOURCES, DEVELOPMENT AND CONFLICT

Given the importance of natural resources for the satisfaction of basic human needs and the creation of economic wealth it would appear that the more natural resources a country had within its territory, the richer that country would be and the higher the development and well-being of its population. A closer look at the distribution of natural resources in the world, however, reveals a very different picture.[198] Natural resources rich countries are in many cases either dominated by corrupt or self-satisfying elites and undemocratic governments which do not invest the revenue from that wealth for the well-being of their citizens or they remain subject to constant conflict and bloodshed with most of the population living well below the poverty line. Angola, Congo, Nigeria, Sierra Leone, and the dictatorships of the Gulf countries seem to point out that having a wealth of natural resources does not amount to an increase in the level of human well-being or development; rather the opposite.[199]

Even in the absence of undemocratic governments natural resources may not contribute positively to a country's wealth in the long run. This phenomenon is known as 'the Dutch disease' or the 'resource curse'[200] and, although not unavoidable, it requires to be addressed by concerted efforts from governments, business and international institutions.[201] The resource curse is a complex phenomenon with three inter-related processes. First, and due to resource revenues, there is a currency appreciation in the country which causes a negative effect on the competitive position of other industries – this is called the 'Dutch disease'. Secondly, a fluctuation in commodity prices worldwide can cause an enormously disruptive effect on the national economy if this is heavily or almost exclusively reliant on a particular commodity. Lastly, riches seem to have an adverse effect on political conditions. The first two are purely economic processes and have been studied extensively, but the third factor needs to be better understood, especially as its impact is far greater than that of the other two.[202] The terminology 'conflict resources' is used in respect of those

---

[198]   Ross, M. (2004), 'The Natural Resource Curse: How Wealth Can Make You Poor', in I. Bannon and P. Collier (eds), *Natural Resources and Violent Conflict*, Washington, DC: World Bank.

[199]   UNEP (2009), 'From Conflict to Peacebuilding: The Role of Natural Resources and the Environment' shows that since 1990 at least 18 violent conflicts, including in Sudan, Congo and Angola, have been fuelled by the exploitation of natural resources.

[200]   Humphreys, M., J.D. Sachs and J. Stiglitz (2007), 'What Is the Problem with Natural Resource Wealth?', in M. Humphreys, J.D. Sachs and J. Stiglitz (eds), *Escaping the Resource Curse*, New York: Columbia University Press, pp. 1–20.

[201]   Humphreys, M., J.D. Sachs and J. Stiglitz (2007), 'Future Directions for the Management of Natural Resources' in ibid. at 322.

[202]   G. Soros in Humphreys et al. (2007), supra, at foreword.

natural resources the control, exploitation, trade, taxation or protection of which contribute to or benefit from the context of armed conflict.[203] The goods themselves are not necessarily illegal; only the use that is made of them. For example in the case of timber, 'conflict timber is timber that has been traded at some point in the chain by armed groups or by a civilian administration involved in conflict or its representatives, either to perpetuate conflict or to take advantage of conflict situations for personal gain'.[204]

Violent secessionist movements are statistically much more likely to occur if the country has valuable natural resources, especially oil.[205] If a particular ethnic group is 'sitting' over a resource it is likely that it will seek to secede and break away from the other ethnic groups, especially if the latter are the dominant group and foster a corrupt government.[206] Minerals, oil, diamonds and timber provide the source of financing which warlords exploit into perpetuating violence.[207] On the other hand the absence of access to natural resources is itself a driver of violence.[208]

But the relationship between violence and access to resources is extraordinarily complex and solutions are not easy or unitary. For example it does not follow that simply curtailing access to resources by belligerent groups will stop armed conflict. In many cases, it has been pointed out that they may intensify attacks on the population and predation of civilians.[209] Unfortunately the opposite is not true, and having plentiful access to resources does not ensure that belligerents engage in a more 'conventional' type of warfare and reject attacks on civilian populations. A tragic example was provided by Sierra Leone where the wealthy revolutionary groups, the Revolutionary United Front (RUF),

---

[203]   Le Billon, P. (2003), 'Getting it Done: Instruments of Enforcement', in I. Bannon and P. Collier (2003), *Natural Resources and Violent Conflict*, Washington, DC: World Bank Publications, World Bank, p. 215.

[204]   Global Witness briefing paper 1 March 2002, 'The Logs of War: The Timber Trade and Armed Conflict', available at: www.globalwitness.org/media_library_datadatabase.php/89/en/the_logs_of_war.

[205]   Biafra in Nigeria, Cabinda in Angola, Katenga in the ex-Congo and Aceh and West Papua in Indonesia are recent examples of violence in oil rich areas.

[206]   This was the case in Nigeria when Biafra tried to declare its independence. Bannon and Collier (2003), supra, at 6.

[207]   Ibid., at 7.

[208]   As can be seen in Darfur where drought and shortages of land are creating an ongoing conflict with millions of people displaced.

[209]   Humphreys, Sachs and Stiglitz (2007), supra, at 322; also Le Billon (2003), supra, at 219–223.

BOX 2.5.   CONFLICT DIAMONDS IN LIBERIA AND SIERRA LEONE

In 1991, Liberian warlord Charles Taylor sponsored the invasion of Sierra Leone by the Revolutionary United Front (RUF), a rebel group whose brutal military campaign was characterized by mass amputations and systematic rape. Taylor not only provided material support to the RUF, but also sent his own troops to fight alongside them, both before and after he assumed the Liberian presidency in 1997. Taylor's support of the RUF was motivated at least in part by his desire to gain control of lucrative Sierra Leonean diamond fields less than 100 miles from the Liberian border. This interest undermined peace in Sierra Leone until 2001, and the Special Court for Sierra Leone later indicted Taylor for participating in a joint criminal enterprise 'to take any actions necessary to gain and exercise political power and control over the territory of Sierra Leone, in particular the diamond mining areas'.

In response to the role of the diamond trade in financing Charles Taylor and the RUF, the UN Security Council imposed sanctions on diamond exports from Liberia in March 2001. This increased pressure on the RUF, which laid down its arms the following year, leaving over 200,000 people dead, more than two million displaced, and thousands maimed. As an unintended side effect of the sanctions, however, Charles Taylor switched to another natural resource – Liberian timber – as his main source of revenue. Reflecting the lack of coherence in the UN's approach to natural resource-fuelled conflicts, it was another two years before sanctions were imposed on Liberian timber exports in July 2003. The following month, with his key funding source cut and rebel groups advancing on Monrovia, Charles Taylor went into exile in Nigeria.

Full appreciation of the role of natural resources in the conflict in Sierra Leone requires scrutiny of the Sierra Leonean government's own track record. In the years preceding the RUF insurgency, massive corruption in Sierra Leone's diamond sector played a more subtle but significant role in setting the stage for complete political collapse. Autocratic ruler Siaka Stevens, who was in power from 1968 to 1985, brought Sierra Leone's lucrative diamond sector under his personal control, overseeing the wholesale diversion of revenues from the state into the pockets of a few individuals. As diamond-smuggling operations overseen by Stevens' cronies skyrocketed, official exports dropped from more than two million carats in 1970 to 48,000 carats in 1988. By the end of Stevens' rule, the Sierra Leonean economy was to all intents and purposes criminalised or destroyed. The situation improved little under the rule of his successor, Joseph Momoh. This looting of the state marginalised large sections of the population, undermined the government's legitimacy and weakened its capacity to maintain peace and stability.

FOR DISCUSSION

- What are the available strategies when dealing with the relationship between natural resources and conflict?
- What is the role of the international community in implementing those initiatives?
- The private sector is said to have an important role in reducing the incidence of conflict in natural resource rich areas. Discuss how this role can be articulated and whether it should be accompanied by mandatory provisions.
- Are voluntary certification schemes effective?

---

used widespread force despite their plentiful sources of finance for the conflict.[210] Sometimes having access to resources may mean that the conflict can come to an end, as happened in Angola when the oil revenues allowed the government to defeat UNITA which could no longer exchange its diamonds.[211]

The problems identified with trying to regulate conflict resources range from the difficulties of curbing financial access for belligerents without impairing social and economic growth for the rest of the population and

---

[210] For a good discussion on natural resources and conflict in Sierra Leone see Schwartz, P. (2009), 'Corporate Activities and Environmental Justice: Perspectives on Sierra Leone's Mining', in J. Ebbesson and P. Okowa (eds), *Environmental Law and Justice in Context*, New York: Cambridge Univesity Press, pp. 429–447.

[211] Le Billon, P. (2001), 'Angola's Political Economy of War', African Affairs, No. 100, pp. 55–80.

defining legality, responsibility and complicity through supply chains and their connections to financial, transport and insurance services.[212] Globalisation allows the sale of resources in the open economy and can, in this respect, fuel wars but it can also provide the necessary tools for controlling it by international pressure and the creation of initiatives which deprive rebels and belligerent groups of finance and markets. In the context of 'conflict resources' command and control or mandatory regulations are particularly effective as they operate in the absence of a level playing field, often with unscrupulous parties. Combining mandatory compliance with voluntary schemes offering strong incentives has also been successful. An example of this is the Financial Action Task Force on Money Laundering, an inter-governmental body which has developed policies to combat money laundering and terrorist financing.[213] But above all actions from local governments which increase governance, poverty reduction, tackling internal corruption and education programmes can do much to reduce conflict. Development and economic well-being are the best insurance against civil or natural resource-spurred war.[214]

The private sector also has a crucial role to play. Multinationals and investors are key players in any conflict resources governance model since they are the crucial elements to the trade in natural resources.[215] Schemes like the Kimberley Certification Process Scheme[216] should make it increasingly difficult for rebel groups to sell diamonds in global markets, and despite its shortcomings it can provide a voluntary and successful model which can be applied to other commodities.[217] International institutions such as the International Finance Corporation (IFC)[218] have a role to play in reassuring reputable companies about the investment security of areas previously involved in armed conflict or with governments with reputations of corruption.[219]

---

[212]   Le Billon (2003), supra, at 220.
[213]   See www.fatf-gafi.org/. The FATF is discussed in more detail in chapter 6.
[214]   Bannon and Collier (2003), supra, at 8.
[215]   Discussed further in chapter 5.
[216]   Discussed above in this chapter.
[217]   Other efforts have been made with certification in timber exports: see www.bureauveritas.com.
[218]   Explained in chapter 4, p. 185.
[219]   See chapter 4, the Chad-Cameron Pipeline project case study, p. 189.

7. CONCLUSION

While progress towards sustainable development has been made through meetings, agreements and changes in environmental governance, real change has been slow. Since 1987 population growth, growing consumption and energy use, from both developed and developing countries, have placed increasing pressure on the environment and natural resource use. We have discussed how a change from resource sovereignty towards resource efficiency is necessary to confront successfully today's natural resources needs.[220]

Sustainable development rests upon the accommodation of economic growth, environmental concerns and the wider social effects of economic activity. It is also useful in including equity considerations (intra- and inter-generational equity) into the process of globalisation. The accommodation of economic and environmental consideration with social needs requires a recognition that unregulated industrialisation and growth created undesirable environmental consequences, especially, perhaps, in developing countries. While those opposing globalisation argue that sustainable development is not possible while the current economic system is in place,[221] it is possible to find that market-based instruments and techniques may enable environmentally sensitive business practices and contribute toward sustainable development.[222]

In order to address environmental problems and resource degradation effectively policy-makers should design policies which tackle *both* pressures to the environment and the drivers behind them. A combination of both economic and non-economic instruments should be used to address human behaviour. While economic instruments such as market creation and charge systems may be used to help spur environmentally sustainable behaviour, valuation of environmental goods and services can help policy-makers make informed decisions about the value of changes to ecosystem services. Non-economic instruments should be used to address issues of equity and access for the poorest segments of the population.

> Developing countries are providing enormous services to the world for which they are not compensated, such as environmental services and preservation of biodiversity. One of these services is in the area of greenhouse gases. Measured

---

[220] See 'Introduction' in this book, p. 7.
[221] See chapter 1.
[222] Esty, D. (1994), *Greening the GATT*, Washington, DC: Institute for International Economics, at 54. Also Carley, M. and I. Christie (2000), *Managing Sustainable Development*, 2nd edn, London: Earthscan, pp. 263–266.

by mechanisms included in the Kyoto Protocol, the value of the carbon services provided by the tropical countries exceeds $30 billion a year. Developing countries now propose that they would submit themselves voluntarily to the provisions of the Kyoto Protocol if they received compensation for environmental services. This needs innovative financing to make it work.[223]

In the next chapter we argue the need for a 'right to natural resources' at the substantive level, coupled with strong participatory and procedural rights linked to generally recognised human rights.

FURTHER READING

Birnie, P., A. Boyle and C. Redgwell (2009), *International Law and the Environment*, Oxford: Oxford University Press.

Blanco, E. and J. Razzaque (2009), 'Ecosystem Services and Human Well-Being in a Globalized World: Assessing the Role of Law', Human Rights Quarterly, 31, 692–720.

Cordonnier-Segger, M.C. and A. Khalfan (2004), *Sustainable Development Law: Principles, Practice and Prospects*, Oxford: Oxford University Press.

Crawford, J. (1988), 'Rights of Peoples: "Peoples" or "Governments"?', in J. Crawford (ed.), *The Rights of Peoples*, Oxford: Clarendon Press.

Sands, P. (2003), *Principles of International Environmental Law*, 2nd edn Cambridge: Cambridge University Press.

Schrijver, N. (1997), *Sovereignty over Natural Resources*, Cambridge: Cambridge University Press.

Stewart, R. (2007), 'Instrument Choice', in D. Bodansky et al. (eds), *Oxford Handbook of International Environmental Law*, Oxford: Oxford University Press.

---

[223]   Stiglitz, J., 'Cleaning up economic growth', The Economic Times, Friday 10 June 2005.

3. Legal framework guiding natural resource management

1. INTRODUCTION

In the realm of natural resource management, both substantive and procedural rights play a crucial role. Sustainable natural resource management requires strong substantive rights supported by inclusive participatory rights. The issue is not only about having a liberal judiciary, strong environmental legislation and explicit constitutional provisions; there should also be public access to decision-making and to information. Over the last few years, a number of legal instruments have influenced the development of procedural rights. Along with Principle 10 of the Rio Declaration,[1] several international and regional treaties include references to public participation in the decision-making process.[2] Although regional in scope, the 1998 Aarhus Convention reflects the increased concern of the international community in the transparency of environmental decision-making and asks the states parties to consult local communities before undertaking development activities.[3]

The move from economic to sustainable globalisation is evident as international actors including the business community acknowledge that a market-based approach alone is not adequate to meet social obligations. Sustainable globalisation emphasises the importance of collaboration among state and non-state actors for the equitable sharing of natural resources and partnership with local communities which promotes good

---

[1] Rio Declaration on Environment and Development (1992), adopted by the UN Conference on Environment and Development (UNCED), UN Doc. A/CONF.151/26 (Vol. I) (1992).

[2] Pring, G. and S.Y. Noe (2002), 'The Emerging International Law of Public Participation Affecting Global Mining, Energy and Resource Development', in D. Zillman, A. Lucas and G. Pring (eds), *Human Rights in Natural Resource Development: Public participation in the sustainable development of mining and energy resource*, Oxford: Oxford University Press, pp. 11–76.

[3] UN/ECE Convention on Access to Information, Public Participation in Decision-Making and Access to Justice in Environmental Matters (1998). This Convention elaborates Principle 10 of the 1992 Rio Declaration.

resource governance. Various international and regional instruments promote mechanisms to involve people, e.g. to challenge corporate privatisation efforts, jointly to manage natural resources, and to protect traditional knowledge and biological resources. A right-based approach to natural resources which includes the right to access, use, explore, exploit and conserve natural resources can empower people to assert their shared sovereign rights over natural resources. However, the substantive resource rights have to be complemented by the procedural right to information, participation and justice.

This chapter explores both the substantive and procedural aspects of decision-making in natural resource management. After a brief discussion in section 2 of the substantive rights that protect natural resources, section 3 examines access to decision-making related to natural resources at the international, regional and national level. This chapter examines international and regional experiences that promote public involvement in decisions on natural resources. By examining these legal instruments, it is clear that there are international and regional mechanisms to ensure people's involvement in decision-making, and various aspects of public participation (e.g. consultation, information, access to court) are linked. Some international institutions, however, provide inadequate mechanisms to allow people to be involved in the decision-making processes. The chapter highlights that regional instruments such as the Aarhus Convention are playing a crucial role in developing effective mechanisms to involve people in the decision-making process.

2.   SUBSTANTIVE RIGHTS AND NATURAL RESOURCE MANAGEMENT

2.1.   Rights-based Approach

Human beings are an inseparable part of the environment. The issue is whether there is a need to have a right-based approach to protect natural resources. A right-based approach provides a better compliance, monitoring and dispute settlement mechanism and creates priority over non-right-based objectives.[4] Rights holders such as individuals or communities, through their actions and legal claims, can invoke their rights individually or collectively. However, a right to natural resources may not be acceptable

---

[4]   Shelton, D. (2008), 'Human Rights and the Environment: Problems and Possibilities', Environmental Policy and Law, 38, 41.

globally as it creates a corresponding duty for governments, private sector and individuals.[5] As a principal duty bearer, states are obliged to respect, protect and fulfil all human rights. There are certain challenges linked to this right-based approach: many states have not incorporated the treaty-based rights in the domestic legal framework; policies and practices at the domestic level may vary and developing countries may not have efficient and cost-effective judicial systems.[6]

A right-based approach to natural resources is a precondition to the enjoyment of a number of human rights: the right to life, right to a healthy environment and right to development. In addition, the human rights courts at the regional level provide some remedies when there is no local remedy or weak international compliance mechanisms to protect natural resources.[7] If the right to natural resources is considered part of the human rights framework, the right-based approach is only ideal if it protects the intrinsic value of the ecosystems and non-human values are integrated into the interpretation of the rights.[8] The right to natural resources should be able to deal with the issues of biological diversity and the protection of non-human species, harm caused to future generations by environmental degradation and the transboundary impact of resource degradation such as climate change, deforestation and transboundary watercourses pollution.

The realisation of certain civil and political rights, e.g. the rights to life, association, expression, property, political participation, personal liberty, equality and legal redress, can make an important contribution to protecting the natural resources. Certain economic, social and cultural rights, e.g. the right to health, can be linked to decent living or working conditions and may also include the protection of ecosystems.[9] Moreover, the right to self-determination can protect natural resources in two ways: providing permanent sovereignty over natural resources and the right of the indigenous community over the natural resources.[10] The people have the right

---

[5]   For example, the 1998 Aarhus Convention (discussed in section 3) applies a right/duty-based approach.

[6]   Shelton (2008), supra, 42.

[7]   Osofsky, H.M. (2005), 'Learning from Environmental Justice: A New Model for International Environmental Rights', Stanford Environmental Law Journal, 24, 107–118.

[8]   Redgwell, C. (1996), 'Life, Universe and Everything: A Critique of Anthropocentric Rights', in M. Anderson and A. Boyle (eds), *Human Rights Approaches to Environmental Protection*, Oxford: Oxford University Press, pp. 71–88.

[9]   Churchill, R. (1996), 'Environmental Rights in Existing Human Rights Treaties', in Anderson and Boyle (eds), supra, pp. 89–108.

[10]   Anderson, M. (1996), 'Human Rights Approaches to Environmental Protection: An Overview' in ibid., 6.

to manage, govern and regulate the use of natural resources.[11] In addition, there is recognition of indigenous peoples' right to give prior and informed consent to activities which may affect their land and natural resources.[12] A state's sovereign rights over its resources must respect these human rights of the people.

The 1966 International Covenant on Economic, Social and Cultural Rights (ICESCR) states that each party has the obligation 'to take steps . . . to the maximum of its available resources with a view to achieving progressively the full realisation of the rights recognised in the present Covenant'.[13] The ICESCR, however, uses qualified language allowing the states to impose restrictions on these rights.[14] Application of this approach means that the right to natural resources could be weighed against other social or cultural rights including the right to development.[15]

The right to natural resources can be an individual (right to property, right to participation) as well as a collective right (right to self determination). The collective nature of the right gives communities or peoples a right to determine how their natural resources should be protected, managed and explored. A collective right means that the beneficiary of the right is a group rather than its individual members.[16] One criticism of the collective right approach is that collective rights 'are so vast that they encompass anything and anybody'.[17] Alan Boyle adds that the collective right approach may devalue 'the concept of human rights' and divert 'attention from the need to implement the civil, political, economic and social rights fully'.[18] However, this collective right to resources is recognised in several treaties: for example, the International Covenant on Civil and Political Rights (Article 47), the UN Covenant on Economic, Social and Cultural Rights (Article 25), ILO Convention 169 concerning

---

[11]   Discussed in the Introduction to this book.

[12]   Articles 28, 29 and 32, Declaration on the Rights of Indigenous Peoples (2007) UN GA Res. 61/295, 2 October 2007. See chapter 9 (Globalisation and biological resources) of this book.

[13]   Article 2 of the ICESCR, adopted 16 December 1966, 993 U.N.T.S. 3, 6 I.L.M. (1967) 360 (entered into force 3 January 1976).

[14]   For example, Articles 2(3) and 4 of the ICESCR.

[15]   Boyle, A. (2007), 'Human Rights or Environmental Rights – A Reassessment', Fordham Environmental Law Review, 18, 471. He also notes the relatively weak supervisory mechanisms of the ICESCR.

[16]   Crawford, J. (1988), 'Rights of Peoples: "Peoples" or "Governments"?', in J. Crawford (ed.), *The Rights of Peoples*, Oxford: Clarendon Press, 64.

[17]   Fitzmaurice, M. (2001), 'International Protection of the Environment', *Recueil des Cours*, Dordrecht: Martinus Nijhoff, 293, 170.

[18]   Boyle (2007), supra, 472.

Indigenous and Tribal Peoples in Independent Countries (Article 15) and the 1981 African Charter on Human and Peoples' Rights (Article 21).

2.2. Substantive Discussion at the International Level

There are three levels of discussion at the international level: general protection of natural resources, specific resource protection under human rights and environmental law, and the protection of transboundary natural resources. The collective nature of the right remains broad as it includes rights to develop, exploit, access, protect and conserve natural resources.

2.2.1. General protection of natural resources

Permanent sovereignty over natural resources sets the tone of a right-based approach to protecting natural resources. The *right to dispose freely of natural resources* is explicitly recognised in the Human Rights Covenants: '[a]ll Peoples may, for their own ends, freely dispose of their natural wealth and resources'.[19] The *right to explore and exploit natural resources* is a corollary to the right to dispose freely of natural resources. As Nico Schrijver adds:[20]

> . . . the right of free disposal of natural resources and wealth is the seminal source of a series of corollary rights of the state, including the right freely to determine and control the prospecting, exploration, development, exploitation, use and marketing of natural resources and to subject such activities to national laws and regulations within the limits of its exclusive economic jurisdiction under prevailing international law.

The International Covenant on Civil and Political Rights (ICCPR)[21] and ICESCR[22] affirm the 'inherent right of peoples to enjoy and utilize fully and freely their natural wealth and resources'. A number of non-binding and binding instruments deal with the right of the state *and* people freely to use and exploit their natural resources.[23] General Assembly

---

[19]   Article 1 of the ICCPR and Article 1 of the ICESCR. ICCPR, adopted on 16 December 1966, 999 U.N.T.S. 171, 6 I.L.M. (1967) 368 (entered into force 23 March 1976). ICESCR, adopted 16 December 1966, 993 U.N.T.S. 3, 6 I.L.M. (1967) 360 (entered into force 3 January 1976).
[20]   Schrijver, N. (1997), *Sovereignty over Natural Resources: Balancing Rights and Duties*, Cambridge: Cambridge University Press, 264.
[21]   Article 47 of the ICCPR.
[22]   Article 25 of the ICESCR.
[23]   GA Res. 626 (VII), Preamble, para. 3, 21 December 1952. GA Res. 1803 (XVII).

Resolution 2158 (XXI) includes the right of developing countries 'effectively [to] exercise their choice in deciding the manner in which the exploitation of their natural resources should be carried out'.[24] The bottom line being that the state, while alienating its sovereignty over natural resources to explore and exploit natural resources, should not affect the interests of the people.[25] If it is the 'people' who possess part of the sovereign right to natural resources, that limits the right of the state to dispose freely of the natural resources without the free prior consent of the people.[26]

Along with these UN resolutions, the 1972 Stockholm Declaration adds:

> States have, in accordance with the Charter of the United Nations and the principles of international law, the *sovereign right to exploit their own resources pursuant to their own environmental policies*, and the responsibility to ensure that activities within their jurisdiction or control do not cause damage to the environment of other states or of areas beyond the limits of national jurisdiction.[27]

Similarly, according to Principle 2 of the 1992 Rio Declaration, states while exploiting their natural resources would have to take into account their environmental and developmental policies.[28] Several UN resolutions also acknowledge the *right to use natural resources for development plans*.[29] UN Resolution 1803 (XVII) states:

> [t]he right of peoples and nations to permanent sovereignty over their natural wealth and resources must be exercised in the interest of their national development and of the well-being of the people of the State concerned.[30]

National development priorities of a country may clash with the well-being of the people. Therefore, it is crucial that people have a *right to conserve natural resources*. Principle 22 of the Rio Declaration notes that

---

[24] Para. 3, GA Res. 2158 (XXI) adopted by the GA on 28 November 1966, available at www.un.org/en/documents/index.shtml (accessed 15 January 2010).

[25] Schrijver (1997), supra, 264.

[26] Crawford (1988), supra, 64.

[27] Principle 21, emphasis added. 1972 Declaration of the United Nations Conference on Human Environment.

[28] 1992 Rio Declaration on Environment and Development, supra.

[29] Preamble, Res. 523 (VI), Integrated economic development and commercial agreements (12 January 1952). Para. 1, GA Res. 626 (VII) on the right to exploit freely natural wealth and resources, 21 December 1952.

[30] Para. 1 of Res. 1803 (XVII). GA Res. 1803 (XVII) of 14 December 1962, Permanent sovereignty over natural resources, available at: www2.ohchr.org/English/law/resources.htm (accessed 15 January 2010).

indigenous people and other communities play a 'vital role in environmental management and development because of their knowledge and traditional practices' and emphasises that states need to recognise and support their identity, culture and interests.[31] The ILO Indigenous and Tribal Peoples Convention No. 169 (1989) states that the rights of the indigenous people to natural resources 'include the right of these peoples to participate in the use, management and conservation of these resources'.[32] According to the UN Declaration on the Rights of Indigenous Peoples (2007), indigenous peoples have the right to natural resources which they have traditionally owned and they have the 'right to own, use, develop and control' resources which they possess.[33] Moreover, the 1992 Biodiversity Convention[34] and the 1994 Desertification Convention[35] refer to roles the indigenous people can play in conserving natural resources.

2.2.2. Specific resource protection

Natural resources such as wetlands or biodiversity are an integral part of the ecosystem. Several multilateral environmental agreements deal with the protection of natural resources such as the wetlands,[36] cultural and natural heritage,[37] endangered species of wild flora and fauna,[38] migratory species of wild animals,[39] genetic resources,[40] climate change[41] and the protection of fragile drylands.[42]

---

[31] 1992 Rio Declaration on Environment and Development. Principles 3 and 4 balance the development and environmental priorities.

[32] Article 15 of ILO Convention (No. 169) concerning Indigenous and Tribal Peoples in Independent Countries, adopted 27 June 1989, 328 U.N.T.S. 247 (entered into force 5 September 1991).

[33] Article 26. UN Doc. A/61/L.67, 7 September 2007.

[34] Preamble, Article 8(j), Convention on Biological Diversity, 31 I.L.M. (1992) 822 (entered into force 29 December 1993).

[35] Preamble, Article 3(a), Article 5(d) and Article 19.1(a), Convention to Combat Desertification in those countries experiencing serious droughts and/or desertification, particularly in Africa, 33 I.L.M. (1994) 1328 (entered into force 26 December 1996).

[36] 1971 Ramsar Convention on Wetlands of International Importance, 996 U.N.T.S. 245; 11 I.L.M. (1972) 963.

[37] 1972 UNESCO Convention Concerning the Protection of the World Cultural and Natural Heritage, 11 I.L.M. (1972) 1358.

[38] 1973 Convention on International Trade in Endangered Species of Wild Fauna and Flora, 993 U.N.T.S. 243; 12 I.L.M. (1973) 1085.

[39] 1979 Convention on the Conservation of Migratory Species of Wild Animals (Bonn) 19 I.L.M. (1980) 15.

[40] 1992 Convention on Biological Diversity, 31 I.L.M. (1992) 818.

[41] 1992 UN Framework Convention on Climate Change, 31 I.L.M. (1992) 851.

[42] 1994 UN Convention to Combat Desertification, 33 I.L.M. (1994) 1016.

Apart from these binding legal instruments, non-binding international guidelines provide protection to specific resources and confirm the links between human rights, environmental degradation and resource depletion.[43] For example, General Comment 15[44] on the right to water notes that water is a limited natural resource and 'should be treated a social and cultural good, and not primarily as an economic good'.[45] Enjoyment of the right to safe drinking water is dependent upon the realisation of other human rights, particularly the rights to housing, health, food, as well as freedom of expression, freedom of association, and participation in public decision-making.[46] In 2005, the draft guidelines for the realisation of the right to drinking water supply and sanitation considered water as a common heritage which had to be used in an equitable manner.[47] These guidelines refer to a right to water for everyone which is of acceptable quality, affordable and physically accessible.[48] While these documents are non-binding, they do create a moral obligation, reaffirm commitments of the international community to use, exploit, develop and access natural resources, and establish a standard of behaviour and obligations.

2.2.3. Transboundary resource protection

The need for a common approach and shared responsibility to manage transboundary natural resources is not new in international law.[49]

---

[43]   See, for example, United Nations, Non-legally binding authoritative statement of principles for a global consensus on the management, conservation and sustainable development of all types of forests. Report of the UN Conference on Environment and Development (1992), A/CONF.151/26 (Vol. III).

[44]   CESCR (Committee on Economic, Social and Cultural Rights), Substantive Issues Arising in the implementation of the international covenant on economic, social and cultural rights, The Right to Water, Articles 11 and 12, E/C.12/2002/11 (20 January 2003). See the further discussion in chapter 7 on water resources.

[45]   Ibid., para. 11.

[46]   See General Comment 4, The right to adequate housing (Article 11(1) of the Covenant), CESCR, UN Doc. HRI\GEN\1\Rev.1 (1994) 53 (para. 12). General Comment 12, The right to adequate food (Article 11) E/C.12/1999/5, 12 May 1999. General Comment 14, The right to the highest attainable standard of health E/C.12/2000/4, 11 August 2000.

[47]   Preamble. Commission on Human Rights, Realization of the right to drinking water and sanitation. Report of the Special Rapporteur, El Hadji Guissé, E/CN.4/Sub.2/2005/25, 11 July 2005.

[48]   Ibid., Guideline 1.

[49]   Sands, P. (2003), *Principles of International Environmental Law*, Cambridge: Cambridge University Press, chapter 6. Birnie, P., A. Boyle and C. Redgwell (2009), *International Law and the Environment*, Oxford: Oxford University Press, pp. 190–205.

Emphasising the need for a 'community of interest' while managing trans-boundary rivers, the Permanent Court of International Justice[50] held that:

> [t]his community of interest in a navigable river becomes the basis of a common legal right, the essential features of which are the perfect equality of all riparian states in the use of the whole course of the river and the exclusion of any preferential privilege of any riparian State in relation to others.

Reference to a right to an equitable share in benefits of transboundary natural resources is found in both binding[51] and non-binding[52] documents. The 1974 Charter of Economic Rights and Duties of States affirms that, while exploiting shared natural resources, each state must exchange information and consult to achieve 'optimum use of such resources'.[53] The UNEP draft principles on shared natural resources state that:

> [i]t is necessary for states to co-operate in the field of the environment concerning the conservation and harmonious utilization of natural resources shared by two or more states. Accordingly, it is necessary that consistent with the concept of *equitable utilization of shared natural resources*, states co-operate with a view to controlling, preventing, reducing or eliminating adverse environmental effects which may result from the utilization of such resources. Such co-operation is to take place on an equal footing and taking into account the sovereignty, rights and interests of the states concerned.[54]

Principle 3 adds that:

> . . . it is necessary for each state to avoid to the maximum extent possible and to reduce to the minimum extent possible the adverse environmental effects beyond its jurisdiction of the utilization of a shared natural resource so as to protect the environment, in particular when such utilization might

---

[50]   *Case relating to the Territorial Jurisdiction of the International Commission of the River Oder*, Judgment of 10 September 1929, Permanent Court of International Justice, Series A, No. 23, Series C, No. 17 (II), Document instituting proceedings: Special Agreement of 30 October 1928.

[51]   Articles 5 and 6. The Convention on the Law of the Non-Navigational Uses of International Watercourses, UN Doc. A/51/869 of 11 April 1997. The Convention was adopted by UN GA Res. 51/229 of 21 May 1997. Not in force.

[52]   Article 35 (Transboundary Natural Resources) of IUCN's 2004 draft of the International Covenant on Environment and Development, Environmental Law and Policy Paper 31, Rev.2.

[53]   Article 3. UN Res. 3281 (XXIX). A/RES/29/3281 (12 December 1974).

[54]   Principle 1. Emphasis added. 'Draft Principles of Conduct in the Field of the Environment for the Guidance of States in the Conservation and Harmonious Utilization of Natural Resources Shared by Two or More States. UNEP/IG12/2 (1978), 19 May 1978. 17 I.L.M. (1978) 1097.

(a) cause damage to the environment which could have repercussions on the utilization of the resource by another sharing State;
(b) threaten the conservation of a shared renewable resource:
(c) endanger the health of the population of another State.

The 1985 World Commission on Environment and Development (WCED) requests states to 'use transboundary natural resources in a reasonable and equitable manner' and 'cooperate in good faith with other states to achieve optimal use of transboundary natural resources'.[55] Legal instruments on protected areas and international watercourses provide some guidance on how to manage these resources at the transboundary level.

Protected areas can be a nature reserve, national park, natural monument, habitat/species management area, protected landscape and managed resource protected area.[56] A number of non-binding[57] and binding[58] documents provide an ecosystem approach for protected areas. An example of transboundary management of protected areas is the Great Limpopo Transfrontier Park which is jointly managed by Mozambique, South Africa and Zimbabwe[59] and aims to preserve ecosystem services

---

[55] Articles 9 and 14. Report of the World Commission on Environment and Development: Our Common Future, Annex 1: Summary of Proposed Legal Principles for Environmental Protection and Sustainable Development Adopted by the WCED Experts Group on Environmental Law. Transmitted to the General Assembly as an Annex to document A/42/427, 4 August 1987.

[56] A transboundary protected area is defined as 'an area of land and/or sea that straddles one or more boundaries between states, sub-national units such as provinces and regions, autonomous areas and/or areas beyond the limits of national sovereignty or jurisdiction, whose constituent parts are especially dedicated to the protection and maintenance of biological diversity, and of natural and associated cultural resources, and managed co-operatively through legal or other effective means'. Sandwith, T., C. Shine, L. Hamilton and D. Sheppard (2001), *Transboundary Protected Areas for Peace and Cooperation*, Best Practice Protected Area Guidelines Series No. 7, World Commission on Protected Areas, Gland, Switzerland and Cambridge, UK: IUCN, 3.

[57] For example, World Commission on Protected Areas (WCPA), Draft Code for Transboundary Protected Areas in Times of Peace and Armed Conflict (2001).

[58] Article 8 (*in situ* conservation) of the Biodiversity Convention calls on parties to develop protected areas. *Protected area* (Article 2) means a geographically defined area which is designated or regulated and managed to achieve specific conservation objectives.

[59] Treaty on the establishment of the Great Limpopo Transfrontier Park (Xai-Xai, Mozambique, 9 December 2002). The agreement makes specific references to the CBD, CITES, the UNCCD, and the Treaty of the Southern African Development Community.

and natural resources productivity. Another example is the La Amistad International Park in Central America which is managed by Costa Rica and Panama.[60] There are concerns that

> . . . while the number and extent of protected areas has been increasing in the past decades, so that around 11 per cent of the world's land surface is currently in protected status, existing systems of protected areas are neither representative of the world's ecosystems, nor do they adequately address conservation of critical habitat types, biomes and threatened species, and, with marine areas particularly under-represented actions need to be taken to fill these gaps.[61]

With its divergent range of approaches, the international law for protected areas is fragmented and not adequately coordinated.[62]

Rules on international watercourses affirm that states' natural resource related activities within their territories should not have a transboundary effect which violates the right of other states.[63] The 2004 Berlin Rules[64] of the International Law Association affirm that sustainable management of transboundary water resources requires cooperation between basin states. They add that:

> Basin states have the right to participate in the management of waters of an international drainage basin in an equitable, reasonable, and sustainable manner.[65]

> Basin states shall in their respective territories manage the waters of an international drainage basin in an equitable and reasonable manner having due regard for the obligation not to cause significant harm to other basin states.[66]

There are, however, several problems with the way transboundary resources are being managed in international law. First: the threshold of transboundary 'harm' is still uncertain, and that may undermine the transboundary impact.[67] However, a number of international treaties now deal

---

[60]   Sandwith et al. (2001), supra, 10.

[61]   Decision VII/28 (2004) of the Biodiversity Convention on Protected Areas (Articles 8 (A) to (E)).

[62]   Gillespie, A. (2007), *Protected Areas and International Environmental Law*, Leiden: Martinus Nijhoff.

[63]   Handl, G. (2007), 'Transboundary Impacts', in D. Bodansky, J. Brunnee and E. Hey (eds), *The Oxford Handbook of International Environmental Law*, Oxford: Oxford University Press, pp. 532–533.

[64]   ILA, Berlin Rules on Water Resources. Chapter II, Articles 10–16 deal with international shared waters. Adopted in 2004.

[65]   Article 10(1).

[66]   Article 12(1).

[67]   Handl (2007), supra, 535.

with the threshold of harm which may provide some guidance to states.[68] Second, the obligation of states to take adequate measures to prevent transboundary harm can also be questioned.[69] Low-level risk of significant transboundary harm may not raise an obligation of prevention.[70] Thus, deforestation or dam building activity in the state of origin may not give rise to an obligation of prevention. Third, there is no universal compulsory jurisdiction to deal with transboundary disputes.[71] It may be difficult for states to bring actions due to 'the complexity and uncertainty of the law of state responsibility'.[72] According to the ILC Draft Articles, significant transboundary harm gives rise to an obligation to cease the conduct and repair the injury if the impact involves wrongful conduct or a lack of due diligence.[73] However, this is a non-binding document and there is resistance by states to enter into a binding document which would set out a liability or responsibility regime.[74]

2.3. Right to Natural Resources at the Regional Level

2.3.1. Regional agreements

Several binding agreements deal with the right to explore, exploit and use natural resources.[75] These regional agreements ask states to cooperate with each other in order sustainably to manage the transboundary natural resources. In order to implement these agreements at the domestic level, parties require adequate support from national policies and law.

The ASEAN Agreement on the Conservation of Nature and Natural Resources recognises the 'interdependence of living resources, between them and with other natural resources, within ecosystems of which they are part'.[76] It asks the parties to take actions to 'preserve genetic

---

[68] Ibid., 535–538.

[69] International Law Commission, Draft Article on the Prevention of Transboundary Harm from Hazardous Activities, ILC Report 2001, GAOR A/56/10.

[70] Handl (2007), supra, 540.

[71] Birnie et al. (2009), supra, 303.

[72] In these circumstances, there may be a possibility for non-state actors to bring an action. See section 3 (procedural rights) of this chapter.

[73] ILC Draft Articles on Responsibility of States for Internationally Wrongful Acts, GA Res. 56/83 of 12 December 2001, and corrected by document A/56/49(Vol. I)/Corr.4. Handl (2007), supra, 544.

[74] Birnie et al. (2009), supra, pp. 316–326.

[75] These arrangements are guided by several international conventions, for example, CITES (Article 5), CBD (Articles 3, 5, 14, 19).

[76] Preamble. Association of South East Asian Nations (ASEAN) Agreement

diversity, and to ensure the sustainable utilization of harvested natural resources'.[77]

The North American Agreement on Environmental Cooperation affirms:

> . . . the sovereign right of States to exploit their own resources pursuant to their own environmental and development policies and their responsibility to ensure that activities within their jurisdiction or control do not cause damage to the environment of other States or of areas beyond the limits of national jurisdiction.[78]

The Transboundary Air Pollution Convention states:[79]

> The Contracting Parties, taking due account of the facts and problems involved, are determined to protect man and his environment against air pollution and shall endeavour to limit and, as far as possible, gradually reduce and prevent air pollution including long-range transboundary air pollution.

The Environmental Impact Assessment Convention states:[80]

> The parties shall, either individually or jointly, take all appropriate and effective measures to prevent, reduce and control significant adverse transboundary environmental impact from proposed activities.[81]

The list of activities includes establishment of a thermal power station, a crude oil refinery, chemical installations, wind farms, large dams, reservoirs; deforestation of large areas; and groundwater abstraction.[82]

The Water Convention[83] states that the member states will take 'appropriate measures to prevent, control and reduce any transboundary impact'

---

on the Conservation of Nature and Natural Resources, 9 July 1985, reprinted in 15 Environmental Policy and Law 64 (1985).

[77]   Article 1.

[78]   North American Agreement on Environmental Cooperation (NAAEC), 14 September 1993, Canada–Mexico–USA, 32 I.L.M. (1993) 1480.

[79]   Article 2. UNECE Convention on Long-Range Transboundary Air Pollution, Geneva, 13 November 1979. Entered into force in 1983. Available at: www.unece.org/env/lrtap/lrtap_h1.htm (accessed 15 January 2010).

[80]   UNECE Convention on Environmental Impact Assessment in a Transboundary Context, Espoo, 25 February 1991. Entered into force 10 September 1997.

[81]   Article 2(1) of the Convention.

[82]   Appendix I to the Convention.

[83]   UNECE Convention on the Protection and Use of Transboundary Watercourses and International Lakes, Helsinki, 17 March 1992. Entered into force 6 October 1996.

on waters and international lakes. The states parties should be guided by the precautionary principle, the polluter pays principle and intergenerational equity and should take appropriate measures 'to prevent, control and reduce pollution of waters causing or likely to cause transboundary impact'.[84]

The 1994 Energy Charter Treaty recognises sovereign rights of states parties over energy resources, in particular, the rights to determine in which areas of their territories exploration and development of energy resources can take place, and 'to participate in such exploration and exploitation, inter alia, through direct participation by the government or through state enterprises'.[85] It affirms the right of each state 'to regulate the environmental and safety aspects' of the exploration and development of energy resources.[86]

A number of regional and bilateral agreements dealing with transboundary resources apply to protected areas as well.[87] By using these agreements, parties can manage cross-border protected areas or common watersheds and control trade in flora and fauna or invasive alien species. Regional arrangements can provide mechanisms sustainably to govern the natural resources. For example, the Nile Basin Initiative seeks to develop the river in a cooperative manner, share substantial socio-economic benefits, share water in a sustainable and equitable way and ensure efficient water management and the optimal use of the resources.[88] In Asia, the Mekong River Agreement [89] between Cambodia, Lao PDR, Thailand and Vietnam sets up a framework for cooperation between the riparian states in all fields of the river basin's sustainable development. However, the developing countries of Asia and Africa face common and shared problems when managing transboundary resources due to, for example, weak institutional capacity, lack of resource inventory, lack of monitoring and ineffective conservation measures.

---

[84]   Article 2 of the Convention.
[85]   Article 18(3), 1994 Energy Charter Treaty, came into force in 1998.
[86]   Ibid.
[87]   Sandwith et al. (2001), supra, Appendix 1 on protected areas.
[88]   The Nile Basin Initiative, adopted on 22 February 1999, is a transnational arrangement established by the Nile Basin states: Uganda, Tanzania, Sudan, Rwanda, Kenya, Ethiopia, Egypt, D.R. Congo, Burundi.
[89]   Agreement on Co-operation for the Sustainable Development of the Mekong River Basin, 5 April 1995. The 4,800 km long Mekong River originates in China, and flows through Myanmar, Lao PDR, Thailand and Cambodia before ending in the Mekong Delta of Vietnam.

2.3.2. Right to natural resources in regional courts

Regional human rights bodies in Europe, the Americas and Africa examined cases which alleged violation of human rights and the degradation of
natural resources.[90] In several cases, the Inter-American Commission and
Court of Human Rights held that indigenous peoples have the right to
enjoy their land and natural resources.[91] In the *Maya Community* case,[92]
the petitioners claimed that the state had violated several provisions of the
American Declaration of the Rights and Duties of Man.[93] In their view,
the state had granted logging and oil concessions in the lands traditionally used and occupied by the Maya people and had failed to recognise
and secure the territorial rights of the Maya people in those lands. Thus,
the state impacted negatively on the natural environment upon which the
Maya people depended for subsistence. The Inter-American Commission
on Human Rights concluded that the state had failed to recognise the
communal property right of the Maya people and to consult with them
before granting logging and oil concession to the lands which they had
traditionally occupied and used. Similarly, the Inter-American Court
of Human Rights, in the *Sawhoyamaxa Indigenous Community* case,[94]
held that indigenous peoples maintain their property rights even where

---

[90] Boyle (2007), supra, 471. Fitzmaurice, M. and J. Marshall (2007), 'The
Human Right to a Clean Environment – Phantom or Reality? The European
Court of Human Rights and English Courts Perspective on Balancing Rights in
Environmental Matters', Nordic Journal of International Law, 76, 103–151.

[91] Inter-American Court of Human Rights, *Case of the Mayagna (Sumo)
Awas Tingni Community.* Judgment of 31 August 2001. Series C No. 79. Inter-
American Court of Human Rights, *Saramaka People v. Suriname.* Judgment
of 28 November 2007. Series C No. 172, paras 88–96. Inter-American Court of
Human Rights, *Yakye Axa Indigenous Community v. Paraguay*, 17 June 2005,
paras 123–156, especially paras 131, 135, 137, 146, 147 and 154. Inter-American
Commission on Human Rights, *Yanomai v. Brazil*, Res 12/85, Case No. 7615,
5 March 1985. Inter-American Commission on Human Rights, 'Human Rights
Situation of the Indigenous People in the Americas', Inter-Am. OEA/Ser.L/V/
II.108, Doc. 62 (2000).

[92] *Maya Indigenous Community of the Toledo District v. Belize*, Case 12.053,
Report No. 40/04, Inter-American Commission on Human Rights, OEA/Ser.L/V/
II.122 Doc. 5 rev. 1 at 727 (2004), paras 85–156.

[93] Articles I (right to life), II (right to equality), III (right to religious
freedom), VI (right to family), XI (right to health), XVIII (right to a fair trial), XX
(right to vote and to participate in government) and XXIII (right to property) of
the American Declaration.

[94] *Sawhoyamaxa Indigenous Community v. Paraguay*, 29 March 2006, paras
117–143. It was alleged that the state had not ensured the ancestral property rights
of the Sawhoyamaxa Community.

they have been forced to leave or have otherwise lost possession of their traditional lands. The Court affirmed

> . . . the close ties of indigenous peoples with their traditional lands and the native natural resources thereof, associated with their culture, as well as any incorporeal element deriving therefrom, must be secured under Article 21 of the American Convention. [95]

A bold approach can be found in the African Commission on Human Rights as it applies the 1981 African Charter on Human and Peoples' Rights.[96] In the *Ogoniland* case,[97] (see Box 3.1 below) the African Commission dealt with the disposal of toxic waste which caused poisoning to soil and water and affected human health. The Commission noted that the right to a satisfactory environment under Article 24 'imposes clear obligations upon a government', requiring 'the State to take reasonable and other measures to prevent pollution and ecological degradation, to promote conservation, and to secure an ecologically sustainable development and use of natural resources'.[98]

Within the European Court of Human Rights (ECtHR), the claims are primarily based on the violation of the right to privacy and home.[99] The European Convention on Human Rights (ECHR) does not include any reference to resource protection or nature conservation.[100] Article 8(1) provides that 'everyone has the right to respect for his privacy, his home and his correspondence'. This right under Article 8 can be restricted

---

[95] Ibid., para. 121.

[96] Article 21 of the African Charter states: 'All peoples shall freely dispose of their wealth and natural resources. This right shall be exercised in the exclusive interest of the people. In no case shall a people be deprived of it.' African Charter on Human and Peoples' Rights, adopted 27 June 1981, 1520 U.N.T.S. 217, 21 I.L.M. (1981) 59 (entered into force 21 October 1986).

[97] Decision regarding Communication 155/96 (*Social and Economic Rights Action Center/Center for Economic and Social Rights v. Nigeria*), Case No. ACHPR/COMM/A044/1, African Commission on Human and Peoples' Rights, 27 May 2002.

[98] Ibid., para. 52.

[99] *Guerra and Others v. Italy* (1998) 26 EHRR 357. *Lopez-Ostra v. Spain* (1994) 20 EHRR 277. *Hatton v. UK* (Judgment of the Grand Chamber, 8 July 2003), (2003) 37 EHRR 28. *Kyrtatos v. Greece* (2003) ECHR 242. *Öneryildiz v. Turkey* (2004) ECHR 657. *Fadeyeva v. Russia* (2005) ECHR 376. *Taskin v. Turkey* (2006) 42 EHRR 50.

[100] European Convention for the Protection of Human Rights and Fundamental Freedoms, opened for signature 4 November 1950, 213 U.N.T.S. 222 (entered into force 3 September 1953).

BOX 3.1. THE OGONI PEOPLE AND THE PROTECTION OF NATURAL RESOURCES

Oil production in Nigeria has had severe environmental and human consequences for the indigenous peoples including the Ogonis who inhabit the areas surrounding oil extraction sites. The southwestern oil producing areas of Nigeria are severely damaged by environmental pollution from oil spills, dumping of waste products, burning of excess gases, pipe-line leaks, oil well blowouts, and gas-flaring operations. The Nigerian government is involved in the oil production through the state oil company, Nigerian National Petroleum Company, and part of a consortium with the Shell Petroleum Development Company (SPDC).

The Ogonis have a long history of preserving their environment, which they regard as sacred. They claimed that the oil extraction activities and disposal of toxic waste had damaged the tropical rain forest, destroyed mangrove vegetation and biodiversity, polluted soil, air and drinking water, destroyed the local fishing industries and led to severe health problems. They also claimed that there was no consultation by the government or the oil companies about the development of their land. They had not received any compensation for environmental damage or economic benefits from the profits made from the oil production and were not informed of any potential danger posed by oil extraction in that area. The government also failed to protect the Ogoni people from environmental pollution and the national regulation for petroleum industries does not apply international environmental standards.

The Ogonis protested against the Nigerian government and oil industries including Shell Oil, the major oil producer in the country. The campaign group, Movement for the Survival of the Ogoni People, was met with violent reprisals. In 1996, the Social and Economic Rights Actions Centre and the Centre for Economic and Social Rights sent Communication 155/96 to the African Commission on Human and Peoples' Rights alleging violation of the African Charter by the Nigerian government. In 2002, the African Commission found Nigeria to have violated, inter alia, the right to life (Article 4), right to property (Article 14), right to health (Article 16), and right to satisfactory environment favourable to development (Article 24) of the African Charter. In 2008, the Nigerian government decided to replace the SPDC as operator of oil concessions in Ogoni areas.

Source: http://ccrjustice.org/files/4.6.09%20Case%20Against%20Shell%20 Factsheet.pdf.

if the activity falls under Article 8(2) of the ECHR.[101] For example, the *Hatton* case[102] deals with noise pollution from Heathrow airport. The initial Chamber judgment found that the noise from increased flights at Heathrow airport between 4 a.m. and 6 a.m. violated the rights of the applicants to respect for their home and family life under Article 8. This judgment was overturned by a Grand Chamber decision in 2003 where the Court held that there was no violation of Article 8. At the same time, the Grand Chamber (with one dissenting vote) upheld the initial Chamber's finding of a violation of Article 13 and awarded some costs and fees to the applicants.[103] When faced with the competing interests of the right to privacy and the right to development, the ECtHR applied the 'fair balance' test while balancing the economic interests (i.e. economic contribution from flights) of the country with the rights of the affected individuals (i.e. noise pollution).

The cases decided by the ECtHR show that states have positive duties to take all appropriate and reasonable measures to prevent environmental pollution from seriously interfering with the right to life or privacy.[104] The Court has not established any general duty to protect the environment; rather the duty is owed to the individuals whose rights will be affected by the state's failure to reduce or eliminate pollution.[105] These ECtHR decisions also show that there is a need for express provision in order to protect the environment and natural resources (as in the African Charter) in the binding instrument. Express provisions on the right to natural resources may make it easier for the affected individuals to bring a claim in the Court and somewhat less challenging for the Court to reach a fair balance between competing rights.

---

[101]   Ibid., Article 8(2) provides the permissible grounds for limiting the exercise of the right.

[102]   *Hatton v. UK*, supra, note 99.

[103]   Article 13 deals with the right to an effective remedy.

[104]   Birnie et al. (2009), supra, 282–285.

[105]   Ibid., 285.

2.4. Right to Natural Resources at the National Level

Similar to the regional courts, there are national level courts where environmental policies, rights and responsibilities conflict, for example, with the human rights to development, food, privacy and property.[106] In many of these cases, the national court has to balance the right to explore and extract natural resources and the right to protect and preserve the resources for the benefit of future generations.

Over 60 national constitutions include provisions to protect the environment.[107] Not all of them expressly mention natural resources.[108] The constitutional provisions dealing with the sustainable exploitation and management of natural resources are found in the constitutions of Afghanistan (2004), Albania (1998), Bahrain (1973), Cambodia (1993), China (1982), Cuba (1992), Peru (1993), Portugal (1976) and South Africa (1996).[109] The Bolivian Constitution (2009) includes a collective right to natural resources.[110] Constitutional provisions relating to the management of species and ecosystems can be found in the constitutions of Brazil (1998), Colombia (1991), Ecuador (1998), Namibia (1990) and Panama (1972).[111] Some of these constitutions create a justiciable right and some contain purely aspirational provisions.[112] Constitutional provisions of Albania (1998), Argentina (1994), Bolivia (1967), Brazil (1998), Iran (1979), Malawi (1994), Norway (1814), South Africa (1996) and Uganda (1995) recognise the rights of future generations by means of environmental protection and the sustainable development of natural resources.[113]

The constitutional right to protect natural resources offers an opportunity to promote environmental and resource concerns at the highest and most visible level of the legal order. Addressing environmental and resource protection at the constitutional level as a *right* means that the protection of the environment and natural resources does not depend

---

[106] Razzaque, J. (2007), 'Linking Human Rights, Development and Environment: Experiences from Litigation in South Asia', Fordham Environmental Law Review, 18, 587–608.

[107] O'Gara, R. et al. (2007), *Human Rights and the Environment*, Geneva: Earthjustice, Appendix.

[108] However, some national constitutions include the right to water. This substantive right to water is discussed in chapter 7 (Water resources).

[109] O'Gara et al. (2007), supra, 126–147.

[110] Article 349.

[111] O'Gara et al. (2007), supra, Appendix.

[112] Ibid., 126–147. Justiciability means the right is enforceable in a court of law. Aspirational provisions are not binding on the states.

[113] Ibid., 126–147.

on the liberal or conservation interpretation of the judiciary. On the one hand, with constitutional provisions by its side, the community affected by a development decision may argue that the principle of intergenerational responsibility is legally justiciable.[114] The express provision in the Constitution provides them with legal capacity to sue on behalf of the present and future generations. There is, however, difficulty in defining the nature, content and scope of the right to natural resources. Where the right to natural resources is not spelt out, the affected community or individual may have to depend on a liberal interpretation of 'right to life' or 'right to a healthy environment' by the judiciary. For example, in the absence of an express right to environment or natural resources, the Indian judiciary has interpreted the right to life to include the right to quality of life, the right to live with dignity and the right to livelihood.[115] Lack of an express and binding provision in the Constitution means that if the right to access natural resources is defined inadequately or imprecisely it will not be enforced effectively by the public agencies.

3. PROCEDURAL RIGHTS TO NATURAL RESOURCES

Realisation of the substantive right to natural resources requires adequate information and participation of affected communities to protect and manage natural resources. In natural resource management, participation in the decision-making process creates a sense of 'ownership' in the decision itself and various participatory techniques assist communities to achieve a sustainable outcome. This section examines the development of procedural environmental rights, and reviews the approaches of procedural rights in international and national laws. Procedural rights deal with the process through which an administrative or judicial decision is taken and encompass public consultation, information provision and access to the courts.[116] Procedural fairness allows people to be part of the process, and community empowerment enables people to take an active role in decisions affecting their lives. Access to information, public participation,

---

[114] *Oposa v. Factoran*, GR No. 101083, 224 SCRA 792 (30 July 1993) (Phil).
[115] Razzaque, J. (2002), 'Human Rights and the Environment: National Experiences', Environmental Policy and Law, 32, 99–111.
[116] Ebbesson, J. (1997), 'The Notion of Public Participation in International Environmental Law', Yearbook of International Environmental Law, 8, Oxford: Oxford University Press, 70–75.

and access to justice improve the credibility, effectiveness and accountability of governmental decision-making processes.[117]

> *Right to participation* allows people to be part of the decision-making process through consultation and comments, and to have their opinions heard. Participation enables the participating communities to hold public authorities accountable for implementation and improves efficiency and credibility to government processes. Commonly used participatory tools include public hearings, notice and consultation, citizen ombudsmen and judicial review mechanisms . . . Right to participation needs to be supported by a right to information that is accurate, accessible, timely and comprehensive . . . *Right to information* includes right to seek information from public authorities with a corresponding duty of public authorities to collect and disseminate information . . . This right can enable citizens to participate meaningfully in decisions that directly affect their livelihood and promote accountability and transparency in environmental decision-making . . . Right to information and participation will have little meaning if the public lacks access to justice. *Right of access to justice* allows people to enforce environmental laws and remedy any breach – thus, establishes a right to clean environment . . . To be effective, this right needs to be fair, timely, affordable, and include effective remedies. Access to justice allows affected communities and environmental activists to challenge decisions adopted by public authorities or businesses that have failed to comply with environmental laws . . .[118]

According to Benjamin Richardson and Jona Razzaque,[119]

> Different models have been proffered to analyse the range of forms of public participation. One model, known as Arnstein's 'ladder', shows the spectrum of participation opportunities, beginning with mere notification, and extending to consultation and even joint decision-making power.[120] The lowest levels of participation may effectively amount to non-participation.[121] The highest level of participation, says Arnstein, is where the public has the power to negotiate with decision-makers and to veto proposed decisions. Another model of participation distinguishes between 'top-down' and 'bottom-up' approaches.

---

[117] Petkova, E., C. Maurer, N. Henninger and F. Irwin (2002), *Closing the Gap: Information, Participation, and Justice in Decision-making for the Environment*, Washington, DC: World Resources Institute, pp. 121–132.

[118] Razzaque, J. (2009), 'Human Rights to a Clean Environment: Procedural Rights', in M. Fitzmaurice, D. Ong and P. Marcouris (eds), *Research Handbook on International Environmental Law*, Cheltenham, UK and Northampton, MA, USA: Edward Elgar, chapter 14. Footnotes omitted.

[119] Richardson, B. and J. Razzaque (2006), 'Public Participation in Environmental Decision-making', in B.J. Richardson and S. Wood (eds), *Environmental Law for Sustainability: A Reader*, Oxford: Hart, 167. Footnotes included.

[120] Arnstein, S.R. (1969), 'A Ladder of Citizen Participation', Journal of American Institute of Planning, 35(4), 216.

[121] Ibid., 217.

The former is where the government initiates participation, the latter where communities do so.[122]

At the international level, both non-binding and binding instruments have influenced the normative development of procedural rights. At the national level, national constitutions include rights to information, participation and justice, and some of these provisions are linked to the right to natural resources. The national laws and regulations also elaborate these rights and may include specific procedures ensuring information and participation and providing guidelines on consultation and post-project monitoring. Some of these national laws allow citizens access to administrative or judicial remedies to challenge a private or governmental act or omission. Moreover, these laws may also provide a right to seek a judicial review when access to information or public participation is wrongfully denied.

This chapter examines a number of human rights and environmental conventions in international (section 3.1) and regional law (section 3.2) to identify the nature and scope of procedural rights to protect natural resources. The discussion then concentrates on procedural mechanisms available at the national level (section 3.3).

3.1.   Public Participation at the International Level

Major international environmental policy statements[123] and international financial institutions[124] call for increased community involvement in decision-making. Richardson et al. state:[125]

During the 1970s and early 1980s, commentators increasingly emphasised the value of a 'bottom-up', people centred approach to economic development.[126]

---

[122]   Langton, S. (ed.) (1978), *Citizen Participation in America*, Lexington, MA: Lexington Books.

[123]   See e.g. World Commission on Environment and Development (1987), *Our Common Future*, Oxford: Oxford University Press. World Conservation Union (1990), *Caring for the Earth*, Gland: IUCN. Stockholm Declaration, 11 I.L.M. (1972) 1416. Rio Declaration on Environment and Development, 31 I.L.M. (1992) 874. Declaration of the World Summit for Sustainable Development (2002). UNECE Convention on Access to Information, Public Participation in Decision Making and Access to Justice in Environmental Matters (Aarhus Convention), 38 I.L.M. (1999) 517, discussed below.

[124]   World Bank (2003), 'Water Resources Sector Strategy: An Overview', available at: http://lnweb18.worldbank.org/ESSD/ardext.nsf/18ByDocName/Strategy (accessed 15 January 2010).

[125]   Richardson et al. (2006), supra, 168–169. Footnotes included.

[126]   Spyke, N. (1999), 'Public Participation in Environmental Decision Making

. . . By the 1990s, consultation and participation became the buzzwords of successful environmental decision-making, feeding into broader discourses on 'good governance', 'environmental justice' and 'environmental citizenship' . . . Numerous societal conflicts over development choices in the 1970s and 1980s fuelled popular demands for more participation in decision-making.

Several human rights treaties include provisions on procedural rights. For example, the Universal Declaration of Human Rights provides rights of access to information and justice.[127] The International Covenant on Civil and Political Rights guarantees citizens the 'freedom to seek, receive and impart information and ideas of all kinds'.[128] Human rights instruments, such as the Declaration on Indigenous Peoples[129] and the General Comment 15 on water,[130] assert the right of the people to participate in the decision-making on natural resources.

A number of non-binding instruments[131] recognise the important role of procedural rights to protect the environment and natural resources. While the 1972 Stockholm Declaration indirectly refers to public participation,[132] the 1992 Rio Declaration summarises emerging public participation norms in its Principle 10:[133]

---

at the New Millennium: Structuring New Spheres of Public Influence', Boston College Environmental Affairs Law Review, 26, 269.

[127] Articles 8, 10 and 19. Universal Declaration of Human Rights, adopted 10 December 1948, UN GA Res. 217 (AIII), UN GAOR, 3rd Session, pt 1, at 71, UN Doc. A/ 810 (1948).

[128] Article 19(2) ICCPR.

[129] UN Declaration on the Rights of Indigenous Peoples (2007), adopted by GA Res. 61/295 (13 September 2007).

[130] General Comments 15. Substantive Issues Arising in the Implementation of the International Covenant on Economic, Social and Cultural Rights (Twenty-ninth session, Geneva, 11–29 November 2002). See chapter 7 of this book.

[131] 1978 Draft Principles of Conduct in the Field of Environment for Guidance of States in the Conservation and Harmonious Utilization of Natural Resources Shared by Two or More States, 19 May 1978, UN Doc. UNEP/IG12/2 (1978), 17 I.L.M. (1978) 1097. 1982 World Charter for Nature, 28 October 1982, GA Res. 37/7 (Annex), UN Doc. A/37/51, 22 I.L.M. (1983) 455. 1986 WCED Experts Group on Environmental Law of the World Commission on Environment and Development, Legal Principles for Environmental Protection and Sustainable Development, UN Doc. WCED/86/23/Add. 1 (1986). 1987 UNEP Goals and Principles of Environmental Impact Assessment, UN Doc. UNEP/Z/SER.A/9 (1987). 1991 IUCN Draft Covenant on Environmental Conservation and Sustainable Use of Natural Resources, UN Doc. A/CONF.151/PC/WG.III/4 (1991).

[132] Preamble, Declaration of the United Nations Conference on the Human Environment (1972), UN Doc. A/CONF/48/14/REV.1.

[133] Supra. Emphasis added.

Environmental issues are best handled with the *participation of all concerned citizens*, at the relevant level. At the national level, each individual shall have appropriate *access to information* concerning the environment that is held by public authorities, including information on hazardous materials and activities in their communities, and the opportunity to participate in decision-making processes. States shall facilitate and encourage public awareness and participation by making information widely available. Effective *access to judicial and administrative proceedings*, including redress and remedy, shall be provided.

In addition, Agenda 21 (1992) relies heavily on the role of civil society in developing, implementing, and enforcing environmental laws and policies.[134] Agenda 21 emphasises the need for strengthening the role of major groups as critical to the effective implementation of sustainable development and outlines the different forms of procedural mechanisms.[135] References to access to information, public participation and access to justice appear throughout Agenda 21.[136]

Among the binding documents, the Climate Change Convention asks the parties to 'promote and facilitate . . . public access to information on climate change and its effects'.[137] The 2000 Biosafety Protocol to the Biodiversity Convention relies on access to information[138] and public participation[139] for effective implementation. Provisions on participation can be found in the Climate Change Convention, Biodiversity Convention and Desertification Convention.[140] Provisions on access to justice are found in the Civil Liability Convention[141] and Convention on International Watercourses.[142] These international environmental instruments impose positive obligations on states to take measures to exchange information

---

[134] Agenda 21, Report of the UNCED, I (1992) UN Doc. A/CONF.151/26/Rev.1, 31 I.L.M. (1992) 874.

[135] For example, chapter 26 (Recognising and Strengthening the Role of Indigenous People and their Communities), chapter 27 (Strengthening the Role of Non-Governmental Organisations: Partners for Sustainable Development).

[136] Chapters 12, 19, 26, 27, 36, 37, and 40 of Agenda 21.

[137] Article 6(a)(ii). UN Framework Convention on Climate Change, 9 May 1992, 31 I.L.M. (1992) 849.

[138] Articles 20, 23(1) and (3). Protocol on Biosafety (Cartagena), 39 I.L.M. (2000) 1027 (entered into force 11 September 2003).

[139] Articles 23(2) and 29(8), ibid.

[140] Article 6 (a) (iii), Climate Change Convention. Article 14 (1) (a), Biodiversity Convention. Article 19, Desertification Convention.

[141] Articles 1 and 18, 1993 Convention on Civil Liability for Damage Resulting from Activities Dangerous to the Environment, 21 June 1993, 32 I.L.M. (1993) 1228.

[142] Article 32, 1997 Convention on the Law of Non-Navigational Uses of International Watercourses, 21 May 1997, UN Doc. A/51/869, 36 I.L.M. (1997) 700.

on environmental matters.[143] These provisions, however, do not create an enforceable right which can be asserted by an individual.[144]

In contrast to the International Court of Justice, other international courts and tribunals are allowing people to participate in court proceedings.[145] These submissions may be to challenge a breach of international law or failure of an organisation to enforce its own policies. It is possible to participate in the proceedings directly or indirectly.

- Direct participation is allowed, e.g. in the World Bank Inspection Panel, where private citizens, including NGOs, who believe that their interests have been or could be directly harmed by a project financed by the World Bank can bring an action.[146]
- Indirect participation, e.g. procedures to bring amicus curiae briefs in the International Tribunal for the Law of the Sea,[147] and acceptance of amicus briefs in the WTO Dispute Settlement Body[148] allowing submissions from NGOs, industries and academics. The International Centre for the Settlement of Investment Disputes is another forum where submissions from people are accepted by the Tribunal.[149]

---

[143]   For example: 1987 Montreal Protocol on Substances that Deplete the Ozone Layer (Article 9). 1992 Climate Change Convention Article 4(1)(h), Biodiversity Convention Article 13.

[144]   Sands, P. and J. Werksman (1995), 'Procedural Aspects of International Law in the Field of Sustainable Development: Citizens' Rights', in K. Ginther, E. Denters, and P.J.I.M. de Waart (eds), *Sustainable Development and Good Governance*, London: Martinus Nijhoff, 185.

[145]   Sands, P., R. Mackenzie and Y. Shany (1999), *Manual on International Courts & Tribunals*, London: Butterworths.

[146]   Hunter, D. (2003), 'Using the World Bank Inspection Panel to Defend the Interests of Project-Affected People', Chicago Journal of International Law, 4, 201.

[147]   Articles 77, 82 and 84 of the Rules of the Tribunal. International Tribunal for the Law of the Sea, ITLOS/8, 17 March 2009.

[148]   Appellate Body Report, *United States – Import Prohibition of Certain Shrimp and Shrimp Products*, WT/DS58/AB/R, adopted 6 November 1998, DSR 1998:VII, 2755, paras 104, 105 and 106. Panel Report, *Australia – Salmon*, WT/DS18/RW, adopted 18 February 2000, paras 7.8 and 7.9. Appellate Body Report, *United States – Imposition of Countervailing Duties on Certain Hot-Rolled Lead and Bismuth Carbon Steel Products Originating in the United Kingdom*, WT/DS138/AB/R, adopted 7 June 2000, DSR 2000:V, 2595. Panel Report, *United States – Imposition of Countervailing Duties on Certain Hot-Rolled Lead and Bismuth Carbon Steel Products Originating in the United Kingdom*, WT/DS138/R and Corr.2, adopted 7 June 2000, as upheld by the Appellate Body Report, WT/DS138/AB/R, DSR 2000:VI, 2623.

[149]   Rule 37(2) (submissions from non-disputing parties) provides certain conditions. Rules of Procedure for Arbitration Proceedings (2006), Washington, DC:

3.2.　Procedural Rights in Regional Law

The African Charter on Human and Peoples' Rights guarantees that citizens have the rights of access to information, participation and justice.[150] Similar provisions on information and justice can be found in the European Convention on Human Rights.[151] In addition, a number of non-binding and binding instruments in Europe include provisions on information,[152] participation[153] and justice.[154] The right of communities to participate in the consultation on major new projects is entrenched in the environmental impact assessment (EIA) processes.[155] For example, the 1991 UNECE Convention on Environmental Impact Assessment in a Transboundary Context (Espoo Convention) provides provisions on participation and information. Members of the public situated in the state which is likely to be affected by the activity have the right to receive information and participate in the environmental impact assessment of the proposed activity to be conducted in the state of origin.[156]

ICSID. *Aguas Argentinas, S.A., Suez, Sociedad General de Aguas de Barcelona, S.A. and Vivendi Universal, S.A. and the Argentine Republic,* ICSID Case No. ARB/03/19, Order in response to a petition for transparency and participation as amicus curiae, 19 May 2005 (paras 17–29). *Aguas Provinciales de Santa Fe SA and ors v. Argentina,* Order in Response to a Petition for Participation as Amicus Curiae, ICSID Case No. ARB/03/17, 17 March 2006.

[150]　Articles 3, 7, 9(1) and 13, supra.

[151]　Articles 6 and 10, supra.

[152]　Provisions on access to information are found in 1985 ASEAN Agreement on the Conservation of Nature and Natural Resources, 2003 EC Directive on Access to Environmental Information OJ L41/26 (2003), 1992 Convention for the Protection of the Marine Environment of the North East Atlantic (OSPAR Convention) and 1993 North American Agreement on Environmental Cooperation (NAAEC).

[153]　For example, provisions on environmental impact assessment are found in the 1985 EC Directive on Environmental Impact Assessment (as amended by 97/11/EC and 2003/35/EC), OJ L175/40 (1985), 1985 ASEAN Agreement on the Conservation of Nature and Natural Resources, 1991 UNECE Espoo Convention, 1993 North American Agreement on Environmental Cooperation. These provisions ensure the participation of people at the project preparation level.

[154]　1974 Convention on the Protection of the Environment between Denmark, Finland, Norway and Sweden (Nordic Convention), 1993 North American Agreement on Environmental Cooperation.

[155]　See Holder, J. (2004), *Environmental Assessment: The Regulation of Decision Making,* Oxford: Oxford University Press.

[156]　Articles 2 and 3. UNECE Convention on Environmental Impact Assessment in a Transboundary Context (Espoo, 1991). Text available at: www.unece.org/env/eia/ (accessed 15 January 2010).

In 1998, the UNECE Aarhus Convention adopted a right-based approach to information, participation and justice.[157] The Convention makes reference to a substantive right to a healthy environment and allows people to enforce their procedural and substantive environmental rights in court.[158] Although the Convention is regional in scope, it is open to accession by any UN member state.[159] The Aarhus Convention deals with activities which may significantly affect the environment (e.g. construction of a power plant), or policies, programmes and plans relating to the environment.[160] Influenced by Principle 10 of the Rio Declaration, the Convention endorses three pillars of public involvement in environmental governance:

- *Access to environmental information:* public authorities[161] have a duty to make information available to the public when requested and the Convention lays out time frames for responding to these requests.[162] Article 4 creates a presumption in favour of information disclosure and public authorities can deny a request for information only on the basis of a list of specific grounds for refusal.[163] The public authority may refuse to disclose information which would impair the ability of a person to receive a fair trial, or would adversely affect national defence or public security.[164] Denials of requests for information must be subject to a review consistent with the access to justice provisions of the Convention.[165] The governments should establish a publicly accessible database to provide information on a range of activities including water, energy and other resource use.[166]

---

[157] UNECE Convention on Access to Information, Public Participation and Access to Justice in Environmental Matters, adopted at Aarhus, Denmark, 25 June 1998, entered into force 30 October, 2001. 38 I.L.M. (1999) 515.

[158] The procedural rights conferred on the public are to be applied without discrimination as to citizenship, nationality or domicile. Article 3(9).

[159] The Aarhus Convention can be acceded to by any UN member with the approval of the Meeting of the Parties. Article 19.

[160] Articles 6–7 of the Aarhus Convention. Annex I lists those activities which must be subject to the requirements under Article 6.

[161] Public authority is defined under Article 2(2). It covers any government body or any natural or legal persons performing public administrative functions, and may include privatised companies providing public services. Stec, S. and S. Casey-Lefkowitz (2000), *The Aarhus Convention: An Implementation Guide*, Geneva: UNECE, 44.

[162] Articles 4 and 5.

[163] Article 4(3).

[164] Article 4(4).

[165] Article 9.

[166] Article 5(9). For example the 2003 Protocol on Pollutant Release and

- *Participation in the environmental decision-making:* the public should be able to participate in the decision-making of a project, plan, policy or programme relating to the environment.[167] According to the Convention, public participation can be ensured with an early notice of the decision-making process when 'all options are open' to people to provide comments or input into the process.[168] Public authorities need to take public participation into account in the final decision. Article 6 outlines the type of information to be included in the notice to the public concerned, and failure to take public input into consideration could be a basis for legal challenge.[169]
- *Access to justice in environmental matters:* the Convention allows individuals and NGOs to seek recourse to an administrative or judicial remedy when public authorities or corporations do not comply with the Aarhus obligations.[170] NGOs are explicitly included under the definitions of 'the public' and 'the public concerned',[171] although their standing will ultimately depend on the criteria laid down in national law.[172] Closely linked to the provision on information and public participation, this pillar mandates the establishment of procedures which are fair, equitable, timely and not prohibitively expensive.[173]

The Aarhus Convention provides a useful framework for public participation, and the participatory rights are linked to the legal, political and administrative arrangements at the national level. While the Convention has the potential to strengthen environmental rights, successful national implementation of the Aarhus Convention will require strong political support.

Transfer Register of the Aarhus Convention aims to enhance public access to information. The PRTR Protocol was adopted at an extraordinary meeting of the MOP in Kiev on 21 May 2003, and entered into force on 8 October 2009.

[167]	Article 6 and Annex 1 deal with specific activities. Article 7 deals with plans, programmes and policies. Also, Article 8 deals with public participation during the preparation of executive regulation. Article 2(4) defines public.

[168]	Article 6.

[169]	Article 9(2).

[170]	Article 9.

[171]	Article 2(4) and (5).

[172]	The Synthesis Report from the Aarhus Convention Secretariat shows that, at the national level, there is a trend to narrow the interpretation of the public concerned and standing criteria for NGOs. Economic Commission for Europe, Synthesis Report on the Status of Implementation of the Convention, ECE/MP.PP/2008/4, 21 May 2008, para.106.

[173]	Article 9(4).

As a party to the Aarhus Convention,[174] the European Union (EU) has adopted binding instruments aligning EU legislation to the requirements of the Aarhus Convention.[175] The EU has adopted a directive concerning public access to environmental information reflecting the first pillar of the Aarhus Convention.[176] In addition, two important pieces of EU environmental legislation[177] have been amended to take account of the public participation in certain environmental decision-making procedures. The European Commission has also adopted a proposal for a directive to address the requirements of access to justice in environmental matters which is expected to contribute to the implementation of the Aarhus Convention within the EU.[178] Along with these directives to implement the Aarhus obligations within the EU, there are examples of other environmental directives which include provisions on public participation.[179]

---

[174]   The EU approved the Convention in early 2005. Other regional conventions such as the 1991 Espoo Convention, 1999 Protocol on Water and Health and 2003 UNECE Protocol on Strategic Environmental Assessment have also influenced the development of EU law.

[175]   Regulation (EC) 1367/2006 of the European Parliament and of the Council on the application of the provisions of the Aarhus Convention on Access to Information, Public Participation in Decision-making and Access to Justice in Environmental Matters to Community institutions and bodies, OJ L264/13 (2006).

[176]   Directive 2003/4/EC of the European Parliament and the Council of 28 January 2003 on public access to environmental information and repealing Council Directive 90/313/EEC, OJ L41/26 (2003). This Directive imposes stricter obligations upon Member States regarding dissemination of environmental information by public authorities and extends the right of access to information from citizens of the EU to any person regardless of residence.

[177]   Directive 85/337/EEC (as amended by Directive 97/11/EC) OJ L175/40 (1985) concerning the environmental impact assessment for certain public and private projects was amended by Directive 2003/35/EC of the European Parliament and of the Council of 26 May 2003 providing for public participation in respect of the drawing up of certain plans and programmes relating to the environment and amending with regard to public participation and access to justice Council Directives 85/337/EEC and 96/61/EC. Directive 2008/1/EC (codified version) of the European Parliament and of the Council of 15 January 2008 OJ L34/8 (2008) concerning integrated pollution prevention and control.

[178]   Commission proposal for a directive on access to justice, COM(2003)624, full text available at the European Commission's website: http://europa.eu.int/comm/environment/aarhus/ (accessed 15 January 2010).

[179]   Article 14 and Annex VII of Directive 2000/60/EC of the European Parliament and of the Council of 23 October 2000 establishing a framework for Community action in the field of water policy, OJ L 327/1 (2000). Article 6 of Directive 2001/42/EC of the European Parliament and of the Council on the Assessment of the Effects of Certain Plans and Programmes on the Environment, OJ L197/30 (2001).

Several regional courts and tribunals allow individuals, NGOs or groups of individuals to come to the court as a party to the proceedings or submit amicus briefs:

- Party to the proceedings: the ECtHR allows individuals, NGOs or groups of individuals to come to the court if they are victims of any violation.[180] The Inter-American Court of Human Rights allows only the Inter-American Commission on Human Rights or the states parties to bring an action.[181] Individuals can submit a petition to the Commission.[182] Similarly, the African Commission on Human and Peoples' Rights allows petitions from victims of any violation.[183] The dispute settlement mechanism established under the 1993 North American Agreement on Environmental Cooperation allows any non-governmental organisation or person to make a submission to the Commission for Environmental Cooperation against governments if they are not enforcing their own environmental regulations.[184]

- Non-party via oral or written submissions: the ECtHR allows individuals and NGOs to submit amicus curiae briefs[185] during the written procedure and, in some cases, take part in oral hearings.[186] Both the Inter-American Court on Human Rights[187] and the NAFTA tribunal[188] allow amicus briefs.

---

[180]   For example: *Guerra and Others v. Italy*, 1998-I ECHR, Judgment of 19 February 1998; *Lopez-Ostra v. Spain*, ECHR (1994), Series A, No. 303C; *Hatton v. UK* (Judgment of the Grand Chamber, 8 July 2003). See: Fitzmaurice, M. (2002), 'Some Reflections on Public Participation in Environmental Matters as a Human Right in International Law', Non-State Actors & International Law, 2, 1–22.

[181]   Article 61(1) of the American Convention on Human Rights.

[182]   Article 44 of the Convention states that any person or group of persons or any non-governmental entity legally recognised in one or more member states of the Organisation may lodge a petition with the Commission.

[183]   Decision Regarding Communication 155/96 (2001), *Social and Economic Rights Action Center/Centre for Economic and Social Rights v. Nigeria*, Case No. ACHPR/COMM/A044/1.

[184]   Articles 14 and 15.

[185]   The amicus or friend of the court is a bystander without any direct interest in the litigation, intervening on his own initiative to make a suggestion to the court on matters of fact and law within his knowledge. An amicus brief contains material additional to that submitted by the parties.

[186]   Article 44(3) of the Rules of the European Court of Human Rights, June 2010.

[187]   Articles 2(3) and 44 of the Rules of Procedure (2009). Amicus briefs were submitted in the Case of the *Constitutional Court v. Peru*, Merits, Reparations and Costs. Judgment of 31 January 2001. Series C No. 71; *Case of Claude-Reyes et al. v. Chile*. Merits, Reparations and Costs. Judgment of 19 September 2006. Series C No. 151.

[188]   *Methanex Corporation v. United States of America: Decision of the Tribunal*

3.3. Procedural Rights in National Law

Participation in the decision-making process could be formal or informal. Formal procedures such as participation in policy-making include the involvement of the public in the consultation process. Informal methods include writing or calling elected officials, attending public hearings, commenting on agency rules, or lobbying on specific legislation. Participation in the implementation and enforcement of decisions includes common law rights to initiate criminal or civil proceedings, statutory rights allowing citizens to bring actions against government agencies and judicial review. Procedural rights to protect the environment or natural resources

> . . . can be built into general laws (administrative law, civil code, penal code), as well as into specific environmental legislation or other specific laws (sectoral law dealing with air and water; framework environmental law and environmental impact assessment procedures). General laws may provide formal (judicial reviews, class action, public inquiries), or informal or quasi-judicial forums (mediation, arbitration) for legal redress. In addition, they outline procedural issues such as standing in public interest litigation or class action and legal aid. Sectoral legislation may provide separate mechanisms (consultation, public inquiry) for people to participate in the EIA procedures. The effectiveness of public participation is directly related to the information available and related provisions can be found in freedom of information laws.[189]

Along with international and regional documents highlighting the importance of community participation, national plans, programmes and policies include provisions for communities to participate in environmental planning, conservation of shared natural resources and activities relating to waste disposal, energy facilities and dams. For example, Joint Forest Management in India is an integral part of forestry schemes to ensure people's participation in afforestation activities, and a large number of state governments have developed mechanisms for public participation in the management of degraded forests.[190]

---

on petitions from third persons to intervene as 'Amici Curiae', 15 January 2001. where NAFTA's chapter 11 investor–state arbitral tribunal accepted amicus written submissions under Rule 15(1) of the UNCITRAL Arbitration Rule.

[189]   Razzaque (2009), supra, chapter 14. Footnotes omitted.

[190]   Report to the Commission on Sustainable Development by India (2002). Text available at: www.un.org/esa/agenda21/natlinfo/wssd/india.pdf (accessed 15 January 2010).

3.3.1. Constitutions and national legislation

Constitutional rights integrate human rights such as freedom of information, expression and assembly, and people can use these provisions to protect natural resources. The right to access courts is included in the constitutions of several EU Member States such as Austria, France, Germany, Greece, Ireland, Italy, Portugal and Spain.[191] Some constitutions accommodate provisions on the right to information and public participation. For example, the constitutions of Uganda, South Africa and Thailand guarantee the right of the public to information.[192]

Some countries have specific freedom of information legislation and environmental protection laws with specific provisions on information.[193] In addition, by 2006, nearly 70 countries worldwide had passed access to information legislation.[194] In some countries, such as South Africa and Thailand, environmental protection laws provide specific provisions for environmental information[195] complementing access to information laws. There are also examples of countries having specific legislation on access to environmental information[196] which can be used to protect natural resources.

The EIA legislation at the national level may include provisions on information and participation of communities in the decision-making process. EIA procedure allows public consultation and participation at the screening and scoping stage of the EIA process.[197] The success of information gathering and analysis under the EIA process depends on clear

---

[191]   Ebbesson, J. (2002), *Access to Justice in the Environmental Matters in the EU*, The Hague: Kluwer.
[192]   Petkova et al., supra, 33–64. Banisar, D. (2006), 'Freedom of Information around the World: A Global Survey of Government Information Laws around the World', available at: www.freedominfo.org/documents/global_survey2006.pdf (accessed 15 January 2010).
[193]   For example, Mexico, South Africa, and Thailand. See Petkova et al., supra, chapter 3., available at: www.accessinitiative.org (accessed 15 January 2010).
[194]   Banisar (2006), supra, 6.
[195]   World Resources Institute (2004), *World Resources 2002–2004 Decisions for the Earth: Balance, Voice and Power*, Washington, DC: WRI, chapter 3.
[196]   In the UK, the Environmental Information Regulations 2004 came into force in early 2005 to implement the EU Directive on Access to Environmental Information. Under the regulations, the public has a right of access to environmental information held by public authorities and a charge may be made for providing the information provided it is reasonable. Text of the legislation is available at: www.opsi.gov.uk/si/si2004/20043391.htm (accessed 15 January 2010).
[197]   See Holder (2005), supra. Glasson, J., R. Therivel and A. Chadwick (2005), *Introduction to Environmental Impact Assessment*, Oxford: Routledge.

guidelines and financial assistance for stakeholders.[198] Having an effective public involvement mechanism means the project is less likely to become controversial in the later stages of the process. Identifying the social, economic and environmental impacts at an early stage can help both developers and public authorities to improve the quality of project planning.[199] While public involvement may slow down the EIA process, it may also strengthen the EIA procedure by attaining transparent decisions.[200] As EIA is project based and does not consider policy options, it may be too late to result in major changes in the proposed activity. This inherent limitation of EIA suggests that, in some cases, the strategic environmental assessment (SEA) may be more beneficial as it allows people to participate at the policy (or plan or programme) making level.[201]

National implementation plans of Multilateral Environmental Agreements (MEAs) are another avenue for people to participate in implementing the MEAs at the national level. The national reports to the secretariats of some of the MEAs have highlighted the need for greater participation of people at the planning, preparation and implementation of MEA national implementation plans.[202] These implementation plans offer opportunities for the local community to participate in the decision-making through village level workshops, public hearings and consultation, and prioritise activities.[203] Involving people to develop the priority areas of the national implementation plans could ensure compliance, develop

---

[198]   Donnelly, A., B. Dalal-Clayton and R. Hughes (1998), *A Directory of Impact Assessment Guidelines*, Nottingham: Russell Press, chapter 1.

[199]   Wood, C. (2002), *Environmental Impact Assessment: a Comparative Review*, Harlow: Prentice Hall. Chapters 2, 3 and 5.

[200]   Tilleman, W.A. (1995), 'Public Participation in the Environmental Impact Assessment Process: A Comparative Study of Impact Assessment in Canada, the United States and the European Community', Columbia Journal of Transnational Law, 33, 337.

[201]   Case studies on the application of SEA in 15 developed countries show that SEA practice differs greatly among countries and sectors. SEA and Integration of the Environment into Strategic Decision-Making (2001), European Commission Contract No. B4-3040/99/136634/MAR/B4, available at: http://ec.europa.eu/ environment/eia/sea-studies-and-reports/sea_integration_main.pdf (accessed 15 January 2010).

[202]   See: the national report from member states to the UN Convention to Combat Desertification, Ramsar Convention, Climate Change Convention and Biodiversity Convention secretariats.

[203]   Razzaque, J. (2009), 'Participatory Rights in Natural Resource Management: The Role of Communities in South Asia', in J. Ebbesson and P. Okowa (eds), *Environmental Law and Justice in Context*, Cambridge: Cambridge University Press, pp. 117–138.

local capacity and assess the impact of measures under MEA including environmental effects on local communities.[204]

3.3.2. Procedural routes to domestic courts

Constitutional provisions, environmental laws or general administrative law provide the possibility for individuals or NGOs to challenge acts and omissions by public authorities or private actors. In many developing countries, the judiciary is willing to hear arguments from environmental groups and concerned individuals who have no direct economic interests at stake. For example, the Indian judiciary, since the 1970s, has permitted actions by any member of the public who has not suffered any violation of their own rights but who has brought an action on behalf of those who suffered a legal wrong or injury.[205]

Public interest litigation (PIL) is a legal mechanism which allows the public to enforce constitutionally guaranteed rights.[206] PIL dealing with environmental issues originated in the US and it is common now in many African, Asian and Latin American countries enabling poorer sections of the community to access courts.[207] When the collective rights of the public are affected, PIL can be brought by any individual or NGO without the need to show any direct injury to any individual member of the public.[208] PIL is widely practised in India. It is facilitated by the inclusion in the Constitution of fundamental duties to protect the environment and the adoption of various social-justice related laws.[209] In addition, public officials and agencies in India are not always capable of policing the environmental system due to insufficient funds, inadequate staff and lack of expertise.[210] The Indian judiciary has taken an inquisitorial role and appointed commissions of enquiry, monitored its own directions,

---

[204] Bruch, C. and E. Mrema (2006), *Manual on Compliance with and Enforcement of Multilateral Environmental Agreements*, Nairobi: UNEP, 120–121, available at: www.unep.org/dec/docs/UNEP_Manual.pdf (accessed on 15 January 2010).

[205] Baxi, U. (1985), 'Taking Suffering Seriously: Social Action Litigation in the Supreme Court of India', Third World Legal Studies, 107.

[206] Cassels, J. (1989), 'Judicial Activism and Public Interest Litigation: Attempting the Impossible?', The American Journal of Comparative Law, 37, 498.

[207] Richardson et al. (2006), supra, 183–184. Examples of case law are available from www.elaw.org (accessed 15 January 2010).

[208] Sorabjee, S.J. (1999), 'Introduction to Judicial Review in India', 4 Judicial Review, 128.

[209] Divan, S. and A. Rosencranz (2001), *Environmental Law and Policy in India: Cases, Materials and Statutes*, Oxford: Oxford University Press, 133–152.

[210] Razzaque (2007), supra, 590–591.

initiated *suo motu* proceedings,[211] accepted amicus curiae briefs, supervised implementation of its orders and awarded compensation to the aggrieved.[212]

One of the criticisms of PIL is that it gives too much power to the judiciary. This criticism becomes more relevant when the judiciary is not accountable to people or not entirely 'separate' from the executive or legislative body.[213] Moreover, PIL has to be accessible and affordable to people. If legal proceedings are expensive to most people, lengthy and time consuming, access to court fails to provide 'justice' to people.[214] In these instances, access to courts may not ensure procedural justice or a just substantive outcome.

Judicial review is another route for people to challenge government decisions. As Richardson et al. opine:[215]

> Judicial review is a procedure by which decisions of public bodies exercising environmental responsibilities can be challenged in court and a means by which the courts can supervise public bodies' exercise of their statutory authority. Judicial review is usually concerned with the decision-making process rather than the decision itself.[216] The basic principle is that it is not for the judges to interfere in the decision as this is within the remit of the decision-maker, unless the decision is 'manifestly unreasonable' or the way in which the decision was arrived at is flawed.[217] But the success of a judicial review application may not secure the desired outcome. A court may find the agency's decision to be unlawful and, while reconsidering the matter, the public body may come to the same conclusion in a lawful way.[218] In judicial review proceedings in common law systems, such as in the UK, courts do not directly consider the merits of any public decision, act or omission.[219] However, in some cases they will indirectly consider the merits through the doctrine of 'manifest unreasonableness'.[220] Judicial review proceedings do not therefore usually examine whether

---

[211]   In order to provide 'complete justice', the Constitution of India allows the Supreme Court (Article 142) and the High Court (Article 226) to take account of letters and petitions from individuals or groups and move the matter as PIL.

[212]   Razzaque, J. (2004), *Public Interest Environmental Litigation in India, Pakistan and Bangladesh*, The Hague: Kluwer, chapter 5.

[213]   Razzaque (2007), supra, 603.

[214]   Ibid., 605.

[215]   Richardson et al. (2006), supra, 182–183. Footnotes included.

[216]   Lord Woolf, J. Jowell and A.P. Le Sueur (1999), *De Smith, Woolf and Jowell's Principles of Judicial Review*, London: Sweet and Maxwell, Part I.

[217]   Supperstone, M. and J. Goudie (1997) *Judicial Review*, London: Butterworths, chapter 3.

[218]   Ibid.

[219]   Southey, H. and A. Fulford (2004), *Judicial Review*, Bristol: Jordan, chapter 1.

[220]   Supperstone and Goudie, supra, chapter 3.

the decision taken was good or bad from a broad policy or ethical perspective, but merely check to see whether the public body has acted within its statutory powers.

This narrow focus of judicial review could be frustrating for community groups if this is the only avenue available for them to challenge a public decision.[221] In addition, examples from Europe show that the litigation cost, lawyers' fees, lack of legal aid for environmental cases as well as a strict interpretation of the standing rule remain major obstacles to bringing a matter to the court.[222]

These domestic avenues could be used successfully if the judiciary relaxed the standing rule to allow the individual into the judicial process.[223] If there is a specialist environment chamber or tribunal at the national level, that may also resolve an environmental dispute allowing affected communities to bring in 'public interest' claims.[224] A number of countries have successful use of such specialist courts or tribunals.[225] In addition, states may establish mechanisms whereby legal costs of environmental cases would be paid for by the government or by the legal services programme. For example, in New South Wales in Australia, legal aid is offered for environmental litigation and the loser may not have to pay the costs of the other side.[226] Although there are provisions for legal aid in developed countries such as the UK and many developing countries such as India, the scheme

---

[221] For example from the UK see: Report by the Environmental Justice Project, produced by WWF, Leigh Day and Co and the Environmental Law Foundation (2004) 33, available at: www.ukela.org/content/doclib/116.pdf (accessed 15 January 2010).

[222] European Commission for Europe, Synthesis Report on the Status of Implementation of the Convention, ECE/MP.PP/2008/4, 21 May 2008.

[223] Richardson et al. (2006), supra. 185–187.

[224] Carnwarth QC, R. (1992), 'Environmental Enforcement: The Need for a Specialist Court', Journal of Environment and Planning Law, 798. Lord Woolf (1991), 'Are the Judiciary Environmentally Myopic?', Journal of Environmental Law, 4, 1.

[225] For example, the Land and Environmental Court of New South Wales, the Environment, Resources and Development Court in South Australia, the Planning and Environment Court in Queensland and the Environment Court in New Zealand. Grant, M. (2000), *Environment Court Project: Final Report*, UK: DETR. Executive Summary 4–11.

[226] McGrath, C. (2008), 'Flying Foxes, Dams and Whales: Using Federal Environmental Laws in the Public Interest', Environmental and Planning Law Journal, 25, 335. Boer, B. (1986), 'Legal Aid in Environmental Disputes', Environmental and Planning Law Journal, 3, 22. Section 47 of the Legal Aid Commission Act 1979 (New South Wales).

rarely caters for environmental litigation.[227] Moreover, legal aid does not cover the whole cost of the litigation and, sometimes, fails to attract experienced lawyers to take on environmental cases.[228]

4. CONCLUSION

The effect of economic globalisation, such as privatisation of natural resources, can lead the state to alienate people and adopt decisions which may not be for the well-being of the present and future generations. While states require regulation to protect their resource sectors, the substantive law of the state needs to promote the right of the people, including the communities and NGOs, to natural resources. Strong procedural rights alone cannot protect natural resources – these rights will have to be complemented by substantive rights to natural resources.

At the international level, the absence of a global treaty on procedural environmental rights and lack of any international compliance mechanism mean that procedural rights depend a lot on the national legal system, courts and other government agencies. Regional bodies, such as the UNECE, Association of South East Asian Nations and the African Commission on Human and Peoples' Rights, could play an important role in strengthening substantive and procedural environmental rights. For example, the 1998 UNECE Aarhus Convention has influenced the development of regional and national instruments on procedural rights to information, participation and justice. With an inadequate legal regime to manage natural resources and increased pressure from the private actors to influence a decision on development activities, regional initiatives can offer some guidance to developing countries to push for transparent and accountable decisions. At the same time, transboundary shared resources, e.g. rivers, wetlands, lakes, could be better managed with EIA and other participatory mechanisms (e.g. SEA), adequate information and access to courts in any of the affected countries. The regional platforms could be instrumental in sharing experiences among countries with similar legal systems and economic development in order to develop, explore and manage natural resources sustainably.

---

[227] Jeffrey QC, M.I. (2002), 'Intervenor Funding as Key to Effective Citizen Participation in Environmental Decision-Making', Arizona Journal of International and Comparative Law, 19, 643. Also, G. Pring and C. Pring (2009), *Greening Justice: Creating and Improving Environmental Courts and Tribunals*, Washington, DC: The Access Initiative, World Resources Institute.

[228] Jeffrey (2002), supra.

Legal development at the international and regional level has influenced the substantive and procedural law at the national level. Regional and national courts have also taken an active role in ensuring that the public, including civil society, the local community and NGOs, have a right to access information and other legal remedies. At the national level, some countries have advanced procedural tools while some national legal frameworks do not provide adequate mechanisms for access to information, participation and justice. Even if there is an effective judicial system, in many instances it is not cost effective and legal assistance is rarely available for environmental cases. Sometimes, the public are not even aware of their procedural rights and fail to participate actively in the decision-making processes. The development of the procedural rights, to a large extent, depends on knowledge sharing among the public bodies, judiciary, private sectors and NGOs.

FURTHER READING

Barton, B. (2002), 'Underlying Concepts and Theoretical Issues in Public Participation in Resource Development', in D. Zillman, A. Lucas and G. Pring (eds), *Human Rights in Natural Resource Development: Public Participation in the Sustainable Development of Mining and Energy Resource*, Oxford: Oxford University Press, 77–121.

Birnie, P., A. Boyle and C. Redgwell (2009), *International Law and the Environment*, Cambridge: Cambridge University Press, 271–311.

Ebbesson, J. (1997), 'The Notion of Public Participation in International Environmental Law', Yearbook of International Environmental Law, 8, 51–97.

Fitzmaurice, M. (2002), 'Some Reflections on Public Participation in Environmental Matters as a Human Right in International Law', Non-State Actors & International Law, 2, 1–22.

Petkova, E., C. Maurer, N. Henninger and F. Irwin (2002), *Closing the Gap: Information, Participation, and Justice in Decision-making for the Environment*, Washington, DC: World Resources Institute.

Pring, G. and S.Y. Noe (2002), 'The Emerging International Law of Public Participation Affecting Global Mining, Energy and Resource Development', in D. Zillman, A. Lucas and G. Pring (eds), *Human Rights in Natural Resource Development: Public Participation in the Sustainable Development of Mining and Energy Resource*, Oxford: Oxford University Press, 11–76.

Razzaque, J. (2009), 'Human Right to a Clean Environment: Procedural Rights', in M. Fitzmaurice, D. Ong and P. Marcouris (eds), *Research Handbook on International Environmental Law*, Cheltenham, UK and Northampton, MA, USA: Edward Elgar, chapter 14.

Richardson, B. and J. Razzaque (2006), 'Public Participation in the Environmental Decision-making', in B.J. Richardson and S. Wood (eds), *Environmental Law for Sustainability: A Reader*, Oxford: Hart Publishing, 165–194.

PART II

Challenges

4. Global governance and sustainable natural resource management through states and international institutions

1. INTRODUCTION

Globalisation has led to important changes in governance models and in the distribution of power between state and non-state actors. This process has been aided and accompanied by the creation of new supranational forums where private–public partnerships collaborate in the gathering of information, exchange of facilities, formulation of policies and implementation of projects. This evolving process of power redistribution requires a reassessment of the roles of both 'traditional' or state actors and institutions and non-state actors in global affairs[1] and their contributions to globalisation and natural resource governance, as well as their political, economic and social interactions.

This chapter focuses on states, international organisations and intergovernmental actors. Other non-state actors are considered in the next chapter.

2. STATES

Nation states, emerging from the post-Westphalia peace, have been for centuries the main actors in international relations with a well developed theory in international law about their powers and prerogatives as well as limits to their actions. This central role in the international sphere began

---

[1] By traditional we mean states and international institutions thought to be the subjects of public international law, while individuals were called objects. This terminology has been long challenged by a preferred view which considers all those who participate in the supranational sphere as 'participants'. See Higgings, R. (1994), *Problems and Processes: International Law and How We Use It*, Oxford: Oxford University Press, 39.

to be challenged in the mid-1990s when globalisation rose to dominate the social and political discourse and calls for an 'end of the nation-state' became commonplace.[2] It was then argued that national frontiers no longer made sense and that unconstrained market forces and transnational political and social movements were creating a new economic and social order beyond the control of nation-states.[3]

Much of the discussion in this book revolves round the need for greater cooperation between and beyond states and national borders in areas such as environmental protection, the management of transboundary natural resources, the provision of global public goods and the integration of trade and investment with natural resource governance. We also consider whether transnational institutions which include both state and non-state actors would be better equipped to deal with several of the challenges of global governance. However nation-states remain, to date, the main source of regulatory power and retain vital ingredients to bind societies and peoples together, providing a sense of identity and legitimacy which supranational organisations still lack. States adopt and ratify treaties, with their practice and *opinio iuris* they provide the basis for the formation of customary international law, and many principles of international environmental law are derived from principles of national environmental law.[4]

The changed economic climate of 2008 and 2009 provided the background for a change in focus about the relative roles of the state and the market. As anger in countries with traditional laissez-faire policies and market-based economic models mounted towards the risk-taking attitudes of industry and the private sector, the state has been forced to intervene, acquiring or re-acquiring a parcel of power in economic regulation. The

---

[2]   There is an ample literature round the theme of 'the end of the nation-state' in the 1990s. See for example Guehenno, J.M. (1995), *The End of the Nation-State*, Minneapolis, London: University of Minnesota Press, and, more legally focussed, Falk, R. (1998), *Law in an Emerging Global Village*, Ardsley, New York: Transnational Publishers.

[3]   For a discussion on the role of the nation-state in globalisation which challenges the usual 'end of the nation-state' discourse see Hirst, P., G. Thompson and S. Bromley (2009), *Globalization in Question*, 3rd edn, Malden, MA: Polity, especially chapter 8.

[4]   Marauhn, T. (2007), 'The Changing Role of the State', in D. Bodansky, J. Brunee and E. Hey (eds), *The Oxford Handbook of International Environmental Law*', New York and Oxford: Oxford University Press, p. 733. This is despite the influence that the participation of NGOs in international environmental conferences has had on the substance of the law. See the discussion in chapter 3 on NGOs and other non-state actors.

so-called 'market state' of the last two decades[5] seems to have arrived at a dead end, and a new role and opportunity for the state as a regulator of the national and international economy in conjunction with international institutions is now greeted by those traditionally advocating the laissez-faire of market forces.[6] States are now seen as playing a crucial role of mediators between markets and societies. '[O]nly a state can correct the negative consequences of globalisation for the community of individuals living in its territory . . . [a]nd ensure a minimum of social sharing of wealth and national solidarity'.[7]

While in the economic field states see their possibility of manoeuvre certainly reduced due to the multilateral trading regime and the expansion of the economic system of investment liberalisation,[8] in the area of natural resource protection and management states, at least nominally, retain much of their power over resources in their territory.[9] Economic imperatives such as the need to receive inflows of foreign investment may constrain states' sovereignty and independence when formulating energy policies or environmental standards, but the principle of permanent sovereignty over natural resources[10] and the lesser number and reach of Multilateral Environmental Agreements (MEAs) compared to the comprehensive rules of the multilateral trade system allow states a wider margin of manoeuvre, leaving states as the crucial actors in the formulation of natural resources policies, both nationally and supranationally and the main agents for their enforcement.[11] Against this view many would contend that, with

---

[5] Term coined by Rowan Williams, The Guardian, 27 February 2003.

[6] For a discussion on the changing role of the state and the rule of law in political economy see Trubeck, D.M. (2009), 'The Political Economy of the Rule of Law; The Challenge of the New Developmental State', Hague Journal on the Rule of Law, 1, 28–32.

[7] Stern, B. (2000), 'How to Regulate Globalisation', in M. Byers (ed.), *The Role of Law in International Politics*, New York; Oxford University Press, 247 at 251.

[8] Discussed in chapter 1.

[9] In general, Schrijver, N. (1997), *Sovereignty over Natural Resources*, Cambridge: Cambridge University Press.

[10] Discussed in chapters 1 and 2. See also French, D. (2002), 'The Role of the State and International Organizations in Reconciling Sustainable Development and Globalisation', International Environmental Agreements: Politics, Law and Economics, 2, 135–140.

[11] No discussion about the role of the nation-state serves any purpose unless a distinction is made between the type of state or group of states that we are referring to. Small states hardly have any voice in multilateral negotiation forums and international institutions like the WTO, the World Bank or the UN, while economically powerful states such as the United States or the European states acting through the

the exception of powerful states, individual states are rather powerless to influence policy or oppose trends, negotiations and regulation at the global level. States, they argue, have become 'implementing agencies of international mandates that no longer have the monopoly of command and control type instruments but rather are subject to increasing numbers of guidelines, soft-law rules and regulations that require them to acquire a reporting and supporting role'.[12] But globalisation, while creating problems, also offers solutions, and collaborative networks enable states to join initiatives with other like-minded states and global companies in areas such as eco-labelling or public-performance rating.[13]

3.　INTERNATIONAL INSTITUTIONS

International cooperation and collective action has traditionally been articulated through international institutions. These institutions can be either intergovernmental organisations such as the UN or the Bretton Woods institutions or can be informal group settings such as the G-7, G-8, G-22, or G-77.[14] In some cases these informal groupings of countries have considerable power and exert influence in many areas such as global finance, energy or climate change.[15] We will focus here on the United Nations and its specialised agencies and programmes on natural resource management, treaty bodies, the IMF and World Bank and the WTO.

European Union have a considerable impact in political and economic design well beyond their borders.

[12]　See Marauhn (2007), supra, pp. 732–735.

[13]　Veeman, S. and D. Liefferink (2005), 'Different Countries, Different Strategies: "Green" Member States Influencing EU Climate Policy', in F. Wijen, K. Zoeteman and J. Pieters (eds), *A Handbook of Globalisation and Environmental Policy. National Government Interventions in a Global Arena*, Cheltenham, UK and Northampton, MA, USA: Edward Elgar Publishing, at 519–544.

[14]　For all of them see 'Factsheet – A Guide to Committees, Groups, and Clubs', available at: www.imf.org/external/np/exr/facts/groups.htm (accessed 15 November 2009).

[15]　The G-8 is a powerful actor in global politics and decisions are taken at its meetings which impact on global natural resource management. For example, at the Heiligendamm Summit in 2007, it acknowledged a proposal from the EU for a worldwide initiative on energy efficiency. The G-8 agreed to explore, along with the International Energy Agency, the most effective means to promote energy efficiency internationally. A year later, on 8 June 2008, the G-8, along with China, India, South Korea and the European Community, established the International Partnership for Energy Efficiency Cooperation, at the Energy Ministerial meeting hosted by Japan, holding the 2008 G-8 Presidency, in Aomori.

3.1. The United Nations

The UN, created in 1945, sought to represent the equal and sovereign nations of the world, but its mandate – preserving international peace and security[16] – has been heavily distorted by politics and geopolitical tensions since its inception. From its very beginning the UN was founded upon an imbalance of power by giving to the five permanent members of the Security Council, France, the United States, China, Russia and Great Britain, the power of veto. Historically tensions in the UN operated in two axes: the North–South and the East–West. During the Cold War the tensions between East and West,[17] communism and capitalism, provided a balance of power between the two groups. With the collapse of communism and the dramatic changes experienced by ex-communist countries in the 1990s the geopolitical situation changed, creating a world dominated by a single superpower, the United States, and a single political and economic model: corporate capitalism. Tensions also existed between the North and the South, with the rich countries of the North trying to control the political and, especially, economic development of their ex-colonies and other natural resource rich developing countries. The North–South divide had its most important manifestations in the General Assembly, where the 'one country one vote' rule allowed countries from both sections – the developed and the developing world – to block and obstruct decisions which would influence economic design. In the 1970s the approval of a Declaration on the New International Economic Order (NIEO)[18] which included proposals for South–South cooperation, transfer of technology, increased aid and the global regulation of multinational corporations, drew resistance from the North.[19]

Over the years various reforms have been suggested in order to make

---

[16]   Preamble, Charter of the United Nations 1945.

[17]   The East–West divide manifested itself mostly in respect of the Security Council actions under Chapter VII of the Charter in the areas of authorising interventions to maintain peace and security and responding to breaches of these. See Falk, R. (2002), 'The United Nations System: Prospect for Renewal', in D. Nayyar (ed.), *Governing Globalisation*, New York: Oxford University Press, pp. 183–186.

[18]   GA, Declaration on the Establishment of a New International Economic Order, A/RES/S-6/3201 (1 May 1974).

[19]   Especially in respect of the initiatives to control corporations, see chapter 5, pp. 217–220 and Kennedy, D. (2006), 'The "Rule of Law", Political Choices and Development Common Sense', in D.M. Trubek and A. Santos (eds), *The New Law and Economic Development: A Critical Appraisal*, Cambridge: Cambridge University Press, 116.

the UN more efficient, democratic and legitimate.[20] From these, several common themes arise. First, most commentators coincide in suggesting that membership of the Security Council must be enlarged and the veto powers changed or eliminated altogether.[21] Secondly, the creation of a proper 'Peacekeeping Force' which would operate under the UN mandate and execute the decisions of a new enlarged Security Council in respect of maintaining peace and security has also been advanced.[22] Some more radical ideas for reform include the creation of a forum for people's representation parallel to the General Assembly, which will remain an assembly of states. This new assembly – a Global Peoples' Assembly (GPA) – could be modelled on the European Parliament.[23] The growing consensus on the importance of the economic dimensions to the world order and the deficiencies and shortcomings of the current international financial institutions to avert recent crises have made calls for the creation of a central or global institution, a type of 'Economic Security Council' within the UN, very attractive. There are good reasons to support the theory that with a growing integration of the world economy it is necessary to have a system of integrated and global direction and control. Common to all critics is an imperative need to explore alternative methods of independent financing which would deprive economically powerful states of the control which they exercise over the UN and related institutions. Ideas advanced to achieve this independent finance have included the introduction of a 'Tobin tax' over transactions of the stock market, the use of the global commons or foreign exchange transactions.

3.1.1. Specialised agencies and programmes
UN specialised agencies and programmes were created to reflect new institutional concerns in the areas of trade, development and the environment.

(a) UNEP. The United Nations Environment Programme (UNEP) defines its mission as 'to provide leadership and encourage partnership in caring for the environment by inspiring, informing, and enabling nations and peoples to improve their quality of life without compromising that of

---

[20] See for example Michie, J. (2003), *The Handbook of Globalisation*, Cheltenham, UK and Northampton, MA, USA: Edward Elgar Publishing, at 22.
[21] Falk (2002), supra, at 186.
[22] Ibid.
[23] Falk, R. (2001), 'On the Creation of a Global People's Assembly: Legitimacy and the Power of Popular Sovereignty', Stanford Journal of International Law, 36, 191–220 and Falk, R. and A. Strauss (1997), 'For a Global People's Assembly', International Herald Tribune, 14 November 1997.

BOX 4.1.   FINANCING THE CHANGES: THE TOBIN TAX[1]

In 1978, James Tobin, a Nobel Prize-winning economist, first proposed the idea of a tax on foreign exchange transactions which would be applied uniformly by all major countries. A tiny amount (less than 0.5%) would be levied on all foreign currency exchange transactions to deter speculation on currency fluctuations. While the rate would be low enough not to have a significant effect on longer term investment where yield is higher, it would cut into the yields of speculators moving massive amounts of currency round the globe as they seek to profit from minute differentials in currency fluctuations. The tax would:

- reduce the volatility of exchange rates,
- reduce the power that financial markets have over national governments to determine fiscal and monetary policies, and
- raise revenue.

A tax to curb speculation in foreign currency exchange is an innovative and fair proposal which will contribute to restoring democratic control over national economies. The tax should be administered by an accountable democratic structure such as could be found within the UN system, with the revenue collected used for genuine social development.

See: http://tobintax.org/factsheet.htm.

Note:
1.   See Tobin, J. (1996), 'Foreword', in M. ul Haq, I. Kaul and I. Grunberg (eds), *The Tobin Tax: Coping with Financial Volatility*, New York: Oxford University Press.

Source: Elliott, L. (2009), 'The Time is Ripe for a Tobin Tax', 27 August, available at: www.guardian.co.uk/business/. . ./turner-tobin-tax-economic-policy.

FOR DISCUSSION

There have been growing calls for the introduction of a Tobin tax:

- Which institution(s) would be better equipped to administer such tax?
- How should the revenue it generates be used?

future generations'.[24] Six priority areas constitute the focus of UNEP's work: climate change, disasters and conflict, ecosystems management, environmental governance, harmful substances and resource efficiency. For the development of its work in these focus and related areas UNEP works closely with civil society and relevant stakeholders in order to formulate policies which are relevant, effective and capable of being implemented at the local level. UNEP works with a variety of actors in each of their priority areas, for example in its 'ecosystem management programme' UNEP works closely with the FAO, IUCN, or the UNDP. In the area of climate change UNEP has developed close work with the UNFCC Secretariat, the IPCC Secretariat, UNDP and the World Bank by playing a more active role in the World Bank Climate Investment Funds.

Collaboration is close with other United Nations agencies with complementary mandates such as the UNEP–UNDP–FAO Collaborative Programme on REDD[25] under which the three agencies are undertaking all of their REDD activities jointly, based on their distinct but complementary roles. Activities such as adaptation mainstreaming will be undertaken through mechanisms such as the UNEP–UNDP Poverty Environment Initiative to ensure a coordinated country approach which is fully in line with the Nairobi Framework.[26]

UNEP's work has been criticised by some as ineffective, diffuse and unfocused.[27] Some of UNEP's failures have their root in the fragmentation of agencies and departments which operate in the same or similar areas with little, and in many cases no, coordination.[28] UNEP spends lots of effort and time on specific country programmes which, according

---

[24]   http://unep.org.

[25]   Reducing Emissions from Deforestation and Degradation in Developing Countries (REDD) is now widely recognised as a critical issue for climate change mitigation. However, many questions remain regarding the social and environmental risks and benefits to countries and communities. UNEP, through the joint UNEP–UNDP–FAO UN–REDD Programme, is supporting capacity development, analysis and policy dialogue at country and international levels to find answers to these fundamental questions and ensure the environmental integrity of emerging REDD schemes. See www.unep.org/climatechange/UNEPsWork/REDD/.../Default.aspx.

[26]   www.unep.org/climatechange/Actors/tabit/231/language/en-US/default.aspx.

[27]   Esty, D.C. (2007), ' Global Environmental Governance', in C.I. Bradford Jr., and J.F. Linn (eds), *Global Governance Reform: Breaking the Stalemate*, Washington, DC: Brookings Institution Press, at 109.

[28]   This is now being at least partially addressed with initiatives such as the UN-REDD Programme. UNEP is working on Climate Change with a variety of UN and non-UN actors, see www.unep.org/climatechange/LinkClick.aspx?link=231&tabid=1.

to critics, would be best served by agencies such as UNDP or the World Bank, while it neglects what should be its role of information gathering and policy formulation in leading areas of global environmental concern. Proposals for the 'upgrading' of UNEP from a programme to a specialised agency have been put forward by France and Germany which advocate the creation of an environmental organisation within the UN: a United Nations Environmental Organisation (UNEO). Other proposals favour the creation of a Global Environmental Organisation (GEO) or a Global Environmental Mechanism (GEM). The GEM could consolidate the diverse and to date fragmented environmental activities of a multitude of entities, including environmental treaties' secretariats. It could also offer an inclusive forum by creating a support network of outside experts which would include civil society, NGOs and business alongside government officials, and which would contribute to information gathering and policy formulation.[29] Whether through a revived and revamped UNEP or through another newly created environmental agency, the main challenges that a global environmental agency must address are creating a suitable forum for information gathering and exchange, norm creation and dispute resolution. Unlike international trade, environmental concerns and problems lack the basic pillars of a good governance structure and rely on general principles of international law which obstruct the resolution of disputes in cases of transboundary resources management or transboundary pollution.[30] Institutions such as the WTO and the OECD provide useful guidance on how effective mechanisms of dispute resolution are and what are adequate forums for norm creation which can be used in the environmental sphere.

The creation of a global environmental organisation or mechanism would help simplify the existing confusing system of programmes and treaty secretariats and would encourage reluctant parties to take part if the norms created were fair, and took into account the common but differentiated responsibilities of its members, especially those of developing countries.[31] It is also imperative to create effective dispute resolution systems that can be easily accessed by those who are suffering from violations of environmental standards. The success of the compliance regime of

---

[29]   Esty (2007), *supra*, at 111.

[30]   See the discussion in chapter 6.

[31]   One of the obstacles to general participation in environmental and natural resource management regimes is the reluctance of developing countries to adhere to environmental commitments. Developing countries have repeated in a variety of forums that any environmental commitments should be conditional on the transfer of technology and more equitable terms in international trade. See chapter 1, pp. 31–34 and chapter 2, pp. 101–104.

the WTO has led some commentators to suggest that the GEM could be linked to the WTO dispute settlement body (DSB) and decisions against one state for breach of environmental commitments could be enforced by imposing countervailing duties which would not normally be authorised under normal WTO principles.[32]

(b) UNDP. The United Nations Development Programme (UNDP) is the UN's global development network. It focuses on helping developing countries to attract and use aid efficiently and to find solutions to the challenges of democratic governance, poverty reduction, environment and energy, HIV/AIDS and crisis prevention and recovery.[33] It plays an important role in linking and coordinating global and national efforts to reach the MDG's and publishes the annual *Human Development Report*[34] which offers analysis, tools and policy proposals on development issues.

(c) The FAO. The Food and Agriculture Organization of the United Nations (FAO) leads international efforts to defeat hunger.[35] The FAO serves as a knowledge network, collecting, analysing and disseminating data which aid development. It devotes particular attention to rural development since 70 per cent of the world's poor and hungry people live in rural areas, and helps member countries in devising agricultural policy, supporting planning, drafting effective legislation and creating national strategies to achieve rural development and hunger alleviation goals. In crisis situations, it works side-by-side with the World Food Programme and other humanitarian agencies to protect rural livelihoods and help people rebuild their lives.

The FAO's activities and mandate extend beyond agriculture to economic and social development, fisheries and aquaculture, forestry, natural resources and technical cooperation in matters related to the above. As a consequence it exercises a considerable influence on the development of natural resources policy in these areas. The FAO played a big role in the development of international fisheries law and its implementation,[36]

---

[32] Esty (2007), supra, pp. 111–12.

[33] www.undp.org/about/.

[34] www/hrd.undp.org/en.

[35] www.fao.org.

[36] Especially the 1993 Agreement to Promote Compliance with International Conservation and Management Measures by Fishing Vessels on the High Seas. Birnie, P., A. Boyle and C. Redgwell (2009), *International Law and the Environment*, Oxford: Oxford University Press, pp. 73–74.

and in the negotiation of the 2001 International Treaty on Plant Genetic Resources for Food and Agriculture in the context of biological diversity.

(d)   UNCTAD. The United Nations Conference on Trade and Development (UNCTAD) is a specialised agency of the UN GA and currently has 193 members. Established in 1964, UNCTAD promotes the development-friendly integration of developing countries into the world economy. Its work was seriously compromised during the 1980s and it ceased its operations. A renewed UNCTAD has progressively evolved into an authoritative knowledge-based institution the work of which aims to help shape current policy debates and thinking on development. UNCTAD has three key functions: it provides a forum for intergovernmental deliberations aimed at consensus building; undertakes research, policy analysis and data collection for debate between government representatives and experts; and provides technical assistance tailored to the specific requirements of developing countries. In its thematic quadrennial conferences it addresses many of the issues of the trade, environment and natural resources axis: the opportunities and challenges of globalisation for development were looked at in Accra:[37]

> 3.   For developing countries to reap the benefits of globalization in the future, there is a need to address the impact of commodity dependence, including the volatility of prices, the pro-poor and transparent allocation of revenues as well as the diversification of production structures in economies dependent on a few commodities. All developing countries, in particular the least developed, have to build productive capacity, ensure access to basic services and strengthen their legal and regulatory frameworks and institutions.

Its *Trade and Development Reports* and the *World Investment Reports* add to the knowledge base in areas of trade, development and natural resources with suggestions on how to move from a greenhouse gas-intensive model of production and consumption to more climate-friendly models with opportunities for developing countries from the new and fast-growing markets in environmental goods[38] to the latest trends in foreign direct investment around the world[39] or the extractive industries.[40]

---

[37]   Twelfth session GE.08-70399, Accra, Ghana, 20–25 April 2008.
[38]   *Trade and Development Report 2009 – Responding to the Global Crisis Climate Change Mitigation and Development*, available at: http://unctadorg/en/docs/tdr2009_en.pdf.
[39]   *World Investment Report 2009*, available at: http://unctad.org/en/docs/wir2007_en.pdf.
[40]   *World Investment Report 2007: Transnational Corporations, Extractive Industries and Development*, available at: http://unctad.org/en/docs/wir2007_en.pdf.

3.2. International Institutions of Natural Resource Management

There are a number of international organisations which exercise a role of stewardship or trusteeship and subordinate individual natural resource exploitation by the state to certain parameters which have been agreed collectively.[41] They usually correspond to those natural resources that are said to be common heritage of mankind, common concern, or which are of a transboundary nature.[42] Having organisations that operate in a model of international trusteeship could potentially overcome the problems that states' control and sovereignty over natural resources pose for the conservation and management of natural resources which are largely of global concern. However, common property regimes in natural resources are problematic and the existence of these organisations is rooted in deep controversy with considerable political opposition to them. The regime of international fisheries illustrates this well – fish stocks falling within the exclusive economic zone have now been removed from the common property regime and are considered to be under national sovereignty.[43]

The best example of natural resource management organisation is perhaps the International Seabed Authority (ISBA) created by UNCLOS.[44] The ISBA is concerned with the exploitation of the deep seabed mineral resources,[45] over which it exercises total control by creating rules and regulations which aim to ensure the effective protection of the marine environment. Disagreements over the ISBA delayed the entry into force of UNCLOS. Only the approval of the 1994 Implementation Agreement of Part XI of UNCLOS[46] made possible the start of operations of the ISBA. Similar bodies were envisaged for the exploitation of Antarctica's natural resources[47] and

---

[41]   Birnie, Boyle and Redgwell (2009), supra, pp. 94–97.

[42]   See chapter 4 for a definition of these concepts.

[43]   Common property regimes have also been discussed in chapter 1. See on this point Birnie, Boyle and Redgwell (2009), supra, p. 97.

[44]   1982 United Nations Convention on the Law of the Sea, 21 I.L.M. (1982) 126, Articles 156 to 170.

[45]   Ibid. See Birnie, Boyle and Redwell (2009), supra, p. 95 and, for more detail, Freestone, Barnes and Ong (eds) (2006), *The Law of the Sea*, Oxford: Oxford University Press, chapter 5.

[46]   Agreement Relating to the Implementation of Part XI of the United Nations Convention on the Law of the Sea. 28 July 1994, New York.

[47]   A Protocol to the Antarctic Treaty in 1991 bans all mineral activities in the Antarctic for 50 years but fails to provide an organisation similar to the ISBA. A proposed Antarctic Mineral Resource Commission was never created due to opposition by France and Australia. See Francioni, F. and T. Scovacci (eds) (1996), *International Law for Antarctica*, Cambridge: Cambridge University Press.

the Moon and other celestial bodies,[48] but the problems encountered over the agreements in respect of the ISBA were if anything amplified in respect of both Antarctica and the Moon and celestial bodies.

3.3. Treaty Bodies, Mechanisms and Secretariats

Many MEAs establish permanent bodies as their preferred institutional machinery. Of these bodies the Conference of the Parties (COP) together with secretariats are perhaps the best known. These bodies are not just intergovernmental conferences due to their permanent nature but they are not traditional intergovernmental organisations (IGOs) either. They have the advantage of flexibility and the fact that without a permanent seat they can convene meetings at a variety of locations. For some commentators the trend towards the establishment of permanent treaty bodies may be interpreted as a general trend towards the institutionalisation of cooperation between states to solve common problems.[49] COPs play a crucial role in standard setting, and together with their subsidiary bodies and secretariats have been very successful in providing frameworks through which environmental cooperation can take place in a 'non-bureaucratic and dynamic' manner.[50] Issues such as state consent, the legitimacy of decision-making under MEAs[51] and the role of public participation and scientific knowledge still need to be addressed further, but for the time being these dynamic bodies have greatly advanced cooperation in pressing and common environmental problems.

Several MEAs allow their COPs to adopt new measures or to amend annexes to the MEA or its protocols subject to non-acceptance of these decisions by individual states. Examples of this can be found in CITES[52] and the Montreal Protocol.[53] The most advanced model of decision-making and the adoption of binding obligations by an MEA body is the Montreal Protocol, which allows in its Article 2.9 the adoption of new

---

[48] The Moon Treaty of 1979 envisaged the creation of such an organisation for the exploitation of mineral resources of celestial bodies. See Birnie, Boyle and Redgwell (2009), supra, at 96.

[49] Ulfstein G. (2007), 'Treaty Bodies', in Bodansky et al. (eds) (2007), supra, p. 888.

[50] Ibid., at 889.

[51] Bodansky, D. (1999), 'The Legitimacy of International Governance: A Coming Challenge for International Environmental Law?', AJIL 93, 596.

[52] 1973 Convention on the International Trade of Endangered Species of Wild Fauna and Flora, 12 I.L.M. (1973) 1085.

[53] 1987 Protocol on Substances that Deplete the Ozone Layer, 26 I.L.M. (1987) 1550.

obligations by a double majority of developed and developing states.[54]
Further integration and cooperation between these bodies is the next
challenge of international law in addressing environmental and natural
resource governance.

3.4. Other Institutional Arrangements: The Global Environment Facility (GEF)

The Global Environment Facility was established in October 1991 as a
$1 billion pilot programme in the World Bank to assist in the protection of
the global environment and to promote environmental sustainable development. The GEF would provide new and additional grants and concessional funding to cover the 'incremental' or additional costs associated
with transforming a project with national benefits into one with global
environmental benefits.

The United Nations Development Programme, the United Nations
Environment Programme, and the World Bank were the three initial
partners implementing GEF projects. In 1994, at the Rio Earth Summit,
the GEF was restructured and moved out of the World Bank system
to become a permanent, separate institution. The decision to make the
GEF an independent organisation enhanced the involvement of developing countries in the decision-making process and in implementation of
the projects. The World Bank has remained involved in the GEF as the
Trustee of the GEF Trust Fund and provides administrative services.

As part of the restructuring, the GEF was entrusted to become the
financial mechanism for both the UN Convention on Biological Diversity
and the UN Framework Convention on Climate Change. In partnership
with the Montreal Protocol of the Vienna Convention on Ozone Layer
Depleting Substances, the GEF started funding projects which enable
the Russian Federation and nations in Eastern Europe and Central Asia
to phase out their use of ozone-destroying chemicals. The GEF subsequently was also selected to serve as the financial mechanism for two
more international conventions: the Stockholm Convention on Persistent
Organic Pollutants (2001) and the United Nations Convention to Combat
Desertification (2003).

---

[54]　Ulfstein (2007), supra, at 882.

4. INTERNATIONAL FINANCIAL INSTITUTIONS (IFIS)

4.1. The World Bank

4.1.1. The World Bank Group

The World Bank Group (WBG) is a group of five agencies: the International Bank for Reconstruction and Development (IBRD, 1945), the International Development Agency (IDA, 1960), the International Finance Corporation (IFC, 1956), the International Centre for the Settlement of Investment Disputes (ICSID, 1966) and the Multilateral Investment Guarantee Agency (MIGA, 1988).[55] What is referred to commonly as 'the World Bank' (WB) is the IBRD which has its origins in the Bretton Woods Agreements. The IBRD was to be one of three pillars[56] upon which the war-ravaged economies were to be reconstructed supported by a system of liberalised trade free of protectionism and of fluctuating foreign exchange.[57] Since its creation in 1944 as the International Bank for Reconstruction and Development the IBRD has evolved into a group of five closely connected development institutions with the main aim of alleviating world poverty. In the Bank's own words, 'poverty reduction through an inclusive and sustainable globalization remains the overarching goal of our work'. Unlike other financial institutions the WB does not operate for profit. The IBRD lending comes from selling its triple 'A' rated bonds in the financial markets and from lending its own capital which has been accumulated over the years through contributions of its 185 members (they are shareholders).[58]

In 1960 the International Development Agency (IDA) was created to concentrate on loans to the poorer countries. Its interest-free loans to the world's poorer countries are recycled once they are paid into further relending.[59] The IFC was created in 1956 with the purpose of furthering

---

[55] www.worldbank.org/.

[56] Together with the International Monetary Fund (IMF) and the failed International Trade Organisation (ITO).

[57] Article I Articles of Agreement IBRD (as amended, effective 16 February 1989), available at: http://worldbank.org/.

[58] The IBRD focuses on middle income and creditworthy poor countries.

[59] The IDA focuses on the poorest countries in the world. The IBRD and the IDA provide low-interest loans, interest-free credits and grants to developing countries for a wide array of purposes which include investments in education, health, public administration, infrastructure, financial and private sector development, agriculture, and environmental and natural resource management. See http://web.worldbank.org/WBSITE/EXTERNAL/EXABOUTUS/.

economic development through the encouragement of productivity of private enterprises in member countries.[60] The IFC finances private sector investment and provides advisory services to businesses and governments. For example in 2003 the IFC approved finance for the Baku–Tbilisi–Ceyhan (BTC) pipeline.[61]

The MIGA provides services mostly to private investors with the aim of increasing FDI in poor countries, especially those which are not attractive to foreign investors because of perceived or real political risks. Its services range from providing political risk insurance to investors to technical assistance to improve the investment climate to governments and the provision of dispute resolution services through mediation.[62] In 2007 its technical assistance services were integrated into the Foreign Investment Advisory Service (FIAS), another World Bank Group entity. With 20 years of experience FIAS strategy revolves round the simplification of regulation in recipient countries in order to make these more attractive to foreign investors.[63] Examples of projects in which FIAS has been involved include the simplification of obtaining licences for trading and investment, the reduction of taxes for business and the reduction of administrative burdens to investment.[64] In respect of its mediation on investment disputes MIGA will use its good offices and try to find an amicable settlement to any investment dispute between the host country and the investor. If a resolution is not possible the investor may be able to claim under the investment guarantee and MIGA reserves for itself the right to seek a recovery of costs against the host country.[65] Governments are not insured by the MIGA against non-performance by the investor.[66]

The ICSID[67] is an autonomous international institution established under the Convention on the Settlement of Investment Disputes between

---

[60]   www.ifc.org/.

[61]   The IFC's investment in the BTC pipeline consists of a loan of up to $125 million for its own account and a loan of up to $125 million in commercial syndication. The total project cost of the BTC is approximately $3.6 billion. See www.ifc. org/btc/. This project is discussed as a case study in chapter 6.

[62]   www.miga.org/.

[63]   www.fias.net/icfext/fias.nsf/Content/Home/.

[64]   See the website above for examples of these projects, available at: www. miga.org.

[65]   See www.miga.org/guarantees/index_sv.cfm?stid=1549.

[66]   Of course governments can and do use private instruments such as performance bonds to insure the performance of private contractors.

[67]   Visit: www.icsidworldbank.org/ICSID. The ICSID is discussed in chapter 6 in the context of foreign investment disputes, pp. 256–261.

States and Nationals of Other States.[68] The Convention entered into force on 14 October 1966 and sets out ICSID's mandate, organisation and core functions. The main purpose of ICSID is to provide facilities for conciliation and arbitration of international investment disputes. There are currently 155 signatory states to the ICSID Convention. Of these, 143 states have also deposited their instruments of ratification, acceptance or approval of the Convention to become ICSID Contracting States.[69] To date the ICSID has resolved 162 cases[70] and 125 are pending resolution. The number of cases submitted has multiplied every year.[71]

4.1.2.   Mandate, criticisms and its role in natural resource governance

Initially the Bank funded mostly infrastructure projects, especially those connected with transportation and electricity. In the 1960s the bank diversified into social projects and particularly into funding for policy reform and knowledge dissemination.[72] In the 1990s it became debatable whether the World Bank was actually needed or not. The growth of the private sector, both NGOs and business, with the increase of private capital flows challenged its role of directing flows of capital to less developed countries.[73] The World Bank responded to this takeover from private capital by refocusing its work on knowledge exchange and on helping countries in the creation of policies and business environments which would promote and attract foreign private capital.

The Bank has been criticised for the lip service that it pays to environmental and natural resource governance and the weakness of its procedures for stakeholder participation and monitoring within its agencies.[74] Despite the enormous effect that most projects in which the World Bank is involved have on the immediate environment for those concerned, consultation procedures are poor and EIAs and monitoring through project

---

[68]   The Washington Convention was adopted by resolution of the Executive Directors of the World Bank in 1965. The text of the Convention is published at 4 I.L.M. (1965) 524.

[69]   For general information on the ICSID see Schreuer, C. (2001), *The ICSID Convention: A Commentary*, Cambridge: Cambridge University Press.

[70]   Correct on 19 May 2009.

[71]   The ICSID dispute resolution procedure is discussed in chapter 6.

[72]   Stiglitz, J. (2002), 'Globalization and the Logic of International Collective Action: Re-examining the Bretton Woods Institutions', in Nayyar (2002), supra at 212.

[73]   Ibid., at 238. Stiglitz noted that most private capital went to a few countries and none of it to Africa.

[74]   See the discussion below and the case study on Indonesia and the Wilmar Audit at p. 192.

BOX 4.2.   THE NARMADA PROJECT AND THE WORLD BANK

India's most controversial dam project, the Narmada project, was first envisaged in the 1940s by the country's first Prime Minister, Jawaharlal Nehru, but several legal and logistical arguments between various Indian states delayed the project until 1979.

The multi-million dollar project involves the construction of some 3,200 small, medium and large dams on the Narmada River which originates in the central Indian state of Madhya Pradesh and empties into the Arabian Sea after flowing through Maharashtra and Gujarat states. The Sardar Sarovar is the biggest dam on the river and its construction has been fiercely opposed.

Controversy
The Narmada Bachao Andolan (Save the Narmada Movement – NBA), spearheading the protest, argued that the project would displace more than 200,000 people and damage the fragile ecology of the region. The dams will submerge forest farmland, disrupt downstream fisheries and possibly inundate and salinate land along the canals, increasing the prospect of insect-borne diseases. Some scientists have added to the debate saying the construction of large dams could cause earthquakes.

But those in favour of the project say that the project will supply water to 30 million people and irrigate crops to feed another 20 million people.

In what was seen as a major victory for the anti-dam activists, the World Bank withdrew from the Narmada project in 1993. An independent review, commissioned by the Bank and completed in June 1992, found that the resettlement and environmental aspects of the project were not being handled in accordance with Bank policies. Responding to the review, the Bank made its continuing support for the dam contingent on the borrower's achievement of performance standards for resettlement and economic rehabilitation of displaced people, and for environmental protection. In March 1993 the Bank cancelled the remainder of its loan for the project at the request of the Indian authorities. Several other international financial institutions also pulled out, citing human and environmental concerns. The construction of the Sardar Sarovar dam itself was stopped soon afterwards.

Source: Independent Evaluation Group, World Bank, 'Learning from Narmada', available at: www.lnweb18.worldbank.org.

implementation are weak, with a large discretion being given to private operators and companies in the execution of the environmental aspects of the project. The controversial Narmada Project led to the review of the Bank's participation procedures and the creation of an Inspection Panel.

The Bank influences natural resource governance through its policies which encourage pro-market reforms, the protection of investors and the privatisation of resources. For example the privatisation of water supply in Tanzania, Armenia, Zambia and India and the creation of large-scale commercial farms in Africa[75] have had serious environmental consequences, as do projects such as the Chad–Cameroon pipeline[76] or the Baku pipeline.[77] In Tanzania World Bank-supported privatisation of water services resulted in sharply higher water prices, little improvement in supply and the eventual termination of the contract with UK-based multinational Biwater in 2005. Biwater took Tanzania to arbitration in the ICSID[78] in a case in which investors' gains, expectations, stabilisation clauses and the human right to water had to be balanced by the tribunal. The Bank also plays a big indirect role in natural resource governance in those countries in which it operates through the lending of money to finance certain projects. Although its environmental record has been severely criticised it has begun to pay more attention to the environmental impact of its activities.[79] If initially the type of large-scale infrastructure

---

[75] A topic which has received recent renewed attention: The World Bank (2009), 'Awakening Africa's Sleeping Giant', *Prospects for Commercial Agriculture in the Guinea Savannah Zone and Beyond*, available at: www.siteresources.worldbank.org/EXTARD/Resources/336681-1231508336979/SleepingGiantFinal.pdf.

[76] www.foe.org/camps/intl/institutions/chadcameroon.htm.

[77] Discussed in chapter 6.

[78] *Biwater Gauff (Tanzania) Ltd v. United Republic of Tanzania* (ICSID Case No. ARB/05/22). On 24 July 2008, the arbitral tribunal issued its final decision in this case. The tribunal declared that the Tanzanian government had violated the terms of its bilateral investment treaty with the UK. However, the tribunal declined to award BGT the monetary damages requested.

[79] The World Bank has pulled out of several projects due to negative environmental consequences.

projects favoured by the Bank such as the Narmada project had serious environmental and social consequences,[80] today several initiatives such as its participation in the climate change funds[81] and tighter environmental and social controls over the effects of its lending suggest that the World Bank may play a positive role in development, natural resource governance and environmental protection.[82]

4.1.3.   Monitoring of the World Bank activities: the Compliance and Advisory Office (CAO)[83] and the Inspection Panel

The CAO is an independent office with direct reporting to the President of the WBG. Its main aim is to review complaints from communities affected by development projects undertaken by the private sector lending agencies, IFC and MIGA, about the social and environmental impacts. The Ombudsman's role is the main role of the CAO and its objective is to provide an accessible and effective mechanism of complaint to all persons affected or likely to be affected – either socially or environmentally – by an IFC or MIGA sponsored project.[84] The CAO's role is not to allocate blame but rather to identify the problems and offer practical remedial actions which will lead to a solution. Once a complaint is received it is fully assessed and the CAO will respond to the complainant with suggestions as to how to take the matter forward. The CAO has not the power to withdraw the IFC from a project. For example in the Bolivia–COMSUR complaint in respect of the Don Mario mine the CAO suggested that the IFC should contribute to capacity building of COMSUR in order to ensure that the rights of indigenous peoples and local communities were respected, and that consultation and participation channels were established, as well as compliance with environmental impact assessment according to international standards.[85]

---

[80]   Discussed below.

[81]   The Climate Investment Funds – the Strategic Climate Fund (SCF) and the Clean Technology Fund (CTF) – are a unique pair of financing instruments designed to support low-carbon and climate-resilient development through scaled-up financing channelled through the African Development Bank, Asian Development Bank, European Bank for Reconstruction and Development, Inter-American Development Bank and World Bank Group. See www.climateinvestmentfund.org/cif/ (accessed 15 January 2010).

[82]   Opschoor, H. (2005), 'Globalisation and Policies/Politics towards Sustainable Development in Developing Countries', in Wijen et al. (2005), supra, pp. 288–289.

[83]   http://cao-ombudsman.org/html-english/compliance.htm.

[84]   www.cao-ombudsman.org/html-english/ombusdman.htm.

[85]   www.cao-ombudsman.org/html-english/complaintCOMSUR.htm.

CAO-Compliance oversees project-level audits of the social and environmental performance of the IFC and MIGA. The focus is on how the IFC/MIGA assured themselves of the project's performance and that the policies, standards and conditions for the involvement of these agencies have been implemented. Compliance audits can be initiated by senior management of the IFC/MIGA, the president of the WBG or the CAO Vice-President or, more frequently, by transfer from a complaint to the ombudsman which has not been resolved.[86] The process starts by an appraisal by CAO-Compliance to assess whether an audit is merited. If it is, an audit will be opened and monitoring of the situation will start and continue until actions by IFC/MIGA move the project back into compliance. Then the audit will be closed.[87]

A close look at some of the cases where the CAO has initiated an audit shows a pattern whereby the monitoring of compliance procedures by both the IFC and MIGA were weak and inconsistent and there was a lack of channels of communication or procedures whereby interested and affected parties could be heard, either at the time of categorisation of projects, or later, during the monitoring process.[88] Defects were for example found on the Democratic Republic of Congo–Difushi Copper Silver Mine project,[89] where the audit pointed out that MIGA's due diligence with respect to security and human rights was compromised. Although MIGA followed its own underwriting assessment procedures it did not address whether the project would influence the dynamics of conflict in the region or whether security provision for the project could lead indirectly to adverse effects in the community. The follow up of its Environmental and Social Review Procedures (ESRP) was also found to be particularly weak.

The Inspection Panel was established by the Executive Directors of the International Bank for Reconstruction and Development (IBRD) and the International Development Association (IDA) on 22 September 1993. The primary purpose of the Inspection Panel is to address the concerns of

---

[86] Ibid.

[87] A list of projects currently under appraisal, under audit or with an audit already closed is available at the CAO-Compliance website, available at: www.cao-ombudsman.org.

[88] See, for example, the Brazil–Amaggi case where an audit into the categorisation in terms of environmental and social impact of a soya bean investment supported by the IFC was found to be defective. For details see www.cao-ombudsman.org/html-english/complaint_amaggi.htm.

[89] For full details of the audit and its background and related documentation see www.cao-ombudsman.org/html-english/DemocraticRepublicofCongo.htm.

BOX 4.3.   THE INDONESIA–WILMAR AUDIT

Representatives of 20 Indonesian and international NGOs filed a complaint in 2007 to the CAO Ombudsman with respect to a series of investments by the IFC in companies of the Wilmar Group, an agribusiness specialising in the production of palm oil, and the social and environmental effects that its operation was having. The claimants stated that Wilmar subsidiaries were not complying with national laws (a requirement of IFC policies and standards), that there were no social and environmental impact assessments or action plans publicly available for Wilmar subsidiaries, that the IFC did not give any attention to the policy of involuntary resettlements when assessing the projects or to the policies and guidelines on preserving biodiversity nor to prior policy on indigenous people.

Further adverse effects by Wilmar include clearance of primary forests, and of areas of high conservation value; the takeover of indigenous peoples' customary lands without due process; the failure to carry out free, prior and informed consultations with indigenous peoples which would have led to broad community support; failure to negotiate with communities or abide by negotiated agreements; failure to establish agreed areas of small-holdings; repressive actions by companies and security forces following social conflict due to the above actions; and clearance of tropical peat and forests without legally required permits.[1]

Note:
1.   www.cao-ombudsman.org/html-english/documents/CAO_Appraisal_
Report_C_I_R6_Y08_F096_II_ENGLISH.pdf.

---

the people who may be affected by Bank projects and to ensure that the Bank adheres to its operational policies and procedures during the design, preparation and implementation phases of projects.

The Inspection Panel consists of three members who are appointed by the Board for non-renewable periods of five years. Members are selected on the basis of their ability to deal thoroughly and fairly with the requests brought to them, their integrity and independence from the Bank management, and their exposure to developmental issues and living conditions in developing countries.

4.2.   The International Monetary Fund (IMF)

4.2.1.   Functions and mandate

The IMF is a specialised agency of the United Nations, with its own charter, governing structure and finances. The purposes of the IMF are defined in Article 1 of its Articles of Agreement[90] and include the promotion of monetary cooperation, exchange stability to avoid competitive exchange depreciation, the elimination of foreign exchange restrictions that hamper the growth of world trade and making the general resources of the Fund temporarily available under adequate safeguards and providing members with the opportunity to correct maladjustments in their balance of payments. The IMF has 185 member countries which are represented through a quota system based on their relative size in the global economy. This has given an unbalanced power to the big economies since each member's quota determines its voting power (the US, for example, has 16.83 per cent of the total voting power). The quota also determines the amount of financing which a member can obtain from the IMF. In general a member can borrow up to 200 per cent of its quota annually and 600 per cent cumulatively. This may be increased under exceptional circumstances. In May 2008 the IMF agreed on a rebalancing of the quota system to reflect changing global economic reality and increase the quota of countries like Mexico, China or India, but the system, is still heavily unbalanced.[91]

Its main operations can be divided into three groups: surveillance, technical assistance and financial assistance.[92] The deployment of these three operations has resulted in the IMF making money available to countries by imposing heavy conditions which have been blamed in many cases for economic and financial disaster in those countries. The IMF has encouraged financial austerity, reducing trade deficits and running surpluses, and with its draconian non-public expenditure conditions precipitated financial crises which have, ironically, made it much more likely that loans will not be repaid as the economies of those countries affected plummet. When the main borrowers from the IMF were the European countries in the post-war years conditionality was strictly rejected, and due to European opposition it was not included in the Articles of Agreement.

---

[90]   Adopted at the United Nations Monetary and Financial Conference, Bretton Woods, New Hampshire, 22 July 1944. Entered into force 27 December 1945, as amended.

[91]   The IMF is pressing ahead with what is envisaged to be a two-year process of reform designed to update the representation of members and modernise the voting systems. www.imf.org/external/pubs/ft/survey/so/2007/NEW057B.htm.

[92]   http://imf.org.

But as developing countries started to succeed European countries as borrowers conditionality crept in, as the political weight of the new customers could not match that of the countries of the old Europe. In 1952 the IMF started to apply conditionality in its loans, although as a principle it was not legally sanctioned until 1969 when the Articles of Agreement were reformed to include it.[93] In the 1980s the Bretton Woods institutions became not just financial institutions but policy drivers in all areas of political and social life in those countries which they lent to, and in doing so they eroded the democratic process. Amongst the most contested of the IMF's policies have been those which have encouraged (or forced, in many cases) capital and financial market liberalisation without ensuring that there is a sufficient regulatory framework or risk absorption capacity. Forced privatisation of state assets nearly bankrupted Argentina and led to the oligarchies in Russia,[94] while the state was deprived of sufficient income to run the most basic social services for its people.

4.2.2. Criticisms of the IFIs

Criticisms of the World Bank and IMF are extensive. Two criticisms merit special attention: the issue of conditionality in their lending and the undemocratic systems of internal governance of both institutions.

Conditionality had always been present in the Bank's lending. This tended to be focused on specific sectors to which the project related, but this approach changed in 1979. Throughout the 1980s the Bank imposed detailed and explicit conditionalities and began to focus on balance of payments problems, traditionally the realm of the IMF,[95] while the IMF moved closer to development financing and structural reforms.[96] Packages of IMF/WB support would demand fiscal and monetary austerity, devaluation of the currency, trade and financial liberalisation, privatisation, labour market de-regulation, tax reform and subsidies cuts, creating social problems and furthering poverty in many countries.[97]

The IMF has also been severely criticised in its handing of economic crises – in some cases created by its own misguided advice. But the most

---

    [93]   Jong-Il You (2002), 'The Bretton Woods Institutions: Evolution, Reform and Change', in Nayyar (ed.), supra, at 220.
    [94]   Stiglitz, J. (2006), *Making Globalisation Work*, London: Penguin, chapter 8.
    [95]   See for a good discussion of conditionality in the IFIs, Kapur, D. (1997), 'The new conditionality of the international financial institutions', *International Monetary and Financial Issues for the 1990s*, Vol. VIII, New York and Geneva: United Nations.
    [96]   Crook, C. (1991), 'The IMF and the World Bank', *The Economist*, 12 October.
    [97]   Jong-Il You (2002), supra, at 214.

important call for reform of the IMF is in its governance. The IMF is really not accountable in *any democratic* sense. IMF policies are not subjected to public scrutiny from independent bodies. For example the much maligned conditionality which has eroded democracy in many countries and reduced social spending creating humanitarian catastrophes is not subject to scrutiny by the country that is to receive the money. Talks remain confidential with finance ministers and secret to the outside world. The World Bank has got better monitoring mechanisms in place through its Compliance and Advisory Bureau (CAO) and the Inspection Panel (IP),[98] which allow for public participation and challenging of the Bank's procedures in its development projects if these do not comply with the Bank's own guidelines for social and environmental impacts.

It is also suggested that one of the problems of IMF operations is that it operates in conditions of monopoly, and as such it is inefficient. This monopoly gives the IMF an increased power as its decisions about lending to a particular country can have an inordinate weight with investors who may interpret a refusal to lend from the IMF as a sign that the country does not have strong or sound policies. In many cases countries which do not need the money are forced to agree to irrational and unjustified demands in the form of conditionality from the IMF in order to send a signal to international private investors that they have IMF approval.[99] A sad example of this power is reflected in the case of Ethiopia which, despite sound fiscal policies, fell out of favour with investors when the IMF stopped programmes after its government refused to proceed to a liberalisation which would have ruined its poor farmers by increasing the cost of borrowing.[100]

4.3.   International Financial Institutions: The Way Forward

Today the World Bank needs to redefine its primary task and focus on responding to the development crisis and providing capital to countries and sectors which do not have access to capital markets.[101] For the

---

[98]   Both discussed in this chapter.

[99]   This was the case of Chile, which had enough funds of its own but did not want to alienate foreign investors.

[100]   Although Stiglitz points out that political interests such as those of the US would have been behind this refusal of further funding since Ethiopia had, in a sound economic move, repaid an American loan early, but without first seeking US approval. See Stiglitz (2002), supra, at 247.

[101]   The literature on the redefinition and change of the World Bank is quite extensive. See among others Nayyar, D. (2002), 'The Existing System and Missing Institutions', in Nayyar (ed.), supra, at 363.

WB to be able successfully to focus its work on development and poor countries more representation of these countries in its governance model and better accountability channels are necessary. Currently most of the voting rights in the WB go to rich industrialised countries, while the main stakeholders are arguably those countries which are the direct beneficiaries of WB involvement and projects, and they have little say in terms of voting despite providing by their interest payments most of the Bank's actual capital. Voting systems need to be changed, perhaps to require a double majority which will require a majority of both quotas and votes.[102] Conditionality should also be abandoned and replaced by a partnership in which the diversity of local conditions is recognised and locals by local participation express their needs for development.

In order to break the IMF's monopoly some suggest that functions such as 'advice' or 'surveillance' can be carried out by other independent agencies, maybe at a regional level.[103] It may also be an area where civil society can participate and provide its expertise. Monitoring and compliance systems which ensure respect for human and environmental rights need to strengthen. While the World Bank's programmes are subject to review through the Inspection panel and the CAO,[104] for the IMF there is only a monitoring of a fund arrangements (MONA) database which contains the most comprehensive history of conditionality in IMF-supported programmes. Its publication was part of the IMF board's response to the Independent Evaluation Office's (IEO) criticisms of IMF structural conditionality.[105] But the MONA database is limited as it includes only data from loans where the letter of intent has already been made public by country authorities. It excludes conditions included in secret side letters and conditions from programmes before 2002. The IEO reviewed all of the Fund's lending operations between 1995 and 2004 and found that IMF programmes, for both middle- and low-income countries, had an average of 17 structural conditions.

5.   THE WTO

Since the inception of the multilateral trading system under the auspices of the limited GATT which sought to facilitate market access at the border

---

[102]   Woods, N. (1998), 'Governance in International Organisations: The Case for Reform of the Bretton Woods Institutions', *International Monetary and Fiscal Issues for the 1990s*, Vol. IX, Geneva: United Nations.

[103]   Stiglitz (2002), supra, at 249.

[104]   See above.

[105]   www.brettonwoodsproject.org/art559953.

for trade in goods, to the institutional machinery of the WTO, world trade has played a crucial role in the shaping of today's global economy. While the old GATT was restricted to the cross-border sale of goods and avoided intrusions into domestic policy, the WTO goes well beyond trade in goods. It encompasses trade in services and intangibles and has direct effects on the domestic policy of member states.[106] The Preamble to the WTO states several noble objectives to which its members commit: improved standards of living, full employment, expanded production and trade of goods and services, sustainable development and an enhanced share of participation of developing countries in world trade.[107] It aims to achieve those objectives by lowering barriers to trade between member states. Its mandate has extended from trade regulation to other international matters such as intellectual property or the protection of foreign investments. This expansive policy space has a detrimental effect on developing countries which have limited capacity to negotiate and understand these large agendas.[108] It also leaves a diminishing national space, with the consequence that populations across the world have to adhere to regulations they do not agree with.[109] Up to the Uruguay Round and the entry into force of the WTO in 1995, developing countries' commitment to free trade and their immersion into the system had been casuistic, but in 1995 with the Single Undertaking after any transition periods had expired developing countries became subject to all the rules and undertakings which had been previously agreed.

The WTO is based upon the general principles of reciprocity and non-discrimination[110] which crystallised round the most-favoured nation clause (MFN)[111] and the principle of national treatment.[112] These principles prohibit the parties to the WTO from having any rule or standard

---

[106] Narlikar, A. (2005), *The World Trade Organization: A Very Short Introduction*, Oxford: Oxford University Press, p. 2.

[107] For a detailed account of the WTO see Van den Bossche, P. (2008), *The Law and Policy of the World Trade Organization*, 2nd edn, Cambridge: Cambridge University Press.

[108] This was the case with the Singapore Issues, see Stiglitz, J. and A. Charlton (2004), *Fair Trade for All*, New York: Oxford University Press, p. 85.

[109] For example the regulation of GMOs: see Narlikar, supra, at 131.

[110] Article I.1. GATT.

[111] Article I of GATT, Article II of GATS. The most-favoured nation principle requires that if special treatment is given to the goods and services of one country, it must be given to all WTO member countries. No one country should receive favours that distort trade.

[112] Article III of GATT, Article XVII of GATS. The principle of national treatment requires that the goods and services of other countries be treated in the same way as those of the host country.

which is discriminatory or a disguised restriction to trade. Thus, the WTO agreements curtail the capacity of the countries to adopt national legislation which may become a 'unilateral restriction' or barrier to trade. There are exceptions, albeit limited. For example, the GATT allows national measures restricting trade if these measures are 'necessary to protect human, animal or plant life or health' or 'relating to the conservation of exhaustible natural resources'.[113] Such measures, however, cannot be 'applied in a manner which would constitute a means of arbitrary or unjustifiable discrimination between countries where the same conditions prevail, or a disguised restriction on international trade'.[114] If an environmental measure conforms to Article XX(b) or (g) and the chapeau of Article XX (i.e., no arbitrary or unjustifiable discrimination and not a disguised restriction), the measure may be allowed.[115] The measure should not be arbitrary or an unjustified discrimination, and multilateral (or bilateral, plurilateral) rather than unilateral restrictions or measures are encouraged.[116]

Its very successful Dispute Settlement System (DSS)[117] has encouraged some commentators to consider the WTO as a global model from which to construct the basis for a system of global governance.[118] This system of global governance will be modelled in many ways on the European Union which grew from a customs union in the 1950s to become the most successful model of political and economic integration. If this proposal were to be followed it would require an ever growing expansion of the organisation's mandate, and expansion which would not be met without disagreement by its current members. While developed countries have traditionally led the process of expansion of the WTO's mandate in order to fulfil their economic needs, developing countries find it difficult even to keep up to date with the existing agreements and oppose further matters becoming regulated by the organisation.[119]

---

[113] Article XX(b) and (g) of GATT, 1947, 55 U.N.T.S. 194.

[114] Article XX, Chapeau or preambular para.

[115] A similar exception is found in GATS: Article XIV(a), 'necessary to protect public morals or to maintain public order' and (b) 'necessary to protect human, animal or plant life or health'. This exception does not include any provision to conserve natural resources.

[116] See chapter 6, pp. 255–256 and chapter 8, pp. 354–357.

[117] Discussed in chapter 6.

[118] See, among others, Sampson, G.P. (ed.) (2002), *The Role of the World Trade Organisation in Global Governance*, Tokyo, New York and Paris: United Nations University Press.

[119] See Narlikar (2005), supra, at 129. Stiglitz and Charlton (2004), supra, pp. 86–89.

5.1. Trade and the Environment

The debate on the possible expansion of the WTO mandate is polarised not only between developed and developing countries. Some NGOs and civil society criticise the WTO's focus on trade and would like to see it operating in matters such as human rights, environmental protection, development, labour standards or gender equality[120] mostly due to its very effective DSS. Trade policy has been used under the current WTO system to enforce environmental standards. The *Shrimp/Turtle* case[121] addressed the issue of the role of the WTO in sustainable development[122] and the relationship between trade and environmental standards. In the case the US imposed unilateral measures which had the aim of preserving the turtle populations which were killed during shrimp fishing. The measures were found to be possible and consistent with the exception under Article XX(b) and (g) of the GATT[123] even though in this particular case they were found by the Appellate Body not to be acceptable under the WTO agreement because they discriminated between Asian countries (which brought the dispute) and Caribbean countries (which were given three years to adopt the measures).

Trade has also been used increasingly on multilateral environmental agreements as a tool for environmental protection,[124] raising questions about the relationship between the commitments under the WTO and commitments under multilateral environmental agreements. Different scholars have opposing views on the position of WTO rules vis-à-vis other provisions of international law. Van den Bossche summarises the debate on the relationship between WTO law rules and other international law (including environmental law) agreements into two main scholarly positions. At one end of the spectrum are those who think that in practice most WTO provisions should be able to be read in a manner which avoids

---

[120]   In all these aspects see Sampson (2002), supra.
[121]   Appellate Body Report WT/DS58/AB/R, adopted 6 November 1998.
[122]   In the preamble to the 1994 Marrakech Agreement the parties recognise that the institutional framework for the development of trade needs to take place in accordance with sustainable development and the protection and preservation of the environment.
[123]   Measures to protect human animal and plant life, Article XX(b), or conserve natural resources, Article XX(g). See chapter 6 for further discussion of the case.
[124]   For example by banning the use and trade of CFCs by the Montreal Protocol for the Protection of the Ozone Layer, or restricting trade of protected species in CITES or of hazardous waste by the Basel Convention.

conflict with other treaties.[125] At the other end are those who think that multilateral environmental agreements (MEAs) or human rights norms may often prevail over WTO norms since the obligations under the WTO agreements are essentially reciprocal in nature, and as such may be departed from by parties to a multilateral agreement if they do not infringe rights of third parties.[126] In the middle are those who argue that the answer lies within the general principles of public international law[127] as contained in the Vienna Convention on the Law of Treaties[128] and the general principle against conflict interpretation. It is important to note, though, that even if human rights rules or provisions of environmental protection from MEAs prevail over WTO rules it does not imply that a WTO panel will *apply* environmental or human rights provisions, as has been proposed by some authors.[129] These rules may constitute a defence against an allegation of breach of WTO provisions, but never serve to initiate a legal claim under the WTO Dispute Settlement Mechanism.

The situation is slightly more complex if one of the WTO members is not a signatory to the multilateral environmental agreement, and the outcome would very much depend on the nature of the MEA and the provisions which are sought to be enforced. It is thought that multilateral agreements may be applicable even to countries which have not signed them if these are of a global nature and reflect global consensus on a matter. An example of this would be the application of the Montreal Protocol prohibition of trade in CFCs which has been ratified by a majority of countries and over which there is a wide global consensus.[130]

---

[125]   On this matter see Marceau, G. (2001), 'Conflicts of Norms and Conflicts of Jurisidiction: The Relationship Between the WTO Agreement and MEAs and Other Treaties', Journal of World Trade, 35(6), 1129.

[126]   Van den Bossche (2008), supra, pp. 61–62 and Pauwelyn, J. (2003), *Conflict of Norms in Public International Law: How WTO Law Relates to Other Norms of International Law*, Cambridge: Cambridge University Press, 476–491.

[127]   'The WTO, its treaty provisions and their implementation confirm the absence of any hierarchy between WTO norms and those norms developed in other forums: WTO norms do not supersede or trump other international norms.' Lamy P. (2007), 'The Place of the WTO and its Law in the International Legal Order', European Journal of International Law, 17(5), 978.

[128]   Articles 30 and 31.3(c) Vienna Convention on the Law of Treaties.

[129]   See Petersmann, E.-U. (2005), 'Human Rights and International Trade: Defining and Connecting the Two Fields', in T. Cottier, J. Pauwelyn and E. Burgi (eds), *Human Rights and International Trade*, New York: Oxford University Press, 29.

[130]   See Birnie, Boyle and Redgwell (2009), supra, pp. 766–769.

5.2.   The WTO and Development: A Fairer Trade System

The WTO has focused on trade liberalisation and expansion, forgetting the creation of employment and the eradication of poverty, some of the objectives which it proudly stated in its Preamble. Trade has become an end in itself instead of a means to the end of development and prosperity, and this has resulted in a widening gap between poor and rich countries. The WTO recognises the special needs of developing countries through the 'special and differential treatment' provisions (SDT) which afford special rights to developing countries and allow developed countries to treat developing countries more favourably. But in general the WTO agreement and rules have been drafted by developed countries with their interests in mind, with a quick liberalisation of trade in goods of interest to developed countries (manufactures and services), but while liberalisation of labour-intensive goods (such as textiles) of interest mostly to developing countries lags behind.[131] In November 2001 the WTO deliberations in Doha focused upon the needs of developing countries in order to ensure, at last, that free trade could bring development, economic growth and a reduction of poverty. It was called the 'Doha Development Agenda'.[132] This development agenda contrasted starkly with the developments hitherto which had taken place in the WTO, clearly focused on the trading interests of developed nations like TRIPs and rules on intellectual property protection,[133] and the refusal to reduce tariff peaks and agricultural subsidies in OECD countries.[134] The development round of the WTO at Doha collapsed as developed countries refused to reduce or eliminate agricultural subsidies. In fact, in 2002, the USA doubled its agricultural subsidies with a new Farm Bill.[135]

The failure to conclude the Doha trade round has serious consequences which go well beyond the reduction of agricultural subsidies. The World Bank has pointed out that:

---

[131]   Stiglitz and Charlton (2004), supra, at 93.

[132]   See Hoekman, B. (2004), 'Developing Countries and the WTO Doha Round: Market Access, Rules and Differential Treatment', in B. Guha-Khasnobis (ed.), *The WTO, Developing Countries and the Doha Development Agenda: Prospects and Challenges for Trade-Led Growth*, New York: Palgrave Macmillan, pp. 10–33.

[133]   See chapter 8.

[134]   Hoeckman (2004), supra, p. 10.

[135]   Stiglitz (2004), supra, p. 80. The US spends $4 billion subsidising loss-making cotton production which could be imported from Africa at half the price. Farmers make up 1.7% of the US population. The European Commission spends 40% of its budget on an inefficient industry which employs 2% of the workforce.

> The Doha Round must be concluded not because it will produce dramatic liberalization but because it will create greater security of market access . . . [T]here are also environmental benefits to be captured, in particular disciplining the use of subsidies that encourage over-fishing and lowering tariffs on technologies that can help mitigate global warming. An agreement to facilitate trade by cutting red tape will further expand trade opportunities. Greater market access for the least-developed countries will result from the 'duty free and quota free' proposal and their ability to take advantage of new opportunities will be enhanced by the Doha-related 'aid for trade' initiative. Finally, concluding Doha would create space for multilateral cooperation on critical policy matters that lie outside the Doha Agenda, most urgently the trade policy implications of climate change mitigation.[136]

Reforms at the WTO and fairer trade agreements go beyond blanket reductions in subsidies. For example, the elimination of developed countries' agricultural subsidies will increase the price of agricultural products, which will benefit developing country producers of such products but will hurt those developing countries which import them. Impact assessment of how agreements are going to hit the least developed countries is thus necessary as implementation and adjustments costs are likely to be much higher in developing countries due to their high risk markets and lower social safety nets.[137]

Trade can and should promote development, but this would be possible only if a fairer trade system were to substitute for the existing one. This new system should allow access to technology for poor countries and fewer restrictions on labour mobility to match the almost unfettered mobility of capital.[138] To date the WTO has been described as a 'mercantilist institution that has worked on a principle of self-interested bargaining'.[139] A progressive agenda of trade integration could be based on the 'Doha Market Access Proposal'[140] which suggests a special and differential treatment for developing countries without marginalising them from the system or from the gains of South–South liberalisation. In general terms the proposal would involve providing free market access in all goods to all countries with a lower GDP per capita. This proposal requires significant

---

[136]　http://go.worldbank.org/Y9JT2CI8G0.
[137]　Ibid. at pp. 74–76.
[138]　Stiglitz and Charlton (2004), supra, at 67.
[139]　Ibid.
[140]　Based on Charlton, A. (2005), 'A Proposal for Special Treatment in Market Access for Developing Countries in the Doha Round', in J.M. Curtis and D. Ciuriak (eds), *Trade Policy Research*, Ottawa: Department of International Trade. See Stiglitz and Charlton (2004), supra, at 94–105 for a discussion of the MAP proposal.

South–South liberalisation from middle income countries and very little from the poorest ones. It also allows countries to protect their infant industries and to stagger adjustment costs.

6. REGIONAL INSTITUTIONS

Regional institutions vary enormously as to their role, functions and influence in global governance and on natural resource management. In theory regional institutions should present advantages over global institutions since they are closer to the local level and to the people they represent. The localisation of issues can mean that member countries are likely to share the same or very similar concerns, and it would be easier to make decisions and take action in respect of shared natural resources or about activities one of the consequences of which will be felt quite homogeneously within the region. Regional organisations also have the advantage of grouping states and peoples with a shared history, culture and in many cases ethnicity, making the possibility of transfer of powers to the organisation easier.

Of all regional organisations the most important in terms of scope, volume of trade and geopolitical influence in global affairs is the European Union. The European Union is unique in the measure of powers which states have transferred to the different European institutions and, despite critics, its very successful model supra-state integration. The range of activities and areas in which the EU legislates and its unique institutional structure deserve much longer and more detailed treatment than this book can afford, and therefore we will refer the reader to some of the main works in the area while making brief comments in those areas of legislation or actions in which the EU has shown unique leadership or initiative. Other regional institutions with variable degrees of integration in policies beyond trade are NAFTA, ASEAN and MERCOSUR and the different regional organisations in Africa such as ECOWAS, OAS and ECAS.[141]

The relationship between trade and the environment and the integration of environmental concerns into the trade agenda of free trade areas and other types of regional agreements present distinct characteristics in those cases such as ECOWAS, MERCOSUR and ASEAN in which all members

---

[141] See the United Nations Economic Commission for Africa (UNECA) and its work on African Regional integration at The Economic Community of West African States integrated by 16 members, http://ecowas.int/ for general and further information.

of a regional organisation are developing countries, and those regional institutions integrated mostly or solely by developed countries such as the EU. Developing countries are mostly worried about market access and their development needs and aspirations.[142] Their preoccupation about the environment revolves usually round how the environment can be preserved *without* affecting growth rates and liberalization.[143]

Free trade facilitated through regional (and global) agreements is also likely to produce more environmental destruction in developing countries, since their export structures are more likely to be based on natural resources (for example, agriculture, mineral extraction, timber)[144] and the level of domestic environmental protection and public concern is likely to be lower than in developed countries. When countries with different levels of environmental protection enter into a free trade agreement or other form of regional integration a process of adjustments takes place with compromises to be made, but in general with a tendency towards enhanced environmental protection.[145] We will look briefly at some of the main regional institutions in Europe, America and Asia due to their developments and work towards environmental protection.

6.1. Europe: The European Union (EU)

The EU is the most successful model of governance beyond national borders, with high degrees of integration and delegation of powers.[146] Although this model is impossible to replicate globally due to the diversity of cultures, interests, economic development and geopolitical history, some valuable lessons can be learnt from it and solutions extrapolated to other regional models. It is arguable that the model could be translated to the global sphere. The EU plays an active role in energy regulation, setting of environmental standards and natural resources protection. It is also one of the main political players on world trade.

---

[142]   See chapter 1, pp. 39–40.

[143]   Tushie, D. (ed.) (2000), *The Environment and International Trade Negotiations. Developing Country Stakes*, New York, St Martin's Press/ International Development Research Center, pp. 1–9.

[144]   In MERCOSUR for example agriculture, mining and energy products account for more than half of their total imports. See Hochstetler, K. (2003), 'Fading Green: Environmental Politics in the Mercosur Free Trade Agreement', Latin American Politics and Society, 45(4) (Winter), pp. 1–32.

[145]   Wijen (2005), supra, Introduction.

[146]   See in general on EU environmental law Lee, M. (2005), *EU Environmental Law: Challenges, Changes and Decision-Making*, Oxford: Hart Publishing.

The EC[147] shares the competence to negotiate treaties in environmental matters with its Member States. The EC Treaty contains many environmental provisions, especially in its Article 2 where it declares its commitment to a 'high level of protection and improvement of the quality of the environment'. The EC acts mostly by adopting legally binding regulations, directives and decisions[148] which are binding on either Member States or individuals depending on the instrument chosen. Proposals for regulations regarding the environment fall within the competence of the Commission. Its proposals are then considered by the Council and the European Parliament. The EC has adopted legislation in almost all areas of environmental policy. This legislation is adopted, mostly by majority of 70 per cent of the Member States, which makes the process much more dynamic than agreeing to international environmental standards according to the rules of public international law. The improved management of natural resources is one of the seven key challenges towards a sustainable development of the EU identified in 2006 by the European Council in the 'Renewed EU Sustainable Development Strategy'.

6.2. America: NAFTA

The North American Free Trade Agreement between Mexico, the United States and Canada entered into force on 1 January 1994.[149] The agreement was to remove most barriers to trade and investment among the United States, Canada, and Mexico.[150] One of its promises was that it would alleviate the pressure of illegal immigration as wealth would be redistributed towards Mexico. In practice the income differences between the two countries grew bigger in the first ten years of the agreement[151] as NAFTA eliminated tariffs to agricultural products but did not eliminate all other

---

[147]   After the Lisbon Treaty, the EU has legal personality (Art. 45 TEU) and would have exclusive competence for the conclusion of international agreements (Arts. 216–218 TFEU). See Steiner, J. and L. Woods (2009), *EU Law*, 10th edn, Oxford: Oxford University Press, p. 63.

[148]   Article 249 EC Treaty.

[149]   www.nafta-sec-alena.org/ (accessed 15 December 2009).

[150]   Under the NAFTA, all non-tariff barriers to agricultural trade between the United States and Mexico were eliminated. In addition, many tariffs were eliminated immediately, with others being phased out over periods of 5 to 15 years. This allowed for an orderly adjustment to free trade with Mexico, with full implementation beginning on 1 January 2008. See www.fas.usda.gov/itp/Policy/nafta/nafta.asp/.

[151]   See, for extensive criticism of the agreement on all fronts, www.citizen.org/trade/nafta/ (accessed 15 December 2009).

non-tariff measures, and heavily subsidised corn flooded Mexico, sending thousand of poor Mexican corn farmers into poverty. On the other hand when cheap Mexican tomatoes made a good break into the US market, Florida tomato growers pressurised the Clinton Administration and this threatened to take action on the basis of anti-dumping. As Mexico could not afford to defend the case in the Secretariat it agreed to increase the price, with the result that the Mexican tomato farmers lost their share of the market.[152]

In its Preamble it commits the parties to attaining the trade goals of the agreement 'in a manner consistent with environmental protection and conservation', while also including in NAFTA's goals that of promoting sustainable development and strengthening the development and enforcement of laws and regulations. The North American Agreement for Environmental Cooperation (NAAEC), sometimes referred to as the NAFTA Environmental Side Agreement, has been praised by some for its citizen submission process[153] which allows private individuals to trigger an official international investigation into a NAFTA government's failure effectively to enforce its environmental laws. Although it remains one of the most advanced institutional mechanisms aimed at addressing international environmental issues relating to trade liberalization and has been described by some as an example of an environmentally sensitive regional trade and investment agreement,[154] problems of transboundary enforcement remain to be solved.[155]

6.3.   Asia's Regional Integration: ASEAN

As world power, economic and strategic weights shift decidedly towards Asia the lack of institutional capacity of the region contrasts with its increased and unprecedented economic growth. Tensions revolve round the role of China in the region and its disproportionate economic weight

---

[152]   Stiglitz and Charlton (2004), supra, p. 64.

[153]   See Articles 14 and 15 of NAAEC. For citizens' participation in general see chapter 5.

[154]   Baughen, S. (2006), 'Expropriation and Environmental Regulation: The Lessons of NAFTA Chapter Eleven', Journal of Environmental Law, 18, 207.

[155]   Yang, T. (2004), 'The Effectiveness of the NAFTA Environmental Side Agreement's Citizen Submission Process: A Case Study of the Metales y Derivados Matter' (15 October) available at: SSRN: http://ssrn.com/abstract=552483 or DOI: 10.2139/ssrn.552483. See also chapter 6 for a general discussion on transboundary enforcement problems. Kibel, P. (2002), 'Awkward Evolution: Citizen Enforcement at the North American Environmental Law Commission', Environmental Law Reporter, 32, 7 at 14.

in relation to neighbouring countries. For many the inclusion of countries such as Russia and even the US would act as a power check and serve to balance interests. Discussed options include the creation of either a bilateral (China and Japan) or trilateral (+ South Korea) free trade area (EAFTA) which could potentially be extended to other members.[156] To date ASEAN has been dominating the institutional structure, although China's and India's economic and strategic power now eclipses the group. Perhaps a wider group such as EAS which could be expanded to include Russia and the US will serve to balance China's seemingly unstoppable power.

Established in 1967, ASEAN – the Association of South East Asian Nations – consists of ten member states, namely, Brunei, Cambodia, Indonesia, Laos, Myanmar, Malaysia, the Philippines, Singapore, Thailand and Vietnam.[157] The aims of the Association are to accelerate economic growth, social progress and cultural development in the region and to promote regional peace and stability. The ASEAN leaders view the protection of the environment and the sustainable use and management of natural resources as essential to the long-term economic growth and social development of their countries and the region. The ASEAN Vision 2020 calls for 'a clean and green ASEAN with fully established mechanisms for sustainable development to ensure the protection of the region's environment, the sustainability of its natural resources and the high quality of life of its peoples'.[158] ASEAN recognises the synergistic benefits in addressing common environmental problems on a regional basis, and has since 1977 developed a series of ASEAN Sub-regional Environmental Programmes (ASEP I, II, and III), followed by the Strategic Plan of Action on the Environment, 1999–2004 (SPAE). ASEAN Vision 2020 and the current Vientiane Action Programme 2004–2010 (VAP), the successor to the Ha Noi Plan of Action 1999–2004 (HPA), have further elaborated 12 strategies and 55 programme areas and measures to achieve the twin objectives of promoting environmental sustainability and sustainable natural resource management.

Half a billion people in ASEAN depend directly on access to natural resources for economic and social development and livelihood. In many

---

[156] 'The cause of regional integration in Asia faces better odds than in a long while', The Economist, 12 December 2009, p. 65.

[157] See www.aseansec.org/. The ASEAN region has a population of about 560 million, a total area of 4.5 million square kilometres, a combined gross domestic product of almost US$ 1,100 billion, and a total trade of about US$1,400 billion. Ibid.

[158] ASEAN Vision 2020, Kuala Lumpur, 15 December 1997, available at: www/aseansec.org/1814.htm (accessed 15 December 2009).

ASEAN countries, land resources and terrestrial ecosystems are under increasing stress due to growing population and extension of agricultural land into forest and other ecologically sensitive areas. This is compounded by pollution due to accelerated industrialisation and urbanisation in ASEAN member countries and other countries in the region, especially China. These environmental problems are complex in nature and transcend national boundaries which call for increased regional and global cooperation.

In the context of environmental governance, the ASEAN Way is generally typified by soft laws rather than hard laws. The burden of implementation, compliance and enforcement lies with the member states as there is no central ASEAN bureaucracy. A 'survey of ASEAN's efforts in the protection and management of natural resources in the region demonstrates more of a convergence than divergence, not so much in terms of integration (at least not in the context of environment – perhaps more in the economic field) but rather towards the harmonization of policies, programmes, plans of action, strategies and guidelines'.[159]

For the moment a lack of a definite institutional framework besides that of ASEAN makes it difficult to evaluate the importance that the proposed regional institution could have on natural resource management. With much of the focus on environmental matters, and not only in respect of climate change, turned towards China, it is clear that whatever form this regional institution will take it will be a crucial player on world trade matters. It rests only to hope that it will incorporate mechanisms for enforcement and compliance on environmental standards such as those of the NAAEC and be firmly rooted on the principles of sustainable development.

The Agreement Establishing the ASEAN – Australia – New Zealand Free Trade Area (AANZFTA)[160] will liberalise and facilitate trade in goods, services and investment between New Zealand, Australia and the ASEAN (Association of Southeast Asian Nations) economies. It contains

---

[159] Kheng-Lian Koh (2007), 'ASEAN Environmental Protection in Natural Resources and Sustainable Development: Convergence versus Divergence?', Macquarie Journal of International and Comparative Environmental Law, 4, 43, at 45.

[160] The AANZFTA will enter into force on 1 January 2010 for (and between) the following countries: Australia, Brunei, Malaysia, Myanmar, New Zealand, Singapore, the Philippines, and Viet Nam. It will enter into force for the remaining four ASEAN member countries (Cambodia, Indonesia, Lao PDR, and Thailand) 60 days after they provide formal notification of the completion of their internal ratification procedures.

measures to improve business flows and promote cooperation in a broad range of economic areas of mutual interest.

7.   CONCLUSION

Several problems afflict existing institutions. On the one hand there is a gap of powers either due to the principle of sovereignty retained by states and recognised in international law[161] or to the existence of private actors which operate largely unregulated.[162] On the other hand there is an overlap of functions within the existing institutions which results in inefficacy in respect of the goals and objectives sought. This is especially true in the area of natural resource and environmental governance and development and poverty alleviation, where UN agencies, the World Bank and private actors engage in sometimes conflicting programmes in a wasteful use of resources.[163] Moreover global institutions are not democratic and to date represent the interests of the richer and more powerful countries.

Global governance also needs to be inclusive of all actors that represent and shape the current world order. It also needs to be democratic. And today, looking at the existing institutions and rules we need to conclude that it is not. Developing countries with 80 per cent of the world's population and 50 per cent of the world's output have only a marginal voice in the existing global institutions. All the main institutions existing today suffer from this undemocratic system and all, unavoidably, produce unfair and asymmetrical rules. The UN is politically dominated by geopolitical groups and controlled by an obsolete post-World War II right of veto which blocks any possibility of effective global action. The WTO allows subsidies which distort an allegedly free trade system and leave intra-firm trade largely unregulated. The IMF and the World Bank with their unequal voting systems in their power structures are controlled by the US and a few other industrialised countries. Wherever we look we see an illegitimate, unfair but somehow pervading system which is much to blame for today's poverty and underdevelopment in the world.[164]

---

[161]   In this sense the UN has been described as a watchdog without teeth.

[162]   The ability of the IMF and WB to manage international liquidity is jeopardised by the international financial markets which are largely unregulated and outside the control of any state or international institutions, and by the growing number of private providers which overlap into their spheres of development and poverty reduction.

[163]   Nayyar (2002), supra, p. 9.

[164]   This assertion does not ignore the fact that developing countries could and

It does not come as a surprise that institutions dominated by a few countries produce rules that benefit mostly those countries. Since the financing of international institutions seems to be the key to holding power in the decision-making of these, there is a sense of urgency in looking for non-nationally bound systems of finance, which makes alternatives such as the Tobin tax extremely attractive.

In the area of management of natural resources the disparities of power between the different actors and their conflicting interests result in paralysis. This paralysis translates itself into the lack of a truly global organisation which could coordinate multilateral environmental commitments and serve as a forum for policy analysis, knowledge exchange and advice in natural resource management. Suggestions for such an institution have been made, but progress is slow and yet, without an institution backed up with an effective dispute settlement mechanism and enforcement procedures for the monitoring of compliance human development and well-being, become severely compromised. States needs to realise that trade cannot subsist, nor can development, without a proper and coordinated approach to management of the Earth's over-stretched, endangered and in many cases finite resources upon which all human life ultimately depends.

FURTHER READING

Bodansky, D., J. Brunnee and E. Hey (eds) (2007), *The Oxford Handbook of International Environmental Law*, Oxford and New York: Oxford University Press.

Desai, B.S. (2000), 'Mapping the Future of International Environmental Governance', Yearbook of International Environmental Law, 13, 21.

Desai, B.S. (2004), *Institutionalizing International Environmental Law*, Ardsley, NY: Transnational Publishers.

Charnovitz, S. (2002), 'A World Environmental Organisation', Columbia Journal of Environmental Law, 27, 323.

Esty, D.C. (2007), 'Global Environmental Governance', in C.I. Bradford Jr. and J.F. Linn (eds), *Global Governance Reform: Breaking the Stalemate*, Washington, DC: Brookings Institution Press, at 109.

Lee, M. (2005), *Environmental Law: Challenges, Change and Decision Making*, Oxford: Hart.

Nayyar, D. (ed.) (2002), *Governing Globalisation*, New York: Oxford University Press.

Petersmann, E.-U. (2005), 'Human Rights and International Trade: Defining

should do much internally to help themselves in areas such as governance, democracy and anti-corruption.

and Connecting the Two Fields', in T. Cottier, J. Pauwelyn and E. Burgi (eds), *Human Rights and International Trade*, New York: Oxford University Press, 29.

Sampson, G.P. (ed.) (2002), *The Role of the World Trade Organization in Global Governance*, Tokyo, New York and Paris: United Nations University Press.

Schrijver, N. (1997), *Sovereignty over Natural Resources*, Cambridge: Cambridge University Press.

Stiglitz, J. and A. Charlton (2006), *Fair Trade for All*, New York: Oxford University Press.

Van den Bossche, P. (2008), *The Law and Policy of the World Trade Organization*, 2nd edn, Cambridge: Cambridge University Press.

Veeman, S. and D. Liefferink (2005), 'Different Countries, Different Strategies: "Green" Member States Influencing EU Climate Policy', in F. Wijen, K. Zoeteman and J. Pieters (eds), *A Handbook of Globalisation and Environmental Policy. National Government Interventions in a Global Arena*, Cheltenham, UK and Northampton, MA, USA: Edward Elgar Publishing.

5. Multinational corporations, civil society and non-state actors: participation, governance and accountability

1. INTRODUCTION

The advances in communications and information technology that have been crucial in the development of the current phase of globalisation have also facilitated the emergence and empowerment of non-state actors: civil society, multinational corporations, NGOs and even indigenous peoples can communicate, conduct transactions and associate with a speed and ease that was unthinkable a few decades ago. Despite not having any formal recognition or having been devoted independent chapters in the main texts on international law or international environmental law, non-state actors play a crucial and growing role in all matters of policy formulation, monitoring and compliance at the international and national levels: 'with some recognised de iure rights non-state actors are de facto international actors for all intents and purposes'.[1]

Agenda 21, Chapter 27, paragraph 27.143 and Principle 10 of the Rio Declaration called for a greater role of non-state actors in enforcing international environmental law obligations in national courts, giving them an important role in ensuring compliance with agreed rules and standards.[2]

Multinational corporations (MNCs) have developed and grown in the last couple of decades to become powerful participants in global affairs and symbolise globalisation itself: the freedom to establish operations where production is most efficient in economic terms, the capacity to

---

[1] Sands, P. (2000), 'International Law, the "Practitioner and Non-State Actors"', in C. Wickremasinghe (ed.), *The International Lawyer as Practitioner*, London: British Institute of International and Comparative Law.

[2] The role of non-state actors in compliance procedures is examined both in this chapter and in chapter 6.

reach worldwide markets and the ability to operate beyond national borders in terms of production, workforce, distribution and sales. Their economic power translates into a political and social weight which, for the time being, is insufficiently regulated. MNCs are often blamed as profit driven and destructive in social and environmental terms, but they have the potential to be engaged in responsible global governance systems and to contribute to both social and economic development, sustainability and poverty eradication. In many cases MNCs are the only actors with sufficient technological know-how to be able to explore, access and exploit natural resources. This can be done in an environmentally friendly manner or not. Multinational corporations have also driven regulatory changes towards greater sustainability through voluntary codes of conduct (VCC) and can be engaged in sustainable responsible investment (SRI).

In this chapter we argue that multinational corporations are key to any effective system of global governance and to environmental protection. MNCs are capable of producing high levels of pollution but can also develop advanced technologies which contribute to positive environmental protection.

Individuals feel in many cases closer to those with common or shared interests through the activities of civil society organisations than to their own co-nationals. These networks have the potential to approach issues from non-state-centric perspectives, focusing on common or shared interests and can provide the much needed global solutions. Indigenous peoples have emerged in the current landscape of transnational action as important players in the struggle against both state governments and multinationals in defence of their way of living. Alliances are forged between NGOs, indigenous associations and individuals. Human rights and the development of participatory rights are at the core of much of the resistance against the dark side of globalisation.[3] But it is not only in the resistance against globalisation that NGOs and civil society play an important role. More dynamic arrangements such as those which include cooperative approaches to business and which may lead to joint standard setting or to the development or achieving of particular goals have also been developed in recent years.[4]

---

[3]   See, especially, chapter 3 of this book for a development of these themes.

[4]   Newell, P. (2001), 'Environmental NGOs, TNCs and the Question of Governance', in D. Stevis and V.J. Assetto (eds), *The International Political Economy of the Environment: Critical Perspectives*, Boulder, CO: Lynne Reinner Publishers, p. 85. These issues will be developed in this chapter.

2. MULTINATIONAL CORPORATIONS (MNCS)

2.1. What is a Multinational Corporation?

The growing literature on 'multinationals' and the varied instruments suggested for regulation and control suffer from a terminological disparity in the description of the phenomenon of corporate activity beyond national borders. In the economic literature the term 'multinational enterprise' is uniformly used to refer to 'any corporation which owns (in whole or in part), controls or manages income generating assets in more than one country'.[5] Economists favour the term 'enterprise' over 'corporation' due to the variety of forms (not just incorporated) that international production can take.[6]

Non-economists have not shown such a consistent preference for a denomination. The United Nations initially defined 'multinational corporations' as 'enterprises which own or control production or service facilities outside one country in which they are based. Such enterprises are not always incorporated or private; they can also be cooperatives or state owned enterprises.'[7] Later discussions led to the distinction between 'multinational corporations' (MNCs) – as enterprises owned and controlled by persons or entities of more than one country and 'transnational corporations' (TNCs) as those owned and controlled by persons and entities of one country but operating across national borders.[8] The OECD chose the term 'multinational enterprises' when it published its Guidelines for Multinational Enterprises[9] and defined them as 'companies or other entities established in more than one country and so linked that they may coordinate their operations in various ways'. This definition encompasses both uni-national enterprises with operations in other countries and firms of multiple national origins such as Royal-Dutch Shell. Multinational enterprises are firms which engage in foreign direct investment (FDI) outside their home country.[10]

---

[5] Dunning, J.H. (1993), *Multinational Enterprises and the Global Economy*, Wokingham, UK: Addison Wesley, 3–4.

[6] Muchlinski, P. (2007), *Multinational Enterprises and the Law*, 2nd edn, Oxford: Oxford University Press, at 5.

[7] Report of the UN Group of Eminent Persons, *The Impact of Multinational Corporations on Development and on International Relations*, UN Doc. R/5500/ Add1 (part I), 24 May 1974, at 25.

[8] Muchlinski (2007), supra, at 6.

[9] 1976 OECD Declaration on International Investment and Multinational Enterprises, Paris, 21 June 1976; 15 I.L.M. (1976) 967, 969.

[10] As opposed to enterprises which engaged only in portfolio investment. Muchlinski (2007), supra, at 5.

This terminological disparity reflects the variety of forms that the corporate form can take in transnational operations. Each nomenclature has the advantage of depicting one of the aspects of multinational corporate operations. We will use the term multinational corporation or multinational companies (MNC) since the corporate structure is used in most of, if not all, the situations which we will refer to in this book.

2.2. The Rise of the Multinational Corporation

The removal of trade and investment barriers within states heralded by the expansion and consolidation of the EC (which became the EU in 1992) and the signing of NAFTA between Canada and the USA (later extended to Mexico in 1992), provided a significant impetus to foreign direct investment. The removal of trade barriers coupled with the advances in technology and the speed of communications marked what commentators call the transition from a 'state-centred' world to a 'market dominated' world.[11] In trade terms a turbulent couple of decades of recession and rocketing fuel prices were followed by a 'new world order' epitomised by the creation of the World Trade Organization following the Uruguay Round of talks with its sophisticated dispute settlement mechanism, and its ancillary agreements on trade in services (GATS) and trade related intellectual property rights (TRIPS).[12] As globalisation progressed so did the power of multinationals, which could now establish operations and specialise production wherever labour was cheaper, more educated or plentiful or wherever environmental controls were lower.

The expansion of multinational corporations has been accompanied by a worldwide shared concern about their increasing power. On the one hand their economic superiority[13] puts MNCs above states, allowing them to impose demands on legitimately elected governments, creating

---

[11] Gilpin, R. (2002), *The Challenge of Global Capitalism*, Princeton, NJ: Princeton University Press, p. 22.

[12] About WTO see the discussion in chapters 1 and 4.

[13] Of the top 100 largest world economies 51 are corporations. The top 200 corporations generate 27.5% of the world's gross domestic product and their combined annual revenues are greater than those of the 182 states which contain 80% of the world's population. The combined sales of four of the largest corporations in the world exceed the gross domestic product of the whole of Africa. Shamir, R. (2002), 'Corporate Social Responsibility: A Case of Hegemony, and Counter-Hegemony' in B. Souza Santos and C. Rodriguez-Garavito (eds) (2005), *Law and Globalization from Below*, Cambridge: Cambridge University Press, p. 92.

concerns about sovereignty, power and economic dependency.[14] These concerns extend to both developed and developing countries: in developed countries big corporations influence law making through lobbying and the funding of political campaigns;[15] in developing countries bribery of officials and governments coupled with impositions made to governments faced with economic imperatives has put multinationals in the spotlight of anti-globalisation activists and NGOs for the little regard they pay to local populations or the environment and their complicity and participation in the violation of human rights.[16]

Tensions in the relationship between home states, host states and multinationals were expressed by the Economic and Social Council of the UN over 30 years ago as:

> Home countries are concerned about the undesirable effects that foreign investment by multinational corporations may have on domestic employment and the balance of payments, and about the capacity of such corporations to alter the normal play of competition.
>
> Host countries are concerned about the ownership and control of key economic sectors by foreign enterprises, the excessive cost to the local economy which their operations may entail, the extent to which they may encroach upon political sovereignty and their possible adverse influence on socio-cultural values. Labour interests are concerned about the impact of multinational corporations on employment and workers' welfare and on the bargaining strength of trade unions. . . . [T]he multinational corporations themselves are concerned about the possible nationalization or expropriation of their assets without adequate compensation and about restrictive unclear and frequently changing government policies.[17]

Muchlinski traces the mistrust of MNCs in Europe to the post-war years when many US corporations expanded business into war devastated Europe. Dislike of and opposition to the Americanisation of culture was big in continental Europe and has, to a large extent, lasted until today. For most Europeans multinational corporations were synonymous with American

---

[14]   Zerk, J.A. (2006), *Multinationals and Corporate Social Responsibility. Limitations and Opportunities in International law*, Cambridge: Cambridge University Press, at 7.

[15]   Ratner, S. (2001), 'Corporations and Human Rights: A Theory of Legal Responsibility', Yale Law Journal, 111, 443 at 462.

[16]   Korten, D. (1995), *When Corporations Rule the World*, Bloomfield, CT: Kumarian Press. See also the discussion below.

[17]   'The Impact of Multinational Corporations on Development and on International Relations', UN Doc. E/5500/Rev.1., ST/ESA/6 (New York: UN, 1974), 13 I.L.M. (1974), 800, p. 26.

corporate power.[18] At the end of the last century the balance between the host, the home state and MNCs had changed. Foreign investment became more difficult to obtain after the fall of the Soviet Union and a shift in the balance of power took place. Efforts in the 1970s which had sought greater economic equality and some historical justice for developing and resource rich states[19] turned round again, this time with MNCs as the clear winners.[20] The United States was elevated to the position of only superpower and extended the reach of its BITs to any country which sought to attract American money and investment, while it pushed for the signature of regional (NAFTA) and multilateral trade agreements which allowed the free flow of capital and investment with very little risk for Western investors. The number of BITs signed in the last 20 years has made most states vulnerable to be taken to international arbitration by an MNC – without further state consent and without having to exhaust the remedies offered by the domestic courts.[21] More importantly, due to the difference in economic power between the host state and the investor and the concentration of available investment in a few countries, a so-called race to the bottom took place whereby cash-strapped countries would seek foreign investment at any cost and would be willing to create a favourable climate to foreign investors which in some cases could amount to violations of the human rights commitments of the host state in respect of labour rights or environmental protection.

Weak corporate governance is combined with the corruption and cronyism that is widespread in many developing countries, which gravely distorts the efficient allocation of resources and the opportunity to compete on a level playing field, hindering both long-term development and ultimately investment in the host country.[22]

2.3. The Challenges: Regulating MNCs and the Relationship between MNCs and Human Rights

2.3.1. Regulating multinational corporations

The relationship between MNCs and states is important when formulating proposals for the regulation of MNCs. Multinationals are often

---

[18] Muchlinski (2007), supra, at 15–17. Zerk (2007), supra, at 9, cites a study of European public opinion which reflected a perception that most multinationals were American (meaning North American) or based on an American model.

[19] See 'Introduction', pp. 5–7.

[20] Ratner (2001), supra, at 458.

[21] See chapter 6, pp. 257–261.

[22] Lodge, G. and C. Wilson (2006), *A Corporate Solution to Global Poverty*, Princeton, NJ: Princeton University Press, p. 140.

identified with the interest of the state of origin or the 'home' state.[23] However what emerged from the globalisation and post-globalisation era was a conception of multinational corporations as stateless entities. '[T]he Multinational Enterprise (MNE) . . . has been described as a challenge to the nation-state, a creature with no loyalties except to itself, an entity that caused economic, social and political disruption in both the host and the home countries, and that aimed to global dominance . . .'.[24] Multinationals have become more and more independent of any state's control. They may have their headquarters in one country but their majority shareholders may be based in another and the bulk of their operation in a third or fourth country. Laws liberalising companies' registration and foreign investment have paved the way for a race to the bottom in all aspects of multinational companies' establishment and operations. MNCs are often registered in countries where taxation is favourable to them, where company laws are suitable and where the total economic cost of the operation is more afford-able. They do not 'belong' to any country in many cases, and talking about the 'home' state may be a reminiscence of the past when in colonial times companies, i.e. the Royal Dutch company, were effectively based in one country even if they operated abroad. This independence makes states wary of imposing regulations and of enforcing them against corporations which only 'on paper' have domicile in their jurisdictions, particularly for acts committed abroad.[25] Companies know that, and in many cases have questioned the duties and rights of the state.[26] However, it is also arguable that MNCs and states are closely connected and that states do much to pave the way for the smooth operation of MNCs.[27] These two contrasting views are both articulated in the piecemeal regulation on MNCs and the tortuous channels for ensuring their accountability.

In the 1970s, coinciding with a growth in MNC expansion and with

---

[23]   Barnet, R. and R. Muller (1974), *Global Reach: The Power of the Multinational Corporations*, New York: Simon & Shuster, p. 75. For example revelations about United Fruit Company's and International Telephone and Telegraph's roles in destabilising, respectively, the governments of Guatemala in the 1950s and Chile in the early 1970s shows a pursuit of US political interests.

[24]   Muchlinski, P. (1999), *Multinational Enterprises and the Law*, Oxford: Blackwell, p. 7.

[25]   See chapter 6, litigation against MNCs, pp. 276–285.

[26]   Strange, S. (2004), *The Retreat of the State: The Diffusion of Power in the World Economy*, Cambridge: Cambridge University Press, at 49–50.

[27]   See McCorquodale, R. and P. Simmons (2007), 'Responsibility Beyond Borders: State Responsibility for Extraterritorial Violations by Corporations of International Human Rights Law', MLR 70, 598–625. This is discussed in chapter 6.

the approval of the NIEO, attempts were made to regulate corporations at the international level. Work on a Draft Code began at the UN;[28] the OECD in 1976 issued a set of Guidelines on Multinational Enterprises;[29] and in 1977 the ILO Tripartite Declaration of Principles Concerning Multinational Enterprises and Social Policy was published.[30] The UN Draft Code, while recognising some rights for investors, emphasised the need for foreign investors to obey host country law, follow host country economic policies, and avoid interference in the host country's domestic political affairs. By contrast the OECD Guidelines were much more biased in favour of investors and were, in addition, non-mandatory.

None of them resulted in a binding code or set of principles, and a change in political and economic direction in the 1980s and 1990s displaced the focus of international institutions from trying to control and regulate corporate activity towards facilitating capital movements and investment as capitalism grew global. Parallel to developments on the regulation of world trade, negotiations on a Multilateral Agreement on Investment (MAI) were launched by governments at the Annual Meeting of the OECD Council at ministerial level in May 1995. The proposed objective of the MAI was to provide a broad multilateral framework for international investment, with high standards for the liberalisation of investment regimes and investment protection with effective dispute settlement procedures. The MAI was so biased towards multinationals and their interest that it encountered fierce opposition in both developed and developing countries.[31] Critics point out that the MAI was an 'essentially anachronistic instrument based on old perceptions of the inventor and investor protection belonging to the decolonization period'.[32] Perhaps the most obvious of the imbalances proposed by the MAI came from its proposed enforcement and compliance regime. In addition to placing serious restrictions on a country's ability to favour domestic industries or

---

[28]   Draft United Nations Code of Conduct on Transnational Corporations, UN ESCOR, Spec. Sess., Supp. No. 7, Annex II, UN Doc. E/1983/17/Rev.1 (1983).

[29]   This was annexed to the 1976 OECD Declaration on International Investment and Multinational Enterprises, Paris, 21 June 1976, I.L.M. (1976) 15 967, 969.

[30]   17 I.L.M. (1978) 422.

[31]   McDonald, J. (1998), 'The Multilateral Agreement on Investment: Heyday or Mai-Day for Ecologically Sustainable Development', Melbourne University Law Review 22, 617; Friends of the Earth (1999), 'The World Trading System: Winners and Losers', November, available at www.foe.co.uk/campaigns (last accessed 15 November 2009).

[32]   Muchlinski, P. (2000), 'The Rise and Fall of the Multilateral Agreement on Investment: Where Now?', International Lawyer 34, 1033, esp. 1049.

place restrictions on foreign direct investment in any sectors, for example water or energy which it wanted to keep under national control, the MAI extended a rule existing in many BITs whereby multinationals can take states to the World Bank's ICSID should they pass any laws to enforce tighter environmental or social controls, on the basis that those measures will diminish their profit and may be termed indirect expropriations.[33] This was a missed opportunity for devising a multilateral instrument which would regulate multinational corporations' actions.

At the same time worries about the increased numbers of violations of human rights committed in the context of multinational corporations' operations, be it by the companies themselves, by the host state where the companies operate, or by a combination of state and corporate activities, brought the issue of the relationship between multinationals and human rights to the forefront of international attention. The last two decades have seen an increase in the resort to human rights to protect individuals, not only against state action but also against the actions of multinational corporations.[34] As private actors encroach into areas previously reserved for public powers it is necessary to accommodate claims against abuses committed in this context in the current human rights system.[35] Clapham builds upon these important trends, in terms of both direct and indirect duties on private entities to respect human rights, to support a human rights regime which challenges exclusive focus on the state:

> [T]he emergence of new fragmented centres of power, such as associations, pressure groups, political parties, trade unions, corporations, multinationals . . . and quasi-official bodies has meant that the individual now perceives authority, repression, and alienation in a variety of new bodies . . . This societal development has meant that the definition of the public sphere has had to be adapted to include these new bodies and activities.[36]

2.4.   Corporate Social Responsibility and Voluntary Codes of Conduct

As attempts to regulate MNCs internationally failed due to political opposition from the developed countries, most of them home countries

---

[33]   Ibid.

[34]   Clapham, A. (2006), *Human Rights Obligations of Non-State Actors*, New York: Oxford University Press, esp. pp. 195–270.

[35]   Some of the approaches to this problem are discussed in chapter 6 in the context of state responsibility for acts committed by MNCs, and litigation in domestic courts for human rights abuses committed by MNCs.

[36]   Clapham, A. (1993) *Human Rights in the Private Sphere*, New York: OUP, p. 157.

to MNCs, and to pressure from MNCs themselves, a new concept – that of allowing companies to regulate themselves – grew in popularity during the 1990s. Corporate Social Responsibility (CSR) and Voluntary Codes of Conduct (VCC) emerged as the answer to the vacuum of regulation of MNCs.[37] Companies and governments of countries like the US and the UK – capital exporting countries – gave their prompt and full support to the initiative. After disasters such as Bhopal[38] or the public outcry after the involvement of Royal-Dutch Shell in Nigeria in the assassination of Ogoni leader and activist Ken Saro-Wiwa,[39] multinationals have been in the spotlight of consumer, activist and NGO attention and have seen their reputation and profits endangered by public pressure. They are thus particularly keen to be seen as drivers of progress and good practice in their particular industry and see CSR initiatives and VCC as powerful tools which will enable them to control their own regulation in certain areas of activity while providing essential PR tools for improving their image and attracting investors.[40]

Codes of conduct can be divided into five main types: company codes, trade association codes, multi-stakeholder codes, model codes and intergovernmental codes. Codes vary considerably in scope. Many do not even cover all of the International Labour Organization's core labour standards. Company codes and trade association codes often have a more limited scope than those developed in conjunction with other stakeholders. There are also differences in the coverage of codes. Although many do cover the firm's suppliers, they often do not extend all the way along the supply chain, and very rarely cover home-based workers. Provisions for the implementation of a particular code, and for effective monitoring, are crucial if it is to have any real impact, but only a small proportion of codes make provision for independent monitoring.[41] Problems with regulation

---

[37] See also chapter 2 for a discussion on voluntary instruments in natural resource management, pp. 111–116.

[38] Visit http://Bhopal.com/ for information about the disaster and links to legal documents. The case also is discussed in chapter 6 in the context of jurisdiction over MNCs.

[39] Shell now has a webpage on 'Safeguarding human rights' despite accusations of its involvement in human rights abuses in Nigeria. Visit www.shell.com/home/content/responsible_energy/society/using_influence. . ./human_rights/dir_human_rights_16042007.html. The company stood trial in New York in May 2009 for alleged collusion in human rights abuses dating back to the 1995 hanging of the writer and activist Ken Saro-Wiwa. He had campaigned against Shell's operations in his native Niger Delta region.

[40] See criticism of CSR at pp. 275–276.

[41] Jenkins, R. (2005), 'Corporate Codes of Conduct: Self Regulation in a

of MNC activities through voluntary codes of conduct are discussed in the context of some of the attempts to devise codes of international reach.

2.4.1. Companies and human rights, from violations to 'human rights entrepreneurialism'

While the relationship between human rights and corporations remains controversial and a large proportion of people reflect the direct or indirect involvement of multinationals in human rights violations, the concept of 'human rights entrepreneurialism' has been coined to describe the new trend on voluntary commitments and declarations of adherence to human rights by companies.[42]

> The issue of human rights is central to good corporate citizenship . . . [M]any companies find strength in their human rights records; others suffer the consequences of ignoring this vital part of corporate life. Today, human rights are a key performance indicator for corporations all over the world.
>
> One of the great ironies of this period in history is that, just as technology remakes our world, the need to maintain the human dimension of our work, and a company's sense of its social responsibility, is growing at an equally rapid pace. Harmonizing economic growth with the protection of human rights is one of the great challenges we face today. It is a challenge which, if met, can harness the great power of economic growth to the great principle of human dignity . . .'[43]

Multinationals now voluntarily proclaim some commitment to human rights even if their report of performance is uneven. The oil and gas sector has been among the leading industries in championing corporate social responsibility (CSR):

> [O]il companies have initiated, funded and implemented significant community development schemes . . . [O]il companies now help build schools and hospitals, launch micro-credit schemes for local people and assist youth-employment development programmes in developing countries. They participate in partnerships with established development agencies such as the United States development agency (USAID) and the United Nations Development Programme

---

Global Economy', United Nations Research Institute for Social Development (UNRISD), at 44, available at: www.elsis.org/static/DOC 9199.htm.

[42] Steinhardt, R. (2005), 'Corporate Responsibility and the International Law of Human Rights: The New Lex Mercatoria', in P. Alston (ed.), *Non-State Actors and Human Rights*, New York: Oxford University Press, at 5.

[43] 'Business and Human Rights: A Progress Report'. Preface by Mary Robinson, UN High Commissioner for Human Rights, available at: www.unhchr.ch/business.htm#preface.

UNDP, while using NGOs to implement development programmes on the ground.[44]

A good example is provided by Chevron, denounced by several campaigners and NGOs as one of the worst corporate human rights violators, it having been involved in litigation in respect of its operations in Burma, Nigeria and Ecuador,[45] but which has launched a website proclaiming its commitments to human rights.[46] Shell, another company involved in some of the worst allegations of human rights violations and pollution,[47] has also launched an eye-catching website,[48] while standing trial in New York[49] in May 2009 for alleged collusion in human rights abuses dating back to the 1995 hanging of the writer and activist Ken Saro-Wiwa. Shell also faces legal action in the Netherlands, the first time the Anglo-Dutch energy group has had to defend itself in a Dutch court. Friends of the Earth Netherlands and Nigerian plaintiffs are bringing an action over repeated oil spills in the Niger Delta.[50]

While national regulation of multinational corporations' activities is uneven and erratic due to economic constraints and the need for foreign investment, critics of voluntary mechanisms stress in the first place the vagueness of the principles and their non-binding nature.

---

[44] Frynas, J.G. (2005), 'The False Developmental Promise of Corporate Social Responsibility: Evidence from Multinational Oil Companies', International Affairs, 81, 581–598, at 581.

[45] http://www.globalexchange.org/getInvolved/corporateHRviolators.html.

[46] http://www.chevron.com/globalissues/humanrights/. The website proclaims 'Chevron's Human Rights Statement, adopted in 2006, reaffirms our long-standing support for universal human rights' . . . adding 'While the ultimate responsibility for protecting human rights rests with governments, Chevron also has a role to play.'

[47] See amongst others Okonta, I., O. Douglas and G. Monbiot (2003), *Where Vultures Feast: Shell, Human Rights and Oil*, London and Brooklyn, NY: Verso, for an excellent account of the tragedy in Nigeria's oil exploitation by foreign multinationals, and Shell in particular.

[48] www.shell.com/home/content/responsible_energy/society/using_influence.../human_rights/dir_human_rights_16042007.html.

[49] On 26 May 2009, oil multinational Shell stood trial in a Federal District Court in New York for complicity in human rights abuses in Nigeria, including the summary execution of writer and activist Ken Saro-Wiwa and eight of his Ogoni colleagues on 10 November 1995. The other charges against Shell included complicity in crimes against humanity, torture, arbitrary arrest and detainment. This landmark human rights case was filed by the US based Center for Constitutional Rights (CCR) and Earth Rights International (ERI).

[50] Smith, K. (2009) 'Ken Saro-Wiwa: The day of truth?', The Guardian, 19 May, available at: www.guardian.co.uk.

BOX 5.1.   CORPORATE SOCIAL RESPONSIBILITY
AND BRITISH PETROLEUM

'In recent years, British Petroleum (BP) has been working hard
to remake its public image. Their well-crafted print and television
ads feature upbeat electronic music and a vibrant new yellow
and green starburst logo. With its cutting-edge content on human
rights, biodiversity and macro-economic theory, their website is
designed to look like that of a developmental think-tank.

In reality, BP is the world's third largest oil and gas company
and one of the largest polluters on the globe. Exploration and
production of crude oil and natural gas are the company's main
activities and it operates in 100 countries in Europe, North and
South America, Asia and Africa. Its revenues for 2003 were over
$16 billion; its profits were over $10 billion. BP's profits come with
enormous human cost and environmental damages.'

Source: Hannan Ellis, Corporate Watch, June 2005, available at: www.corp-
watch.org/articlephp?id=12340.

'Good governance, good citizenship, or social responsibility can mean
anything to anyone'.[51] For many, CSR is nothing more than a new and
effective public relations instrument used by corporations to improve
their damaged public image in front of Western consumers.[52] Voluntary
codes of conduct, furthermore, can act as deflection devices which fail
to address the underlying issues or change any of the situations that
produce problems while producing positive and valuable publicity for
MNCs.[53]

2.4.2.   The UN Global Compact
In 1999 Kofi Annan (then UN Secretary-General) launched the Global
Compact in order to encourage corporations to commit to following a
minimum list of principles in their activities.[54] The Global Compact is
not a regulatory instrument but a voluntary initiative. It relies on public

---

[51]   Addo (1999), supra, p. 14.
[52]   Rowell, A. (1996), *Green Backlash*, London: Routledge, at 105.
[53]   Dine (2005), supra, especially chapter 2.
[54]   See www.unglobalcompact.org.

accountability, transparency and disclosure to complement regulation.[55] It seeks to align business practices with ten universally accepted principles of human rights, labour, environment and anti-corruption. It relies on companies voluntarily signing up to it and contributing financially to its work. The Global Compact asks companies to embrace, support and enact, within their sphere of influence, a set of core values in the areas of human rights, labour standards, the environment, and anti-corruption. The principles derive from the Universal Declaration of Human Rights,[56] the International Labour Organization's Declaration on Fundamental Principles and Rights at Work of 1998, the 1992 Rio Declaration on Environment and Development[57] and the United Nations Convention Against Corruption.[58]

The Global Compact is a multi-stakeholder instrument which seeks to bring together business, civil society, labour organisations and the United Nations in ensuring that business advances in a way which benefits economies and societies worldwide and that corporations are not complicit in human rights abuses. It has been criticised on several fronts with arguments ranging from its misuse by MNCs for 'bluewashing' without actually changing their practices,[59] to the lack of actual enforcement mechanism or sanctions for those who do not comply with the principles. While these allegations are undoubtedly true it is important to remember that the Compact is not a regulatory instrument as such, and the imposition of sanctions is beyond its realm. It is also important to realise that the imposition of too high a threshold for companies to adhere to would have a detrimental effect, and while monitoring procedures could and probably should be improved its value resides in bringing awareness of the implications that corporate action has over human rights and the

---

[55] www.unglobalcompact.org/docs/news_events/8.1/GC_Brochure_FINAL. pdf, at 2.

[56] Universal Declaration of Human Rights, GA. Res. 217A (III), UN Doc. A/810 at 71 (1948).

[57] UN Doc. A/CONF.151/26 (vol. I); 31 I.L.M. (1992) 874. Rio Declaration on Environment and Development (1992) adopted by the UN Conference on Environment and Development (UNCED). UN Doc. A/CONF.151/26 (Vol. I) (1992).

[58] UN GA, United Nations Convention Against Corruption, 31 October 2003, A/58/422, available at: www.unhcr.org/refworld/docid/4374b9524.html (accessed 20 January 2010).

[59] Companies like Bayer which subscribe to the Global Compact have been accused of using powerful and damaging pesticides and of lobbying against the introduction of generic drugs which would endanger their profits. Bigge, D.M. (2004), 'Bring on the Bluewash', International Legal Perspectives, 16, 6.

environment and on providing a forum for information and best practice sharing.[60]

2.4.3. OECD Guidelines on Multinational Enterprises

The origin of the OECD Guidelines[61] (the Guidelines) can be tracked down to two different sets of reasons. The first was a reaction in the 1970s against the wave of nationalisations and controls that newly independent countries sought to impose on foreign MNCs in the context of the New Economic International Order.[62] The U.S., especially, sought a form of MNC regulation which would move away from MNC control after the UN Economic and Social Council set up a commission with the task of creating a binding Code of Conduct for Transnational Corporations.[63] At the same time some OECD countries[64] and the Trade Union Advisory Committee (TUAC) wanted stricter control and regulation of the operations of MNCs.[65]

The Guidelines are addressed to multinational 'enterprises' operating in or from the 33 adhering countries and are to be applied to business operations worldwide. They are intended to 'supplement' the applicable law and to 'complement and reinforce' codes of conduct and other private efforts to implement responsible business conduct. The first chapter is careful to state that 'Governments adhering to the guidelines should not use them for protectionist purposes nor use them in a way that calls into question the comparative advantage of any country where multinational enterprises exist'.[66] The revised Guidelines have added human rights obligations in the context of general policies. The Guidelines have been criticised on several fronts. They are non-binding under international or

---

[60] On the Global Compact see, Petersmann, E.U. (2002), 'Time for a United Nations "Global Compact" for Integrating Human Rights into the Law of Worldwide Organisations: Lessons from European Integration', EJIL 27, 621; Oshionebo, E. (2007), 'The UN Global Compact and Accountability of Transnational Corporations: Separating Myth from Realities', Florida Journal of International Law, 19, 1; Ruggie, J. (2001), 'The Global Compact as Learning Network', Global Governance, 7, 371.

[61] The first version was published in 1976 and is reproduced in 15 I.L.M. (1976) 961–980. The current version (at the time of writing) is from 2000 and can be found at www.oecd.org/dataoecd/56/36/192248.pdf.

[62] See 'Introduction', p. 5, and chapter 1, p. 47.

[63] Muchlinski (2007), supra, at 659.

[64] Canada, Holland and the Scandinavian countries.

[65] Muchlinski (2007), supra, 118.

[66] 'Business and Human Rights: An Update', www.unhchr.ch/businessupdate.htm.

national law but at the same time are imposed externally defeating the purpose of 'self-regulation'.[67] They ignore the problem of the status of corporations under international law and 'their adherence to "the wider principle of sustainable development" makes it difficult to imagine how companies that are driven by the underlying principle of maximising shareholder profit can or should assume a vague notion of redistributional equity'.[68] But perhaps the biggest criticism is that they do not establish any basis on which responsibility can be imposed on companies which fail to fulfil the Guidelines.[69]

2.4.4.   The UN Norms on the responsibilities of transnational corporations and other business enterprises with regard to human rights[70]

A further attempt to regulate the responsibility of corporations for human rights violations was the publication in 2003 of the UN Norms following criticism that instruments such as the Global Compact were ineffective and that violations of human rights increased at an alarming rate. 'The Norms' received a mixed response which ranged from an endorsement from several NGOs[71] and academics[72] as an appropriate basis to develop corporate accountability to severe criticisms.[73] Governments in both the developed and developing countries reacted negatively to them on the

---

[67]   They are, in the words of Dine, 'a form of outside exhortation that is unlikely to be effective'. Dine, J. (2005), *Companies, International Trade and Human Rights*, Cambridge: Cambridge University Press, p. 237.

[68]   Ibid., 237–239.

[69]   See ibid. and Addo, M. (1999), *Human Rights and Transnational Corporations*, The Hague: Kluwer International, p. 14 on the basis for attributing social responsibility to companies as first an extension of individual responsibility and, second, an attribution of responsibility to the company itself as an independent entity capable of exercising control and making decisions.

[70]   UN Sub-Commission on the Promotion and Protection of Human Rights, Norms on the responsibilities of transnational corporations and other business enterprises with regard to human rights, UN Doc. E/CN.4/Sub.2/2003/12/Rev.2 (26 August 2003).

[71]   Amnesty International, Human Rights Watch and the International Commission of Jurists were amongst those who supported the norms. See Steiner, H. and P. Alston (2007), *International Human Rights in Context*, New York: Oxford University Press, at 1404.

[72]   Kinley, D. and R. Chambers (2006), 'The UN Human Rights Norms for Corporations: The Private Implications of Public International Law', Human Rights Law Review, 6, 447.

[73]   Baxi perhaps being one the most vocal of the critics, see Baxi, U. (2005), 'Market Fundamentalisms: Business Ethics at the Altar of Human Rights', Human Rights Law Review, 5, 1; and discussion in Steiner and Alston (2007), supra, at 1404–1405.

basis that they were either unnecessary, overreaching or would impair their chances of economic development.[74] The UN Commission on Human Rights responded by appointing a Special Representative, John Ruggie, on the issue of human rights and transnational corporations. In his critical initial report[75] he pointed out that the Norms did not differentiate adequately between responsibilities of states and responsibilities of corporations, imposing in many instances higher obligations on the latter than on states.

In his final report[76] Ruggie identified four main problems in the area of human rights and multinational corporations. The first problem is that voluntary accountability mechanisms are too varied and dispersed, which only creates frustration and lack of certainty about their value, effects and standing. Secondly, there is a lack of generalised market participation in existing mechanisms. This particularly applies to firms from emerging markets, notably China, but there are plenty of laggards in industrialised countries. Third, there are no viable grievance and alternative dispute settlement mechanisms in the area and, last, he found out that very few firms conduct human rights impact assessments (HRIAs).

> [F]or business with large physical or societal footprints, accountability should begin with assessments of what their human rights impact will be. This will allow companies and affected communities to find ways of avoiding negative impacts from the start. . . . [O]nly one company, BP, has ever made public even a summary of an HRIA. No single measure would yield more immediate results in the human rights performance of firms than conducting assessments when appropriate.[77]

Some of the above findings, especially that pointing out the absence of suitable mechanisms for settlement of disputes, have encouraged scholars to argue that a World Court of Human Rights to which non-state actors could become parties is necessary.[78] Corporations will be invited and encouraged to accept the binding jurisdiction of the court in relation to selected human rights, for example, forced and child labour or the prohibition of discrimination, in their sphere of activity. A slightly different proposition is that of creating a Human Rights Unit (HRU) under the UN auspices to deal with human rights cases arising in the context

---

[74] Ibid.
[75] UN Doc. E/CN.4/2006/97 (2006).
[76] UN Doc. A/HRC/4/35 (2007).
[77] Ibid., at 76.
[78] Nowak, M. (2007), 'The Need for a World Court of Human Rights', *Human Rights Law Review*, 7, 251.

of private–public partnerships (PPP). This HRU will set standards for projects and monitor these uniformly, creating accountability where there is now only confusion and different standards inadequately monitored.[79] None of these proposals has been taken forward.[80]

2.5. Multinational Corporations and Natural Resources

There is a close relationship between MNCs and natural resource exploitation. Historically foreign companies were involved in natural resource extraction in colonial and overseas territories. Higher prices for many minerals have led to renewed investor interest in the extractive industries. MNCs, including some of the world's largest corporations, play a key role in the mining of metals and in the extraction of oil and gas. Privately owned MNCs dominate the harvesting of metal minerals, while state-owned companies from developing and transition economies are key players in oil and gas. Many such state-owned firms are emerging as MNCs in their own right.

Articulating a legal framework and a transparency regime to regulate MNCs' role in natural resource extraction in host countries is crucial. Whether the involvement of MNCs in natural resource exploitation is beneficial to the host country and its population has to do with several factors: first whether profits obtained from a country's natural resources remain in the country or are exported via corporate profits; second the special conditions created by the MNC for its workers and, third, the environmental impact which extractive industries have. Much litigation against MNCs involves accusations of environmental damage, degradation of natural resources and ecosystems and damage to health.

Lastly, MNCs can play a great role in the prevention and eradication of corruption and the reduction of conflict around natural resources. Multinationals and investors are key players in any conflict resources governance model since they are crucial elements to the trade in natural resources.[81] For example one of the ways for rebels to obtain finance is the sale of 'booty futures', this is the sale of what the rebels plan they will obtain if successful. It is a practice which happens on the fringes of the corporate world, with reputable companies usually not engaging into such practice. The OECD Guidelines on MNEs ban the so-called

---

[79] Likosky, M. (2006), *Law, Infrastructure and Human Rights*, Cambridge: Cambridge University Press, chapter 9.

[80] Further discussion of compliance and enforcement mechanisms in respect of multinationals can be found in chapter 6, pp. 273–285.

[81] See the discussion in chapter 1.

'facilitation payments', but it is suggested that the prohibition should go further and this practice should be made a criminal offence in the home country of the corporation[82] following the precedent set by the OECD to criminalise bribery.[83] This will reduce the access of belligerents to finance and decrease the likelihood of conflict. Multinationals can also help in transparency efforts by participating in 'publish what you pay' (PWYP) campaigns, whereby firms are required to produce adequate reporting and proof of payments to the government.[84] In this way governments cannot divest revenue from natural resource concessions while multinationals have their possibilities of 'bribery' reduced.

2.6.   The Role of MNCs in Development and Poverty Alleviation

The rise of MNCs as centre-stage actors in the global world has brought about a perception that their power entails duties: duties which may not be reflected in any legally binding instrument at the national or international level, but duties nevertheless. MNCs themselves have been quick to take this perception on board: '[s]ocial issues are not so much tangential to the business of business as fundamental to it. . . . Companies that ignore public sentiment make themselves vulnerable to attack'[85] and to include social responsibilities in their agendas.

The corporate social responsibility initiative embraced eagerly by most Western based corporations is an example of this movement, but the growth of corporate activity and power demands looking beyond responsibility for their actions or the voluntary involvement of companies in socially beneficial projects in the areas where they operate. For many, as corporations have more powers and resources than many of the govern-

---

[82]   See Le Billon, P. (2003), 'Getting it Done: Instruments of Enforcement', in I. Bannon and P. Collier (2003), *Natural Resources and Violent Conflict*, Washington, DC: World Bank Publications, World Bank, p. 228 and OECD Recommendation for Further Combating Bribery of Foreign Public Officials in International Business Transactions, of 9 December 2009, available at: http://oecd.org/.

[83]   OECD Convention on Combating Bribery of Foreign Public Officials in International Business Transactions of 21 November 1997. DAFFE/IME/BR(97)20.

[84]   See: http://publishwhatyoupay.org. The 'PWYP' campaign is a civil society led coalition which aims to help citizens in resource rich countries to benefit from the exploitation of those resources and at the same time reduce bribery and corruption.

[85]   Ian Davies, managing director of McKingsey and Company, in The Economist, 26 May 2005.

ments of the states where they conduct operations, they should take on some of the provision of services traditionally left to governments in areas such as education, the building of roads or hospitals. In many parts of the developing world, especially in Africa, weak states have *de facto* delegated much of their role to multinational corporations, aid agencies and international organisations and the locals expect these to fulfil many of the roles which in other societies would traditionally have been performed by the state.

While there is a high degree of suspicion around any relationship between the United Nations or its agencies and the corporate world,[86] partnerships between the UNDP and leading MNCs is a growing phenomenon which requires attention and careful consideration before dismissing it as an attempt at publicity by the corporations. The 'Growing Sustainable Business for Poverty Reduction' framework under the auspices of the UNDP seeks to facilitate and encourage 'greater private sector contributions to poverty reduction and sustainable development through commercially viable alternatives . . . [i]increased investments and business activities in developing countries that link large companies to local small and medium size enterprises, along with communities and other relevant partners'.[87]

While projects like this present an encouraging avenue to articulate the relationship between business, society and sustainable development and to integrate economic productivity and MNCs' profits with the advancement of the MDGs, many obstacles remain before a proper partnership between MNCs and traditional development institutions in the UN system can operate together.[88]

3.   EXPORT CREDIT AGENCIES, PRIVATE FINANCE AND DEVELOPMENT BANKS. IS SOCIALLY RESPONSIBLE INVESTMENT A REALITY?

Export Credit Agencies (ECAs) are public agencies which provide government-backed loans, guarantees and insurance to corporations

---

[86]   See the above comments about the Global Compact.

[87]   'Growing Sustainable Business for Poverty Reduction' (2004), p. 1 available at: http://undp.or/partners/business/gsb.

[88]   See Lodge, G. and C. Wilson (2006), *A Corporate Solution to Global Poverty*, Princeton, NJ; Princeton University Press, for a spirited discussion of the possibilities offered by business to eradicate poverty.

BOX 5.2.   RURAL ICT IN TANZANIA

While mobile telephone services in the Republic of Tanzania have been growing rapidly, as of 2005 more than 90 per cent of the country's area and 75 per cent of its population were unable to access existing networks.

One of the major challenges for potential investors and operators in rural connectivity projects is the lack of reliable information about forecast revenues. Even if initial costs are lowered, there remain many uncertainties regarding willingness to pay and affordability of services. The risk associated with these uncertainties has discouraged investors from entering the Tanzanian market and investing in the ICT infrastructure in the United Republic of Tanzania.

The GSB solution

To resolve issues concerning access to reliable information, the Growing Sustainable Business (GSB) initiative of the United Nations Development Programme (UNDP) funded a feasibility study to identify potential locations to initiate the project, to assess the socio-economic impacts of investment and existing demand, and to identify key issues and challenges. GSB facilitated partnerships between several players, identifying common goals and areas of collaboration and enabled risk sharing among various stakeholders. GSB also organised a Rural ICT Forum to ensure local company buy-in.

Ericsson and other telecommunications providers invested in a 'shared communication network', which is leased to multiple service providers and controlled by a neutral network supervisor. Rural Netco is a local entity created to manage the investments. The operators are then charged for consumed network resources or traffic, on the basis of communicated data amounts, used bandwidth, and/or connection time.

As of 11 May 2008, two telecom operators in the United Republic of Tanzania have agreed to use the shared network model, and another two are expected to join soon. In the next few years, Ericsson will initiate the roll-out of the network and begin operations. At a later stage of the project, Subscriber Service Applications will be implemented and developed by local expertise and according to local needs.

Development impact

The main objective of the Rural ICT project is to ensure access to affordable telecommunications services in the rural regions of the United Republic of Tanzania. Sharing a network greatly reduces the expenses borne by each company, and this in turn reduces the cost of the service for customers. Furthermore, one single network enables Ericsson and its partners to focus their resources on the rapid and wide expansion of network access, thus reaching a greater number of rural inhabitants.

The Rural ICT project specifically addresses the Millennium Development Goals (MDGs) by increasing telephone and cellular access (MDG 8 on global development), as well as MDG 1 on poverty reduction. In a typical developing country, an increase of 10 mobile phones per 100 people boosts growth of the gross domestic product by 0.6 per cent. Access to telecommunications can facilitate entrepreneurship opportunities, private sector development and new jobs, thereby increasing incomes.

---

from their home country when these seek to do business overseas in developing countries or emerging markets. All industrialised countries have at least an ECA[89] and newly industrialised countries have quickly developed their own export credit agencies.[90] The importance of export credit agencies contrasts with the relative lack of public attention devoted to them compared to that commanded by multilateral banks such as the World Bank Group. Yet, collectively, they exceed the size of multilateral lending and fund the majority of private sector projects in the developing world, while they are subject to very little surveillance. ECAs will often lend in those areas or projects abandoned by the World Bank or the regional development banks (European Bank for Reconstruction and Development, African Development Bank, Asian Development Bank, Inter-American Development Bank) because of their social or environmental cost.

They are studied here despite their public nature because of their close

---

[89] CESME (Spain), Coface (France), ECGD (UK), EDC (Canada), ENK (Sweden), Eximbank (USA), Atradius (The Netherlands), Nexi (Japan), SACE (Italy).

[90] For example the ECGA in Oman and the Export-Import Bank of India (I-Eximbank). For a full list see: www.people.hbs.edu/besty/projfinportal/ecas.htm.

relation with MNCs as they are the necessary financing arm to the private activities of investors abroad.

Projects funded by ECAs can cause important social and environmental disruption. In the absence of a mechanism for challenging this lending several non-governmental organisations have sought to reform the way ECAs operate in order to bring them closer to the guarantees now existing within the multilateral banks.[91] Demands of debt cancellation, curbing of abetting corruption, and explicit human rights criteria have also been made. The Jakarta Declaration[92] provided basic criteria for demands of transparency, public disclosure and consultation on all ECA policies. ECAs responded by introducing the Common Approach in 2003[93] where some social and environmental standards were introduced. The Working Party on Export Credits and Credit Guarantees (ECG) has agreed a Revised Recommendation on Common Approaches to the Environment and Officially Supported Export Credits, which was adopted by the OECD Council in June 2007. This latest Recommendation, which replaces one agreed in 2003, sets out strengthened environment-related requirements for export deals to qualify for support from OECD members' Export Credit Agencies.

Large investment banks, whether private or semi-public, are also of crucial importance in natural resource management. These invisible actors of globalisation hold the fate of multinational and state alike by deciding to provide finance for certain projects, developments and industries. Their refusal to invest in a country could have a great effect on its economy and, consequently, its politics.

Large private banks are not included in the definition of MNCs that we have given above as they do not engage in direct investment and only have a financial stake in the foreign venture without any managerial control.[94]

The idea that investment can be responsible and contribute to the attainment of social and environmental goals has gained adherents in the

---

[91] See the CAO and inspection panels of the World Bank in chapter 2.

[92] Jakarta Declaration for Reform of Official Export Credit and Investment Insurance Agencies.

Over 50 representatives of Indonesian and international non-governmental organisations (NGOs), and social movements convened in Jakarta and South Sumatra on 1–7 May 2000 for a strategy meeting on official export credit and investment insurance agencies (ECAs). See www.escrnet.org/usr_doc/Jakarta_Declaration.doc.

[93] http://eca-watch.org/problems/fora/oecd/eca-watchmemo_25oct07.pdf (accessed 15 January 2010).

[94] See Muchlinski (2007), supra, for a distinction between foreign portfolio investment and FDI and UNCTAD (1997), *World Development Report 1997*, New York and Geneva: United Nations, chapter III.

last decade.[95] The SRI 'movement' seeks desired changes through investments. Socially responsible investment is closely related to the concept of
sustainable development. Although SRI represents only a minority of all
investments[96] it is arguable that if introduced through suitable regulatory
reform of the financial markets it could represent the single most important factor in achieving sustainable development.

4.   CIVIL SOCIETY

4.1. NGO Participation in Governance, Regulation and Compliance Procedures

It is unquestionable that globalisation has contributed to the emergence
of a civil society with expanding networks of citizens, labour, media and
transnational businesses. Although civil society is not easy to define it
involves collective action of individuals in the public sphere and seems to
include the organisations commonly known as non-governmental organisations (NGOs).[97] It has been defined as '[a]n intermediary entity, standing
between the private sphere and the state. . . . It is distinct from society in
general in that it involves citizens acting collectively in a public sphere to
express their interests . . .'.[98]

Most of civil society action takes place through what are known as non-
governmental organisations or NGOs. Their definition remains equally
elusive.[99] Beyond being 'non-governmental' NGOs are also generally
considered to be non-profit organisations, thereby excluding business and
corporate entities.[100] The various and multifaceted roles and approaches to

---

[95]   Richardson B. (2008), *Socially Responsible Investment Law; Regulating the Unseen Polluters*, New York: Oxford University Press.

[96]   Ibid., at 3.

[97]   Spiro, P.J (2007), 'NGOs and Civil Society', in Bodansky, D., J. Brunnee and E. Hey (eds), *The Oxford Handbook of International Environmental Law*, New York: Oxford University Press, p. 772.

[98]   Diamond, L. (1996), 'Towards Democratic Consolidation', in L. Diamond and M. Platter (eds), *The Global Resurgence of Democracy*, Baltimore: The Johns Hopkins University Press, 2nd edn, 228.

[99]   Ruggie suggests that we abandon the term NGO altogether and use the more accurate and encompassing 'civil society organisations' in Ruggie, J.G. (2004), 'Reconstituting the Global Public Domain – Issues, Actors and Practices', European Journal of International Relations, 10, 449 at 501.

[100]   But not business organisations such as the World Business Council for Sustainable Development (WBCSD), a CEO-led, global association of some 200

action of NGOs make it difficult to find a suitable definition. On the one hand the public is usually familiar with what are commonly called 'activist' NGOs such as Greenpeace, Amnesty International and many south based NGOs. These organisations seek to politicise issues and in many cases even to bring 'regime change'.[101] Other NGOs are what can be called 'expert' or 'advisory' NGOs which are close to the phenomenon known as 'epistemic communities'.[102] An epistemic community is a network of professionals with recognised expertise and competence in a particular domain and an authoritative claim to policy-relevant knowledge within that domain or issue area. Epistemic communities are important in natural resource conservation and management as they group experts in different areas and provide high degrees of specialisation. For example, epistemic communities were directly involved in the creation of the Board of Plant Genetic Resources.[103] They have a direct effect on agenda setting in intergovernmental organisations and indirect effect on the behaviour of small countries.

NGOs were recognised as actors in international relations in 1945 by article 71 of the UN Charter which directed the Economic and Social Council to 'make suitable arrangements for consultation with non-governmental organizations which are concerned with matters within its competence'. Since then NGOs have grown both in number and in strength and today they are an incontestable force in international policy-making, policy implementation, compliance monitoring and dispute settlement processes.[104] NGOs can provide information and expertise acting as 'intellectual competitors' to governments in the quest for optimal policies.[105] They can also 'increase legitimacy and public confidence in certain

---

companies dealing exclusively with business and sustainable development which provides a platform for companies to explore sustainable development, share knowledge, experiences and best practices, and advocate business positions on these issues in a variety of forums, working with governments, non-governmental and intergovernmental organisations. See www.wbcsd.org/.

[101]   Spiro (2007), supra, at 773.

[102]   Haas, P.M. (1992), 'Epistemic Communities and International Policy Coordination', International Organization, 46, 1–35 and, more recently, Haas, P. (2007), 'Epistemic Communities', in Bodansky et al. (eds) (2007), supra, pp. 792–895.

[103]   Sauve, R. and J. Watts (2003), 'An Analysis of IPGRI's Influence on the International Treaty on Plant Genetic Resources for Food and Agriculture', Agricultural Systems , 78, 2, pp. 307–327.

[104]   The constituent instruments of some international organisations, such as the United Nations Conference on Trade and Development (UNCTAD) and the International Labour Organization (ILO), explicitly provide for engagement with NGOs. The World Bank (WB) and the International Monetary Fund (IMF) do not provide an explicit legal basis for NGO involvement.

[105]   Esty, D. (1995), 'Why the WTO needs Environmental NGOs', paper

institutions like the WTO where there is a public perception of mistrust towards the way in which decisions are "bargained" between states'.[106] NGOs represent, as we have pointed out, transnational interests instead of states' interests, and in that sense they may contribute towards more balanced solutions and policies. But greater participation of NGOs in international organisations is not devoid of criticisms as NGO involvement may lead to the capture of the decision-making process by special interests.[107] One of the main worries over NGO participation in international organisations is lack of legitimacy: NGOs are self-appointed entities not accountable to any electorate or representative in a general way. The interests they advocate are usually narrow and, unlike governments, they do not balance all of society's interests.[108] There is also a degree of suspicion from developing countries towards environmental NGOs of developed countries as their interests may conflict with developing countries' industrialisation policies. These justified concerns about the legitimacy, accountability and politics of NGOs could be eliminated, or at least mitigated, by introducing a homogeneous system of accreditation of NGOs[109] in addition to the existing rules at the organisations where they seek to participate. The essence of the debate over (greater) NGO involvement in international organisations is captured in the Background Paper for the Cardoso Report:

> well handled involvement of NGOs in the policy deliberation and decision-making processes of international organizations 'enhances the quality of decision-making, increases ownership of the decisions, improves accountability and transparency of the process and enriches outcomes through a variety of views and experiences'. However, 'handled badly, it can confuse choices, hamper the intergovernmental search for common ground, erode the privacy needed for sensitive discussions, over-crowd agendas and present distractions at important meetings.

NGO or civil society participation in decision-making and in the formulation of environmental and natural resource policy is usually looked at in what has been described as a linear process.[110] This process

---

published by the ICTSD. Available at: http://ictsd.net/downloads/2008/04/esty.pdf (accessed 15 January 2010).

[106]   See Van den Bossche, P. (2008), 'NGO Involvement in the WTO: A Comparative Perspective', Journal of International Economic Law, 11, 717.

[107]   Van den Bossche summarises these in the context of the WTO but the criticisms are applicable to other organisations. Ibid.

[108]   Ibid.

[109]   Ripinski, S. and P. Van den Bossche (2007), *NGO Involvement in International Organisations: A Legal Analysis*, London: BIICL.

[110]   This classification has been criticised by Spiro as reductive as it fails to

looks at the participation of civil society at the different stages of the law making and enforcement process. NGOs with their issue-orientated focus, expertise and information gathering abilities play an important role in the agenda setting stage. In some organisations such as the United Nations Development Programme (UNDP)[111] and the World Bank,[112] there are permanent bodies through which a formal dialogue between the institution and civil society, including NGOs, can take place. In UNEP, organisations which have been accredited[113] receive the unedited working documents of the UNEP Governing Council sessions at the same time as the Committee of the Permanent Representatives (CPR), for their review and comments. This consultation with civil society prior to the Governing Council provides an opportunity for civil society to contribute to the discussions on thematic and policy issues.

NGOs also participate during the actual formulation of policies. NGOs have observer status in all major environmental treaty regimes, which allows them to intervene in public treaty negotiating sessions and proceedings including attendance at the annual conferences of the parties.[114] For example the Council of the GEF allows for participation of NGOs[115] and UNEP allows NGOs to comment on its working documents.[116]

In some treaty regimes like CITES, NGOs play a fundamental role in monitoring treaty compliance,[117] performing roles which some states would

---

address foundational questions, agency relationships and casual chains. Spiro (2007), supra, at 774. We will still use the classification here as it illustrates clearly the stages of NGO involvement and we will try to conclude some of what Spiro calls foundational aspects in the explanation.

[111]   UNEP has replaced the name Global Civil Society Forum by the Global Major Groups and Stakeholders Forum (GMGSF) in order to include all major stakeholders in discussions. See http://unep.org/civil_society/GCSF/index.GCSF/1.asp.

[112]   Civil Society Global Policy Forum, available at: www.siteresources.worldbank.org/CSO/Resources/CS_Forum/SUMMARY_REPORT_FINAL.pdf.

[113]   Rule 69 of the rules of procedure of the UNEP Governing Council states that the organisation should be a 'civil society organisation . . . and . . . [h]ave an interest in the field of the environment'. For the full text of rule 69 see http://unep.org/civil_society/PDF_Docs/Rule69.pdf (accessed 15 January 2020).

[114]   Spiro (2007), supra, at 781. For example the European Environmental Bureau (EBB) or the International Union for the Conservation of Nature (IUCN).

[115]   The GEF–NGO network was established in May 1995 with the aim of enhancing relations between the Council, secretariat and Assembly of the GEF and civil society organisations. See www.gefngo.org/.

[116]   www.unep.org/civil_society/2ndGCSF_CS_Statement_GMEF.pdf.

[117]   See TRAFFIC at: www.traffic.org/cites/ a joint venture by the Worldwide Fund for Nature (WWF) and the World Conservation Union (WCU) which provides capacity building and monitoring for CITES.

be unable or unwilling to perform. This role of supporting states in their interstate relations in respect of environmental and natural resource governance has particularly been taken by organisations such as Greenpeace or FIELD.[118] The latter was pivotal in the creation of AOSIS and its influential role in climate negotiations. The wealth of expertise and resources of developed countries-based NGOs has been used to drive environmental policy, acting in some cases through 'states of convenience'.[119]

NGO participation in dispute resolution is also a growing phenomenon. It is common for NGOs to submit briefs in dispute resolution forums where issues relating to their areas of activity are being discussed. These written briefs are known as amicus curiae ('friends of the court') briefs. Their admissibility and the value that the tribunal, panel or court dealing with specific disputes attaches to them vary widely. Their advantage resides in the fact that these briefs provide both a legal and factual analysis beyond that of the parties to the dispute and place the dispute in a wider context which takes into account society's (or at least certain sectors of society's) interests.[120] This type of participation is to be welcomed, particularly in natural resource disputes as society's interest is often obscured behind the parties' confrontation and bilateral interests. Despite the few procedural rules acknowledging the value of these amicus curiae briefs they are accepted in a growing number of courts and tribunals. It is interesting to note that in forums where states have an interest in controlling the dispute under a state-centric prism, for example the European Court of Justice, there is still a firm reluctance to accept NGOs' statements as amicus curiae briefs in disputes between states.[121] The inter-state forum par excellence, the International Court of Justice (ICJ), does not have rules on the formal acceptance and consideration of amicus curiae briefs submitted by individuals or NGOs[122] but its Practice Direction XII provides that the ICJ makes those written statements and/or documents available to the states and intergovernmental organisations that are involved in the same advisory proceedings, although it adds that 'such statement and/

---

[118]   The Foundation for International Environmental Law, FIELD, is a London based NGO which was instrumental in the creation of AOSIS – the Association of Small Island States. See http://field.org.uk/.

[119]   A term used by Chayes, A. and A. Handler (1995), *The New Sovereignty: Compliance with International Regulatory Agreements*, Cambridge, MA: Harvard University Press, at 265, cited in Spiro (2007), supra, at 783.

[120]   Van den Bossche (2008), supra, at 729.

[121]   Article 40 of the Statute of the European Court of Justice (March 2008), available at: http://curia.europa.eu/en/instit/txtdocfr/index.htm.

[122]   Ibid. Article 62 of the Statute of the International Court of Justice on third party interventions.

or document is not to be considered as part of the case file'.[123] Arbitrations under the ICSID accept amicus curiae submissions in certain cases,[124] and the Inter-American Court of Human Rights has the power both to invite and grant leave to any state, organisation, or person to appear before it and to make submissions on any issue specified by the court[125].

In the context of the WTO in the *US – Shrimp* dispute,[126] the Appellate Body came to the conclusion that panels have the authority to accept and consider amicus curiae briefs if they consider them useful to the case.[127] If this seems a promising development it must be contrasted with recent findings about briefs being rejected in most cases,[128] despite the report of the Warwick Commission suggesting that panels and the Appellate Body should be open to the consideration of amicus curiae briefs submitted by NGOs, especially in those disputes which involve conflicts between economic and non-economic values.[129]

4.2. Cooperation and Participation of Civil Society and Other State Actors in Regulation: 'Civil Regulation'

The term civil regulation encompasses the emerging trend which involves the participation of NGOs in the process of policy development, implementation and compliance monitoring discussed above. Of particular interest are the cooperative approaches developed between civil society and businesses devoted to pursuing particular environmental policy goals or the development of specific projects.[130] Examples of this include the cooperative work of NGOs, corporations and UN agencies with government bodies in the water industry in the context of privatisation of water

---

[123] Practice Direction XII, www.icj-cij.org/documents/index.php?p1=4& p2=4& p3=0 (as amended on 6 December 2006).

[124] See rule 37 of the Rules of Procedure for Arbitration Proceedings (Arbitration Rules), ICSID Convention, Regulation and Rules, www.worldbank. org/icsid/basicdoc/basicdoc.htm.

[125] Treves, T., M. Frigessi di Rattalma, A. Tanzi, A. Fodella, C. Pitea and C. Ragni (eds) (2004), *Civil Society, International Courts and Compliance Bodies*, Cambridge: Cambridge University Press, 338. Cited and discussed in Van den Bossche (2008), supra, at 729.

[126] *US – Shrimp*, WT/DS58/AB/R, adopted on 6 November 1998.

[127] On the basis of Articles 13, 12, and 11 of the DSU.

[128] Van den Bossche (2008), supra, 729.

[129] Warwick Commission (2007), *The Multilateral Trade Regime: Which Way Forward?*, Report, Warwick: University of Warwick, 34.

[130] Newell, P. (2001), 'Environmental NGOs, TNCs and the question of Governance', in D. Sevis and V. Assetto (eds), *The International Political Economy of the Environment: Critical Perspectives*, Boulder, CO: Lynne Reiner, 85.

supply.[131] While governments, encouraged by the World Bank, have proceeded to the privatisation of the water supply, Water Aid and other NGOs are acting to ensure that the commercial activity does not encroach on human or environmental interests.

Other examples are the Forest Stewardship Council (FSC) integrated by environmental NGOs, forest industry representatives, community forest groups and forest certification groups. They aim to ensure that only certified timber is sold by its members.[132]

NGO–business partnerships are likely to grow in the future as governments retreat from certain functions within the market economy,[133] but questions arise as to the effectiveness of this type of regulation and their legitimacy and independence. Once a partnership between an NGO and a business sector or industry has been achieved it may be difficult for the NGO to assert its independence and act critically.

4.3.   Civil Society and Globalisation

Besides NGO participation in international organisations and the setting of natural resource policy civil society participates in global governance through a variety of spaces. Opposition and resistance to economic globalisation and transnational rules have been exercised by civil society through the market-mediated exercise of consumer power,[134] by coordinated action enhanced by information technology[135] and by resorting to units of government at the local or sub-national level.[136]

Globalisation has created 'market' or 'economic citizens' that belong to a 'transnational capitalist class' which includes both natural and legal persons (especially multinational corporations).[137] These citizens benefit

---

[131]   Muchlinski (2007), supra, at 551–552. See also chapter 7.

[132]   Although the scheme has been subject to criticism due to its voluntary character which allows many companies, especially those from developing countries, to operate outside the scheme.

[133]   Likosky, M. (ed.), (2005), *Privatising Development: Transnational Law Infrastructure and Human Rights*, Leiden: Martinus Nijhoff.

[134]   Klein, N. (1999), *No Logo: Taking Aim at the Brand Bullies*, London: Picador.

[135]   Opposition to the MAI is a good example of civil society resistance facilitated by information technology.

[136]   Schneiderman, D. (2008), *Constitutionalising Economic Globalization. Investment rules and Democracy's Promise*, Cambridge: Cambridge University Press, at 186.

[137]   These market citizens enjoy mostly civil rights – to contract and to own property very similar to the civil rights of the eighteenth century. Ibid., at 190.

from the rules of non-discrimination of the investment and trade regimes. The global market has also created another type of citizens – consumer, who is partly complicit with the system through the consumption of goods and services but who has, according to some authors, a power of resistance.[138] This 'resistance' or 'action through consumption' poses important questions of equity and participation. On the one hand, the majority of the world population is excluded from this group or 'consumer class' – as those who are too poor to consume are not able to act as full citizens. The second type of issue has to do with the effectiveness of 'consumer action' and the actual amount of resources needed to investigate abuses of power by other more powerful actors (states or multinationals). Lastly, large amounts of resources are needed to mobilise the 'consumer society' through media and awareness campaigns.[139]

Civil society also operates at the sub-national or supra-national level. While states are said to concentrate their efforts on paving the way for the globalisation of trade and investment, other units of political power (local or transnational) may be better equipped and more willing to reflect society's interests and concerns. Examples such as the fight against the Multilateral Agreement on Investments (MAI) by British Columbia while the Canadian government was busy negotiating its terms at the OECD or the Massachusetts selective purchasing laws directed at the military regime in Burma illustrate the potential for this action.[140] Opposition to the MAI provides a good example of civil society action directly related to globalisation governance. For many, the failure of the MAI was made possible though the combined effort of opposition groups which saw the MAI as the triumph of corporate rule and a danger to democracy.[141]

---

[138]   Klein, N. (1999), supra, at 375–376 gives examples of how Nike changed some of its production practices to appease the indignation of Western consumers when they learned about the starvation wages of workers and the use of child labour in its factories.

[139]   A massive effort was required to improve the conditions in just one of the Nike plants around the world. See Schneiderman (2008), supra, at 194 and www.workersrights.org/. The Workers' Rights Consortium monitors local production practices in factories around the globe and conducts investigations and issues reports detailing local abusive practices on labour rights for products sold in the United States.

[140]   See Schneiderman (2008), supra, at 197. The latter were challenged by the EU and Japan in the WTO claiming that they violated the 1994 GPA which forbids states to use non-economic criteria in public procurement.

[141]   Sassen describes mobilisation against the MAI as a 'largely digital event' in Sassen, A. (2006), *Territory, Authority, Rights: From Medieval to Global Assemblages*, Princeton, NJ: Princeton University Press, at 339 and see the general discussion in Schneiderman (2008), supra, at 201.

While '[r]epresentative democracy, in which citizens periodically elect their representatives across the full spectrum of political issues, is now supplemented by participatory democracy, in which anyone can enter the debates that most interest them, through advocacy, protest and in other ways',[142] the main obstacle to effective civil society participation in global governance is the lack of institutions that represent civil society or where civil society can have a voice outside the interstate system and beyond protests and campaigning.

5.   INDIVIDUALS

People are without doubt the least regulated of all globalisation actors. Cross-border movement of people is restrained by immigration laws which do not match the freedom afforded to goods or services, which can enjoy the advantages of globalisation and the efficiency of finding the best place for production in the global marketplace. Only in regional spaces such as the European Union are people free to move within the intra-union borders.[143] Other regional organisations lag behind in allowing freedom of movement to individuals.[144]

If the situation is erratic at the regional level things get worse as we move to the global sphere. There is no multilateral agreement mirroring the WTO which regulates the transboundary movement of people. This disparity between the freedom of goods and capital to cross borders and the restrictions on individuals to do the same works mostly against developing countries which, with growing populations, see their best productive asset, their workforce, blocked from entering the working space of the developed world. In economic terms this makes no sense. Labour

---

[142]   Report of the Panel of Eminent Persons on United Nations–Civil Society Relations, *We the People, Civil Society, the United Nations and Global Governance* (Cardoso Report), A/58/817, 11 June 2004, para. 13, available at: http://documentsddsny.un.org/doc/UNDOC/GEN/N04/376/41/pdf/N0437641. pdf?OpenElement.

[143]   European Parliament and Council Directive 2004/38/EC of 29 April 2004 on the right of citizens of the Union and their family members to move and reside freely within the territory of the Member States amending Regulation (EEC) No. 1612/68 and repealing Directives 64/221/EEC, 68/360/EEC, 72/194/EEC, 73/148/EEC, 75/34/EEC, 75/35/EEC, 90/364/EEC, 90/365/EEC and 93/96/EEC.

[144]   NAFTA, despite its promises, failed to address the issue of immigration in respect of Mexican citizens, while ASEAN is more concerned with the movement of skilled workers while keeping strong immigration controls for unskilled workers.

movements should create the same efficiency predicated in respect of capital movements by neoclassical economic theory, and provisions which allow the establishment of corporate entities should also allow the establishment of individuals.[145] Yet arguments of self-determination, social and cultural cohesion are used to limit what would otherwise be the human right of free transit in the planet. With the exception of the UNHCR,[146] there are no agencies or international institutions which govern the cross-border movement of people. While international migration is a reality the only regulation to date, the International Convention on the Protection of the Rights of All Migrants and their Families,[147] has been ratified by only 43 countries, all of them labour-exporting. In his report on the 'Strengthening of the United Nations – an agenda for further change', UN Secretary-General Kofi Annan identified migration as a priority issue for the international community and a Global Commission on International Migration (GCIM) was launched.[148] The GCIM has highlighted the contradictions existing in today's globalised world between markets and states in respect of migration. While the corporate world would like to be able to access labour in the same way as it accesses goods, states' concerns are connected to local politics; '[they] may acknowledge the economic case for a more liberal approach to international migration, many governments are also worried that admitting additional numbers of foreign nationals, even on a temporary basis, will have negative consequences for the stability of society and ultimately the security of the state'.[149] The Commission pointed out that this 'tension between markets and the state, between the corporate sector and government, between the global and the local, between national interests and the globalization process, will be an increasingly important element of the discussion on international migration in years to come',[150] although it acknowledged at the same time that international migration[151]

---

[145]　Nayyar, D. (2002), 'Cross-border Movement of People', in D. Nayyar (ed.), *Governing Globalisation*, New York and Oxford: Oxford University Press, pp. 166–167.

[146]　Created in 1950 with the purpose of protecting refugees.

[147]　International Convention on the Protection of the Rights of All Migrant Workers and Members of their Families, New York, 18 December 1990. Doc. A/RES/45/158.

[148]　http://gcim.org/en.

[149]　Report of the GCIM (2005), 'Migration in an Interconnected World: New Directions for Action', Switzerland, para. 29, Introduction, available at: www.gcim.org/en/finalreport.html.

[150]　Ibid., at para. 30.

[151]　Ibid., para. 33.

[i]s a controversial matter because it highlights important questions about national identity, global equity, social justice and the universality of human rights. International migration policy is difficult to formulate and implement because it involves the movement of human beings, purposeful actors who are prepared to make sacrifices and to take risks in order to fulfil their aspirations. Its challenges are radically different from those that arise in managing the movement of inanimate objects such as capital, goods and information.

Besides migrants, war or environmentally displaced refugees, individuals engage in the globalisation discourse through information technology, international networks and civil society. As holders of both substantive and procedural rights individuals have a certain voice and control over the policies which inform their lives. The growing recognition of procedural and participatory rights,[152] added to the traditional remedies for violation of constitutional or human rights[153] which have been extended through judicial interpretation, to also encompass non-state actors' actions, allows them a certain control over the negative effects that the global system has on their everyday lives.

6.   INDIGENOUS PEOPLES

The expansion of global capitalism into new territories and economic activities as a consequence of a growing need for resources fuelled by the affluence and consumption patterns of the rich countries has created a new threat to the lives of the millions of indigenous peoples that live in the increasingly less remote regions of the world. Indigenous people resisted the first wave of European colonisation and remained unaffected by modernity, living in harmony with their immediate environment according to their millenary cultures and traditions.

The policies imposed by neoliberal economics and the structural adjustment programmes of the international lending institutions had a devastating effect on indigenous peoples.[154] On the one hand budding efforts at land reform and recognition of land rights of indigenous peoples which had been taking place in many countries, especially in Latin America, were halted. On the other hand the politics of individualism propagated by capitalism and the Washington consensus signified the end to the system

---

[152]   See chapter 3.
[153]   Now extended to litigation against MNCs. See the discussion below.
[154]   de Souza Santos, B. and C. Rodriguez-Garavito (2005), 'Law, Politics and the Subaltern', in Santos and Rodriguez-Garavito, supra, at 5.

of communitarian land ownership which extends over much indigenous land. A focus on crops for export followed by the fall in the commodity prices put enormous pressure on land resources and eventually forced a turn towards resource extraction in many Latin American countries: timber, oil and minerals were the only commodities that could help service the increasing external debt.[155] The rise in mineral, timber and oil extraction had catastrophic consequences for indigenous peoples. As most of these resources are found in indigenous land, states and companies pushed to evict indigenous communities or push them to the frontiers of their land. Extractive activities, the growing of cash crops and consumer patterns in the developed world have generated climate change, environmental degradation and widespread pollution which have a particularly harmful impact on indigenous peoples due to their close dependence on the land they inhabit. Indigenous peoples have had to wage a double battle against the state and against foreign multinationals to stop the rate of resource extraction and destruction of their land which risks their very survival.[156]

In this battle indigenous peoples have come to symbolise the unique cultural, political and legal confrontations between the globalisation discourses. The current transnational movement of indigenous peoples has been galvanised as a protest against the predatory forms of global capitalism. While indigenous peoples have been traditionally excluded from the Western legal discourse, globalisation has made possible the revitalisation of their struggle and public concern, advocacy and pressure campaigns have allowed for the recognition of collective rights to land and natural resources that have been embodied in constitutional reforms in some countries with indigenous populations and recognition of indigenous rights in international instruments.[157] The struggle of the U'wa people symbolises both the possibilities and contradictions of global legal action for the protection of indigenous rights.

---

[155]   Brysk, A. (2000), *From Tribal Village to Global Village: Indian Rights and International Relations in Latin America*, Stanford, CA: Stanford University Press, p. 151.

[156]   Examples range from the Huaroani, Cofran and Secoya in Ecuador trying to make Texaco accountable for oil spills in their territory to the Mayagnas in Nicaragua trying to protect their timber against Korean TNCs.

[157]   Several Latin American Constitutions recognise indigenous rights: Brazil (1988), Bolivia (1994), Mexico (1991), Peru (1993), Colombia (1991) and Venezuela (2000). International Instruments are discussed below in this section.

BOX 5.3.   THE U'WA PEOPLE

The U'wa people occupy a land extending to approximately 60,000 hectares in the northeast of Colombia. Throughout the 1970s and 1980s the U'wa people had pressed the Colombian government for the recognition of their collective title to the land. In 1991 the Colombian constitution recognised the rights of indigenous peoples to their land and territories, and that brought a revival of the U'wa people's demand for a united territory where all members of the U'wa community could live in peace without outside interference.

In 1992 Oxy entered the scene by signing an agreement with Texaco and Ecopetrol – Colombia's oil company – to exploit an oil site called Samore Block which partially overlapped the U'wa homeland.

The U'wa people requested that the Colombian government stop oil drilling, arguing that their right to 'free prior informed consent' recognised in the 1991 constitution[1] had been violated and that no licence for oil exploration could be granted without their consent. After a meeting in 1992 between a representative of Ecopetrol, government officials and Oxy and indigenous leaders a communiqué was published recognising the rights of the U'wa to participate in the management of the project.

Before a second scheduled meeting took place the government unilaterally granted the licence for oil exploration, and the dispute became judicialised and gained international attention when the U'wa people announced that in the face of the collusion between the government and Oxy they would commit mass suicide.

The ombudsman's office took over the case which had raised its international profile and attracted the attention of foreign and national NGOs working on indigenous issues. The ombudsman brought two legal challenges against the government arguing that the licence granted violated the right of the U'wa to participate in the process and asked the Constitutional Court to issue a writ ordering the immediate cessation of operations in U'wa homeland. The Constitutional Court ruled in 1997 that indigenous rights stand on a par with individual human rights and, according to ILO Convention 169 and the Constitution, indigenous peoples' rights of cultural survival needed to be respected. It also ordered that a consultation between the government, Oxy and U'wa representatives be arranged within 30 days of the ruling.

Parallel to that a case was being decided in the Council of State, a traditional, administrative type of court, since the decision by the government to grant a licence was basically a matter of administrative law. The Council of State ruled that the right of consultation recognised in respect of indigenous peoples had been satisfied by the meeting being held since it did not include a guarantee that the demands of indigenous peoples in the consultative meeting would be met.

With two conflicting decisions at the national level the U'wa struggle became international as the case was taken up by the TAN – transnational advocacy network, a group of international NGOs – to the global scene. Tours of indigenous leaders through Europe and America, a well orchestrated press campaign and the submission of an official complaint to the Inter-American Commission on Human Rights quickly raised the international profile of the U'wa people and their plight. An unsuccessful attempt to find a negotiated solution through the involvement of the Organization of American States (OAS) and the granting of a further licence to Oxy to operate drilling adjacent to U'wa land forced the U'wa into several actions of civil disobedience and the intensification of the international campaign against Oxy and the Colombian government.

Feeling the pressure Oxy unilaterally withdrew in 2001, returning the concession to the Colombian government. This was interpreted as a great victory by the international coalition of NGOs involved in supporting the U'wa struggle, but the victory was short-lived as Ecopetrol, the state company, took over the activities of Oxy. This time, however, international interest had moved to other causes and struggles and the U'wa failed to raise the same type of support that they had obtained in the past.

Note:
1.   And also in the 169 ILO Convention and later in the UNDRIP.

Source: Rodriguez-Garavito, C. and L.C. Arenas (2005), 'The Struggle of the U'wa People in Colombia', in B. de Souza Santas and C. Rodriguez-Garavito (eds), *Law and Globalisation from Below*, Cambridge: Cambridge University Press, pp. 241–266.

7. CONCLUSION

There is ample literature on the negative consequences of global economic activities on the environment. Multinational corporations are frequently denounced by the media and have been brought to account in courts for human rights violations and direct environmental destruction in developing countries,[158] and the international economic system with its institutions and rules has been accused jointly by a section of public opinion and academia of being the main culprit.

The liberalisation of trade, and particularly of foreign investment, has made it possible for multinational companies to establish operations in any country that fits their economic plans. In many cases the damage to the environment takes place because polluting industries relocate to places with lower or non-existent environmental standards, the so-called 'race to the bottom'. In others, it is the system of free trade and consumerism, with its associated increase in the use of fossil fuels, higher transportation costs and the increased demand for goods and services, which is blamed for pollution or increased natural resource consumption. Perhaps, though, the most serious of criticisms are those which blame the current trade and investment regimes for the economic inequalities which they create between nations, and force developing countries into unsustainable and environmentally damaging production strategies in a desperate attempt to survive economically. Examples of this abound, ranging from the system of subsidies to agriculture in developed countries to stabilisation clauses in investment contracts, the system of intellectual property rights imposed in the WTO context or the conditions imposed by the IFIs in their loans and finance to developing countries.

For some the emergence of civil society reflects a trend in global society development: 'this growth of NGO activity may indicate an emerging transformation of the international legal and political system – a decline in the importance of the sovereign state and the state system and an accompanying rise of governance by a dynamic global civil society'.[159]

The shift from states to markets has made political players of MNCs.[160] This political role goes well beyond the usual allegations of influence on the foreign or domestic policies of states and focuses on the political relationship of MNCs with society through their involvement at every stage

---

[158] Discussed in chapters 3, 6, 7, 8 and 9.

[159] Raustiala, K. (2997), 'The "Participatory Revolution" in International Environmental Law', Harvard Environmental Law Review, 21, 537, at 539.

[160] Strange (2004), supra, at 44.

of production, as technical innovators or employers.[161] Until this relationship is understood, articulated and reflected in the national and supranational legal systems, multinational corporations, the most mobile, powerful and versatile of global actors, operate in uncharted territory, largely unregulated, subject only to the limited constraint of national laws while taking full advantage of the benefits offered by the corporate structure and the global economy.

FURTHER READING

Addo, M. (1999), *Human Rights and Transnational Corporations*, The Hague: Kluwer International.

Clapham, A. (1993), *Human Rights in the Private Sphere*, New York: Oxford University Press, pp. 83–130.

Dine, J. (2005), *Companies, International Trade and Human Rights*, Cambridge: Cambridge University Press.

Muchlinski, P. (2007), *Multinational Enterprises and the Law*, 2nd edn, Oxford: Oxford University Press.

Ruggie, J.G. (2004), 'Reconstituting the Global Public Domain – Issues, Actors and Practices', European Journal of International Relations, 10, 449.

Schneiderman, D. (2008), *Constitutionalizing Economic Globalization. Investment Rules and Democracy's Promise*, Cambridge: Cambridge University Press.

Spiro, P.J. (2007), 'NGOs and Civil Society', in D. Bodansky, J. Brunnee and E. Hey (eds), *The Oxford Handbook of International Environmental Law*, New York: Oxford University Press.

Steinhardt, R. (2005), 'Corporate Responsibility and the International Law of Human Rights: The New Lex Mercatoria', in P. Alston (ed.), *Non-State Actors and Human Rights*, New York: Oxford University Press.

Van den Bossche, P. (2008), 'NGO Involvement in the WTO: A Comparative Perspective', Journal of International Economic Law, 11.

Zerk, J.A. (2006), *Multinationals and Corporate Social Responsibility. Limitations and Opportunities in International Law*, Cambridge: Cambridge University Press.

---

[161]   Ibid.

6. Compliance

1. INTRODUCTION

In natural resource and environmental matters sustainable use and conservation of natural resources require regimes and systems which focus on the prevention and control of environmental harm rather than on providing reparation for damage already suffered. The unsustainable use of natural resources has consequences which are difficult to quantify in economic terms and which are unsuitable for resolution by resorting to the channels of state responsibility or the imposition of fines or other sanctions. It is much more important that all parties involved agree to a regime which allows the sustainable use of resources without depleting them. Sustainable use, in turn, needs to be based on fair and equitable access to resources, and economic measures and incentives should be implemented together with the necessary safeguards in respect of the poor and vulnerable.[1] Environmental damage is often subtle, cumulative and long term[2] and therefore requires 'equitable and preventative measures'.[3]

In order to have an effective system of compliance it is necessary to have an agreed system of rules and standards. The two are mutually and intrinsically connected. The more successful the agreement on standard setting, the more likely it is that parties will comply with the rules and the less the need for enforcement mechanisms. Strong governance institutions and forums for fostering agreement are the first step towards effective compliance mechanisms. Effective compliance mechanisms must also include provisions which enable enforcement of the regulatory regime, if necessary, by all interested affected parties.[4] Natural resources regulation takes

---

[1] See chapter 2, 'Sustainability', pp. 93–95.
[2] Birnie, P., A. Boyle and C. Redgwell (2009), *International Law and the Environment*, 2nd edn, Oxford: Oxford University Press, p. 212.
[3] Ibid., citing Bilder (1975), 'The Settlement of Disputtes in International Law', *Recueil des Cours* 144, III, at 225.
[4] These may be not only states but also individuals, communities or multinational corporations. See for example Articles 14 and 15 of the NAEEC: see chapter 3, p. 143.

place at different levels: national, regional and international. These levels are inter-related. National mechanisms are sometimes used to enforce international regulation, while measures or provisions of national regulation will have a global dimension due to the interconnectedness of natural processes. This interconnectedness requires consensus to be at the centre of any potential regime.

If the regulation and compliance regimes on natural resource matters need to be amicable, non-confrontational, equitable and aimed at promoting sustainability, the enforcement of trade and investment laws obeys very different principles and policies. Certainty, deterrence and economic imperatives are articulated into the WTO Dispute Settlement System where violations of the rules of the multilateral trade regime are dealt with efficiently. Foreign investors find themselves streamlined into the arbitration system of the ICSID whereby they can bring states to account for any actions that endanger their profits or change the conditions of their investment.

The variety of compliance mechanisms in national and international law reflects the variety of actors and stakeholders in global trade, investment and natural resource use and management. Different mechanisms have different degrees of effectiveness, and this, in turn, is often linked both to economic incentives for compliance and the importance placed on conservation of the resource by users. This chapter addresses compliance mechanisms and classifies them on methods of accountability and compliance in respect of states and non-state actors in order to assess whether procedures for compliance, enforcement and accountability are adequate to meet the needs of global trade and natural resource activities.

2.   STATE COMPLIANCE

States, however diminished, changed or threatened their position is said to be, retain characteristics which are not shared by non-state actors. States keep the monopoly of law production and enforcement at the national level, and as 'traditional' subjects of public international law states sign treaties, are subject to the law of state responsibility and are subject to the compliance mechanisms of multilateral and bilateral agreements.

The developed system of global governance in trade and foreign investment matters ensures that making states comply with the global rules is easy. The power of private investors, multinationals and the rich states they come from has contributed to putting in place an effective framework of compliance and enforcement. On natural resource matters the issues are more complex, as we will see throughout this chapter.

2.1. State Compliance with the World Trade System. The WTO Dispute Settlement System

At the global level, the most successful enforcement regime is said to be the Dispute Settlement System (DSS) at the WTO. The WTO regime is extremely successful in promoting compliance by providing a swift, accessible and rule-based system of dispute settlement which allows those who think they are suffering damage by the violation of trade laws by another member of the multilateral trade system to bring a complaint to the WTO DSS.[5] If it is decided that a breach of obligations has indeed taken place the 'victim' state can retaliate and impose countervailing duties against the products of the offending state. This acts as a strong deterrent to deviations from compliance, although critics point out that small and poor states are, as usual, at a disadvantage since the countervailing duties or trade boycotts which they can impose against powerful, market dominating states like the United States or the European Union would have a minimal impact on the economies of those two big trading blocs, while the opposite situation would bring economic chaos and great losses to a small state if its products were to be blocked or heavily taxed by a big trading partner.

The prompt settlement of disputes is 'essential to the effective functioning of the WTO and the maintenance of a proper balance between the rights and the obligations of Members . . . [i]t is central to providing security and predictability to the multilateral trading system'.[6] Disputes are always initiated by the members. The WTO does not have a supervisory body which can or should initiate non-compliance procedures if a member state departs from applying some of the rules of the system. The WTO is, in this respect, member-driven. Disputes are first referred to consultations (Article 4 DSU) or alternative dispute settlement mechanisms such as good offices, mediation or arbitration (Articles 5 and 25 DSU). If none of these are successful the dispute will be adjudicated by a panel and subject to appeal to the Appellate Body (Articles 6, 17 DSU). The Dispute Settlement Understanding (DSU) departs from the GATT's old rule that

---

[5] General Agreement on Tariffs and Trade 1994, 15 April 1994, Marrakech Agreement Establishing the World Trade Organization, Annex 1A, The Legal Texts: The Results of the Uruguay Round of Multilateral Trade Negotiations Vol. 17 (1999), 1867 U.N.T.S. 187, 33 I.L.M. (1994) 1153, available at: www.wto.org/English/docs_e/legal_e/legal_e.htm (GATT 1994).

[6] Article 3.3 of the Understanding on Rules and Procedures for the Settlement of Disputes, commonly known as the Dispute Settlement Understanding (DSU). The full text can be found at: http://.wto.org/english/tratop_e/dispu_e/dsu_e.htm.

consensus was necessary in order to have a legally binding decision, which was perhaps its main impediment to being really effective.[7]

There are three types of complaints that members can bring to the Dispute Settlement Mechanism (DSM).[8] First, if there has been a breach of rules by any one member, there is prima facie case for a 'nullification and impairment' of the benefits that were meant to accrue for the aggrieved party. A breach of rules by any one member can be brought to the attention of the dispute settlement body by another member. This accounts for the large number of cases which are brought to the system, usually alleging breach of the principle of non-discrimination.[9]

The second type of complaint is a 'non-violation complaint'. This type of complaint is brought up by a member which thinks that a benefit of the WTO is being nullified or impaired by any rules of the state against which the complaint is made, even if the rules or practices do not constitute a violation of WTO rules per se. This second type of complaint shows an extremely advanced and sophisticated dispute settlement mechanism which is able to move beyond the legalistic application of the provisions of the WTO and will seek to enforce the spirit of the agreement.[10] However it is also a dangerous mechanism which can be overtly invasive of domestic sovereignty. The last type of complaint arises when a member thinks that 'any other situation' which does not fit into the above two categories is undermining its gains from a WTO agreement.[11] Disputants should start consultations which, after 60 days with no result, will automatically trigger the establishment of the panel. Retaliation can be authorised if a respondent does not comply with the recommendations issued by the DSB.[12]

There is no provision or requirement in the DSU for panels that adjudicate on environmental disputes to have environmental expertise. A Committee on Trade and the Environment (CTE) was created by Ministerial Declaration under the auspices of the WTO with the mandate to 'make appropriate recommendations on the need for rules to enhance

---

[7]   For a discussion on the importance of the DSU in protecting security and predictability in the multilateral trading system see Van den Bossche, P. (2009), *The Law and Policy of the World Trade Organization*, Cambridge: Cambridge University Press, pp. 168–172.

[8]   Articles 2–3 DSU.

[9]   Article XVII of the GATT 1994 — 'principles of non-discriminatory treatment'.

[10]   Narlikar, A. (2005), *The World Trade Organization: A Very Short Introduction*, Oxford: Oxford University Press, p. 90.

[11]   Ibid.

[12]   Anderson, K. (2002), 'Peculiarities of Retaliation in WTO Dispute Settlement', World Trade Review, 1, 123–134.

the positive interaction between trade and environment measures for the promotion of sustainable development'.[13] The CTE is more significant for the 'institutionalisation of environmental issues into WTO processes' than for any significant output.[14] Progress is blocked due to the disagreements between the US and the EC on the one hand and developing countries on the other which fear that the introduction of environmental standards and conditions would amount to little more than covert discrimination against their products. Other defences are those which have been discussed in the context of the dispute between the US and the EC over GMOs.[15]

The *Shrimp/Turtle*[16] and *Asbestos*[17] disputes illustrate the progress made by the Appellate Body in meeting environmental concerns. In the first case the Appellate Body considered the role of the WTO in sustainable development and the relationship between trade and environmental standards.[18] And although the unilateral measures imposed by the US were found to be discriminatory they were found to be consistent with the exception under Article XX (b) and (g) of the GATT.[19] The WTO dispute settlement panel and the Appellate Body have repeatedly expressed a preference for the negotiation and signature of MEAs to regulate natural resource conservation and use[20] instead of resorting to trade measures which seek to enforce individual members' views on general obligations.

Article XX of the GATT has been considered in detail by the Appellate Body in cases which directly and indirectly affect a state's choices in respect of environmental standards. Parties are able to impose environmental measures (or trade barriers) if the conditions set out in Article XX of GATT are met:

---

[13] GATT Ministerial Decision of 14 April 1994, 33 I.L.M. (1994) 1267.

[14] Birnie, Boyle and Redgwell (2009), supra, at 763.

[15] See *EC – Biotech Dispute (European Communities – Measures Affecting the Approval and Marketing of Biotech Products)*, Reports of the Panel WT/DS291/R, WT/DS292/R, WT/DS293/R, 29 September 2006 ('Final Panel Report'). The report is available at: www.wto.org/english/news_e/news06_e/291r_e.htm.

[16] *US – Import Prohibition of Certain Shrimp and Shrimp Products*, WT/DS58/AB/R (1998).

[17] *European Communities – Measures Affecting Asbestos and Asbestos-Containing Products*, WT/DS135/AB/R (2001).

[18] In the preamble to the 1994 Marrakech Agreement the parties recognise that the institutional framework for the development of trade needs to take into account sustainable development and the protection and preservation of the environment.

[19] Measures to protect human, animal and plant life: Article XX(b) or conserve natural resources: Article XX(g).

[20] See Birnie, Boyle and Redgwell (2009), supra, at 767.

Subject to the requirement that such measures are not applied in a manner which would constitute a means of arbitrary or unjustifiable discrimination between countries where the same conditions prevail, or a disguised restriction on international trade, nothing in this Agreement shall be construed to prevent the adoption on enforcement by any member of measures . . .

. . . (b) Necessary to protect human, animal or plant life or health;

. . . (g) relating to the conservation of exhaustible natural resources if such measures are made effective in conjunction with restrictions on domestic production or consumption.

To apply the Article XX(g) exception, there must be a 'real' connection between the GATT inconsistent measures to conserve the exhaustible natural resources and their aim, and the measure must not be disproportionately wide in scope.[21]

In the *Asbestos* dispute[22] the legal question revolved round the 'necessity' of the measure – banning asbestos to protect human life and health under Article XX(b) and whether a less restrictive approach, i.e. controlling the use of asbestos, would had been sufficient. In the *Shrimp/Turtle* dispute[23] the Appellate Body considered the environmental implications under the exception in Article XX(g) of the USA's measures to restrict imports of shrimp captured under certain conditions in order to reduce turtle mortality. It concluded that Article XX could 'in principle, provide a legal basis for unilateral trade measures to protect the global environment, in this case endangered species of sea turtles, even when directed against other countries' policies'.[24]

Criticisms of inequality of power and relative strength aside the WTO is an extremely effective system which it would be unwise to ignore when trying to construct effective compliance systems at the global level. This success has fuelled a growing debate about the possibilities offered by the integration of the enforcement of international trade laws and the enforcement of human rights.[25]

---

[21] For example applying *United States – Import Prohibition of Certain Shrimp and Shrimp Products*, WT/DS58/R, 12 October 1998.

[22] *EC – Measures Affecting Asbestos and Asbestos-containing Products*, WT/DS135/AB/R, 12 March 2001.

[23] *United States – Import Prohibition of Certain Shrimp and Shrimp Products*, WT/DS58/AB/R, 12 October 1998.

[24] Howse, R. (2002), 'From Politics to Technocracy – and Back Again: The Fate of the Multilateral Trading Regime', AJIL 96, 94, p. 111. Cited in J. Holder and M. Lee (2007), *Environmental Protection, Law and Policy*, 2nd edn, Cambridge: Cambridge University Press, at 278.

[25] Cottier, T. (2002), 'Trade and Human Rights: A Relationship to Discover', Journal of International Economic Law 5, 111–132.

2.2. International Investment Disputes

As foreign direct investment multiplied in the post-war period it became increasingly apparent that the existing mechanisms of dispute settlement were not satisfactory or sufficient to enable investors to operate with confidence and provide the flow of investment that it was thought would maximise economic development. Expropriations and nationalisations in newly independent countries were also a risk which investors were reluctant to take in their stride as they approached foreign markets.

Under traditional public international law, and despite some authority supporting at least some qualified legal personality,[26] companies or individuals had to resort to what was known as diplomatic protection[27] since individuals and corporations lacked personality to pursue any claims. Diplomatic protection would be exercised by the home state only if political conditions were favourable to the investor and its interests,[28] but also included the so-called exhaustion of domestic remedies rule, or the proof by the investor that all judicial and administrative channels in the host state had been exhausted in order to obtain redress or compensation.[29] The result was that years could pass exhausting domestic remedies in the local courts before diplomatic protection, if ever exercised, took place. The old role of diplomatic protection also placed big companies with powerful lobbying power in a much stronger position than medium sized companies for which the home state might not risk a breakdown of foreign relations with the host state. The home state always retained discretion whether to bring the claim or not, a claim which, once taken, became the claim of the state itself and no longer that of the individuals. This rule also meant that there was no legal obligation for the state to repay any monies eventually obtained:[30] a situation which was not especially favourable to investors.

Diplomatic protection was also particularly problematic in the case of multinational corporations because of the 'nationality rule' which requires

---

[26]   See the Texaco arbitration 17 I.L.M. (1978) 1, Muchlinski, P. (2007), *Multinational Enterprises and the Law*, 2nd edn, Oxford: Oxford University Press, at 704.

[27]   Brownlie, I. (1998), *Principles of Public International Law*, 5th edn, Oxford: Oxford University Press, p. 482.

[28]   Vernon, R. (1978–79), 'The Multinationals: No Strings Attached', Foreign Policy, 33, 121 at 126.

[29]   Brownlie (1998), supra, pp. 472–481.

[30]   O'Connell, D.P. (1970), *International Law*, 2nd edn, London: Stevens, pp. 106–112, thinks that there is a moral duty but, of course, this is unenforceable.

the private entity to be a national of the protecting state,[31] while the international operations of multinational corporations and the complexity of the international corporate structure of branches, subsidiaries and establishments on many occasions made it difficult to establish the necessary link.

Litigation has not traditionally been the most favoured system of dispute resolution on commercial ventures but when one of the parties is a state or state entity litigation becomes even less attractive. In many cases it would be difficult to take the government or one of its agencies to court due to the immunity of jurisdiction which states enjoy. Although this immunity should exclude commercial transactions – the commonly named *ius commercii* – it is nevertheless arguable that the acts which led to the dispute may fall within the realm of *ius imperii* or acts of government (for example the passing of legislation nationalising property, or laws and regulations radically changing the prospects of the investment), and these cannot be challenged in the national courts. Secondly, even if the immunity of jurisdiction hurdle is successfully negotiated investors will find it uncomfortable to litigate in the state's own courts, in many instances alleging lack of independence of the judiciary, delays and lack of resources, undeveloped or unsophisticated legal systems. In order to deal with these problems and encourage foreign direct investment states have negotiated a framework of BITs which in most, if not all, cases contain dispute settlement provisions establishing that disputes between the investor and the host state can be referred to neutral alternative dispute resolution forums such as the ICSID, UNCITRAL arbitration centre or some other international arbitration tribunal for resolution. The ICSID has been chosen as the investor–state dispute mechanism by the majority of BITs.

2.2.1. The International Centre for the Settlement of Investment Disputes (ICSID)

The ICSID[32] is an autonomous international institution established under the Convention on the Settlement of Investment Disputes between States and Nationals of Other States.[33] The Convention entered into force on 14 October 1966 and sets out the ICSID's mandate, organisation and

---

[31]   In the *Barcelona Traction* case [1970], CJ Rep 3, the ICJ held that for the purposes of diplomatic protection the nationality of a company should be established according to the place of incorporation and its seat, and not by the majoritary nationality of the shareholders should the corporate veil be lifted.

[32]   Visit www.icsidworldbank.org/ICSID.

[33]   The Washington Convention on the Settlement of Investment Disputes between States and Nationals of Other States was adopted by resolution of the

core functions. The main purpose of the ICSID is to provide facilities for conciliation and arbitration of international investment disputes. There are currently 155 signatory states to the ICSID Convention. Of these, 143 states have also deposited their instruments of ratification, acceptance or approval of the Convention to become ICSID Contracting States.[34] The Centre itself does not conduct arbitration proceedings, but administers their initiation and functioning.[35] Some other multilateral trade and investment treaties such as the North American Free Trade Agreement, the Energy Charter Treaty, the Cartagena Free Trade Agreement and the Colonia Investment Protocol of Mercosur, also refer to ICSID for disputes arising in investment.[36]

The main features of the ICSID system of dispute resolution are: (a) foreign companies and individuals can directly bring an action against their host state; (b) state immunity is severely restricted; (c) international law can be applied to the relationship between the host state and the investor; (d) the local remedies rule is excluded in principle and (e) ICSID awards are directly enforceable within the territories of all states parties to ICSID.[37]

In 1978 ICSID established the Additional Facility, which allows for arbitration in cases where parties do not fulfil the usual ICSID criteria, i.e., investors are not from ICSID signatory states, or the host country is not an ICSID signatory. The Additional Facility can also accept disputes which are not over an investment[38] per se, but instead 'relate to a

---

Executive Directors of the World Bank in 1965. The text of the Convention is published at 4 I.L.M. (1965) 524.

[34] For general information on the ICSID see Redfern, A. and M. Hunter (2004), *International Commercial Arbitration*, London: Sweet & Maxwell, chapter 11; Muchlinski (2007), supra, pp. 716–742, or for a detailed analysis, see Schreuer, C. (2001), *The ICSID Convention: A Commentary*, Cambridge: Cambridge University Press.

[35] Reed, L., J. Paulson and N. Blackaby (2004), *Guide to ICSID Arbitration*, The Hague: Kluwer Law International, p. 5.

[36] Peinhardt, C. and T. Allee (2008), 'The International Center for Settlement of Investment Disputes: A Multilateral Organisation Enhancing a Bilateral Treaty Regime' in *International Trade Law: Issues and Perspectives*, Hyderabad: ICFAI University Press.

[37] Dolzer, R. and C. Schreuer (2008), *Principles of International Investment Law*, New York: Oxford University Press, at p. 20.

[38] For the ICSID jurisdiction to operate the dispute must be a legal dispute arising directly out of an investment. The term 'investment' is not defined in the Convention but has been given a broad interpretation by ICSID tribunals. See Legum, B. (2005), 'Defining Investment and Investor: Who Is Entitled to Claim?', Paper given at the symposium 'Making the Most of International Investment

transaction having characteristics that distinguish it from an ordinary commercial transaction'.[39]

The ICSID dispute resolution facilities have been severely criticised on various fronts. One of their most recent vocal critics has been Bolivian President, Evo Morales. In a letter to the ICSID[40] he denounced the promotion and protection of foreign investment at all costs with little regard to the costs to democracy, the environment and public welfare and often violating a country's sovereignty, constitution and national laws.[41] Other Latin American countries, following a trend of socialist governments devolving control of the nation's wealth and natural resources to the people, have followed or threatened to follow Bolivia's example and leave the ICSID.[42] Critics also note the ICSID's relationship with the World Bank and the tacit (and express) endorsement that its decisions make to the policies of privatisation, liberalisation and corporate capitalism promoted by Bank and the IMF. The ICSID is seen as little more than the enforcement arm of a system designed to promote and protect the rights of investors. This desire to protect investors has been taken so far as to want to protect them from any investment related risk as evidenced by the amount of damages claimed and awarded when the profits expected by investors are modified due to legislative measures taken by the host country.

In both *Betchel v. Bolivia* and *Biwater v. Tanzania*[43] ICSID arbitration panels had to address public law issues and host state citizen's rights, alongside the private interests of foreign investors. These two cases

---

Agreements: A Common Agenda'. 12 December 2005, Paris, available at: http://. oecd.org/dataoecd/51/10/36370461.pdf.

39   Baker, J.C. (1999), *Foreign Direct Investment in Less Developed Countries: The Role of ICSID and MIGA*, Westport, CT: Quorum Books, p. 61.

40   See Bolivia's letter to ICSID, dated 21 June 2007, available at: www. foodandwaterwatch.org/ water/world-water/right/icsid-letter.

41   On 2 May 2007, Bolivia sent a formal notice to the World Bank's International Centre for the Settlement of Investment Disputes (ICSID) declaring its withdrawal from the ICSID Convention. ICSID News Release, 16 May 2007, 'Bolivia Submits a Notice under Article 71 of the ICSID Convention', available at: http://icsid.worldbank.org/ICSID/FrontServlet?requestType=CasesRH&actionV al=OpenPage&PageType=AnnouncementsFrame&FromPage=NewsReleases&p ageName=Announcement3.

42   On 4 December 2007, Ecuador, under Article 25.4 of the Convention, notified its rejection of ICSID arbitration for future oil, gas and mining disputes, and Venezuela has threatened to take a similar path. See chapter 1 for a discussion on national sovereignty over natural resources and contemporary problems.

43   *Biwater Gauff (Tanzania) Ltd v. United Republic of Tanzania*, Case No. ARB/05/22. See the discussion in chapter 2.

BOX 6.1. AGUAS DEL TUNARI, S.A. v. THE REPUBLIC OF BOLIVIA. ICSID CASE NO. ARB/02/3

In the late 1990s the World Bank imposed a forced privatisation of the water system in Bolivia against the promise of debt relief and aid. Bechtel was the only bidder and was granted a 40 year lease to take over Cochacamba's water supply through its subsidiary company Aguas del Tunari (AdT). AdT imposed price hikes amounting to 25 per cent of the average wages of residents which led to several protests. In 2000 the government of Evo Morales, honouring its electoral promises, terminated the contract.

Bechtel filed a $50 million action (for claims of lost future profits) against the government of Bolivia in the World Bank's International Centre for the Settlement of Investment Disputes. Bechtel had made investments of less than $1 million and therefore the losses claimed were extortionate and aimed at covering lost profit. Battered by several years of bad publicity orchestrated by NGOs and activists, Bechtel settled the $50 million action for a symbolic amount of about 30 cents on 19 January 2006.

---

galvanized external civil society pressure in an effort to control multinational corporations' behaviour.

2.3. Transboundary Regimes and Treaty Compliance in Natural Resource and Environmental Matters

Although it has been argued that '[a] necessary criterion for the validity of any norm of . . . positive international law . . . is the willingness of states and international bodies . . . to enforce i[t]',[44] the most successful regimes of compliance for cross-boundary resources are those which promote dispute avoidance.[45] Most of them rely on institutional inter-governmental

---

[44] Nino, C.S. (1991), 'The Duty to Punish Past Abuses of Human Rights Put into Context: The Case of Argentina', Yale Law Journal, 100, 2619 at 2621, cited in Ratner, S.R. (2001), 'Corporations and Human Rights: A Theory of Legal Responsibility', Yale Law Journal 111, 443 at 473.
[45] UNEP, *Study on Dispute Avoidance and Dispute Settlement in International Environmental Law,* UNEP/GC.20/INF/16 (1999).

commissions with the required capacity to coordinate policy, develop the law and supervise its implementation. One of the most successful of those regimes in the context of air pollution has been that provided by the 1987 Montreal Protocol to the 1985 Vienna Convention on the Protection of the Ozone Layer. Its compliance regime has been heralded as consensual, amicable and conciliatory, focusing on meeting the agreed targets voluntarily, encouraging self-reporting and leaving mechanisms of dispute settlement or sanctioning as the very last resort.[46] The Montreal Protocol was the first multilateral environmental agreement that provided a formal non-compliance procedure based on self-reporting, monitoring and cooperation between the parties in order to meet agreed standards. The compliance procedure under the Protocol can be invoked by any party to the agreement, the secretariat or the party which envisages any compliance problems itself. The Implementation Committee under the protocol will gather all required information and will issue a report to the Full Meeting of the Parties which decides on the steps to take to ensure compliance. These steps may include the provision of technical or financial assistance.[47] There are no other dispute settlement provisions (for example resort or arbitration or international adjudication) in the Protocol, demonstrating the importance of cooperation in complying with environmental standards.[48]

The Aarhus Convention compliance procedure is similar to that of the Montreal Protocol but includes the innovative feature of allowing members of the public and NGOs to bring complaints before the non-compliance committee.[49] Compliance within the Climate regime devised by the Kyoto Protocol is slightly more complex.[50] It differs from the Montreal Protocol's non-compliance procedure in that it seeks not only to facilitate and promote compliance but also to 'enforce' it,[51] making it

---

[46]   Article 8, and Annex IV adopted in Copenhagen in 1992 and amended in 1998. For a discussion see Birnie, Boyle and Redgwell (2009), supra, 246–247 and 351–356.

[47]   See Koskenniemi, M. (1997), 'Breach of Treaty or Non-Compliance', Yearbook of International Environmental Law, 3, 123–162, at 123.

[48]   Birnie, Boyle and Redgwell (2009), supra, at 354.

[49]   Article 15 Aarhus Convention. Birnie, Boyle and Redgwell point out that in many ways this compliance procedure is closer to that of the UN Human Rights Committee than the Montreal Protocol due to the participation of individuals and NGOs. Ibid. at 254.

[50]   See Werksman, J. (1998), 'Compliance and the Kyoto Protocol', Yearbook of International Environmental Law, 9, 48 for a discussion of the difficulties associated with compliance under the Framework Convention on Climate Change.

[51]   Article 18 Kyoto Protocol: 'approve appropriate and effective procedures and mechanisms to determine and to address cases of non-compliance with the provisions of this Protocol, including through the development of an indicative

less of a consensual method of compliance and more similar to procedures such as those of enforcement of obligations under the world trade regime.[52] Compliance questions are directed to a 'Compliance Committee' elected by the parties either by the party which is in breach or by any other party. The Committee then has a choice of how to deal with the non-compliance: it can either offer advice, financial resources or technology transfer and capacity building in a fashion similar to that of the compliance committee of the Montreal Protocol or it can adopt a quasi-judicial process, imposing penalties on the non-compliant party.[53]

Other examples of transboundary compliance regimes in natural resource management are the Convention on International Trade in Endangered Species (CITES)[54] which relies heavily on the participation of non-state actors or the UN Fish Stock Agreement 1995 and the FAO Code of Conduct for Responsible Fisheries.[55]

2.4. State Responsibility

The traditional principles of state responsibility in international law which focus on judicial resolution of disputes and adjudication of damages for environmental harm offer limited scope and possibilities of success for sustainable natural resource management. Although this mechanism may provide economic compensation to the victim if this is easily identifiable and act as a deterrent for the infractor state which may decide to change its policy and put an end to damaging activities, its effectiveness is limited by its nature as an inter-state channel which does not allow access to individuals, by the length of time that decisions take and the fact that environmental damage and natural resource depletion are in most cases a process of continuous effects, long-term and diffuse damage.[56]

---

list of consequences, taking into account the cause, type, degree and frequency of non-compliance'.

[52] See the discussion on the WTO DSS.

[53] These penalties can be an increase in the obligation to reduce emissions, suspension from participating in emission trading or the clean development mechanism. See chapter 8 on the CDM.

[54] Birnie, Boyle and Redgwell (2009), supra, 685–692.

[55] Which ensures compliance and enforcement by relying on the state where the vessel is matriculated (flag) irrespective of where the violation took place. States can board and inspect vessels including using force 'to the degree necessary to ensure the safety of inspectors in the exercise of their duties, and can also detain the vessel if there is sufficient evidence of a violation.

[56] See Birnie, Boyle and Redgwell (2009), supra, at 214–237 for an excellent account and discussion of the law in this area.

2.4.1. State responsibility for transboundary harm

Recognition of responsibility for transboundary environmental damage is tracked down to the *Trail Smelter Arbitration*,[57] where transboundary air pollution by a private operator set the parameters for subsequent cases of transboundary environmental damage. States have resorted to international law and the ICJ to resolve disputes which have had an indirect effect on the conservation and management of natural resources. A recent example is provided by the *Gabcíkovo-Nagymaros* case,[58] the first case in which the ICJ had to consider environmental monitoring and risk management as central to its decision, and which ended in the Court requiring the parties to negotiate a solution. Birnie, Boyle and Redgwell point out when discussing state responsibility that no modern pollution disaster has ever been resolved by adjudication against the state involved:

> [T]he main reason for discussing state responsibility at all in this book is thus not its immediate practical utility but because an understanding of what it can and cannot offer is essential to an explanation of other developments in the international legal system that have largely taken its place. However, the possibility that states might have recourse to international claims against their neighbours may itself exercise an influence on the negotiations of environmental agreements and the settlement of disputes.[59]

The basis for establishing responsibility in international law is the breach of an existing obligation. This international law obligation can arise out of a treaty or customary law. Even if the activity which results in environmental harm is conducted by a private party as was the case in the *Trail Smelter* case, the responsibility is that of the state which has a duty of prevention and cooperation.[60] Due to the limited practical application of state responsibility in cases of transboundary environmental damage we will concentrate on the issue of whether states can be held responsible for the activities of private operators, namely multinational corporations which cause damage in the territory of another state.

2.4.2. State responsibility for acts committed by MNCs

The incidence of states contributing to violations of human rights by corporations and other states abroad is sadly increasingly frequent. Both the privatisation of state services and the engagement in competitive

---

[57] *Trail Smelter Arbitration*, AJIL 33 (1939) 182 and AJIL 35 (1941) 684.
[58] [1997] ICJ Rep. 7.
[59] Birnie, Boyle and Redgwell (2009), supra, p. 212.
[60] Ibid., at 214.

delivery of investment services promoted and encouraged by the globalisa-tion of foreign investment have created more opportunities for abuse. It is common for states to insist on contracts before their companies invest in certain foreign countries considered to be risky. When investments refer to a long-term project involving infrastructure investors, backed up by their governments, insist that the host country government signs off its rights to improve labour conditions or other rights and other measures which may increase the cost of the investment.[61] This has led to severe criticism from academics, human rights activists and the NGO sector.[62]

There is established case law that acknowledges the responsibility of the state under international law for the actions of its nationals abroad if it can be proved that the subjects were under the authority and jurisdic-tion of the state.[63] The concept of 'under the jurisdiction and control of the state' has evolved from the findings of the ICJ in the *Nicaragua* case to a more modern and flexible formulation,[64] but when multinationals are involved one of the problems of establishing state responsibility is the cor-porate structure itself. A corporation established in a state may operate in another via a subsidiary – an entity with separate legal personality which will probably be incorporated in the host state according to the laws of that state.

In those cases establishing responsibility of the parent company has presented difficulties of its own.[65] Establishing responsibility of the home state of the parent company may seem, to some, a step too far. In the *Barcelona Traction* case it was established, for the purposes of exercising

---

[61] Amnesty International (2005), 'Contracting Out of Human Rights: The Chad Cameroon Pipeline Project', London, September, available at: www.amnesty.org/library/Index/engpol340122005.

[62] McCorquodale, R. and P. Simmons (2007), 'Responsibility Beyond Borders: State Responsibility for Extraterritorial Violations by Corporations of International Human Rights Law', MLR 70, 598–625 at 613.

[63] *Lozidou v. Turkey* (Merits) (App No 15318/89) 23 EHRR (1997) 513; *Democratic Republic of Congo v. Uganda* (Merits) 45 I.L.M. (2006) 271. The ICJ stated in relation to Uganda's actions in the Democratic Republic of Congo that the obligations under international human rights instruments and all human rights that are part of customary international law apply in relation to the acts of a state outside its territory.

[64] *Prosecutor v. Tadic*, Case No. IT-94-I-A, para. 137 (Int'l Crim. Trib. for Former Yugoslavia Appeals Chamber, 15 July 1999), available at: www.un.org/icty/tadic/appeal/judgement/index.htm. *Lozidou v. Turkey*, 310 ECtHR (ser. A) at 23–24 (1995) and Article 8 ILC 2001 Draft Articles, supra pt. I, ch. 1, For a discus-sion on this point see Ratner (2001), supra, at 499.

[65] Litigants fought to establish the liability of the parent company Union Carbide (USA) in the context of the Bhopal disaster. See the discussion below.

diplomatic protection, that 'a subsidiary is a separate legal entity and in international law parent and subsidiary are each subject to the exclusive jurisdiction of their respective states.'[66]

Difficulties aside, there are sound theoretical and practical reasons for making states responsible for the acts of MNCs abroad. MNCs are closely tied up with the trade and finance departments of states. Their financial power carries considerable political weight and governments in home states are reluctant to pass legislation or engage in actions which may jeopardise the interests of multinationals. Considerable regulatory and financial measures are taken by the home states in order to facilitate the operations of MNCs abroad. These include negotiations for multilateral regimes such as the WTO which enable companies to sell products world-wide, the negotiation and signature of bilateral investment treaties and the financing and tax allowances made to facilitated FDI abroad: 'if a state is so involved and has so many interests tied up with those of MNCs it should also be responsible for its actions and share into the liability when these much favoured actors commit violations of international human rights law'.[67]

In order to activate the mechanism of state responsibility in international law a state must have broken an international legal obligation.[68] The International Law Commission (ILC) adopted in 2001 the Articles on the Responsibility of States for Internationally Wrongful Acts.[69] In the case of corporations the attribution of responsibility to the state rests upon several conditions.[70] First the corporation must have been empowered to exercise elements of public authority (Article 5 ILC Articles on State Responsibility); second, the corporation must act on the instructions or under the control of the state (Article 8); and, third, the state must be complicit through aiding or assisting the corporation to violate human

---

[66] [1970] ICJ Rep 3, 42.

[67] McCorquodale and Simmons (2007), supra, at 598. The authors give the examples of the acknowledgement by the UK, Canada, Australia and the US and their role and interests in promoting and assisting their corporations to win foreign contracts and lobby against the establishment of regulatory and political barriers in other states.

[68] Brownlie (1998), supra, at 436.

[69] Report of the International Law Commission on the work of its 53rd Session, A/56/10, August 2001, UN GAOR. 56th Sess. Supp. No. 10, UN Doc. A/56/10(SUPP) (2001) (ILC Articles). Most, but not all, articles reflect customary international law. For the most detailed commentary on the articles see Crawford, J. (2002), *The International Law Commission Articles on State Responsibility: Introduction, text and Commentaries*, Cambridge: Cambridge University Press.

[70] McCorquodale and Simmons (2007), supra, at 606.

rights in the territory of another state (Article 16). In all cases the tests applied in respect of the involvement of a state in the acts of corporate subjects abroad is extremely high. This is particularly true in respect of cases falling into the second category where 'instructions or control' by the state is required.[71]

It has been argued that there are at least two situations where a state may be said to have constructive knowledge of violations of human rights committed abroad by subsidiaries of home companies.[72] The first is when a corporation invests in a conflict zone or in a country with a failed state or a repressive regime.[73] The second is when a home state negotiates and signs a BIT with a developing country. It has already been discussed that BITs may restrict the host state's ability subsequently to pass laws to enhance the social, environmental and labour rights of its citizens, as these laws can be interpreted as hindering or diminishing the projected profits of the investor.[74] It has also been suggested that if a home state has negotiated a BIT which will provide for suitable conditions of investment for its corporations and will potentially ban any scrutiny of their actions, as this may be seen as an imposition of particular conditions by the host state not allowed under the 'most-favoured nation clause', then the home state should have constructive knowledge of the potential for human rights violations and an obligation to exercise due diligence in respect of the human rights impact of actions of the country's corporations or their subsidiaries. It has also been argued that under those conditions the home state should provide a remedy to all those affected by the companies' activities in its own courts.[75] This may involve a modification of the normal rules of jurisdiction.[76]

---

[71] The main test was established by the ICJ in the *Nicaragua* case, *Military and Paramilitary Activities in and against Nicaragua (Nicaragua v. United States of America)* (Merits) [1986] ICJ Rep 14. In this case the involvement of the United States in financing, training and supporting the Contras against the legitimate government of Nicaragua was proven, but although the Court found that the U.S. participation in certain actions had been 'preponderant and decisive' it was not enough to support a claim of state responsibility against the US for acts of the Contras. McCorquodale and Simmons (2007), supra.

[72] Ibid., at 620–621.

[73] For example in 2003 the UK government requested Premier Oil and British American Tobacco to cease investment in Burma due to serious concern about human rights abuses in the area. The Guardian, 7 September 2003.

[74] See chapter 1.

[75] McCorquodale and Simmons (2007), supra, 621. See the discussion later in this chapter.

[76] See below.

BOX 6.2.   THE BAKU–CEYHAN PROJECT

'BP is the lead shareholder in the 1,100-mile long oil pipeline, which runs from Baku, Azerbaijan, through Georgia to the Turkish seaport of Ceyhan. In addition to opening up an alternative supply to the US (which has long been in search of an oil source outside the Middle East), the project has led to allegations of human rights abuses, sparked regional conflict, and deprived local people of their livelihoods and land. By 2010, the pipeline is scheduled to deliver an estimated one million barrels of oil a day, predominantly to the already saturated Western markets. The pipeline legal agreements also give BP effective governing power over a strip of land 1,750 miles long, where the company will likely override all national environmental, social, and human rights laws for the next 40 years.

70 percent of the $3.3 billion it cost to build the pipeline came via loans from banks. A large proportion of this debt came from public financial institutions led by the International Finance Corporation (IFC), and the European Bank of Reconstruction and Development. This allowed BP to secure further private investment funding from private banks like Citigroup. The additional thirty percent came in the form of equity (capital provided by the oil companies which hold shares in the project). Construction began in May 2003 and the pipeline was officially declared open two years later, some 16 months behind schedule.

The construction of the pipeline has been monitored by the Baku–Ceyhan Campaign, a consortium of NGOs including the Kurdish Human Rights Project, The Corner House, Friends of the Earth and Environmental Defence. The campaign has uncovered 173 violations of the World Bank's environmental and social standards in the Turkish section of the project during the design stage alone.

The project is governed by an Inter-Governmental Agreement (IGA) between the governments of Azerbaijan, Georgia and Turkey, which was drafted by BP's lawyers, and by individual Host Government Agreements (HGA) between each of the three countries and the BP-led consortium. These agreements have largely exempted BP and its partners from local laws – and allow BP to demand compensation from the governments should any law (including environmental, social or human rights law) make the pipeline less profitable. There is also concern that, rather than adding to the local economies in the areas surrounding the pipeline, BP will pressure the three nations to give them tax breaks.'

Source: Hannan Ellis, *Corporate Watch*, June 2005, available at: www.corpwatch.org/articlephp?id=12340.

FOR DISCUSSION

- Is the UK responsible for the human rights violations that have taken place in the construction of the pipeline?
- Should the statements given by the ECS that the human rights and social impact of a project have been taken into account be interpreted as constructive knowledge on the part of the state should a violation of human rights take place later?

The case law of the European Court of Human Rights (ECHR)[77] and the Inter-American Court of Human Rights (IACHR)[78] has held that states are responsible for not preventing the violation of human rights committed by private parties. States have a duty to protect rights through legislation, preventive measures or the provision of a remedy. The question which is more difficult to answer is which actions and abuses exactly fall within this category.

In the area of environmental harm Francioni has suggested that the state of origin of a company causing environmental harm in another country should be held responsible.[79] This would have a strong deterrent effect on both 'exporting' countries and companies.

To conclude, several points need to be defined before state responsibility

---

[77] In *Guerra v. Italy*, 1998 (1 ECtHR 210) Application number 14967/98. Italy's failure to prevent a fertiliser company from releasing toxic gases violated the right of privacy of the petitioner.

[78] In the famous *Velasquez Rodriguez* case, 1 Inter-Am. Ct H.R. (Ser. C) N 4 (1988), Honduras was held responsible for not preventing and punishing the disappearance of individuals at the hands of private parties (whether or not they were government agents).

[79] Francioni, F. (1991), 'Exporting Environmental Harm through Multinational Enterprises: Can the State of Origin Be Held Responsible?', in F.

can be resorted to as a helpful option for controlling MNCs' activities: which cases amount to a sufficient violation of human dignity in order to make the state accountable, when is a state complicit, what is the standard of fault, and what would be the redress adequate for the victims?[80]

Moving away from the law of state responsibility in international law, another possibility is to hold host states responsible for damage caused by multinational corporations. This can indeed act as an incentive to states to step up their control over individuals and business to ensure that no human rights violations take place within their territory, but in order to be truly effective it would need to be articulated through judicial systems which permit public interest litigation.[81]

3. COMPLIANCE BY MEMBER STATES WITH EU LAW

Although international organisations do not have per se the means to force states to comply with their rules and norms the EU is by virtue of the power deferred to it by states able to ensure compliance with its ever growing body of rules. Different enforcement mechanisms are available to ensure the compliance of state members.[82] There is a system of centralised enforcement through the Commission and the European Court of Justice based on Article 226 EC Treaty (ECT) and a system of decentralised enforcement through the domestic courts of each Member State based on Article 234 ECT.

State compliance with EU law on environmental matters is left mostly to the Commission which has a role of guardian of the implementation of treaties (Article 211 EC Treaty), and which can ultimately bring the matter to the European Court of Justice (Article 226 EC Treaty).

The Commission has made wide use of its implementation powers, and since 1978 has opened more than 20,000 implementation procedures

---

Francioni and T. Scovazzi (eds), *International Responsibility for Environmental Harm*, Oxford: Hart Publishing, pp. 275–288.

[80] Anderson, M. (2002), 'Transnational Corporations and Environmental Damage; Is Tort Law the Answer?', Washburn Law Journal 41, 339. Anderson points out that monetary compensation may not satisfy the victims and criminal law sanctions may provide a better sense of redress. Also Ratner, S.R. (2001), 'Corporations and Human Rights: A Theory of Legal Responsibility', Yale Law Journal, 111, 443 elaborates on the same point.

[81] See chapter 5, pp. 217–218.

[82] See, in general, Tallberg, J. (2003), *European Governance and Supranational Institutions. Making States Comply*, New York: Routledge.

against Member States.[83] Before the Commission opens proceedings it needs to have sufficient evidence of an infringement, and for this it relies on complaints lodged by a variety of actors: citizens, firms, public interest groups and in some cases petitions and queries sent to the European Parliament.[84] If the Commission finds enough evidence it will start proceedings, and if those proceedings do not end with a settlement whereby the state which is being challenged for its infringement of community laws changes its actions, the Commission will refer the state to the ECJ. Once a case is referred to the ECJ there is ample evidence that suggests that a negative ruling against the state will follow.[85]

It has been pointed out that in its mission of assessing implementation of environmental laws and regulations the Commission is in a difficult position,[86] since it lacks the powers that it has in the competition field such as Community environmental inspectors,[87] and has thus to rely on the complaint system in order to start a process of investigation into compliance with and implementation of the relevant laws. Relying on the complaint system makes the Commission's role largely reactive, which, as has been discussed at the beginning of the chapter, is never a good option on environmental or natural resource problems. Complainants find themselves in a contradictory and pivotal position in compliance procedures. On the one hand the Commission has to rely on them as it is impossible for the Commission to ascertain the practical implementation of the law.[88] On the other the Commission has remained 'aloof and unresponsive to complainants'.[89] The situation has improved relatively as the Commission has set time limits for replying to complainants and providing basic information,[90] but the complainant is basically powerless to initiate judicial proceedings which remain at the absolute discretion of the Commission according to Article 226 ECT.

---

[83] Borzel, T. (2006), 'Participation Through Law Enforcement: The Case of the European Union', *Comparative Political Studies*, 39, 128 at 133.

[84] Ibid.

[85] Ibid.

[86] Holder, J. and M. Lee (2007), *Environmental Protection, Law and Policy*, 2nd edn, Cambridge: Cambridge University Press, p. 404.

[87] Macrory, R. (1992), 'The Enforcement of Community Environmental Laws: Some Critical Issues', *Common Market Law Review*, 29, 347.

[88] Holder and Lee (2007), supra, at 404.

[89] Rawlings, R. (2000), 'Engaged Citizens, Citizen Action and Institutional Attitudes in Commission Enforcement', *European Law Journal*, 6, 8–28 at 28.

[90] European Commission (2002), *Communication on Relations with the Complainant in Respect of Infringements of Community Law*, COM 141 final. Cited in Holder and Lee (2007), supra, at 405.

Further to this the very nature of the Commission, which is a political organ which takes political decisions, makes decisions on proposals and, above all, seeks compromises in the taking of its decisions, has been challenged as the most adequate organ to control the enforcement machinery. Should this type of organ with its multiple roles and functions be in charge of the implementation of environmental law and enforcement of community standards against states? Or would this function be better given to a different type of body, to a specialised agency? Proposals have been made for the creation of a powerful specialised enforcement agency with environmental inspectors equipped with adequate powers – for example powers of search or seizure[91] which could take action directly against infringing national authorities or individual and corporate polluters. While these proposals highlight those areas and shortcoming of existing mechanisms it is unlikely that radical reform will take place in the near future. Evolution rather than revolution seems to be the motto in respect of the enforcement of environmental law at the moment.

In 1996 the Commission published a report setting priorities for the enforcement of environmental law[92] and has made efforts at better and more transparent procedures.[93] The Commission encourages citizens to bring incidents of non-compliance before the domestic courts of the state[94] since, given its limited resources, it needs to prioritise cases according to its own political or institutional interests.[95]

Individuals, citizens' groups and firms can sue a state government or public authorities in their national courts for violating EU law according to Article 234 ECT.[96] This is based in two crucial pillars of European law; the doctrine of supremacy of European law[97] and the direct effect of EU law at the domestic level.[98] The Commission has made serious efforts to inform citizens on the procedures available to safeguard and enforce their rights under EU law including initiatives such as 'Citizens First' or the

---

[91]   See Williams, R. (1994), 'The European Commission and the Enforcement of Environmental Law: An Invidious Position', *Yearbook of European Law*, 14, 351 at 398.

[92]   See Hattan's comment on the report in Hattan, E. (2003), 'The Implementation of EU Environmental Law', Journal of Environmental Law, 15, 271.

[93]   See European Commission (2002), supra, at 141.

[94]   Discussed below.

[95]   Conant, L.J. (2002), *Justice Contained. Law and Politics in the European Union*, Ithaca, NY: Cornell University Press, cited in Borzel (2006), supra, at 134.

[96]   Which allows for a preliminary ruling on whether EU law has been violated by domestic laws or authorities.

[97]   Established by the ECJ in 1964.

[98]   See in general for a discussion on these points Conant (2002), supra.

Robert Schumann Project.[99] Together with this the Access to Information Directive (AI)[100] and the Environmental Impact Assessment Directive (EIA)[101] aim to provide channels for citizen and group participation in the implementation of environmental laws in the EU.[102]

What are the lessons that we can learn from the shortcomings and difficulties of enforcement of environmental laws in the most integrated of political and legal supranational spaces in the world today? Perhaps that politics are never completely dissociated from legal issues when states are involved and that negotiation and settlements are to be encouraged and are, without doubt, the best way of resolving infringement incidents. The Commission understands this well and has multiplied occasions for settlement before it decides to take a state to the ECJ. To the opportunity to submit observations awarded by Article 226 ECT the Commission has added what has been called a 'pre-litigation phase'[103] where some agreement and accommodation with the Member State is sought. Participation by citizens and groups in the enforcement process is welcomed and encouraged, although studies have shown that significant differences in access to information and ease of access to courts exist within EU Member States,[104]and that certain groups and therefore interests are privileged – because of knowledge, access to economic means and national variations in participating in the enforcement process.

4. MULTINATIONALS, ACCOUNTABILITY AND COMPLIANCE AT THE NATIONAL AND INTERNATIONAL LEVELS

4.1. International Corporate Responsibility

In the absence of regulatory instruments at the international level which create obligations for MNCs[105] it is difficult to establish the international

---

[99] The project was aimed at improving awareness and knowledge of EU law among national judges, prosecutors and lawyers. See Borzel (2006), supra, at 135.

[100] Council Directive 90/313/EEC. See the discussion in chapter 3.

[101] Council Directive 85/337/EEC. See the discussion in chapter 3.

[102] Even though implementation of the directives themselves has had to be challenged at the national level. Greenpeace challenged the implementation of the Directive in the Spanish courts and obtained a favourable judgment (Sentencia 106/91 of 30 June 1993 of the Audiencia Nacional).

[103] Rawlings (2000), supra.

[104] Borzel (2006), supra, 147.

[105] See chapter 3, pp. 217–218.

responsibility of companies. The nature of their operations and the difficulties and uncertainties of national litigation are factors which suggest that a potential regime for international liability would be an optimum response to the problems created by the transnational actions of multinationals.

From the many theories advanced in the context of accountability of corporations under international law perhaps the most interesting work is that of Goodwin,[106] upon which several scholars build.[107] Goodwin focuses on the ex ante duties of the actors involved to ensure that certain harms do not take place. He departs from the classical distinction between 'evil' intent and 'negligence' that leads to criminal and civil liability respectively. This departure from looking at 'intention' is particularly useful in constructing a theory of corporate liability because it does not matter what the corporation, its directors or the individuals involved 'intended'. What matters really is the corporation's potential for violating human rights, whether adequate rules were in place to avoid this and were these adhered to.[108] Corporate liability, it has been argued, can be more effective than individual or state liability since it can be monitored by shareholders and provide a strong economic incentive to compliance.[109] Corporations act as organisations and are not simply the sum of individuals working for them '[t]hey have autonomy of action, including the capacity to change their policies. They can be held responsible for the outcome of these policies'.[110]

Ratner elaborates upon Goodwin's theory and proposes a theory of corporate responsibility which is grounded on international law rather than on the national law or domestic law of the different states where litigation or violations may occur.[111] Four main parties are identified as relevant when trying to create a theory of responsibility; these are the home state of the corporation, the corporation itself, the host state and the population of the host state whose rights may be violated. In relation to these Ratner identifies four main types of issues in determining the obligations of MNCs: the closeness of the relationship between the corporation and the host state, the MNC nexus to the affected populations, the specific

---

[106] Goodwin, R. (1987), 'Apportioning Responsibilities', Law and Philosophy, 6, 167.

[107] Including Ratner, C. Wells and D. French.

[108] For a detailed and excellent discussion of the subject see Ratner (2001), supra, at 442–445.

[109] Ibid. at 443, discussing R. Gunter's work.

[110] Fisse, B. and J. Braithwaite (1998), 'The Allocation of Responsibility for Corporate Crime: Individualism, Collectivism and Accountability', Sydney Law Review, 11, 468.

[111] Ratner (2001), supra, 525.

human right concerned and the place of the individual violating human rights within the corporate structure.[112]

> The theory ultimately results in two sets of duties upon the corporation. First are the complicity-based duties that the corporation not involve itself in illegal conduct by the government; these duties arise in those circumstances in which the corporation's links to the government are akin to those in the doctrine of superior responsibility, to a duty to prevent abuses by government forces. For these duties, the factor of the nexus to the affected populations drops out. Second is a set of duties on the corporation not to infringe directly on the human rights of those with whom it enjoys certain ties, with the possibility of greater duties depending upon the scope of those links . . . The duties of the first group are conceptually simpler insofar as they are grounded in the sort of human rights abuses that fall within the existing paradigm, namely those committed by governments. The duties in the second group are more complex insofar as they do not assume governmental involvement and move human rights into the private sphere.[113]

Ratner draws a parallel between the recognition and regulation of individual responsibility for international crimes in international law and the regulation of corporate liability in international law. Both arose as a result of the perceived shortcomings of the traditional law of state liability in regulating the various serious consequences that actions by individuals or corporations have on the victims.[114] The claim that human rights constitute violations of human dignity committed by the state and that all claims should be directed against the state since it is the state which is directly or indirectly responsible for such violations although a theoretically sound proposition misses the factual element of the relative power of the parties involved. Some states are powerless in the face of the economic might of some multinationals and the political pressure exerted by the home state of some corporations.[115] The conception that human rights violations are committed just by states also ignores the changes that have taken place in the last few decades and the position on MNEs as global actors. There has been a shift in the position that only states are the duty holders of human

---

[112] Ibid.

[113] Ibid., at 525–526.

[114] Ibid., at 461–462.

[115] Because of the very different economic power between the home state and investors a so-called race to the bottom has taken place by which cash-strapped countries will seek foreign investment at any cost and will be willing to create a favourable climate to foreign investors which would in some cases amount to violations of the human rights commitments for the state in respect of labour rights and environmental protection.

rights obligations since it has become sadly apparent that private parties can participate in state actions or by themselves commit actions which violate human dignity.[116]

Holding states responsible can indeed act as an incentive to states to step up their control over individuals and business to ensure that no human rights violations take place in their territory. However several points need to be defined: which cases amount to a sufficient violation of human dignity in order to make the state accountable? What would be redress adequate for the victims? In many cases what the victims seek is a situation in which some sort of justice and punishment of individuals is achieved.

Lack of an international court to take corporations to and make them accountable does not invalidate the claim to a regime of liability but certainly limits its success. If we think of how successful the ICSID system – which allows companies to take states to international arbitration – has been we can easily conceive of a forum where individuals, groups or even states or government agencies could take corporations to court and make them accountable for violations of human rights and international law without having to navigate the jurisdictional rules of each state.

4.2 Litigation in National Courts against MNCs

Judicial instruments have been used to target multinational companies with increased frequency in the last few decades. Individuals and groups affected by the actions of MNCs have resorted to taking them to court either in the host or the home country for violation of human rights, labour or environmental standards.

Litigation has been used in environmental law cases sometimes as an indirect regulatory device. Despite the criticisms against resorting to courts instead of the legislator to regulate an area of activity this is a useful tool which is employed in the context of seeking responsibility from MNCs by victims of their activities. Victims who suffered damage in the country where the MNC operates – the host country – usually seek to bring an action against either the parent company or the subsidiary company itself in the country where the parent company is incorporated. This process has many potential advantages for the victims as the host country may, in addition to poor regulation in areas such as labour standards, pollution or environmental damage, also have an undeveloped, slow, or rudimentary

---

[116] See, in general the excellent book by Clapham, A. (1993), *Human Rights in the Private Sphere*, Oxford: Oxford University Press, esp. pp. 83–130.

judicial system and issues such as difficult or restricted access to courts or legal aid,[117] unavailability of class actions,[118] or lack of sophisticated and modern rules of liability[119] play a crucial role in the success of these types of actions.

But litigation is not necessarily, and despite the attractive points just mentioned, the best way to ensure that in the future the same events will not take place. Big settlements or court orders are a strong deterrent for the company/ies involved and for others operating in the same sector, but they do lack the regulatory power of legislation. There is no guarantee that the courts will issue a similar order in a different case, or that a different multinational could be brought to court in another country. Litigation is, in this context, a purely national remedy, and as such its utility is limited to companies amenable to the courts of a particular jurisdiction.

Examples of litigation against MNCs in home countries abound.[120] From the failed attempt to bring Union Carbide in 1987 to the US courts[121] to the settlement reached in litigation against Unocal in 2005 or Shell in 2009,[122] the success of these cases is measured not just by the potential compensation obtained for the victims, but crucially by the awareness they bring to the wider public of the activities of MNCs abroad and create negative publicity for companies, that may be more damaging and costly in economic terms than the actual damages imposed by any court of law.

Perhaps the most well known and widely used of judicial instruments at the national level are the Alien Torts Claim Act (ACTA)[123] and the

---

[117] See *Lubbe v. Cape plc* [2000] 2 Lloyd's Rep 383, where the decisive factor which persuaded the House of Lords to allow the proceedings to continue in England was the unavailability of legal aid in South Africa which would, in effect, have the effect of precluding access to the courts for the victims. For a discussion of this case see Muchlinski, P. (2001), 'Corporations and International Litigation: Problems of Jurisdiction and the UK Asbestos Cases', International and Comparative Law Quarterly, 50, 1.

[118] On the Bhopal litigation see Muchlinski, P. (1987), 'The Bhopal Case: Controlling Ultra Hazardous Industrial Activities Undertaken by Foreign Investors', MLR, 50, 545.

[119] Ibid. The Indian legal system had a law of tort at the time based on *Rylands v. Fletcher*, while the US system had sophisticated rules of liability and the possibility of punitive damages attached to certain actions.

[120] For an excellent study of litigation in the US courts see Joseph, S. (2004), *Corporations and Transnational Human Rights Litigation*, Oxford and New York: Hart Publishing.

[121] See Muchlinski (1987), supra, for an excellent discussion of the case.

[122] Both discussed below.

[123] The Alien Tort Claims Act (ATCA) of 1789 (as amended) grants jurisdiction

Torture Victims Protection Act (TVPA) in the United States. Both have been used for the enforcement of human rights claim against corporations operating abroad.

Many conditions need to be met for the victims of MNCs' activities to be able successfully to pursue a case in court. First, the country where the MNC has its parent company or headquarters or where it is incorporated must be willing to accept jurisdiction over actions taking place abroad. Not all countries are. Common law systems have, usually, a wider basis of jurisdiction and wider discretion afforded to judges as to which cases to hear and which to dismiss.[124] Countries signatories to Brussels I[125] may, after the ECJ ruling on *Owusu v. Jackson*,[126] see their discretion as to whether to hear or dismiss a case where a tort took place abroad reduced.

Secondly, the judges must be willing to adopt what has been described as a 'world tribunal' role,[127] settling grievances against their own multinationals for actions committed abroad.[128] Thirdly, pressure from the host country, which may be anxious to lose FDI or may be complicit with the foreign company in allowing or perpetrating abuses of human rights violations, may also be a factor against the victims when attempting to start litigation abroad.[129]

But, above all, litigation in national courts involves navigating the rules of jurisdiction of private international law and its different national approaches which are informed by the policy goals of each country. In the USA *Doe v. Unocal* signified a departure from the traditional rule

---

to US Federal Courts over 'any civil action by an alien for a tort only, committed in violation of the law of nations or a treaty of the United States'.

[124]   See Muchlinski (2001), supra.
[125]   EC Council Regulation 44/2001.
[126]   Case C–281/02. In the case the ECJ held that the forum non conveniens doctrine was incompatible with the Brussels Convention. Article 2 is mandatory in nature and can only be derogated from in ways expressly provided for by the Convention, as legal certainty would not be fully guaranteed and the predictability of the rules of jurisdiction would be undermined.
[127]   Muchlinski (2007), supra, p. 566.
[128]   In the U.S., litigation based on the ACTA has developed with judges willing to take this role over the last few decades, and there is now a well-established case law on it. See Joseph (2004), supra, for a comprehensive overview of the topic. Also Muchlinski (2007), supra, especially chapters 4 and 8 and Newell, P. (2001), 'Access to Environmental Justice? Litigation Against TNCs in the South', IDS Bulletin, 32, 83.
[129]   In the cases of both *Shell* in Nigeria and *Unocal* in Burma, the military was involved in torturing and killing civilians and performing other acts of abuse against the locals to facilitate the activities of the MNE. See the discussion below on complicity of states on human rights violations by MNEs in host countries.

of *Piper v. Reyno*[130] which favoured local claimants and made it difficult for foreign plaintiffs to succeed in bringing a case to court. The doctrine of forum non conveniens, as applied in the context of litigation against multinationals brought by foreign plaintiffs, had been applied generally until *Unocal* to the effect of dismissal of those claims in favour of the foreign court on the basis of balancing the public interests of the state with the private interests of the parties.[131] In 2002 in what would have been a landmark human rights case, Judge Victoria Chaney rejected Unocal's attempts to have the case rejected. This was an important decision as it not only allowed Unocal to be held liable for abuses committed overseas, but also because it 'told other multinational corporations that go into business with repressive dictatorships that they may be responsible for their partner's human rights violations'.[132] The action challenged human rights abuses committed by the notoriously brutal Burmese military on behalf of Unocal's Yadana Pipeline project in southern Burma. It was the first case in US history in which a corporation stood trial for human rights abuses committed abroad. Allegations of forced labour, sexual abuse and murder committed by the Burmese military against the local villagers would have been decided by an American jury and the victims of such human rights violations would have obtained compensation according to US standards. The case was settled before a judgment was passed as Unocal feared the damage caused by the already worldwide negative publicity. Before *Unocal*, victims of the Bhopal gas leak disaster saw their prospects of litigation in the US vanish by Judge Keenan's decision.[133] A sign of how much things have changed since the landmark *Unocal* case is the reinstatement on 3 November 2008 by the US Court of Appeals for the Second Circuit of the plaintiffs' claims against Union Carbide Corporation for ongoing, massive water pollution at its infamous plant in Bhopal, India, reversing a lower court's dismissal of the case.[134]

---

[130]   *Piper Aircraft Co. v. Reyno*, 454 U.S. 235 (1981).

[131]   See *Re Union Carbide Corporation Gas Plant Disaster*, 1993 WL 541230 (S.D.N.Y. Dec). Despite the fact that the Indian government was a party to the action in the USA as parens patriae and therefore could hardly be said to have had an interest in having the case litigated in India. See Baxi, U. (1986), *Inconvenient Forum and Convenient Catastrophe: The Bhopal Case*, Bombay: N M. Tripathi Pvt. Ltd, and Cassels, J. (1993), *The Uncertain Promise of Law: Lessons from Bhopal*, Toronto: University of Toronto Press.

[132]   See http://earthrights.org for an account of the case.

[133]   *Re Union Carbide*, supra.

[134]   A poisonous gas leak from this same plant killed thousands of people in 1984. After the 1984 disaster, Union Carbide fled India, leaving vast amounts of untreated toxins at the plant site which have contaminated the drinking water

In Australia a very different application of the forum non conveniens principle requiring 'vexation or oppression' directed at the company against which litigation has been brought has meant that the Australian courts have been slow to dismiss claims by foreign plaintiffs brought against Australian companies.[135] In the UK the courts apply the doctrine of forum non conveniens according to the test established by Lord Goff in *The Spiliada*,[136] and in the context of litigation against MNCs a shift took place with the House of Lords' decision in *Lubbe v. Cape*,[137] where the South African plaintiffs were afforded relief in the UK courts against the parent company of a subsidiary no longer existing in South Africa. The discretion of the UK courts to dismiss cases should now be further restricted due to the ECJ judgment in *Owusu v. Jackson*.[138]

This piecemeal and nationally constricted approach, while providing some hopeful advances in the plight of obtaining justice for the victims, raising worldwide awareness of MNCs' violations of human rights in host countries and creating pressure on MNCs through negative publicity to both settle and amend their behaviour, is full of uncertainties. It relies not only on the private international law or jurisdiction conventions of the states involved as to whether the court will accept jurisdiction to hear and decide a case, but also on the choice of legal rule of each of those national courts as to the law that will be applicable to the resolution of the dispute itself. Perhaps, though, the toughest obstacles to ensuring MNC liability

---

supply of nearby residents. The plaintiffs sued to force Union Carbide to clean up its mess and compensate those injured. The district court decided on its own to evaluate the defendants' evidence at an early stage of the case, and dismissed the case. The Second Circuit overruled that decision, finding the dismissal to be improper because the district court did not give the plaintiffs adequate opportunity to respond to the factual argument the district court raised on its own. The Court of Appeals did not need to reach the plaintiffs' argument that the evidence already in the case was more than sufficient to permit the plaintiffs to present their case to a jury.

[135]   Prince, P. (1998), 'Bhopal, Bougainville and OK Tedi: Why Australian Forum Non-conveniens Approach is Better', *International and Comparative Law Quarterly*, 47, 573–598.

[136]   *Spiliada Maritime Corp. v. Cansulex Ltd* [1987] A.C. 460. Before that decision *The Atlantic Star* [1974] A.C. 436 ruled that if an alternative forum existed where the actions took place litigation should be directed to that forum. See also *MacShannon v. Rockware Glass Ltd* [1987] A.C. 795. The case involved an industrial accident in Scotland but the plaintiffs had been directed by their trade union representatives to bring a claim in England as the damages could be potentially much higher.

[137]   [2000] 1 W.L.R.1545.

[138]   Discussed above.

are national company laws, when applied by the court to determine the connection of the parent company with the acts of its branch, subsidiary or establishment abroad. Until corporate law is standardised and an agreement is reached, perhaps by way of an international instrument which allows the lifting of the so-called 'corporate veil' internationally, it is very difficult to make a company in a home country responsible for the actions of its subsidiary in a host state. The separate legal personality of the different units of an MNC is, of course, what makes the corporate structure so attractive to multinational enterprises which can divide and subdivide assets and liability while preserving the advantages of size and power, wealth and profit behind the carefully crafted shield of corporate law.

Tort litigation against multinationals in national courts is, in conclusion, an attractive prospect, but in practice a prospect which is laden with the problems and technicalities of private international law and cross-country litigation and the privileges afforded by national company laws. One of its major advantages resides in the negative publicity it creates for the companies involved and the pressure that this creates for withdrawing activities, reaching a settlement or engaging in socially and environmentally beneficial projects in an attempt to 'greenwash' their image. There have been calls for global instruments which regulate access to judicial channels worldwide. While there is little consensus on the worldwide regulation of multinationals perhaps a more realistic instrument would be one which regulated jurisdictional access in claims against MNCs.

For many investigating alternative means of bringing MNCs to comply with human rights standards and accountable for their violation requires state involvement and resorting to mechanisms of international law, but these are not devoid of problems,[139] while holding MNCs responsible under the law of the host state ignores the fact that today economic power is as, if not more, important than political power and that many states do not have the will, the capacity or the resources to pursue claims against MNCs. The fear that host states have to cross the line that might upset foreign investors and the consequences that they will have to face from the potential withdrawal of foreign investments is often enough to deter states from challenging MNCs. Further dispute resolution mechanisms such as arbitration under the ICSID highlight the might of corporations in respect of states. The case of Chevron in Ecuador is one of the few cases where an MNC has been taken to court in the host state and high damages are expected.

Some of the above findings, especially that pointing out the absence of

---

[139] See the discussion above.

BOX 6.3.   ROYAL DUTCH SHELL IN NIGERIA

Royal Dutch Shell agreed to a $15.5 million settlement in 2009 to end an action alleging that the oil giant was complicit in the executions of activist Ken Saro-Wiwa and other civilians by Nigeria's former military regime.

Shell, which continues to operate in Nigeria, said it agreed to settle the action in hopes of aiding the 'process of reconciliation'. But Europe's largest oil company acknowledged no wrongdoing in the 1995 hanging deaths of six people, including poet Ken Saro-Wiwa. 'This gesture also acknowledges that, even though Shell had no part in the violence that took place, the plaintiffs and others have suffered', Malcolm Brinded, Shell's Executive Director Exploration & Production, said in a statement.

The action in the US District Court in New York claimed Shell colluded with the country's former military government to silence environmental and human rights activists in the country's Ogoni region. The oil-rich district sits in the southern part of Nigeria and is roughly the size of San Antonio. Shell started operating there in 1958. The primary complaint against Shell focused on activities by the company's subsidiary, Shell Petroleum Development Company of Nigeria Limited. The action said that in the 1990s, Shell officials helped furnish Nigerian police with weapons, participated in security sweeps of the area, and asked government troops to shoot villagers protesting at the construction of a pipeline which later leaked oil. The plaintiffs also say Shell helped the government capture and hang Wiwa, John Kpuinen, Saturday Doobee, Felix Nuate, Daniel Gbokoo and Dr Barinem Kiobel on 10 November, 1995.

Besides compensating the families, the money from Shell will pay for years of legal fees. And a large chunk of the settlement – roughly half – will create a trust which will invest in social programmes in the country including educational endowments, agricultural development, support for small enterprise and adult literacy programmes.

Altogether, the settlement will have a negligible effect on Shell's shareholders, amounting to less than one-hundredth of a per cent of Shell's annual revenue. It is comparable to the annual cost of renting one of the super tankers that Shell uses to deliver Nigerian oil to other countries.

Fourteen years after the Nigerian activists were hanged, Wiwa's son said he thinks Shell has started to acknowledge that it needs a 'social licence' to operate in foreign countries. For example, the company has agreed to pay for a study of environmental damage that drilling has caused the Ogoni region.

FOR DISCUSSION

- Compare with the fate of the Nigerian plaintiffs in *Bowoto v. Chevron* see decisions of Judge Susan Illston of the US District Court for the Northern District of California of 4 March 2009, San Francisco, CA.
- Chevron was found not liable for aiding and abetting human rights abuses after a jury trial last December.

Which were the defining different elements (if any) between both cases?

---

suitable mechanisms for settlement of disputes, have encouraged scholars to argue that a World Court of Human Rights to which non-state actors could become parties is necessary.[140] Corporations will be invited and encouraged to accept the binding jurisdiction of the court in relation to selected human rights in their sphere of activity; for example, forced and child labour or the prohibition of discrimination. A slightly different proposition is that of creating a Human Rights Unit (HRU) under UN auspices to deal with human rights cases arising in the context of private–public partnerships (PPP). This HRU will set standards for projects and monitor these uniformly, creating accountability where there is now only confusion and different standards inadequately monitored.[141] None of these proposals has been taken forward.[142]

---

[140] Nowak, M. (2007), 'The Need for a World Court of Human Rights', Human Rights Law Review, 7, 251.

[141] Likosky, M. (2006), *Law, Infrastructure and Human Rights*, Cambridge: Cambridge University Press, chapter 9.

[142] Further discussion of compliance and enforcement mechanisms in respect of multinationals can be found in chapter 6.

BOX 6.4.   CHEVRON IN ECUADOR

Chevron Corp., which expects to be on the losing end of a long-running environmental lawsuit in Ecuador, is turning its attention to fighting the expected multibillion-dollar verdict in the US.

Chevron itself has never operated in Ecuador, and Texaco pulled out in 1992, leaving behind almost no assets for the court to seize in case of a judgment against the company. Therefore the plaintiffs will need to try to enforce any ruling in a country where Chevron does have assets, most likely the US. Chevron has been reassuring shareholders that it doesn't expect to be forced to pay any judgment imposed by Ecuador. 'We're not paying and we're going to fight this for years if not decades into the future,' Chevron spokesman Don Campbell said in an interview.

After the plaintiffs originally sued Texaco in the US for environmental damage, Texaco convinced a US court that the case should be heard in Ecuador, praising Ecuador's judicial system in court filings. Texaco argued the case should be heard in Ecuador because the evidence and alleged damage were in the country. The plaintiffs argued that Ecuador wasn't equipped to deal with such a complicated case.

To prevent enforcement of a potential judgment in the US, Chevron will likely need to convince a US judge it didn't get a fair trial in Ecuador – something legal experts say won't be easy. Chevron has begun laying the groundwork for such an argument in court filings and letters to investors, questioning the qualifications of the court-appointed expert and arguing that recent incidents – including the adoption last fall of a new constitution that replaced Ecuador's Supreme Court with a new body – have called the entire system into question. The plaintiffs argue Ecuador's court system has become less susceptible to corruption in recent years. Andrew Woods, a lawyer for the plaintiffs, accused Chevron of stalling. Chevron denies stalling, but has stressed to investors that any enforcement will likely take years.

Chevron denies the allegations, arguing that Texaco's operations in Ecuador met local and international standards, that a $40 million cleanup effort in the 1990s resolved any environmental liability the company had there, and that any remaining problems are the responsibility of Petroecuador, the state-run oil company that took over Texaco's operations. Damages of $27 billion would represent roughly a tenth of the company's 2008 revenue, and a record-setting judgment could tarnish Chevron's image at a time when it has been trying to establish itself as environmentally friendly.

The most immediate threat to Chevron, according to analysts, could be the impact a ruling would have on its reputation, particularly as the company seeks permission to drill in other developing countries.

Source: Ben Casselman, Wall Street Journal, 21 July 2009.

5. CONCLUSION

The variety of actors, alongside states, involved in global trade and natural resource management needs reflection in adequate enforcement and compliance regimes, but this is not always the case. On the one hand states can be made accountable under treaty compliance mechanisms, the law of state responsibility or the human rights regime. Other actors, especially international financial institutions, NGOs and multinational corporations, make decisions and take actions of enormous importance for natural resource management and, in the case of corporations, are in a position to engage in human rights violations, and yet they still remain able to navigate the turbulent waters of responsibility between national and international law and, in some cases, escape with impunity.

The most challenging of all aspects of compliance today remains that of creating effective mechanisms and enforcement for multinational corporations. The failure to devise those mechanisms is perhaps linked to the ongoing debate about the changing role of states and corporations[143] and their respective obligations.

Although in the international sphere there are examples of extremely successful compliance regimes there remains a preoccupation with the lack of effective mechanisms which promote common standard setting, monitoring and compliance mechanisms among corporations.

This preoccupation extends to the burdensome mechanisms which at present exist to make corporations accountable for violations of human rights in foreign countries. To date the only viable option is private

---

[143] See chapter 5.

litigation under tort law if enabled by universal jurisdiction statutes such as the ACTA or wide jurisdictional rules. If that fails the individuals affected need to pursue action against the state through complicity or regulatory negligence for the violation of human rights. Pursuing the channel of state responsibility of the home state under international law for acts of its corporations abroad is an option which, despite strong theoretical arguments in its favour, evokes the problems that pursuing state responsibility under international law always has had and is best left for extreme cases of explicit complicity or wilful ignorance by the home state in respect of the actions of its corporations abroad.

Corporate and voluntary codes of conduct have multiplied in the last few decades and the adoption of rights-sensitive branding and certification is now a big part of marketing and consumer capture.[144] Examples include the Kimberley Process for the certification of conflict diamonds, the rain-forest initiative or Fair Trade Certification in products such as cocoa, coffee, sugar and bananas. Indeed many argue that it is in the self-interest of corporations to bring their practices within human rights standards: '[a] company suffers in capital markets if its shares lose value in increasingly socially conscious investment environments, and it suffers in the retail market through consumer choices at the point of purchase (including boycotts). With the rise of litigation against corporate defendants, it may increasingly suffer in a courtroom.'[145]

The need, thus, remains for the development of bodies which can engage in global governance in the spheres of standard setting, monitoring and ensuring compliance. This need includes new mechanisms of dispute settlements whereby MNCs can really be held accountable. In the same manner in which the ICSID was created to protect the interests of MNCs vis-à-vis states a similar dispute settlement body can be created to protect the interests of individuals or weaker states, vis-à-vis corporations. Progress has been made by the creation of the WTO and its DSB, the IFC, initiatives such as Transparency International and the slow advances brought up by human rights litigation, but the advances are too slow and

---

[144] For a general discussion on labelling schemes and their effectiveness see Liubicic, R.J. (1998), 'Corporate Codes of Conduct and Product Labelling Schemes: The Limits and Possibilities of Promoting International Labor Rights Standards Through Private Initiatives', Law and Policy Review of International Business, 30, 111.

[145] Steinhardt, R.G. (2008), 'Soft Law, Hard Markets: Competitive Self-Interest and the Emergence of Human Rights Responsibilities for multinational Corporations', Brooklyn Journal of International Law, 3, 33, available at: www. brooklaw.edu/news/corpliability/pdfs/Steinhardt.pdf, at 9.

too biased. Only corporate agents have a better set of institutions, rules and mechanisms in which to function. Individuals, communities, and non-corporate groups are left behind on the last legs of an old system based on radically different conceptions of politics, states, economic power and society. The changes in the respective roles of states, corporations and civil society clamour for a change in the traditional structures of both national and international law.

FURTHER READING

Birnie, P., A. Boyle and C. Redgwell (2009), *International Law and the Environment*, 2nd edn, Oxford: Oxford University Press.

Clapham, A. (2004), 'State Responsibility, Corporate Responsibility and Complicity in Human Rights Violations', in L. Bomman-Larsen and O. Wiggen (eds), *Responsibility in World Business: Managing Harmful Side Effects of Corporate Activity*, Tokyo: United Nations University Press.

Cottier, T., J. Pauwelyn and E. Burgi (eds) (2005), *Human Rights and International Trade*, Oxford: Oxford University Press.

Dine, J. (2005), 'The Relationship Between Companies and Human Rights', in J. Dine, *Companies, International Trade and Human Rights*, Cambridge: Cambridge University Press, pp. 167–221.

Joseph, S. (1999), 'Taming the Leviathians: Multinational Enterprises and Human Rights', Netherlands International Law Review, XLVI, 175–177.

Ratner, S. (2001), 'Corporations and Human Rights: A Theory of Legal Responsibility', Yale Law Journal, 111, 443.

Reed, L., J. Paulson and N. Blackaby (2004), *Guide to ICSID Arbitration*, The Hague: Kluwer Law International.

Sands, L. (2003), *Principles of International Environmental Law*, 2nd edn, Cambridge: Cambridge University Press, pp. 171–229.

Skolgy, S. and M. Gibney (2002), 'Transnational Human Rights Obligations', Human Rights Quarterly, 24, 781.

Spar, D. (1998), 'The Spotlight and the Bottom Line: How Transnationals Export Human Rights', Foreign Affairs, 77, 7–12.

Ward, H. (2000), 'Foreign Direct Liability: A New Weapon in the Performance Armoury?', AccountAbility Quarterly, 14(3), 22.

PART III

Approaches

7. Water resources

1. WATER GOVERNANCE AND GLOBALISATION

There are two sets of arguments which are increasingly common in water resource management. The first set considers water as a public good and one that is intimately related to human rights entitlements. The second views water as an economic good and can be tracked down to the Dublin Conference (1992).[1] This second set revolves round the idea that if water is treated as an economic good, problems related to scarcity, quality and availability will be solved. This chapter considers both these arguments, looking at the international, regional and national legal policies and practices relating to water.

At the local level, large infrastructure projects and water service concessions are granted by governments. Water users often have no participation in the decision-making processes relating to water – decisions which often affect their water rights and undermine their livelihoods by displacing them or by restricting their water use. Multinational companies as holders of water services contracts in many developing (and developed) countries control the management of water resources. In addition, multinational banks may prescribe policies promoting full cost recovery of water investments. Water privatisation in Asia, Latin America and African countries gave rise to concerns regarding the availability of water to the poor community, quality and quantity of water resources and accountability of multinational companies.[2] The free trade promoted by the WTO and the liberalisation of foreign direct investment have led, in many cases, to environmental deregulation, causing water pollution and depletion of water resources by over extraction. Individuals and communities affected by water development plans, infrastructure projects and privatisation of water services have increasingly demanded greater consultation, and more transparent and accountable decisions.

---

[1] 1992 Dublin Statement on Water and Sustainable Development, International Conference on Water and the Environment (Dublin, Ireland).
[2] See section 5 of this chapter. Also, chapters 5 and 6 on MNCs and accountability.

Water is treated as a public good in a number of documents adopted by the UN with an affirmation that adequate amounts of clean water, for both consumption and sanitation, are a prerequisite for a healthy life. Chapter 18 of Agenda 21 of the 1992 UN Convention on Environment and Development[3] deals with freshwater resources, focusing on the application of integrated approaches to the development, management and use of water resources.

> Water is needed in all aspects of life . . . The multi-sectoral nature of water resources development in the context of socio-economic development must be recognized, as well as the multi-interest utilization of water resources for water supply and sanitation, agriculture, industry, urban development, hydropower generation, inland fisheries, transportation, recreation, low and flat lands management and other activities.[4]

Citing water as a 'good', Chapter 18 of Agenda 21 (1992) stated as follows:

> The role of water as a social, economic and life sustaining good should be reflected in demand management mechanisms and implemented through water conservation and reuse, resource assessment and financial instruments.[5]

The Millennium Development Goals (MDGs)[6] set three targets relating to freshwater. They aim (i) to halve the proportion of people in the world without access to safe drinking water by 2015, (ii) to halve the proportion of people in the world who have no access to basic sanitation by 2015, and (iii) for each country to develop integrated water resources management and water efficiency plans by 2005. The MDG Report of 2008 states:[7]

---

[3]   Paras 18.2 and 18.3 of Chapter 18 of the UN Programme of Action From Rio (Protection of the Quality and Supply of Freshwater Resources: Application of Integrated Approaches to the Development, Management and Use of Water Resources). See Agenda 21, 1992 Report of the UNCED, I (1992) UN Doc. A/CONF.151/26/Rev. 1, Rio de Janeiro, 14 June 1992.

[4]   Para. 18.3.

[5]   Para. 18.17.

[6]   For each goal, one or more targets have been set, mostly for 2015, using 1990 as a benchmark. Goal 7 dealt with environmental sustainability. This goal was re-emphasised in the WSSD summit. Around 191 countries have signed the UN Millennium Declaration. See UN Millennium Declaration, UN GA Res. 55/2, UN Doc. A/RES/55/2, 8 September 2000.

[7]   UN (2008), The Millennium Development Goals Report, New York, 40, 42.

Water use has grown at more than twice the rate of the population for the past century. Although there is not yet a global water shortage, about 2.8 billion people, representing more than 40 per cent of the world's population, live in river basins with some form of water scarcity. More than 1.2 billion of them live under conditions of physical water scarcity, which occurs when more than 75 per cent of the river flows are withdrawn. . . . Another 1.6 billion people live in areas of economic water scarcity, where human, institutional and financial capital limit access to water, even though water in nature is available locally to meet human demands.

. . .

Since 1990, 1.6 billion people have gained access to safe water. At this rate, the world is expected to meet the drinking water target, which would require that 89 per cent of the population of developing regions use improved sources of drinking water by 2015. Still, nearly one billion people today lack safe sources of drinking water.

Like the MDG, the 2002 World Summit for Sustainable Development (WSSD) reiterates the aim to halve the proportion of people without access to safe drinking water.[8] It includes supporting developing countries and countries with economies in transition in their efforts to monitor and assess the quantity and quality of water resources. It urges national governments to develop national programmes for sustainable development and to empower local communities. At the same time, it talks about increasing access to public services and institutions such as water, education and health. In order to combat desertification and mitigate the effects of drought and floods, it prioritises integrated land, water and natural resources management. Moreover, the Water, Energy, Health, Agriculture and Biodiversity (WEHAB) initiative[9] proposed by the UN Secretary-General prior to the WSSD also plays an important role in achieving the MDGs and the targets set out in the WSSD. The WEHAB initiative seeks to provide impetus to action in these five key thematic areas of crucial global importance, and particularly for poor people throughout the developing world. The MDGs, WEHAB and the Johannesburg Plan of Action offer a unique opportunity to coordinate efforts and combine resources of a range of diverse development partners to achieve sustainable water governance in the developing countries.

---

[8] Para. 6. Plan of Implementation of the WSSD, Report of the World Summit on Sustainable Development, Johannesburg, South Africa (2002), UN Doc. A/CONF.199/20, Res. 2, Annex. Water-related issues are mentioned in Chapter II on poverty eradication and Chapter IV on protecting and managing the natural resource base of social and economic development.

[9] WEHAB Working Group (2002), *A Framework for Action on Water and Sanitation*, New York: United Nations, 5.

In 2005, the UN Report on the realisation of the right to water[10] considered that 'water resources constitute a common heritage and must be used in an equitable manner and managed in cooperation with the users in a spirit of solidarity . . .'. The Millennium Ecosystem Assessment adds that '[w]ater withdrawals from rivers and lakes doubled since 1960; most water use (70% worldwide) is for agriculture'.[11] Reasons for this include the rising demand for water for irrigation and industrial processes and increasing use of water by people as their incomes rise. 'The amount of water impounded behind dams quadrupled since 1960 and three to six times as much water is held in reservoirs as in natural rivers.'[12] It shows that some regions have excess water while some do not, and the crucial issue is how to ensure equitable distribution of the water that is available.

The Draft Guidelines proposed in the 2005 UN Report state that '[e]veryone has the right to a sufficient quantity of clean water for personal and domestic uses' and '[e]veryone has the right to have access to adequate and safe sanitation that is conducive to the protection of public health and the environment'.[13] It includes guidelines for national government and the local authorities as they have a 'responsibility to move progressively and as expeditiously as possible towards the full realisation of the right to water and sanitation for everyone, using practical and targeted measures and drawing, to the maximum extent possible, on all available resources'.[14] States should, at all levels of government:[15]

> . . . [e]stablish a regulatory system for private and public water and sanitation service providers that requires them to provide physical, affordable and equal access to safe, acceptable and sufficient water and to appropriate sanitation and includes mechanisms to ensure genuine public participation, independent monitoring and compliance with regulations.

In 2010, the UN General Assembly adopted a resolution recognising access to clean water as a human right and asked international organisations to assist developing countries, in order to scale up efforts to provide

---

[10]   Commission on Human Rights (2005), Sub-Commission on the Promotion and Protection of Human Rights, 'Realization of the right to drinking water and sanitation', E/CN.4/Sub.2/2005/25, 11 July 2005.

[11]   Millennium Ecosystem Assessment (2005), *Ecosystems and Human Well-being: Synthesis,* Washington DC: Island Press, 2.

[12]   Ibid., 2.

[13]   Commission on Human Rights (2005), supra, Guidelines 1.1. and 1.2.

[14]   Guideline 2.1.

[15]   Guideline 2.3 (e).

safe, clean, accessible and affordable drinking water and sanitation for all.[16]

The above discussion highlights that regulating water resources in a sustainable manner is required mutually to benefit the public bodies, private sector and the local communities (i.e. allocation among different users), and there is a need to regulate the water sectors at the local, national and international levels (i.e. water use efficiency). Moreover, national mechanisms should ensure the involvement of all stakeholders in managing, conserving and sharing water resources (i.e. participation, information and access to justice).

This chapter briefly outlines the international commitments under international and regional conventions on human rights law, environmental law and WTO law (sections 2 and 3).[17] Section 4 explores water rights at the national level with judicial decisions outlining the nature of the right. Section 5 looks at the influence of corporations and international financial institutions on the development of the water sector and water-related services.

2. APPROACHES TO WATER GOVERNANCE IN MULTILATERAL AGREEMENTS

A number of non-binding and binding multilateral instruments guide the international legal regime relating to water. Most of these provisions are aspirational and do not have any enforcement mechanism.

2.1. Non-binding Instruments

The civil society plays a crucial role in the development of the right to water. For example, the ILA Berlin Rules (2004) state that:[18]

> Every individual has a right of access to sufficient, safe, acceptable, physically accessible, and affordable water to meet that individual's vital human needs.

---

[16]   UN General Assembly Resolution on Human Right to Water and Sanitation, UN GA Resolution A/64/L.63/Rev.1, 26 July 2010.

[17]   This chapter does not include issues relating to management of rivers, protection of the marine environment or the protection of water during armed conflicts.

[18]   Article 17. This document is influenced by the Helsinki Rules on the Use of Waters of International Rivers (1966) and the UN Convention on the Law of the Non-Navigational Uses of International Watercourses (1997). International Law Association, the Berlin Rules on Water Resources (2004), 24.

According to the Berlin Rules, the right to water requires that states work towards the progressive realisation of the right.[19] There is no present or immediate duty to provide fully adequate and safe water supplies to all.[20] Water is subject to competing uses and there is an unquestionable link between unsustainable water use and poverty. Several water-related declarations, considered below, emphasise public–private partnerships and collaborative efforts between stakeholders as crucial elements to developing a fair and efficient system of water management.

The First International Conference on Water and the Environment (1992) in Dublin provided input on freshwater issues for the 1992 Rio Declaration.[21] It outlined the importance of involving stakeholders in the decision-making process and asked for the economic value of water to be recognised 'in all its competing uses'.[22] The Hague Declaration (2000) stated that business as usual is not an option.[23] It noted that water resources and the related ecosystems are under threat from pollution, unsustainable use, land-use changes, climate change and many other forces. It also highlighted the link between these environmental threats and poverty.

Held prior to the WSSD, the Bonn Ministerial Declaration (2001) acknowledged that water resources continue to be public goods[24] and focused on practical ideas and identified positive ways forward relating to a wide range of water-related issues. It reviewed the role of water in sustainable development and took stock of progress in the implementation of Agenda 21. Participation of local people, workers, NGOs and the private sector in 'new partnerships', joint action, shared knowledge, and effective regulation and monitoring was recognised as essential for improving the management of water resources.[25] Although there was much expectation,[26]

---

[19]   Ibid., Article 17(3).

[20]   Ibid., 24.

[21]   Dublin Statement (1992), supra.

[22]   Ibid., Principle 4.

[23]   Ministerial Declaration of The Hague on Water Security in the 21st Century (The Hague, Netherlands, 2000).

[24]   International Conference on Freshwater: Water – A Key to Sustainable Development (Bonn, Germany, 2001).

[25]   Ministerial Declaration, International Conference on Freshwater (Bonn, Germany, 2001).

[26]   Expectations were created as the Forum met after the ECOSOC General Comment 15 recognised 'water as a human right', and it was held during the International Year of Freshwater. See Joint Statement by Three Rapporteurs of the UN Commission on Human Rights at the Third World Water Forum, UN Press Release, World Water Council, Kyoto, 2003.

the Third World Water Forum (2003) failed to produce a definite pro-gramme of action and the Ministerial Declaration advocated the building of public–private partnerships for water projects.[27] The Fourth World Water Forum (2006)[28] emphasised the need for collaboration among all actors, including the private sector, NGOs, civil society and international financial institutions. It added that governments have the primary role in improving access to water through improved governance at all levels and regulatory frameworks adopting a pro-poor approach with the active involvement of all stakeholders.[29] Acknowledging water as a cross-cutting issue, the Ministerial Declaration of the 2009 World Water Forum reiter-ates the need for better water demand management, implementation of integrated water resources management, and country led water projects which are environmentally sustainable and socially equitable.[30] It accepts the need for a fair, equitable and sustainable cost recovery strategy and that 'exclusively economic approaches and tools cannot capture all social and environmental aspects in cost recovery'.[31]

2.2. Human Rights Treaties

The right to safe drinking water has been implicitly recognised in a wide range of international documents, including treaties, declarations and other standards.[32] These instruments cover the rights to life, to the enjoy-ment of a standard of living adequate for health and well-being, to protec-tion from disease and to adequate food. If these provisions are examined, it is clear that an express right such as the right to adequate food, human health and development cannot be attained without also guaranteeing access to clean water. For example, Article 25 of the Universal Declaration of Human Rights (1948) states that '[e]veryone has the right to a standard of living adequate for the health and well-being of himself and his family, including food . . .'. This provision does not include any express refer-ence to the right to water.[33] McCaffrey assumes that the right to water is

---

[27] Third World Water Forum Ministerial Declaration (World Water Council, Kyoto, 2003), paras, 3, 5 and 6.

[28] Fourth World Water Forum (World Water Council, Mexico, 2006).

[29] Para. 7.

[30] Paras 2–4 and 22, Fifth World Water Forum (World Water Council, Turkey, 2009).

[31] Para. 21.

[32] For example, Declaration on the Right to Development, UN GA Res. 41/128, New York, 4 December 1986, Article 8.

[33] Universal Declaration of Human Rights, UN GA Res. 217A (III), New York, 10 December 1948.

'implicit in the right to adequate standard of living'[34] and Scanlon is in favour of a right to water falling under the liberal interpretation of the Universal Declaration.[35]

Article 6 of the International Covenant on Civil and Political Rights[36] states that '[e]very human being has the inherent right to life. This right shall be protected by law. No one shall be arbitrarily deprived of his life.' This is a negative right and the government should not to take any action which deprives people of their right. Fitzmaurice argues that there is a possibility of interpreting Article 6 broadly to include positive action by government officials, including access to water.[37]

2.2.1. Express rights

Several international instruments refer to water as a human right.[38] These instruments include:

- The 1979 Convention on the Elimination of All Forms of Discrimination against Women stipulates that states parties shall ensure to women the right to 'enjoy adequate living conditions, particularly in relation to . . . water supply'.[39]
- The 1989 Convention on the Rights of the Child requires states parties to combat disease and malnutrition 'through the provision of adequate nutritious foods and clean drinking-water'.[40]

---

[34]   McCaffrey, S. (1992), 'A Human Right to Water: Domestic and International Implications', Georgetown International Environmental Law Review, 5, 1. Also McCaffrey, S. (2004), 'The Human Right to Water Revisited', in E.B. Weiss, L.B. De Chazournes and N. Bernasconi-Osterwalder (eds), *Freshwater and International Economic Law*, Oxford: Oxford University Press, 93–111.

[35]   Scanlon, J., A. Cassar and N. Nemes (2004), 'Water as a Human Right?', IUCN Environmental Policy and Law Paper 51, Gland, Switzerland and Cambridge, UK: IUCN. 4. Cited Gleick, P.H. (1999), 'The Human Right to Water', Water Policy, 1(5), 487–503.

[36]   International Covenant on Civil and Political Rights, UN GA Res. 2200A (XXI), New York, 16 December 1966.

[37]   Fitzmaurice, M. (2007), 'The Human Right to Water', Fordham Environmental Law Review, 18, 541.

[38]   Articles 20, 26, 29, 46 of Geneva Convention III (1949), Articles 85, 89, 127 of Geneva Convention IV (1949). Scanlon et al. (1994), supra, 35–37.

[39]   Article 14(2)(h), UN Convention on the Elimination of All Forms of Discrimination against Women, New York, 18 December 1979.

[40]   Article 24(2)(a). UN Convention on the Rights of the Child, New York, 20 November 1989.

2.2.2. General Comment 15

In General Comment 15 on the implementation of Articles 11 and 12 of International Covenant on Economic, Social and Cultural Rights,[41] the Committee of Economic, Social and Cultural Rights (CESCR) recognises the human right to water.[42] The CESCR noted that 'the human right to water is indispensable for leading a life in human dignity. It is a prerequisite for the realization of other human rights.'[43] In summary, the right to water puts an obligation on governments to extend progressively access to sufficient, affordable, accessible and safe water supplies and to safe sanitation services. Whereas the right to safe drinking water applies to everyone, states parties need to give special attention to those individuals and groups who have traditionally faced difficulties in exercising the right, including women, children, and indigenous peoples. Moreover, the CESCR states that 'water should be treated a social and cultural good, and not primarily as an economic good'.[44]

The General Comment notes that the right to water is 'inextricably related' to the right to health and right to adequate housing and food.[45] It shows that the enjoyment of the right to safe drinking water is dependent upon the realisation of other human rights, particularly the rights to food, housing, health, work, education, as well as freedom of expression, freedom of association, freedom of residence, and participation in public decision-making.

The General Comment on the right to water imposes three levels of obligations on states parties: the obligations to respect, to protect and to fulfil the right to safe drinking water. The obligation to *respect* requires that states parties refrain from interfering directly or indirectly with the enjoyment of the right to drinking water.[46] The obligation to *protect* requires states parties to prevent third parties from interfering in any way with the enjoyment of the right to safe drinking water.[47] Third parties include

---

[41] General Comment 15. Substantive Issues Arising in the Implementation of the International Covenant on Economic, Social and Cultural Rights. The Right to Water (Articles 11 and 12 of the International Covenant on Economic, Social and Cultural Rights), Doc. E/C.12/2002/11, 20 January 2003.

[42] Ibid., para. 3.

[43] Ibid., para. 1.

[44] Ibid., para. 11.

[45] Para. 3. The right to water is also inextricably related to the right to the highest attainable standard of health (Article 12, para. 1) and the rights to adequate housing and adequate food (Article 11, para. 1). See General Comment 4 (1991), General Comment 14 (2000).

[46] General Comment 15, paras 21–22.

[47] Paras 23–24.

individuals, corporations and other entities as well as agents acting under their authority.[48] States parties need to ensure that third parties operating or controlling water services and resources, e.g. piped water networks, water tankers, water vendors and wells, do not threaten or compromise the sufficiency, safety, affordability or accessibility of the right. It adds that privatisation of water services should be deferred until 'an effective regulatory system is in place, that is in conformity with the Covenant and this General Comment and that includes independent monitoring, genuine public participation and imposition of penalties for non-compliance'.[49] The obligation to *fulfil* requires states parties to adopt the necessary measures directed towards the full realisation of the right to safe drinking water.[50] States parties should adopt comprehensive and integrated strategies and programmes to ensure that there is sufficient and safe water for present and future generations.

The General Comment also notes that the states parties are obliged to monitor effectively the realisation of the right to safe drinking water. The work of human rights advocates and other members of civil society who assist in the realisation of the right, particularly for vulnerable or marginalised groups, should be respected, protected, facilitated, and promoted by states.[51] The General Comment is not a legally binding document and the implementation of this document at the national level will largely depend on the goodwill of states. States, however, do have an obligation to report to the CESCR on their progress in fulfilling the right to water.[52]

2.3.   Multilateral Environmental Agreements

Many multilateral environmental agreements (MEAs) address water resource management and do so in ways which are sometimes overlapping, sometimes complementary, and sometimes in apparent conflict. Although each MEA addresses a specific global or regional challenge using distinct approaches and mechanisms, there is considerable ecological interdependence between the goals and strategies of each agreement. For example, both the 1992 Convention on Biodiversity (CBD) and the 1992 UN Convention on Climate Change (UNFCCC) relate to floods, droughts, and aquatic ecosystems. Similarly, the 1994 Convention to

---

[48]   Para. 23.
[49]   Para. 24.
[50]   Paras 25–29.
[51]   Para. 59.
[52]   Paras 9 and 54.

Combat Desertification (CCD) aims to mitigate the effects of drought and desertification. Making matters still more challenging, different government departments and agencies at the national level have responsibility for the implementation of these MEAs.

The following discussion gives an overview of the relevance of various MEAs to water resource management. International treaties include biodiversity related conventions (Ramsar Convention, World Heritage Convention, Biodiversity Convention and Desertification Convention), an atmospheric convention (Climate Change Convention), and chemical conventions (Basel Convention, Stockholm Convention). Although these MEAs appear to have some common elements, they generally follow an individual sectoral approach. In most cases, specific national priorities and objectives in relation to the MEAs are likely to arise through relevant national planning and strategy processes. Coordination is, therefore, necessary for the efficient and effective implementation of MEAs and must occur at all levels: from international to national to local.

2.3.1. Ramsar Convention[53]

Wetlands have important hydrological functions, such as the recharge of groundwater, filtration and flood control, and they support a rich biodiversity. There is a vital link between water resources, wetlands, and the health and livelihood of human communities. The Convention seeks to ensure the wise use[54] of all wetlands and provides for more stringent conservation of those wetlands listed in the List of Wetlands of International Importance.[55] The Ramsar Convention has adopted a series of recommendations and guidelines on conservation and management of wetlands.[56] For example, Resolution VIII.40 (2002) recognises the critical hydrological and ecological linkages between groundwater bodies and wetland ecosystems, and highlights the impacts that groundwater exploitation and use can have on wetlands.

---

[53] 1971 Convention on Wetlands of International Importance especially as Waterfowl Habitat (Ramsar Convention).

[54] 'The wise use of wetlands is their sustainable utilisation for the benefit of humankind in a way compatible with the maintenance of the natural properties of the ecosystem.' Adopted by COP-3 (1987). See: Ramsar Convention Secretariat (2007), *Wise Use of Wetlands: A Conceptual Framework for the Wise Use of Wetlands.* Ramsar Handbooks for the Wise Use of Wetlands, 3rd edition, Vol. 1. Gland, Switzerland: Ramsar Convention Secretariat.

[55] Articles 2, 3 of the Convention.

[56] See: Res. VI.23 (1996), Res. VII.18 (1999), Res. VIII.4 (2002), Res. VIII.34 (2002), Res. VIII.35 (2002), Res. VIII.1 (2002); Res. IX.1 Annex C(ii) (2005); Res. IX.1 Annex C (2005).

2.3.2.   World Heritage Convention[57]

The World Heritage Convention operates on the basis of specific site-listings which include lake, river, wetlands or the upper catchment of a watercourse.[58] For example, the Pantanal conservation area – which is one of the world's largest freshwater wetland ecosystems – is covered by the Ramsar Convention and is also a World Heritage site.[59] The World Heritage Committee produces a 'World Heritage List' and a list of 'World Heritage in Danger'. This list may include such property forming part of the cultural and natural heritage that is threatened by serious and specific dangers, such as changes in water level, floods and tidal waves.[60]

2.3.3.   Biodiversity Convention[61]

The CBD establishes a comprehensive regime for the conservation of ecosystems and biological resources.[62] The CBD applies to biological diversity of all sources (terrestrial, marine and other aquatic sources) and is, therefore, linked to water resources management. 'Inland waters' was adopted as a CBD thematic area at COP-4 (1998) and the work programme promotes the ecosystem approach, including integrated watershed management, as the best way to reconcile competing demands for dwindling supplies of inland waters.[63]

2.3.4.   Desertification Convention[64]

Desertification influences and is affected by environmental concerns such as deterioration of wetlands, loss of biological diversity and climate change.

---

[57]   1972 Convention Concerning the Protection of the World Cultural and Natural Heritage (World Heritage Convention), in force 1975.

[58]   Examples of inland waters which are part of the heritage list: Los Glaciers and Iguazu (Argentina), Wilandra Lakes Region (Australia), Fertö/ Neusiedlersee (Austria/Hungary), Sundarban (Bangladesh), Upper River Rhine Valley (Germany), Lake Malawi (Malawi), Danube Delta (Romania), Lake Baikal (Russian Federation), Everglades (USA), Mosi-oa Tunya/ Victoria Falls (Zambia and Zimbabwe).

[59]   The Pantanal is the world's largest freshwater wetland extending over 81,000 square miles across the borders of Brazil, Bolivia, and Paraguay.

[60]   Article 11.

[61]   1992 Convention on Biological Diversity (Biodiversity Convention).

[62]   Article 1.

[63]   Decision IV/4 (1998): Status and trends of the biological diversity of inland water ecosystems and options for conservation and sustainable use. Decision IX/19 (2008): Biological diversity of inland water ecosystems.

[64]   1994 Convention to Combat Desertification in those Countries Experiencing Serious Drought and/or Desertification, particularly in Africa (Desertification Convention).

Countries should work towards integrated planning and efforts to combat desertification need to be fully integrated with other development sectors such as agriculture, forestry and water management. The Desertification Convention states that to combat desertification and mitigate the effects of drought in countries experiencing serious drought and desertification

> . . . will involve long-term integrated strategies that focus simultaneously, in affected areas, on improved productivity of land, and the rehabilitation, conservation and sustainable management of land and water resources, leading to improved living conditions, in particular at the community level.[65]

In order to achieve the objectives of the Desertification Convention, government, communities, non-governmental organisations and landholders need to work in partnership, and establish a better understanding of the nature and value of land and scarce water resources in affected areas.[66] Parties should also promote cooperation among affected parties in the fields of environmental protection and the conservation of land and water resources, as they relate to desertification and drought.[67]

2.3.5. Climate Change Convention[68]

There is increasing evidence that global climate change and climate variability affect the quality and availability of water supplies.[69] The Fourth Assessment Report of the Intergovernmental Panel on Climate Change acknowledges the scientific consensus that the gradual elevation in mean temperatures, associated changes in hydrological cycle and longer-term sea-level rise are a reality.[70] Parties under the UNFCCC[71] were asked to

---

[65]   Article 2(2).

[66]   Article 3(c).

[67]   Article 4(2)(d). See: Article 17(1)(g), Thematic Programme Network 4 (TPN-4) in Asia (Water Resources Management for Agriculture in Arid, Semi-arid and Subhumid Areas), the TPN-1 in Africa (Integrated management of international river, lake and hydro-geological basins) and TPN-3 in Latin America and the Caribbean (Integrated water management).

[68]   1992 United Nations Framework Convention on Climate Change (Climate Change Convention), in force 1994.

[69]   Bates, B.C., Z.W. Kundzewicz, S. Wu and J.P. Palutikof (eds) (2008), *Climate Change and Water*, IPCC Technical Paper VI, Geneva: IPCC Secretariat.

[70]   Core Writing Team, R.K. Pachauri and A. Reisinger (eds) (2007), *Climate Change 2007: Synthesis Report*, Geneva, Switzerland: IPCC. Summary for Policymakers.

[71]   The Objective (Article 2) of the Convention is to stabilise 'greenhouse gas concentrations in the atmosphere at a level that would prevent dangerous anthropogenic interference with the climate system'.

develop 'appropriate and integrated plans for coastal zone management, water resources and agriculture, and for the protection and rehabilitation of areas, particularly in Africa, affected by drought and desertification as well as floods'.[72] Parties are required to take climate change into consideration while formulating social, economic and environmental policies and actions.[73] It is therefore, essential for vulnerable countries to identify strategies and integrate responses to climate change in their current water resources management policies and activities.

2.3.6. Basel Convention[74]

The fundamental goals of the Basel Convention are: the reduction of transboundary movements of hazardous and other wastes, the prevention and minimisation of hazardous and other waste generation, the environmentally sound management of such wastes, and the active promotion of the transfer and use of cleaner technologies.[75] Environmentally sound management follows an 'integrated life cycle approach' which involves control during the production, use and trade of chemicals, including the disposal of hazardous waste. Disposal of waste includes final disposal in landfill, incineration or release into a water body.[76] Of the hazardous wastes covered by the Basel Convention there are many which particularly threaten water quality. For example, oils produced from petroleum are used as fuels, lubricants, and industrial fluids. They are persistent and can spread over large areas of land or water.[77] The Basel Convention has issued technical guidelines for minimising, recovering, recycling and safely disposing of many of the listed toxic substances, including household wastes, used oils and organic solvents which threaten water quality.[78] If not handled properly, these toxic substances can leak or spill and contaminate soil and groundwater.

---

[72]   Article 4(1)(e).

[73]   Article 4(1)(f).

[74]   1989 Convention on the Control of Transboundary Movements of Hazardous Wastes and their Disposal (Basel Convention).

[75]   Article 4.

[76]   Annex IV.

[77]   Secretariat of the Basel Convention (2008), *Our Sustainable Future: The Role of the Basel Convention*, Geneva: UNEP. Secretariat of the Basel Convention, 'What does the Basel Convention mean for water?', Geneva: UNEP, available at www.basel.int/pub/water%20brohure.pdf (accessed 15 January 2010).

[78]   See List of Technical Guidelines available from www.basel.int.

2.3.7. Stockholm Convention[79]

The preamble to the Stockholm Convention recognises that persistent organic pollutants (POPs)[80] possess toxic substances which resist degradation and can bio-accumulate. Parties are required to adopt legal or administrative measures to eliminate the production and use of listed toxic chemicals.[81] They are transported, through air, water and migratory species, across international boundaries and deposited far from their place of release, where they accumulate in terrestrial and aquatic ecosystems. POPs can be deposited in marine and freshwater ecosystems through effluent releases, atmospheric deposition, run-off, and other means. Most of the initial twelve POPs have been banned or subjected to severe use restrictions in many countries.[82] Many of them, however, are still in use, and stockpiles of obsolete POPs can cause leaching of these chemicals into the soil, contaminating water resources.[83]

2.3.8. Rotterdam Convention[84]

The Rotterdam Convention ensures the protection of people and the environment from the possible dangers resulting from trade in highly dangerous pesticides and chemicals.[85] Many of these substances cause devastating problems when released into the environment, where they poison water resources, animals, plants and people. The aim of the Convention is to promote a shared responsibility between exporting and importing countries in protecting human health and the environment from the harmful effects of such chemicals.[86] The Convention gives importing countries the

---

[79] 2001 Convention on Persistent Organic Pollutants (POPs Convention).

[80] POPs comprise a large number of chemicals which have a wide range of uses. These POPs are placed in three categories: pesticides, industrial chemicals and by-products. Originally, there were 12 POPs including aldrin, chlordane, DDT, dieldrin, dioxins, endrin, and furans. In 2009, nine more POPs were included in the list. Decisions SC-4/10 to SC-4/18 (2009).

[81] Article 3.

[82] Secretariat of the Stockholm Convention on Persistent Organic Pollutants (2005), *Ridding the World of POPs: A Guide to the Stockholm Convention on Persistent Organic Pollutants*, Geneva: UNEP, 8.

[83] Ibid., 5, 13–14.

[84] 1998 Convention of Prior Informed Consent for Hazardous Chemicals and Pesticides in International Trade.

[85] The inclusion of chemicals in the PIC procedure is decided by the COP. In 2009, the Convention includes 40 chemicals in Annex III: 29 are pesticides (including four severely hazardous pesticide formulations) and 11 are industrial chemicals.

[86] Article 1.

power to decide which chemicals they want to receive and to exclude those they cannot manage safely.[87]

2.3.9.   Watercourses Convention[88]

The Convention applies to uses of international watercourses and their water for purposes other than navigation, and asks parties to 'utilise an international watercourse in an equitable and reasonable manner'.[89] The Convention notes that, in the event of a conflict between uses of water in an international watercourse, special regard shall be given 'to the requirements of vital human needs'.[90] The Statement of Understanding accompanying the Convention declared that, in determining vital human needs, 'special attention is to be paid to providing sufficient water to sustain human life, including both drinking water and water required for production of food in order to prevent starvation'.[91] The Convention requires the optimal and sustainable utilisation of the watercourse and its benefits 'consistent with adequate protection of the watercourse'. While equitably utilising the watercourses, parties need to 'take all appropriate measures to prevent the causing of significant harm to other watercourse states'.[92] Watercourse states are required to take all measures necessary to protect and preserve the marine environment, taking into account generally accepted international rules and standards.[93]

2.3.10.   Inferences

The MEAs discussed above provide various approaches and social and environmental considerations to contribute to sustainable water resource management. They also outline a number of implementation strategies, e.g. law and regulation, building capacity, partnerships and stakeholder participation, for states to strengthen water governance. There is concern that the overlapping objectives and requirements of various MEAs could lead to a duplication of efforts or might undermine MEA implementation

---

[87]   Articles 5 and 10.
[88]   1997 Convention on the Law of the Non-Navigational Uses of International Watercourses, not in force.
[89]   Article 5.
[90]   Article 10.
[91]   Statements of Understanding Pertaining to Certain Articles of the Convention, Report of the Sixth Committee convening as the Working Group of the Whole, Convention on the Law of the Non-Navigational Uses of International Watercourses, UN Doc. A/51/869 (New York, 11 April 1997), para. 8, available at www.un.org/law/cod/watere.htm (accessed 15 January 2010).
[92]   Article 7.
[93]   Article 23.

at the national level.[94] For example, a number of biodiversity-related conventions deal with similar habitats, species and ecosystems: issues relating to wetlands are covered by the Biodiversity Convention, the Ramsar Convention and the World Heritage Convention. In addition, some conventions deal with cross-cutting issues, such as sustainable use (Ramsar Convention, Biodiversity Convention) and restoration of habitats (Ramsar Convention, Biodiversity Convention).[95] A coordinated approach to these overlapping issues would accelerate the national implementation of MEAs. For example: the chemical/waste conventions – the Basel Convention, the Rotterdam Convention and the Stockholm Convention – provide a framework for improved chemical/waste management and their coordinated implementation could contribute to the 'life cycle management' of toxic chemicals. A lack of coordinated effort may mean that decisions adopted to implement the water component of one MEA could pose a threat to the objective of another MEA with a negative impact on water management. For example, mitigation activities, such as afforestation, under the UNFCCC might pose risks of negative impacts on wetland ecosystems if tree species with a high water demand were planted in locations where this might lead to increased water stress and the reduction of water availability to wetlands.[96]

2.4. Water Management and GATS

The 2002 WSSD Plan of Implementation opted for the promotion of public–private partnerships and improving accountability of public institutions and private companies.[97] Simultaneously, it urged governments to support efforts and programmes for energy-efficient, sustainable and cost-effective water projects in developing countries, through such measures as technological, technical and financial assistance and other modalities.[98] The issue of technology transfer, capacity building and public–private partnership is central to the discussion on the 1994

---

[94] For examples of overlapping MEAs see: Chambers, W.B. (2008), *Interlinkages and the Effectiveness of Multilateral Environmental Agreements*, Tokyo: UNU Press.

[95] Ibid.

[96] Res. X.24 (2008) on Climate Change and Wetlands acknowledges the need to strengthen synergies between the Ramsar Convention, CBD, UNFCCC and UNCCD with respect to wetland conservation and wise use, including for reducing vulnerability and increasing resilience to climate change.

[97] Para. 26(g).

[98] Ibid., para. 26(f).

General Agreement on Trade in Services (GATS)[99] and its impact on water services.

GATS aims to promote international trade in services and to remove barriers to such trade.[100] The GATS applies to all services[101] and has three pillars. The first is a framework agreement containing basic obligations which apply to all member countries.[102] The second concerns national schedules of commitments containing specific national commitments which will be the subject of a continuing process of liberalisation.[103] The third is a number of annexes addressing the special situations of individual services sectors. GATS rules are legally binding on governments and can be enforced through the WTO dispute system. GATS is divided into twelve broad service sectors, each of which has a number of sub-categories.[104]

Article II(1) of GATS requires that most favoured nation (MFN) status is to be extended to all WTO members and they are to be treated equally.[105] Under GATS rules, each member must accord to services and service suppliers of any other member treatment which is no less favourable than that it accords to its own like services and service suppliers.[106] This is known as 'national treatment',[107] which is a specific commitment

---

[99]   For a general discussion on the WTO see chapter 4.

[100]   Article I, General Agreement on Trade in Services, The Final Act and Agreement Establishing the World Trade Organization, Uruguay Round (Marrakech, 15 April 1994).

[101]   For example, banking, telecommunication, education, financial, legal, energy and environmental services. There are three exceptions: 'services supplied in the exercise of governmental authority' (Article I:3b) do not fall under GATS. The Annex on Air Transport Services exempts from coverage measures affecting air traffic rights and services directly related to the exercise of such rights. Article XIV (general exceptions) and XIVbis (security exceptions).

[102]   For example, Articles II, III. General obligations apply directly and automatically to all members and services sectors.

[103]   Each WTO member is required to have a Schedule of Specific Commitments which identifies the services for which the member guarantees market access and national treatment and any limitations which may be attached.

[104]   Document MTN.GNS/W/120. Under this classification system, any service sector may be included in a member's schedule of commitments with specific market access and national treatment obligations.

[105]   However, GATS Article II(2) offers some possibilities for member states to maintain measures inconsistent with MFN.

[106]   Macmillan, F. (2001), *WTO and the Environment*, London: Sweet and Maxwell, 201.

[107]   Article XVII contains the national treatment principle, 'each Member shall accord to services and service suppliers of any other Member, in respect of all measures affecting the supply of services, treatment no less favourable than that it accords to its own like services and service suppliers'. See GATS, supra.

for member states. The national treatment rule relates to the market access provision[108] which allows countries to attach limitations to the degree to which foreign services providers can operate in their market.[109] If WTO member states open up water services as part of their specific commitments, GATS rules on national treatment (Article XVII), market access (Article XVI), additional commitments (Article XVIII), domestic regulation (Article VI) and general exceptions (Article XIV) will be relevant to imposing restrictions and mitigating any potential negative effect on the domestic water sector.

Water services became a focus of attention when the WTO Doha Ministerial Declaration[110] made a general commitment to remove all barriers to trade in environmental services[111] and launched a new round of negotiation on global trade liberalisation including services. There is no specific reference to water services in GATS. However, water related services can be part of the 'environmental services' which are included as the sixth sector category among the twelve broad service sectors.[112] Whether this category includes water and water related services is being debated at the WTO and provisional commitments have been made that include water-related services such as waste water and sewage treatment.[113]

If a country fully liberalises the water sector services by removing trade barriers and tariffs, it will have to allow access to other WTO members including large industrialised countries into this sector. It is feared that

---

[108] Article XVI. While members can place limitations on the extent of their market access commitment in a specified sector, the commitment in GATS to progressive liberalisation must be kept in mind (Article XIX).

[109] Six types of restrictions are allowed: number of service suppliers, value of service transactions or assets, number of operations or quantity of output, number of natural persons supplying a service, type of legal entity or joint venture, and participation of foreign capital.

[110] Doha WTO Ministerial Declaration, WT/MIN(01)/DEC/1 (Doha, 20 November 2001).

[111] Environmental Services, Background Note by the Secretariat, Council for Trade in Services, WTO Doc. S/C/W/46 (6 July 1998), para. 6. This classification is mutually exclusive, i.e. services in one sector cannot be covered by another sector (para. 10). This has implications for the cross-sectoral approach to the design and delivery of integrated environmental services.

[112] The Services Sectoral Classification List was developed during the Uruguay Round and is based on the United Nations Provisional Central Product Classification (CPC), S/C/W/46 (6 July 1998) and MTN.GNS/W/120 (July 1991).

[113] Lamy, P. (2008), *Report on Market Access Commitments in Services*, 30 July 2008, JOB (08)/93. See Council for Trade in Services – Special Session – Communication from the European Communities and its Member States – Conditional Revised Offer, TN/S/O/EEC/Rev.1, 29 June 2005.

FOR DISCUSSION

- Is there a human right to water in international law?
- Has General Comment 15 dealt with water in a comprehensive manner?
- As water issues are discussed in a fragmented manner in the MEAs, in what ways can water resource management be coordinated at the international level?
- What are the arguments for and against the concern that commodification of water will lead to the increased privatisation of water services?

---

market access commitments under GATS 'could impose restraints on local and national authorities' ability to effectively regulate water extraction to protect the environment'.[114] In addition, 'market access commitments could limit the right of the governments to restrict quantities of water that companies are allowed to collect from lakes, rivers and groundwater sources'.[115] There is an added concern that the progressive liberalisation under GATS would push national governments to deregulate the services sector.[116] Moreover, exception under GATS does not allow governments to use conservation of natural resources (e.g. water) as a ground to restrict the rights of foreign service providers.[117]

---

[114]   Concannon, T. (2002), 'Stealing our Water: Implications of GATS for Global Water Resources', Friends of the Earth Briefing, London: Friends of the Earth, 3. See Ostrovksy, A., R. Speed and E. Tuerk (2003), *GATS, Water and the Environment: Implications of the General Agreement on Trade in Services for Water Resources*, Gland, Switzerland: WWF.

[115]   Concannon (2002), supra, 4. However, countries can impose market access restrictions under Article XVI of GATS.

[116]   According to the WTO, even if such commitments were made, the governments would have the right to set levels of quality, safety, price or any other policy objectives as they see fit. WTO Secretariat (2001), *GATS – Fact and Fiction*, Geneva: WTO, 9.

[117]   General exceptions under Article XIV(b) include 'human, animal or plant life or health' and, unlike GATT XX(g), GATS does not include 'conservation of exhaustible natural resources' as a ground to restrict trade.

3. WATER MANAGEMENT AT THE REGIONAL LEVEL

3.1. Regional Agreements

Express provision on water is found in the African Charter on the Rights and Welfare of the Child (1990).[118] Several regional instruments implicitly include water as part of right to life or right to a healthy environment.[119] A number of regional bodies have acknowledged the link between human rights and water.[120] For example, the American Commission on Human Rights in its *Report on the Human Rights Situation in Ecuador* (1997)[121] found that inhabitants were exposed to toxic by-products of oil exploitation in their drinking and bathing water which jeopardised their human rights to life and health.[122] In the Ogoniland case, the African Commission on Human Rights accepted the claim that the oil consortium has exploited oil reserves in Ogoniland with no regard for the right to health or environment of the local communities, resulting in the contamination of water, soil and air with serious short and long-term health impacts.[123]

Several binding instruments in Europe deal with the link between human rights and water, the promotion of sustainable water use and water management in relation to groundwater abstraction, impact assessment of

---

[118] Article 14(1).

[119] Scanlon et al. (2004), supra, 7–8. For example, Article 11 of the Additional Protocol to the 1988 American Convention on Human Rights in the area of Economic, Social and Cultural Rights. Article 2 of the 1950 European Convention on Human Rights.

[120] For examples of water related cases, see Scanlon et al. (2004), supra, 10–11. See *Lopez Ostra v. Spain*, Judgment of 9 December 1994, application no. 16798/90 (1994), ECHR Series A, No. 303-C, (1995) 20 EHRR 277. *Zander v. Sweden*, application no. 14282/88 (1993) ECHR, Series A, No. 279B. *Case of the Mayagna (Sumo) Awas Tingni Community v. Nicaragua*, Judgment of 31 August 2001, Inter-Am. Ct. H.R. (Ser. C) No. 79 (2001).

[121] Inter-American Commission on Human Rights (1997), *Report on the Situation of Human Rights in Ecuador*, OEA/Ser.L/V/II.96, Doc. 10 Rev. 1.

[122] Shelton, D. (2002), 'Human Rights and the Environment: Jurisprudence of Human Rights Bodies', Environmental Policy and Law, 32(3–4), 158–167, 161. The Commission stated that 'where environmental contamination and degradation pose a persistent threat to human life and health', the rights to life, to physical security and integrity are implicated. See Inter-American Commission on Human Rights (1997), supra, 88.

[123] Paras 2, 40–42, 50. Communication 155/96, *The Social and Economic Rights Action Centre and the Centre for Economic and Social Rights v. Nigeria*. Fifteenth Annual Activity Report of the African Commission on Human and Peoples' Rights (2001–2002), 31–44.

water related projects, such as dams and pipeline, and access to information. These documents, however, do not create any specific right to water.

3.1.1. UNECE Water Convention

The ECE Water Convention[124] is a framework instrument the primary purpose of which is to foster international cooperation in the area of transboundary water resources in the wider European region. It addresses water-related issues at different levels (e.g. regional, bilateral) and obliges parties to prevent, control and reduce water pollution. It provides parties with guidance on increased region-wide cooperation, technical assistance at the country and river-basin levels, and concrete measures aimed at improving water resources management.[125]

3.1.2. Protocol on Water and Health

The Protocol on Water and Health is a binding subsidiary instrument of the UNECE Water Convention.[126] The Protocol promotes the protection of human health and well-being through improving water management, including the protection of water ecosystems, and by preventing, controlling, and reducing water-related disease.[127] The primary target is access to drinking water and the provision of sanitation for everyone within a framework of integrated water-management systems. To realise these goals, parties are required to establish national and local targets for the standards to be achieved with respect to the quality of drinking water and discharges, as well as levels of performance for water supply and wastewater treatment.[128]

3.1.3. Protocol on Civil Liability

The Civil Liability Protocol[129] provides individuals affected by the transboundary impact of industrial accidents on international watercourses

---

[124] UNECE Convention on the Protection and Use of Transboundary Watercourses, Helsinki, 17 March 1992.

[125] Wouters, P. and S. Vinogradov (2003), 'Analysing the ECE Water Convention: What Lessons for the Regional Management of Transboundary Water Resources', in O. Stokke and Ø.B. Thommessen (eds), *Yearbook of International Co-operation on Environment and Development,* London: Earthscan Publications, 55–63.

[126] Protocol on Water and Health to the 1992 Convention on the Protection and Use of Transboundary Watercourses and Lakes (17 June 1999, London). Entered into force 4 August 2005.

[127] Article 1.

[128] Article 6.

[129] Protocol on Civil Liability and Compensation for Damage Caused by the Transboundary Effects of Industrial Accidents on Transboundary Waters to the

(e.g. fishermen, operators of downstream waterworks) a legal claim for adequate and prompt compensation.[130] Companies will be liable for accidents at industrial installations as well as during transport via pipelines.[131] Physical damage, damage to property, loss of income, the cost of reinstatement and response measures are covered by the Protocol.[132] The Protocol sets financial limits of liability depending on the risk of the activity, i.e. the quantities of the hazardous substances which are or may be present and their toxicity or the risk they pose to the environment.[133] To cover this liability, companies will have to establish financial securities, such as insurance or other guarantees.[134]

3.1.4. Aarhus Convention

While the Aarhus Convention is not primarily about water management, issues relating to water are considered in several provisions. For example, the definition of environmental information includes information on water.[135] The Convention states that the concerned public[136] shall have the right to participate in decisions on specific activities listed in Annex I which are assumed to have significant effects on the environment. The list of activities under Annex I includes inland waterways and ports for inland-waterway traffic, groundwater abstraction or artificial groundwater recharge schemes, works for the transfer of water resources between river basins, and dams and other installations designed for the holding back or permanent storage of water. Thus, states are required to involve people while conducting environmental impact assessments for water activities under Annex I or with potentially significant environmental impact.[137]

1992 Convention on the Protection and Use of Transboundary Watercourses and International Lakes and to the 1992 Convention on the Transboundary Effects of Industrial Accidents (UNECE, Kiev, Ukraine, 2003). Not in force.

[130]   Article 1.
[131]   Article 4.
[132]   Article 2(2)(d).
[133]   Article 9, Annex II.
[134]   Article 11.
[135]   Article 3(a). UNECE Convention on Access to Information, Public Participation in Decision-making and Access to Justice in Environmental Matters (UNECE, Aarhus, Denmark, 1998). Discussed in chapter 3 of this book.
[136]   Article 2(5) defines 'Public concerned'. See chapter 3.
[137]   Article 6(1). When activities are not covered by Annex I but have a significant environmental impact, parties have discretion to apply Article 6.

3.1.5. The PRTR Protocol

The Protocol on Pollutant Release and Transfer Registers requires each party to establish a coherent, nationwide system of pollution inventories or registers on a structured, computerised and publicly accessible database.[138] The register will contain information on releases of pollutants to air, water and land, as well as transfers of waste and pollutants, where emissions exceed certain threshold values and result from specific activities.[139]

3.2. EU Water Framework Directive

The Water Framework Directive is applicable to all Member States of the European Union.[140] The Directive requires that the EU Member States establish competent authorities to prepare catchment plans with the aim of achieving good ecological quality of waters and those plans to be supported by economic analyses. The Directive requires Member States to manage their waters (inland surface waters, transitional waters, coastal waters, and groundwater) in such a way as to achieve the overall objective of 'good water status' within a certain time frame.[141] The Directive adopts a 'river-basin' approach to the management of water resources.[142] The EU Member States are required to manage their waters on the basis of 'river-basin districts'[143] by adopting river-basin management plans.[144] Some Member States (UK, Germany and Spain) already use the river-basin approach and river basins such as the Maas, the Schelde and the Rhine are already managed under cross-border agreements. Where a river-basin district extends beyond the territory of the EU, the Member States concerned

---

[138]   Article 5(9) of the Aarhus Convention and Article 1 of the Protocol. Protocol on Pollutant Release and Transfer Registers to the UNECE Convention on Access to Information, Public Participation in Decision-making and Access to Justice in Environmental Matters (UNECE, Kiev, 2003), entered into force 8 October 2009.

[139]   Articles 4–6 and Annex I.

[140]   Directive 2000/60/EC of the European Parliament and of the Council of 23 October 2000 establishing a framework for Community action in the field of water policy, OJ L327 (2000) 1.

[141]   Article 4.

[142]   Article 2(13): 'River basin' means the area of land from which all surface run-off flows through a sequence of streams, rivers and, possibly, lakes into the sea at a single river mouth, estuary or delta.

[143]   Article 2(15): 'River basin district means the area of land and sea, made up of one or more neighbouring river basins together with their associated groundwaters and coastal waters . . .'.

[144]   Articles 3, 13.

FOR DISCUSSION

- How do the regional instruments and case laws acknowledge the link between human rights and water?
- What are the innovative techniques and deficiencies of the EU Water Framework Directive?
- As a case study, how has the UK (or any other EU country of your choice) implemented the EU Water Framework Directive?

---

are expected to coordinate their activities with the relevant non-member states in order to achieve the objectives of the Directive.

The WFD also stipulates that each river-basin management plan must ensure a balance between the abstraction and recharge of water.[145] All abstraction of either surface water or groundwater will require authorisation except in areas where it can be demonstrated that this will have no significant impact on the status of the water. Member States are required to ensure that the price charged to consumers for freshwater and for the treatment of wastewater will 'take into account' the full environmental costs.[146] In order to accommodate national variations, provision is also made for derogations from full cost recovery. For example, Member States are allowed to provide a subsidised drinking water supply and wastewater services for low-income households.[147]

4. WATER RESOURCE MANAGEMENT AT THE NATIONAL LEVEL

Development of national level water law and policies is influenced by the targets set in international goals (e.g. MDG 2000), commitments made in non-binding declarations (e.g. WSSD 2002), priorities identified in international initiatives (e.g. WEHAB 2002) and regional agreements. Most of these documents prioritise the need for community involvement

---

[145] Page, B. and M. Kaika (2003). 'The EU Water Framework Directive: Policy, Innovation and the Shifting Choreography of Governance', *European Environment*, 13(6), 328–343.

[146] Article 9. It includes three sectoral water user groups: agriculture, industry and domestic.

[147] Ibid.

in decision-making relating to water and framing a right to water which is justiciable. At the domestic level, there can be an express right to water (e.g. South Africa) or an implied right derived from the constitutional 'right to life' (e.g. India). Community participation in the decision-making in the water sector includes access to information, justice and participation in the decision-making processes.

4.1.   Right to Water in National Constitutions

The constitutions of several countries include either a specific right to water or a right to protect natural resources.[148] For example, Article 27(1)(b) of the Constitution of the Republic of South Africa[149] guarantees the right of everyone to have access to sufficient food and water.[150] Article 11 of the Constitution deals with the right to life and Article 24 affirms that everyone has the right to an environment which is not harmful to health or well-being. To realise these constitutional rights and to ensure that water resources are sustainably managed for the benefit of the present and future generations, the National Water Act[151] stipulates that the government will act as the public trustee of the nation's water resources.

In contrast to this express right, the Indian Constitution does not guarantee any 'right to water'. Several judicial decisions have held that the right to water is linked to the constitutional 'right to life' (see box 7.1).[152] It is feared that interpreting the right to water as part of the right to life may dilute the scope of the right to water and encourage governments not

---

[148]   For example, the constitutions of South Africa, Guatemala, Gambia, Uganda, Uruguay, Cambodia, Nigeria, Eritrea, Laos mention the right to water. Earthjustice (2005), 'Environmental Rights Report: Human Rights and the Environment'. Materials for the 61st Session of the United Nations Commission on Human Rights, Geneva. Langford, M., A. Khalfan, C. Fairstein and H. Jones (2004), *Legal Resources for the Right to Water: International and National Standards*, Geneva: Centre on Housing Rights and Eviction.

[149]   Constitution of the Republic of South Africa 1996, Act 108 of 1996 was adopted by the Constitutional Assembly on 4 December 1996, and took effect on 4 February 1997.

[150]   Article 27(2). The state must take reasonable legislative and other measures, within its available resources, to achieve the progressive realisation of each of these rights.

[151]   National Water Act (1998), Republic of South Africa, Act No. 36 of 1998. See also Water Services Act (1997), Republic of South Africa, Act 108 of 1997.

[152]   The right to life is guaranteed under Article 21 of the Constitution of India (1949).

BOX 7.1.   GROUNDWATER ABSTRACTION AND
THE COCA-COLA COMPANY IN INDIA

In 1999, the Hindustan Coca-Cola Beverages Private Limited, a subsidiary of the US based Coca-Cola company, established a plant in Plachimada (Kerala). The Perumatty Grama Panchayat (Village Council) gave a licence to the company to commence production in 2000. Coca Cola drew around 510,000 litres of water each day from boreholes and open wells. Two years after production began, local communities complained that water pollution and extreme water shortages were endangering their lives. Wells had dried up and the depletion of groundwater resources meant less water for drinking and agriculture. This excessive exploitation of groundwater led the Village Council to refuse the renewal of Coca-Cola's licence in 2003.

The Coca-Cola Company challenged this decision in the High Court of Kerala. The Court considered two issues: the question of the over-exploitation of ground water and the justification for the Village Council's decision to revoke the licence. In its 2003 judgment, the High Court recognised that the state as a trustee is under a legal duty to protect natural resources. It considered that these resources, meant for public use, cannot be converted into private ownership. It added that the government had a duty to act to 'protect against excessive groundwater exploitation and the inaction of the State in this regard was tantamount to infringement of the right to life of the people guaranteed under Article 21 of the Constitution of India' (para. 34). The High Court ordered the plant to stop drawing on the groundwater within a month and find alternative sources of water. At the same time, it ordered the Village Council to renew the licence and not to interfere with the functioning of the Company as long as it was not extracting the groundwater and was depending for its water needs on other sources.

When the Village Council refused to renew the licence on the grounds that the Company had not stopped using groundwater, the Company went back to the High Court. In its 2005 decision, the Kerala High Court (Division Bench) permitted the company to draw 500,000 litres of water per day. It ordered the Village Council to renew the licence and not to interfere with the functioning of the Company as long as it was not extracting beyond the permitted level. In 2006, the Village Council reissued a licence to the company for three months but laid out thirteen conditions, the first of which is that the company shall not use groundwater for industrial purposes, or for producing soft drinks, aerated carbonate beverages or fruit juice. The Coca-Cola company has stopped production from the Plachimada plant.

Source: 2004(1)KLT731. Also: www.righttowater.org.uk/code/legal_7.asp (accessed on 15 January 2010).

to take any active step to develop the water sector.[153] Moreover, national judges may be unwilling to make broad 'affirmative entitlements for fear of paving the way to claims of other entitlements – justiciable rights to food, shelter, medicine, and the like'.[154] So far, the Indian judiciary has taken a bold approach. For example, the Supreme Court of India, in *Charan Lal Sahu*,[155] explicitly linked environmental quality and the right to life, and held that the right to life includes the 'right to pollution-free air and water'. However, the Supreme Court did not place any absolute duty on the state, and merely asked the state to 'take effective steps to protect this right'. Later, in *Subash Kumar*, the Bihar High Court observed:

> [The right to life guaranteed by Article 21] includes the right of enjoyment of pollution-free water and air for full enjoyment of life. If anything endangers or impairs that quality of life in derogation of laws, a citizen has the right to have recourse to Article 32 of the Constitution for removing the *pollution of water* or air which may be detrimental to the quality of life.[156]

Through this case, the court recognised the right to water as part of the fundamental right to life. Therefore, the municipalities and other concerned governmental agencies can no longer delay implementing measures for the abatement and prevention of water pollution. They may be compelled to take positive measures to improve the environment.[157]

---

[153]   Anon (2007), 'What Price for the Priceless? Implementing the Justiciability of the Right to Water', Harvard Law Review, 120, 1086.

[154]   Ibid.

[155]   *Charan Lal Sahu v. Union of India*, All India Reporter, (1990) SC 1480, at 1495. See also *F.K. Hussain v. Union of India*, All India Reporter (1990) Kerala 321 at 340 (the Kerala High Court held that the right to water is an integral part of right to life).

[156]   *Subhash Kumar v. State of Bihar* (1991) 1 SCC 598, at 608 (emphasis added).

[157]   *M.C. Mehta v. Union of India* (1998) 9 SCC 589, 607.

4.2. Community Participation in Domestic Water Management

Chapter 18 of Agenda 21 (1992) urges the governments to facilitate 'the active participation of women, youth, indigenous people and local communities in water management'.[158] Moreover, to achieve MDG 7 (environmental sustainability) successfully, governments need to adopt water plans and policies which have the active participation of communities.[159] The Johannesburg Plan of Implementation encourages governments to facilitate access to public information and participation *at all levels*, in support of policy and decision-making related to water resources management and project implementation.[160] General Comment 15 states:[161]

> . . . the right of individuals and groups to participate in decision-making processes that may affect their exercise of the right to water, must be an integral part of any policy, program or strategy concerning water. Individuals and groups should be given full and equal access to information concerning water, water services and the environment, held by public authorities or third parties.

It adds that where domestic water systems are controlled by third parties (which occurs where concessions have been signed), the states parties are required to establish an 'effective regulatory system . . . which includes independent monitoring, genuine public participation and imposition of penalties for non-compliance'.[162]

Some of the MEAs allow people to participate at all levels of decision-making. For example, the preamble to the 1992 Biodiversity Convention affirms the need for the full participation of women at all levels of policy-making and implementation for biodiversity conservation. In order to achieve the objectives of the 1994 Desertification Convention, government, communities, NGOs and landholders need to work in partnership, and establish a better understanding of the nature and value of land and scarce water resources in affected areas.[163] The Ramsar Convention urges

---

[158] Agenda 21 (1992), supra, para. 18.9.

[159] Goal 7 dealt with environmental sustainability which targets to reduce by half the proportion of people without access to safe drinking water and basic sanitation by 2015 (MDG, 2000).

[160] WSSD Plan of Implementation, Report of the World Summit on Sustainable Development (Johannesburg, South Africa, 26 August–September 2002), UN Doc. A/CONF.199/20, Res. 2, Annex, Part IX (Other Regional Initiatives).

[161] Article 48.

[162] General Comment 15, para. 24.

[163] Article 3(c).

parties to strengthen the participation of local and indigenous people in the management of wetlands and groundwater.[164]

At the domestic level, there are formal and informal forums available for the public to participate in the decision and policy-making process.[165] Participatory rights may be guaranteed in the Constitution and in water-specific legislation. At the same time, procedural law may allow the public to bring public interest litigation in the court or tribunal. For example, since the 1980s, the Indian court has dealt with cases on water pollution, encroachment of rivers, mining and water and groundwater management.[166] In addition, people can follow a wide range of informal ways to participate in the decision-making process: organising protests, NGOs and community coalition for political bargaining and effective use of the media.

In some countries, public participation is a common theme in water resource management.[167] For example, water policies in some countries of South Asia emphasise the importance of community participation in water management.[168] These water policies encourage the participation of communities in planning, development and management of water projects including irrigation, drainage, rural water supply, flood protection and drought activities. Similar encouragement is found in the national water policies of the African (e.g. South Africa, Zimbabwe) and Latin American (e.g. Mexico) regions.[169] Although these national level water policies stress the importance of public participation, the issue is whether the public has any participation during the preparation of these policies or whether the

---

[164] For example, Res. X.1 (2009): The Ramsar Strategic Plan 2009–2015. Res. VII.8 (1999): Guidelines for establishing and strengthening local communities' and indigenous people's participation in the management of wetlands. Res. VIII.40 (2002): Guidelines for rendering the use of groundwater compatible with the conservation of wetlands.

[165] See the discussion in chapter 3.

[166] Rosencranz, A. and S. Divan (2002), *Environmental Law and Policy in India,* Oxford: Oxford University Press, chapters 4, 5, 10.

[167] Razzaque, J. (2009), 'Participatory Rights in Natural Resource Management: Role of Communities in South Asia', in J. Ebbesson and P. Okowa (eds), *Environmental Law and Justice in Context,* Cambridge: Cambridge University Press, 117–138.

[168] National Water Policy (1999) of Bangladesh; National Water Policy of India (2002); Water Policy of Pakistan (2004); Water Sector Strategy (2002) of Pakistan.

[169] Nicol, A. and S. Mtisi (2003), 'Politics and Water Policy: A Southern Africa Example', Sustainable Livelihoods in Southern Africa Research Paper 20, Brighton: Institute of Development Studies.

policies are effectively implemented at the national level.[170] In addition, there are water specific laws which include provisions on public participation.[171] Countries such as Malaysia and Pakistan have national legislation for public participation in decisions concerning large projects which may have environmental and social impacts.[172] These laws generally promote the participation of local governments and communities in water resources planning, management and preservation.

Large infrastructure projects, including dams, remain an area where people rarely have any voice. There are examples where the government withdrew from the decision to build dams due to successful public uproar (e.g. the U.S., Hungary, Thailand) and some others, where the authority disregarded the public protest (e.g. the Sardar Sarovar project in India,[173] Itoiz Dam in Spain[174]). A decision to construct a dam can have a great impact on human lives and livelihoods with adverse social, environmental and political consequences. The World Commission on Dams (2000) urges national governments to identify the broad range of stakeholders potentially affected by the dam and ensure their informed participation in the planning and implementation processes.[175] However, priorities given to economic and technical aspects rather than social and environmental concerns alienate affected communities from the project.

Privatisation of water services remains another contested issue.[176] If the privatisation process is not backed by effective regulation and if people

---

[170] Examples of such community and local government level participation can be found in the design of the 1992 National Water Law (Mexico) and the 1998 National Water Act (South Africa). See: Food and Agriculture Organization (2001), *Water Rights Administration – Experience, Issues and Guidelines*, FAO Legislative Study 70.

[171] For examples from domestic legislation see Dubreuil, C. (2006), *The Right to Water: From Concept to Implementation*, Marseilles, France: World Water Council.

[172] Krchnak, K.M. (2005), 'Improving Water Governance through Increased Public Access to Information and Participation', Sustainable Development Law and Policy, 5, 34.

[173] World Commission on Dams (2000), *Dams and Development: A New Framework for Decision-Making*, London: Earthscan, 19.

[174] Worldwide Fund for Nature (2004), *Rivers at Risk: Dams and the future of freshwater ecosystems*, Surrey: WWF, 28.

[175] World Commission on Dams (2000), supra, 215–220.

[176] Privatisation or involving the private sector in water services can take the form of complete privatisation or public–private partnership where the public body remains a stakeholder with some control over the water sector. Fitzmaurice (2007), supra, 558.

are not effectively involved in the decision or policy-making process, it can lead to social protests.[177] Examples of such protests can be found when the public authorities have decided to privatise the water sector without consulting the communities adversely affected by the decision. In Latin America, there are some examples[178] where the governments had to terminate the concession contract with the multinational company and return the water service to the public sector. These public protests also highlight that there is an ongoing struggle between commodification and the human right to water. The success of public protests and the level of community participation largely depend on the system of governance, availability of information, communities' access to justice and a strong civil society.[179] It seems that only a powerful social group can influence the policy-making process and can create a level playing field with local government and other market actors.

5. PARTICIPATION OF INTERNATIONAL NON-STATE ACTORS IN WATER MANAGEMENT

Both the international institutions (e.g. IMF, World Bank) and multinational companies influence water sector management at the international and national levels.[180] Sustainable water resource management requires the international institutions to be transparent in their decision-making and the multinational companies to be accountable.

5.1. Influence of International Institutions

International organisations play an important role in financing large-scale infrastructure projects on water. One of the main sources of financing of private water services in developing countries is the IMF, which demands privatisation of water services in exchange for debt relief.[181] The World

---

[177] Budds, J. and G. McGranahan (2003), 'Are the Debates on Water Privatization Missing the Point? Experiences from Africa, Asia and Latin America', *Environment & Urbanization*, 15(2), 93–94.

[178] In Argentina, Buenos Aires Province and Tucumán, and Cochabamba in Bolivia.

[179] Razzaque, J. (2009), 'Public Participation in Water Governance', in J. Dellapenna and J. Gupta (eds), *The Law and Politics of Water,* New York: Springer-Verlag, 353–372.

[180] Non-state actors are considered in chapters 4 and 5.

[181] Bayliss, K. (2002), 'Privatization and Poverty: The Distributional Impact of Utility Privatization', Annals of Public and Cooperative Economics, 73(4), 605.

Bank is another powerful institution which promotes the commodification of water.[182] The 2003 Water Sector Resources Strategy of the World Bank emphasises the need to decentralise water services and achieve full cost recovery which can act both 'as an incentive to private investment and as a disincentive to waste'.[183]

Since the 1990s and early 2000s, international institutions have promoted private sector involvement in infrastructure projects, with the expectation that this will inject both investment and efficiency into traditional public-sector systems.[184] Critics of privatisation have debated the negative impacts (e.g. price increase, unreliable supply of water) of privatisation, especially to developing countries. Private companies which are given concessions to privatise a particular water sector are motivated by 'full cost recovery' through user fees and will increase water prices to a level which is profitable to them.[185] This tariff increase reduces access to water by poor communities and people who do not have access to networked services. The cost of connection is another hurdle.[186] Privatisation also restricts the ability of a state to meet its human rights obligations.[187] Another concern of privatisation is that it triggers corruption and reduces transparency in the water sector.[188]

In recent years, the World Bank has had to withdraw some of its loans amid public protests against water infrastructure projects which had previously received the Bank's support (e.g. the Sardar Sarovar Dam in India, Three Gorges Dam in China).[189] In some national jurisdictions it is possible for the community groups to challenge the privatisation decision of the government in the national court. There are, however, limited participatory tools available for communities to go to international tribunals challenging the water privatisation contract. For example, ICSID

---

[182] General encouragement towards privatisation can be found in World Bank, 'Private Sector Development Strategy – Directions for the World Bank Group', World Bank, 9 April 2002. Street, P. (2002), 'Global Water Markets and the General Agreement on Trade in Services', Water Law, 13(4), 259–268, 265.

[183] World Bank (2004), *Water Sector Resources Strategy: Strategic Directions for World Bank Engagement*, Washington DC: IBRD/World Bank.

[184] Hall, D., E. Lobina and R. de la Motte (2005), 'Public Resistance to Privatisation in Water and Energy', Development in Practice, 15(3/4), 286.

[185] Ibid., 287. Rosemann, N. (2005), 'Financing the Human Right to Water as a Millennium Development Goal', Law, Social Justice and Global Development Journal, 1.

[186] Bayliss (2001), supra, 614.

[187] Fitzmaurice (2007), supra, 559.

[188] Budds and McGranahan (2003), supra, 112.

[189] World Commission on Dams (2000), supra, 19.

does not allow people to participate directly in the proceedings, although amicus briefs are allowed.[190] The IMF and the World Bank have reformulated their lending procedures to require more information disclosure and consultation with affected parties[191] along with a possibility for the affected communities to challenge the decision of the institution.[192] These initiatives acknowledge civil society's crucial role in making the decision-making processes of international organisations more transparent.[193]

Other international organisations, such as the World Commission on Dams, Global Environment Facility, United Nations Environment Programme and a number of international non-governmental organisations (e.g. IUCN, Global Water Partnership)[194] have developed publicly available information on water management. Regional organisations, such as the UN Economic Commission for Europe, Southern African Development Community and Organization of American States, highlight the importance of public participation in water resource management.[195]

---

[190]   Rule 37(2), ICSID Rules of Procedure for Arbitration Proceedings. International Centre for Settlement of Investment Disputes (April 2006). *Aguas Argentinas, S.A., Suez, Sociedad General de Aguas de Barcelona, S.A. and Vivendi Universal, S.A. and the Argentine Republic*, ICSID Case No. ARB/03/19, Order in response to a petition for transparency and participation as amicus curiae, 19 May 2005 (paras 17–29). *Aguas Provinciales de Santa Fe SA and ors v. Argentina*, Order in Response to a Petition for Participation as Amicus Curiae, ICSID Case No. ARB/03/17, 17 March 2006.

[191]   Barton, B. (2002), 'Underlying Concepts and Theoretical Issues in Public Participation in Resource Development', in D. Zillman, A. Lucas and G. Pring (eds), *Human Rights in Natural Resource Development: Public participation in the sustainable development of mining and energy resources,* Oxford: Oxford University Press, 84.

[192]   For example, the Inspection Panel of the World Bank allows people affected by Bank-funded projects (including dams) to seek redress if the Bank fails to follow its policies. Available at: www.worldbank.org/inspectionpanel (accessed 15 January 2010).

[193]   Oberthür S., M. Buck, S. Müller, S. Pfahl and R.G. Tarasofsky (2002), *Participation of NGOs in International Environmental Governance: Legal basis and practical experience,* Berlin: Ecologic.

[194]   A list of international NGOs involved in water related projects can be found at www.unesco.org/water/water_links/Type_of_Organization/Non_Governmental_Organizations_and_Associations/ (accessed 15 January 2010).

[195]   UNECE has created a number of regional conventions with strong provisions for public participation. Available at: www.unece.org. Information on SADC and OAS is available at www.africanwater.org and www.oas.org.

5.2. Corporate Influence

Studies suggest that water privatisation in developing countries generally has been led by multinational companies.[196] A large number of private investments in water and sanitation infrastructure projects have taken the form of public–private partnerships. These partnerships involve joint ventures between multinational water companies and local governments, in which the former contract to design, build and operate water treatment and supplies for a predetermined period.[197] Globally, there are only a handful of major multinational companies now delivering freshwater services.[198]

One avenue for multinational companies to expand their businesses in developing countries' water sectors is by using bilateral investment treaties (BITs).[199] An example is the BIT between the Netherlands and Bolivia which led to a concession contract between Bolivia and Aguas del Tunari, a multinational water company.[200] The company got the rights not only to supply water to the municipalities' network but also for industrial, agricultural and residential uses in all of Cochabamba province. Within three months, Aguas increased water tariffs by up to 200 per cent in Cochabamba.[201] There are several instances of privatised water services similar to those in Cochabamba where water prices have risen without any consultation with the public and without monitoring whether the service was satisfactory.[202] Foreign direct investment (FDI) is another means of capital inflow through which multinational companies can participate in

---

[196] Hall, D. and E. Lobina (2008), 'Water Privatisation', University of Greenwich: Public Services International Research Unit.

[197] Fitzmaurice (2007), supra, 557–558.

[198] Hall and Lobina (2008), supra, 5–12.

[199] Fitzmaurice (2007), supra, 565–566. Pannatier, S. and O. Ducry (2005), 'Water Concessions, and Protection of Foreign Investment Under International Law', in E.L.B. de Chazournes and N. Bernasconi-Osterwalder (eds), *Fresh Water and International Economic Law*, Oxford: Oxford University Press, 289.

[200] The jurisdiction of the ICSID was heavily contested by Bolivia. The company claimed that it was a subsidiary of International Water Holdings B.V. based in the Netherlands. For a discussion on the control and ownership of the Aguas del Tunari see ICSID ARB/02/03 (21/10/2005), paras 71, 119–192.

[201] This provoked a violent protest resulting in the termination of the contract. Aguas de Tunari took the case to the ICSID tribunal. ICSID Case No. ARB/02/3 (21/10/2005). In 2006, the parties agreed to a settlement and the proceeding was discontinued at the request of Bolivia.

[202] Budds et al. (2003), supra, 110. Hall, Lobina and de la Motte (2005), supra, 288–290.

the infrastructure development in another country.[203] While FDI plays an important role in national and international development activities, the host country may lower the environmental standards to attract the fund leading to diversion of water from agriculture to industry and over-exploitation of groundwater.[204] Moreover, 'since FDIs are commonly denoted in foreign currency, the consumer bears the burden of fluctuations in foreign exchange rates, and water supply becomes less affordable'.[205] Instead of providing sweeping protection to companies, both BIT and FDI need to take into account the socio-economic rights of the people and the environmental standards of the host state.

6. CONCLUSION

There is no doubt that international bodies have recognised the vital importance of water. The UN General Assembly resolution in 2010 has explicitly recognised a human right to water. The right to water is mentioned in various regional and non-binding documents and General Comment 15 on the right to water has established clear obligations on member states. The General Comment stipulates that trade liberalisation should not curtail a 'country's capacity to ensure the full realization of the right to water'.[206] Within the last decade, the focus of various international conferences has shifted towards a more sustainable use of water which underlined that water is not merely an economic good. Along with the constitutional right to water, some tools have been evolved to manage water efficiently, including integrated water resource management, participation in the policy-making and accessible courts.

One issue of concern is the privatisation of water where governments transfer the right of access and use of water to private sectors, thus making it out of reach of the poor. It is crucial that any privatisation process is backed by effective regulation, monitoring and penalties.[207] 'In most cases, crucial decisions about water privatisation and cost recovery are made without the knowledge and consent of citizens. Therefore, an inclusive system of governance and local community participation and partnership

---

[203] UNCTAD (2009), *World Investment Report 2008: Transnational Corporations and Infrastructure Challenge*, New York and Geneva: UN, 102–104.
[204] OECD Centre for Co-operation with Non-Members (1999), *Foreign Direct Investment and the Environment*, Paris: OECD, 53.
[205] Fitzmaurice (2007), supra, 559.
[206] General Comment 15 (2002), supra, para. 35.
[207] Ibid., paras 23, 24.

between local government, community-based organisations and water utilities could offer some solutions to make safe drinking water accessible to all.'[208]

Globalisation with liberalisation of markets and private sector participation influences water management at all levels – international, national and local. While designing laws and policies with effective control over water resources, states need to take into account that water remains available, affordable and accessible to the people. Sustainable globalisation requires states to strengthen water governance with equitable distribution of water, efficient water use and an increased role for the people in water-related decision-making.

FURTHER READING

Dellapenna, J.W. and J. Gupta (2008), 'The Evolving Legal Framework for Global Water Governance', Global Governance, 14(3), 437–453.

Fitzmaurice, M. (2007), 'The Human Right to Water', Fordham Environmental Law Review, 18, 537–585.

McCaffrey, S.C. (2001), *The Law of International Watercourses: Non-Navigational Uses*, Oxford: Oxford University Press.

Razzaque, J. (2009), 'Public Participation in Water Governance', in J. Dellapenna and J. Gupta (eds), *The Law and Politics of Water*, New York: Springer-Verlag, 353–372.

Scanlon, J., A. Cassar and N. Nemes (2004), 'Water as a Human Right?', IUCN Environmental Policy and Law Paper 51, Gland, Switzerland and Cambridge, UK: IUCN.

Shiva, V. (2002), *Water Wars: Privatization, Pollution, and Profit*, Cambridge, MA: South End Press.

Weiss, E.B., L.B. de Chazournes and N. Bernasconi-Osterwalder (eds) (2005), *Fresh Water and International Economic Law*, Oxford: Oxford University Press.

---

[208] Razzaque, J. (2004), 'Trading Water: The Human Factor', Review of European Community and International Environmental Law, 13(1), 26.

8. Renewable energy

1. INTRODUCTION

Energy security and climate change are of high importance for today's societies and a key challenge of the twenty-first century. Noting the importance of the stabilisation of greenhouse gas (GHG) emissions, concerns over access to energy and future energy infrastructure have come to the forefront of public opinion and discussion in international bodies. In the pursuit of developing alternatives to mankind's dependence on fossil fuels, renewable energy has become an increasingly complex area involving wide-ranging issues which explore the relationships and links between energy security, economic growth, poverty alleviation and environmental protection.[1]

Climate change is a global issue with no boundaries. Its impacts include the rise in temperature, extreme weather patterns, increased droughts and floods and sea-level rise. These effects are suffered differently in all parts of the world with no direct geographical correlation between contribution towards the production of GHGs and negative effects of climate change.[2] Globalisation with its increasing trade in goods and services flowing from one country to another, energy intensive production methods, and paradigm of worldwide industrialisation, development, capitalism and consumer-led lifestyle have multiplied the carbon footprint and emissions of most societies. For example, imports of flowers or off-season fruits from another country or manufacturing plants assembling goods in various parts of the world add to the GHG emissions. About 79 per cent of the primary energy supply in the world today still comes from fossil fuels including oil, natural gas and coal.[3] Nuclear power contributes approximately 3 per cent and the rest comes from renewable sources such as biomass, hydropower, wind, solar and geothermal.[4]

---

[1] United Nations (2009), *Millennium Development Goals Report*, New York: UN. UNEP (2007), *Global Environment Outlook 4*, Nairobi: UNEP.
[2] Stern, N. (2007), *The Economics of Climate Change: The Stern Review*, Cambridge: Cambridge University Press, Introduction.
[3] REN21 (2008), 'Renewables 2007 Global Status Report', Paris: REN21 Secretariat and Washington, DC: Worldwatch Institute, 9.
[4] Ibid., 9.

In comparison to conventional energy sources, renewable energy may not be cost-effective due to the incentives from government towards conventional energy sources as well as the high capital cost of renewable energy technologies. There are generally government policies and support in the form of subsidies provided for fossil fuels or nuclear energy which give conventional energy sources a competitive edge.[5] In addition, the cost based pricing of fossil fuels does not internalise environmental and health costs. The success of renewable energy will require technological development to bring down the costs – this is particularly true if the developing countries are to explore and benefit from renewable energy sources. Efficient use of energy as well as using renewable energy sources would allow the poorer communities to access electricity for agriculture and other needs, and play an important role in food production and poverty alleviation. In India, for example, the Punjab Renewable Energy Development Agency installed around 100 solar PV systems to provide a continuous supply of water for agriculture. Farmers previously had had to rely on sporadic connection to the grid or on diesel generators. The newly assured supply of water increased the productivity and income of small and marginal farmers.[6] This example shows that renewable energy promotes diversity of energy sources and contributes to energy security. Efficient use of renewable energy may also reduce the energy related CO_2 emissions, and mitigate and adapt its effects on climate change.

The energy intensive lifestyle of the developed and developing nations requires a sustainable strategy which will allow them to use energy efficiently and develop renewable sources of energy. Countries are taking steps which can lead to energy efficiency such as reducing the use of fossil fuels, using efficient electrical lighting and appliances, developing cleaner technology and increasing the use of public transport.[7] Countries are also creating policies, rules and standards to develop renewable sourced energy.[8] For example, the Clean Development Mechanism (CDM) projects under the climate change regime allow the developed countries or investors to initiate renewable energy projects that reduce the emissions of GHGs in the developing countries. The CDM projects also allow investments

---

[5] UNEP (2008), Reforming Energy Subsidies: Opportunities to Contribute to the Climate Change Agenda, Nairobi: UNEP. Stern (2007), supra, 278–279.

[6] Flavin, C. and M.H. Aeck (2005), *Energy for Development: The Potential Role of Renewable Energy in Meeting the Millennium Development Goals*, Washington DC: Worldwatch Institute, 24.

[7] See the Introduction to this book.

[8] REN21 (2009), *Renewables Global Status Report: 2009 Update*, Paris: REN21 Secretariat, 17–21.

and clean technologies to flow from the North to the South and create a market of cleaner and renewable energy.

This chapter examines renewable energy as a natural resource and its ramifications on global warming and energy security. Hydro-power, wind, geothermal, solar, biomass – these are all considered to be renewable energy sources. Of these sources, hydropower, solar and wind power have attracted both positive and negative attention.[9] This chapter highlights the binding (e.g. Energy Charter Treaty) and non-binding instruments which guide access to, use and the supply of renewable energy. It also explores the link between climate change and renewable energy, and the legal developments in the EU. It examines the role played by international institutions such as the World Bank, WTO and Global Environment Facility to promote renewable energy.

2. SOURCES OF RENEWABLE ENERGY AS NATURAL RESOURCES

Access to reliable and affordable energy services facilitates the eradication of poverty. It is, therefore, crucial to determine the sources of energy as impacts of energy based emissions contribute to air pollution and ecosystem degradation affecting human health and the environment.[10] The conventional sources of energy are non-renewable and have adverse environmental and social consequences. While a number of developed and developing countries are considering nuclear energy as a source of clean energy, there is an increasing concern about the cost, safety and waste disposal of nuclear energy.

Renewable energy sources, on the other hand, are considered sustainable. These resources are 'essentially inexhaustible', have lower emissions of GHGs and are less hazardous to human health.[11] The development of renewable energy depends on various potentials: theoretical, geographical, technical, economic, market.[12] Theoretical potential takes into account the natural and climatic factors. Many renewable resources with

---

[9] Ottinger R.L. and R. Williams (2002), 'Renewable Energy Sources for Development', Environmental Law, 32, 333.

[10] Goldemberg, J. and T.B. Johansson (2004), *Energy Assessment: Overview 2004 Update*, New York: UNDP, 12.

[11] Alexander, G. and G. Boyle (2004), 'Introducing Renewable Energy', in G. Boyle (ed.), *Renewable Energy*, Oxford, Oxford University Press, 2.

[12] Hoogwijk, M. and W. Graus (2008), *Global Potential of Renewable Energy Sources: A Literature Assessment, Background Report*, Utrecht: ECOFYS, 6.

theoretical potential may be restricted by geographical limitations, e.g. land use, land cover. Renewable energy sources with geographic potential may have technical restrictions or may not be cost effective. There is also an additional issue of market restrictions, e.g. demand for energy, competing technologies, policies and measures which countries take into account while deciding the development of renewable energy.

The following discussion provides a brief outline of the various sources of renewable energy.

2.1. Hydropower

This is the largest source of renewable energy with a well-established technology. According to the World Commission on Dams, large dams provide 19 per cent of the world's total electricity supply, with relatively low GHG emissions and a secure source of water supply.[13] Dams also play an important role with 12 per cent of large dams designated for water supply.[14] Once built, they produce cheap electricity, create recreational lakes and reduce the danger of flooding. However, dams built to produce hydroelectricity displace human and non-human habitats, destroy biodiversity, degrade natural ecosystems and alter the livelihood of indigenous people.[15] Indigenous communities are generally very vulnerable to the resettlement processes with loss of land, livelihood and culture.[16] Building these dams requires large investment (e.g. the Three Gorges Dam in China), and the hydroelectric project may need to export electricity to more developed countries to make the project economically viable.[17]

2.2. Solar and Wind Power

Solar and wind power sources are commonly used to generate electricity and both have their advantages and disadvantages. Solar energy can be concentrated by mirrors to provide high temperature heat to generate electricity, which is known as solar thermal energy. Solar radiation can also be converted directly into electricity using photovoltaic (PV) modules.

---

[13] WCD (2000), *Dams and Development: A New Framework for Decision Making*, London: Earthscan. Executive Summary, xxix.

[14] Ibid., 14.

[15] WCD (2000), supra, chapters 3 and 4.

[16] For example, the Sardar Sarovar project in India, the Kao Laem Dam in Thailand. Ibid., 110–112.

[17] WWF (2004), *Rivers at Risk: Dams and the Future of Freshwater Ecosystems*, Surrey: WWF, 6.

While the use of solar energy is limited compared to that of hydropower, the output of solar PV is relatively high compared to that of other renewable energy sources.[18] The solar PV system can be connected to the local or national electricity grid or off-grid to supply power in remote locations. Solar power can be used for various energy services such as residential and industrial electricity, lighting, low/medium voltage electric needs such as telecommunications, pumping or heating water and drying crops.[19] On the advantage side, the set up cost of PV cells has come down in price, solar power plants can be built on an individual basis and they are low on distribution costs as they do not necessarily require a grid system.[20] Developing countries such as India and China are using solar energy as it does not require large investment and receives government support.[21] On the negative side, the cost per kilowatt/hour remains higher than that of fossil fuels and, with government support, the actual costs may be difficult to determine. In addition, solar energy plants may require a vast land area[22] and disrupt wildlife.

Wind is one of the most cost-effective methods of electricity generation available.[23] The use of onshore and offshore wind power is increasing over time. The development of onshore wind power depends on wind resources and land available for the installation of wind turbines. The development of offshore wind power depends on the wind resources offshore and the competition for other functions at sea (e.g. fisheries, oil and gas extraction, natural reserves).[24] In recent years, China has experienced a huge growth in its wind power industries with many companies producing wind turbines and other components.[25] Along with noise and electromagnetic interference, there is concern that wind power may degrade landscape and destroy biodiversity.[26] In addition, both wind and solar power have

---

[18]   Hoogwijk et al. (2008), supra, 23.
[19]   Flavin et al. (2005), supra, 15
[20]   Boyle, G. (2004), 'Solar Photovoltaics', in Boyle (ed.), supra, 84–85.
[21]   REN21 (2009), supra, 9.
[22]   Boyle, G. (2004), supra, 94–95.
[23]   Taylor, D. (2004), 'Wind Energy', in Boyle (ed.), supra, chapter 7, 244.
[24]   Hoogwijk et al. (2008), supra, 18–22.
[25]   REN21 (2009), supra, 8.
[26]   Manguiat, M.S.Z., L. Siegele and D.A. Jacobson (2006), 'Wind Turbines and International Biodiversity-Related Agreements: Emerging Trends and Recommendations', in L. Parker, J. Ronk, B. Gentry, M. Wilder and J. Cameron (eds), *From Barriers to Opportunities: Renewable Energy Issues in Law and Policy*, A Report on the Work of the Renewable Energy and International Law (REIL) Project, 2006–2007, New Haven, USA: Yale School of Forestry and Environmental Studies.

one problem in common: how to store electricity when the sun is not shining or the wind is not blowing. One approach is to use diverse sources at a time (e.g. hydroelectricity, wind and solar) and to use these sources when needed. But this solution adds to the cost of production. Another approach is to connect the renewable energy sources to the traditional grid which may supply electricity when the renewable sources are low in supply.[27]

2.3. Geothermal Energy

Compared to other renewable energy sources, geothermal energy is consistently available without any restriction. This source of renewable energy is independent of the sun as the energy source is found within the Earth. Geothermal energy is extracted via boreholes drilled into the reservoir of hot water or steam trapped in shallow rocks. While it is expensive to build a power station, the operating costs are low, resulting in low energy costs. This source of energy can have direct use (e.g. space heating/cooling, industrial use) or can be used for power generation.[28] Major environmental concerns associated with geothermal energy include, in the short term, noise pollution through drilling, and ground subsidence and gaseous pollution in the long term.[29]

2.4. Biomass

This is the earliest source of renewable energy. The definition of biomass is found in the European Union law as

> . . . the biodegradable fraction of products, waste and residues from biological origin from agriculture (including vegetal and animal substances), forestry and related industries including fisheries and aquaculture, as well as the biodegradable fraction of industrial and municipal waste.[30]

The sources of biomass could be energy crops including woody (e.g. short rotation forestry) and agricultural (e.g. sugar cane, maize, oily seeds,

---

[27] Everett, B. and G. Boyle (2004), 'Integration', in Boyle (ed.), supra, 394–404.

[28] Hoogwijk et al. (2008), supra, 28–30.

[29] Brown, G. and J. Garnish (2004), 'Geothermal Energy', in Boyle (ed.), supra, 373.

[30] Article 2(e), Directive 2009/28/EC of the European Parliament and of the Council of 23 April 2009 on the promotion of the use of energy from renewable sources and amending and subsequently repealing Directives 2001/77/EC and 2003/30/EC, OJ L140/16, 5 June 2009.

grassy plants) crops and waste (e.g. crop waste, animal waste, municipal solid waste, landfill gas). The biomass can be converted to produce heat, electricity and transport fuel. Thus, biomass presents the possibility of producing biogas and biofuel. The use and promotion of biofuel have pros and cons: biofuel can arguably[31] reduce GHG emissions. On the negative side, oily seeds (e.g. rapeseed, linseed, soya) and starch rich plants (e.g. wheat, corn, beetroot, potatoes, barley) can be used to produce biodiesel or bioethanol. That means that food crops are used to produce biofuel as it pays more, instead of feeding hungry people in the developing world.[32] In addition, as with onshore wind power, biomass requires large areas of land limiting land for agricultural use and degrading biodiversity.[33] However, with concerns associated with large hydropower and with the present low baseline for solar and wind energy, energy from biomass is likely to play an increasing role in energy security.

3. USE OF RENEWABLE ENERGY AND SUSTAINABLE DEVELOPMENT

By improving energy security and reducing the environmental impact of energy use and production, renewable energy can address key challenges of sustainable development. Non-technical barriers such as lack of government policy support, lack of consumer awareness, inadequate financial incentives, inadequate workforce skills and training and lack of community participation in energy choices hamper the development of renewable energy sources. It is true that technology for using fossil fuels, such as mines and power plants, is already well established. However, the cost involved in extracting oil from ever deeper reservoirs is increasing and the costs of renewable energy technology are falling with increased investment in this sector. The main arguments for expanding renewable energy sources are energy security, diversity of energy sources, production of clean energy and reduction of the depletion of conventional energy sources.

---

[31] Eide, A. (2008), *The Right to Food and the Impact of Liquid Biofuels (Agrofuels)*, Rome: FAO, 21.

[32] Ziegler, J. (2008), Report of the Special Rapporteur on the Right to Food, Human Rights Council, A/HRC/7/5 (10 January 2008), 20–22.

[33] Larkin, S., J. Ramage and J. Scurlock (2004), 'Bioenergy', in Boyle (ed.), supra, 139.

3.1. Energy Security

Apart from the aim to control global warming and promote sustainable use of energy, energy security and diversification of energy sources are other reasons for using renewable energy. Reliance only on fossil fuel can lead to shortfalls in supply as a result of economic tactics, leading to energy crisis or uncertainty of future supply. Therefore, diversity of energy sources becomes crucial to avoid dependence on the oil producing countries. For example, in the USA, the government is promoting the use of renewable energy and lessening the dependence on oil and gas.[34] Renewable energy contributes to the security of supply by increasing the share of domestically produced energy and diversifying the fuel mix and the sources of energy imports.[35] Countries with a large reserve of oil, gas or coal must also realise that these resources are exhaustible and the increasing use of these resources puts their energy security in peril. From a developing country perspective, it may be easier to increase the use of renewable energy (e.g. energy from wind, solar and hydro-electricity) as these resources are generally within the national sovereignty of a country. Moreover, renewable energy reduces the need to import crude oil, thus saving foreign exchange. Large-scale renewable energy projects also create long-term employment within the country. However, the problem remains with the technology required to procure the energy from the sources and the maintenance of the renewable energy sources.[36] In addition, some renewable energy sources (e.g. large hydroelectricity projects) come with a long list of negative effects on the environment and human health. Alternative energy, such as nuclear, may not always be a viable or cost effective option as it could be extremely expensive, and requires long-term planning, advanced technology and adequate pre and post monitoring.

3.2. Clean Energy

There is no denying that the global concern over environmental externalities of conventional sources of energy is quite high. Conventional non-renewable sources create significant and, to some extent, irreversible damage to the natural environment (land, water, forest, biodiversity, climatic systems) and also to humans (general and occupational health,

---

[34] REN21 (2009), supra, 9.
[35] Commission of the European Communities, Renewable Energy Road Map – Renewable Energies in the 21st Century: Building a More Sustainable Future, COM(2006)848 final, 10 January 2007, 14.
[36] Flavin et al. (2005), supra, 31.

radiation hazard, accidents, environment displacement, property damage). The production of renewable energy is comparatively cleaner and has a less adverse impact on the environment. There are, however, some negative environmental impacts from renewable energy sources, e.g. the wind turbines cause damage to wildlife habitat as well as destroying the beauty of the landscape. Similarly, there are ecological effects of hydroelectric dams or toxic heavy metals used in batteries for solar home systems.[37] It is, however, necessary to take into account the short and long-term effect of a particular renewable energy source and compare it to the serious impacts of producing electricity from fossil fuels or nuclear power.[38]

Financial and other incentives from government can promote the use of renewable energy (see box 8.1). The Stern Report estimates that government's direct support for the deployment of renewable sources worldwide was US$10 billion in 2004.[39] Incentives including subsidies designed to encourage renewable technologies may help reduce noxious and GHG emissions depending on how these incentives are structured.[40] Financial or other incentives for renewable energy by the government may, however, create an artificial market which requires consideration of justifications and weighing of harm and benefits to the environment and human health. One such example is subsidies for liquid biofuels which may not always contribute to the reduction of GHGs if the whole life cycle assessment of production, distribution and use is taken into account.[41]

3.3.   Access to Energy

Accessibility of electricity for all including the poorer section of the community depends on the cost of electricity as well as the generation of power at the national level. For developing countries, economic and social development and poverty eradication cannot be achieved in the absence of adequate and affordable energy resources. In some countries in Asia, Africa and Latin America, poorer sections of the community rarely have any access to electricity.[42] Even where they have access, they may not be able to afford the cost of the electricity or there may not be any guarantee

---

[37]   UNEP (2008), *Reforming Energy Subsidies: Opportunities to Contribute to the Climate Change Agenda*, Nairobi: UNEP, 5.

[38]   Manguiat et al. (2006), supra, 21.

[39]   Stern (2007), supra, 367. The Report estimates that subsidies for fossil fuels worldwide are between US$150 billion to 250 billion each year.

[40]   UNEP (2008), supra, 16.

[41]   Eide (2008), supra, 21.

[42]   See the case studies in Flavin et al. (2005), supra.

BOX 8.1. RENEWABLE ENERGY USE IN CHINA[1]

China is a non-annex I party to the UN Climate Change Convention. It has a coal based energy structure and is likely to use coal in its energy mix over the next few decades. According to a 2006 list produced by the UN Statistics Division, China's carbon dioxide emissions are the highest out of all countries in this study. It is important for China to use renewable energy to reduce GHG emissions without compromising its development goals.

The two main sources of renewable energy for China will be hydropower and wind power. As of 2007, hydroelectricity accounted for 20.7 per cent of total energy capacity; nuclear accounted for 1.2 per cent; geothermal, solar, wind, and biomass combined only accounted for 0.5 per cent of energy capacity.

The China Renewable Energy Law (2005) offers financial subsidies and tax incentives for the development of renewable energy sources, like solar, wind, biomass, and geothermal. The law aims to increase Chinese renewable capacity to 15 per cent by 2020 while investing US$180 billion into renewable energy.

China is already a world leader in manufacturing micro and small wind turbines, and multiple developing countries have established production of solar PV modules with potential to export. China plans to boost renewable energy to cover 10 per cent of its electric power capacity by 2010, raising its green power capacity to 60,000 MW, including 50,000 MW of hydropower and 4,000 MW of wind power.

Note:
1. Meisen, P. and S. Hawkins (2009), *Renewable Energy Potential of China: Making the Transition from Coal-Fired Generation*, California, USA: Global Energy Network Institute. Flavin (2007), supra.

---

as the power supply system is quite unreliable in these parts of the world.[43] Agriculture is affected as farmers do not have access to electricity to use water pumps, and manufacturing industries are affected as they cannot meet the deadlines for their exports. Fossil fuel will not be able to meet the demands of the two billion people in the world lacking access to affordable

---

[43] Goldemberg et al. (2004), supra, 13.

energy and use of renewable energy technology can meet that demand. Production of renewable energy allows off-grid and micro-grid systems to supply electricity to those living in remote areas.[44] Renewable energy projects in many developing countries have directly contributed to poverty alleviation and a better quality of life by providing the energy needed for creating businesses and employment.[45]

The falling cost of the production of renewable energy such as wind and solar power over the last 20 years makes it more affordable to the poorer communities.[46] According to REN21, developing countries share more than 40 per cent of global existing renewable power capacity, 70 per cent of existing solar hot water capacity and 45 per cent of biofuels production.[47] Along with improving energy supply, equitable distribution of energy services is necessary to enable poor communities to benefit from renewable energy.

4. THE 'SOFT LAW' AND RENEWABLE ENERGY

The key message from the non-binding instruments is that developed as well as developing countries need to increase the production and consumption of renewable energy. The increased demand and market for renewable energy can lead to increased investment and technology transfer in the developing countries. The development in the renewable energy sector is influenced by the soft law instruments, such as the UN Declaration on Permanent Sovereignty over Natural Resources,[48] the Declaration for the New International Economic Order,[49] 2002 WSSD and the 2004 Renewable Energy Declaration.[50] These soft laws play an important role in the renewable energy sector as these legal policies, guidelines and standards can lead to binding instruments. According to these soft instruments, states have sovereign rights to exploit their own

---

[44] The case studies in Flavin et al. (2005), supra.

[45] Ibid., 12–25.

[46] EU Renewable Energy Road Map (2007), supra, 15–17.

[47] REN21 (2007), supra, 6.

[48] GA Res. 1803 (XVII) of 14 December 1962, Permanent Sovereignty over Natural Resources.

[49] Declaration on the Establishment of a New International Economic Order (1974), GA Res., UN Doc. A/RES/S-6/3201.

[50] International Conference for Renewable Energies (Bonn, 2004). Renewables 2004 adopted three documents: a Political Declaration, an International Action Programme, and a set of Policy Recommendations for Renewable Energies.

resources[51] including renewable energy sources (e.g. wind for the turbine, river to produce hydro-electricity).

Important environmental declarations such as the 1992 UN Conference on Environment and Development do not explicitly address energy issues.[52] However, aspects of energy in relation to environment and development are addressed in Agenda 21, encouraging states to promote renewable energy systems which are less polluting and more efficient.[53] Similarly, there is no Millennium Development Goal (MDG) on increased access to energy services, but energy related indicators are used to measure progress made on poverty alleviation and environmental sustainability.[54] Reaching the goal to halve the proportion of people living in extreme poverty and to achieve environmental sustainability by 2015 will require significantly expanded access to renewable energy in developing countries. It is estimated that up to one billion people can be given access to energy services from renewable sources, provided that market development and financing arrangements can be enhanced.[55] Renewable energy is a core issue for achieving sustainable development as well.[56] As urban development is heavily dependent on fossil fuels, poorer communities are deprived of electricity, leading to social and health problems. Promotion of renewable energy and strategies in energy efficiency can contribute to reducing the health and environmental impacts of energy production and consumption, and fostering economic development.[57]

This recognition of the importance of energy in achieving sustainable development is reiterated by the Commission on Sustainable Development. It acknowledges that around two billion people, mostly living in developing countries, lack access to energy services, and there are

---

[51] See discussion in the Introduction and chapter 3. For example, Article 21, Declaration of the United Nations Conference on the Human Environment (1972). UN Doc. A/CONF/48/14/REV.1.

[52] Declaration of the United Nations Conference on Environment and Development (1992), UN Doc. A/CONF.151/26/Rev.1, Report of the UNCED, Vol. 1 (New York). Principle 16 (polluter pays principle) can be used to promote renewable energy policies with a sustainable production and consumption method and financing for energy.

[53] United Nations, Agenda 21, 1992. Chapter 9 (Protection of the Atmosphere), para. 9.11.

[54] Flavin et al. (2005), supra. Goldemberg et al. (2004), supra, 80.

[55] Para. 3, Political Declaration, International Conference for Renewable Energies, Bonn, 4 June 2004.

[56] Goal 7 (environmental sustainability). UN GA Res., UN Millennium Declaration, UN Doc. A/RES/55/2, 18 September 2000.

[57] Johansson et al. (2004), supra, 34–41.

wide disparities in the levels of energy consumption within and between developed and developing countries.[58] The action-based recommendations by the Commission on Sustainable Development provided a basis for discussion in the WSSD.[59] During the preparatory process of the WSSD, the then UN-Secretary General, Kofi Annan, introduced the Water, Energy, Health, Agriculture, and Biodiversity (WEHAB) framework to guide the WSSD.[60] The WEHAB energy framework highlighted the linkages between energy and goals related to water, health, agriculture, and biodiversity, and emphasised the interdependence among sustainable development issues. In the Johannesburg Plan of Implementation of the WSSD,[61] states agreed to increase the proportion of renewable energy sources in the total global energy supply, diversify the energy supply mix, and recognised the role of the public sector in establishing supportive policy environments. The Johannesburg Plan of Implementation calls upon all the governments to take action to:[62]

> Para 20 (d): Combine, as appropriate, the increased use of renewable energy resources, more efficient use of energy, greater reliance on advanced energy technologies, including advanced and cleaner fossil fuel technologies, and the sustainable use of traditional energy resources, which could meet the growing need for energy services in the longer term to achieve sustainable development;

> Para 20 (e): Diversify energy supply by developing advanced, cleaner, more efficient, affordable and cost-effective energy technologies, including fossil fuel technologies and renewable energy technologies, hydro included, and their transfer to developing countries on concessional terms as mutually agreed. With a sense of urgency, substantially increase the global share of renewable energy sources with the objective of increasing its contribution to total energy supply, recognizing the role of national and voluntary regional targets as well as initiatives, where they exist, and ensuring that energy policies are supportive to developing countries' efforts to eradicate poverty, and regularly evaluate available data to review progress to this end . . .

---

[58] Commission on Sustainable Development, 9th Meeting, Official Records of the Economic and Social Council, 2001, Supplement No. 9 (E/2001/29) 1, 6–7.

[59] World Summit on Sustainable Development, 2002, Report of the World Summit on Sustainable Development, UN Doc. A/CONF. 199/20 (2002).

[60] WEHAB Initiative (2002) UN Press Release, SG/SM/8239 ENV/DEV/637, 14 May 2002.

[61] WSSD Johannesburg Plan of Implementation. paras 9, 20, and 38 in the respective chapters dealing with poverty eradication (II), changing unsustainable patterns of consumption and production (III), and protecting and managing the natural resource base of economic and social development (IV).

[62] Part III, Changing unsustainable pattern of consumption and production, Johannesburg Plan of Implementation (2002). Available at: www.un.org/esa/sustdev/documents/WSSD_POI_PD/English/POIToc.htm (accessed 15 January 2010).

The Johannesburg Plan of Implementation urges the international financial institutions to support developing countries and countries with economies in transition, so that these countries can have adequate policy and regulatory frameworks for renewable energy.[63] Moreover, it asks governments to explore possibilities by using the Global Environment Facility to provide financial resources to build capacity through training, technical know-how and strengthening national institutions. The Plan of Implementation adds that the global financial institutions and public–private partnerships[64] can assist the least developing countries and small island nations in promoting renewable energy and advanced energy technologies.[65]

After the WSSD, a number of declarations dealt with the multiple benefits of the use of renewable sources of energy for improving access to energy services. While the Bonn Declaration (2004) acknowledges that renewable energies combined with enhanced energy efficiency can significantly contribute to sustainable development,[66] the participating countries did not agree on a global target of renewable energy. The Beijing Declaration in 2005 emphasised that the use of renewable energy can contribute to the eradication of poverty as called for in the MDGs, reduce GHG emissions and combat climate change, enhance energy security and offer a new paradigm for international cooperation.[67] The Declaration acknowledges that there is an 'energy divide' between the poor and the rich as the poorer community lacks information, education, economic opportunity and a healthier livelihood, and that such divide 'erodes environmental sustainability at the local, national, and global levels'.[68] The Declaration calls for 'strengthened support for the commercialization and transfer of technologies through North–South and South–South cooperation'.[69] Successful actions to meet the challenges of renewable energy include: creating supportive policy, legal and institutional frameworks and promoting private sector involvement and a stronger alignment between policy time frames

---

[63] Para. 20(j).

[64] Para. 20(t). For example, the World Bank Carbon Funds, Renewable Energy Policy Network for the 21st Century (REN21), Renewable Energy and Energy Efficiency Partnership (REEP).

[65] Paras 20(n) and 59(b).

[66] Political Declaration, International Conference for Renewable Energies, Bonn, 2004, para. 1.

[67] Beijing Declaration on Renewable Energy for Sustainable Development, 2005, para. 3.

[68] Para. 4.

[69] Para. 7.

and timelines for investment.[70] This Declaration recognises the need for significant financial resources, both public and private, for investment in renewable energy and energy efficiency, including the use of innovative financing mechanisms, such as loan guarantees and the CDM, and market-based instruments which can leverage scarce public funds.

As a follow up to the Bonn and Beijing Declarations, the Washington Declaration (2008) produces an Action Programme with specific pledges from governments, international organisations, private sectors and the civil society.[71] For example, the European Union pledges to increase the share of renewable energy to 20 per cent and reduce GHG emissions by 20 per cent by 2020. Pakistan pledges to achieve a 10 per cent share of renewable energy in the national energy mix by 2012. Uganda pledges to make modern renewable energy a substantial part of Uganda's national energy consumption, up from 4 per cent to 61 per cent.

The developed countries' perspectives on the promotion of renewable energy are found in the Brussels Declaration.[72] The Declaration highlights renewable energy as 'an integral part of the European Energy and Climate Policy to combat climate change, enhance energy security and increase job opportunities and economic growth both in the European Union and worldwide'.[73] The recommendations suggest that the market process of renewable energy needs to reflect true costs including externalities which would provide investment security.[74]

These non-binding instruments highlight some common elements:

- there is an urgent need substantially to increase the global share of renewable energy sources in the total energy supply;
- energy security can be achieved through reliance on domestic energy sources such as biomass, hydro, wind, solar and geothermal;
- expansion of renewable energy through international cooperation and partnership will provide opportunities for poverty eradication; and

---

[70] Para. 8.

[71] Washington International Action Programme, Washington International Renewable Energy Conference (2008), available at: www.wirec2008.gov/documents/WIREC_report_final.pdf (accessed 15 January 2010).

[72] Brussels Declaration on the New Role of Renewable Energy Sources for a Sustainable, Secure and Competitive Energy Future for Europe (2007), 'Conclusions and Recommendations from the EU Renewable Energy Policy Conference'. Available at: www.egec.org/download/FINAL_Brussels_Declaration_2007.pdf (accessed 20 August 2010).

[73] Para. 1.

[74] Para. 2. Environmental externalities may include environmental and social impacts and related costs of energy generation and uses.

- renewable energy will curb global warming and contribute to the protection of human health against air pollution.

5. CLIMATE CHANGE AND RENEWABLE ENERGY

A major drive for developing renewable energy sources is the need to reduce the emission of atmospheric pollutants, in particular GHGs which contribute to climate change. Adequate control of global warming requires the reduction of global GHG emissions, which is linked to the reduction of energy use and enhanced use of all forms of renewable energy. The catastrophic implications of climate change induced by global warming, e.g. the disappearance of arctic ice, extreme weather patterns, forest fires and heatwaves, form the central feature of the future of energy use. With these climate change concerns, there is a greater appreciation of the role that renewable energy can play in helping to move towards a low-carbon economy.[75]

According to the Gleneagles Communiqué on 'Climate Change, Energy and Sustainable Development'[76]

1.   We face serious and linked challenges in tackling climate change, promoting clean energy and achieving sustainable development globally.

(a)   Climate change is a serious and long-term challenge that has the potential to affect every part of the globe. We know that increased need and use of energy from fossil fuels, and other human activities, contribute in large part to increases in greenhouse gases associated with the warming of our Earth's surface. While uncertainties remain in our understanding of climate science, we know enough to act now to put ourselves on a path to slow and, as the science justifies, stop and then reverse the growth of greenhouse gases.

(b)   Global energy demands are expected to grow by 60% over the next 25 years. This has the potential to cause a significant increase in greenhouse gas emissions associated with climate change.

(c)   Secure, reliable and affordable energy sources are fundamental to economic stability and development. Rising energy demand poses a challenge to energy security given increased reliance on global energy markets.

---

[75]   Miller, A. and A. Cabraal (eds) (2007), *Catalysing Private Investment for a Low-Carbon Economy: World Bank Group Progress on Renewable Energy and Energy Efficiency in Fiscal 2007*, Washington DC: World Bank. In addition, energy efficiency can also play a role in increasing supply and moderating demand, thus reducing GHG emissions. See the Introduction to this book.

[76]   G-8 Gleneagles Summit 2005, Scotland, UK. Summit Documents. See Climate Change, Clean Energy and Sustainable Development: Gleneagles Plan of Action (2005), paras 5, 11, 16–17, 24–25.

The aim of this communiqué by the G-8 countries was to reaffirm the commitments to reduce GHG emissions, and work in partnership with other emerging economies such as those of Brazil, China, South Africa and India, to improve the global environment and enhance energy security.

5.1. Climate Change Convention and the Kyoto Protocol

The 1992 UN Framework Convention on Climate Change (UNFCCC) sets out broad principles for tackling climate change and relies upon the 1997 Kyoto Protocol to provide further guidance.[77] By January 2010, 194 parties had ratified the Convention and it divides participating countries into three groups.

- Annex I parties include countries which were members of the Organisation for Economic Co-operation and Development (OECD) in 1992, and countries with economies in transition (EIT).
- Annex II parties include the OECD members of Annex I, but not the EIT parties. Annex II parties provide financial resources to developing countries to reduce GHG emissions and to help them adapt to adverse effects of climate change. In addition, they have to take all practical steps to promote the development and transfer of environmentally friendly technologies to EIT parties and developing countries.
- Non-Annex I parties are developing countries. They are recognised as being especially vulnerable to the adverse impacts of climate change, including countries with low-lying coastal areas and those prone to desertification and drought. There are 49 least developed countries which are given special consideration due to their limited capacity to respond to climate change and adapt to its adverse effects.

The Kyoto Protocol to the UNFCCC sets binding targets for developed countries to reduce overall GHG emissions to an average of 5 per cent against 1990 levels over the period 2008–2012. The non-Annex I parties (developing countries) to the UNFCCC have no binding targets but must report in general terms on their actions.

---

[77] United Nations Framework Convention on Climate Change, 9 May 1992, 31 I.L.M. (1992) 849. Protocol to the United Nations Framework Convention on Climate Change (Kyoto), 37 I.L.M. (1998) 22, 10 December 1997, UN Doc. FCCC/CP/1997/7/Add.1.

What are the commitments under the 1992 UNFCCC that encourage the use of renewable energy? Under the UNFCCC, there is no express provision on the use of renewable energy. Since a large volume of GHGs originate from fossil fuels, there is a strong link between climate change mitigation and the global energy system. The principle of common but differentiated responsibility requires all parties to mitigate and facilitate adequate adaptation to climate change.[78] At the same time, the developed countries need to 'take the lead' in combating climate change and are required to assist the developing countries in capacity building, funding and technology transfer.[79] The discussion on climate change and renewable energy evolves mainly around mitigation, technology transfer and financial mechanisms.

5.2. Mitigation and Renewable Energy

The UNFCCC requires all parties to stabilise GHG concentrations 'at a level that would prevent dangerous anthropogenic interference with the climate system' within a time frame.[80] Sources of GHGs include coal, oil and natural gas, and the Convention requires the parties to find alternative or substitute sources of energy to replace potentially dangerous hydrocarbons.[81] Following the common but differentiated responsibility, the developed countries should have quantified emission limitation and reduction targets, as well as using clean energy to mitigate the adverse effects of climate change.

Under the Kyoto Protocol, the measures to be undertaken by the developed countries (Annex B) to achieve such a reduction include developing sustainable forms of energy. The Protocol provides an indicative list of domestic policies, such as research and development of renewable energy sources and promotion of cleaner technologies, which could be used to reduce emissions.[82] The Protocol creates three market mechanisms, known as flexible mechanisms.

---

[78] Articles 3(1) and (2), 4(1) of the UNFCCC. Bali Action Plan, Decision 1/CP13 (2008). Sands, P. (2003), *Principles of International Environmental Law*, Cambridge: Cambridge University Press, 285–289. Discussed in chapter 2.

[79] Article 4(3)–(5) of the UNFCCC. Sands (2003), supra, 289. Birnie, P., A. Boyle and C. Redgwell (2009), *International Law and the Environment*, Oxford: Oxford University Press, 358–360.

[80] Article 2 of the UNFCCC.

[81] Article 4(1)(c) of the UNFCCC. Article 2(1)(a) and Annex A of the Protocol.

[82] Article 2 (1) (a) of the Protocol.

(i)   Emissions Trading (ET): the GHG emission reduction permits are bought, sold or exchanged by agreement between Annex B parties to the Kyoto Protocol.[83] The emissions trading system allows Annex B parties to acquire units from other Annex B parties where it would be more cost effective to do so and use them towards meeting their emissions targets under the Kyoto Protocol.[84]

(ii)   Joint Implementation (JI): this mechanism provides for Annex B parties to the Protocol to implement projects which reduce emissions in other Annex B parties, in return for emission reduction units (ERUs). The ERUs generated by JI projects can be used by Annex B parties towards meeting their emissions targets under the Protocol.[85]

(iii)   Clean Development Mechanism (CDM): Annex B parties to the Kyoto Protocol receive GHG emission credits by investing in projects in non-Annex I countries reducing GHG emissions.[86] The Certified Emission Reductions (CERs) generated by such projects can be used by the Annex B parties to meet their emissions targets under the Protocol.[87]

These flexible mechanisms may be used for emissions reductions as a supplement to domestic action only. Parties to the UNFCCC cannot achieve the required emission reductions merely by using JI, CDM or international emissions trading.[88] The use of these flexible mechanisms such as the ET has created a global carbon market which has the potential to attract investment for renewable energy projects. Along with the emissions trading mechanism under the Protocol, a number of countries (US, Japan, Canada) have introduced domestic emissions trading schemes. The European Union emissions trading scheme which started in 2005 imposes a cap on emissions of CO_2 from installations or facilities within the EU.[89] This emissions trading scheme can contribute to an

---

[83]   Articles 17, 3(3), 3(4), 3(7), 3(8) of the Kyoto Protocol, Decision 2/cmp.1 (2005), 11/cmp.1 (2005). Parties may be able to trade units in the form of assigned amount units, certified emission reductions, emission reduction units and removal units. Birnie (2009), supra, 367.

[84]   Only Annex B parties to the Kyoto Protocol with emissions limitation and reduction commitments inscribed in Annex B to the Protocol may participate in such trading. Freestone, D. and C. Streck (eds), *Legal Aspects of Implementing the Kyoto Protocol: Making Kyoto Work*, Oxford: Oxford University Press, 3–24.

[85]   Article 6 of the Kyoto Protocol, Decision 9/CMP.1 (2005), 5/cmp.4 (2008), FCCC/KP/CMP/2009/18 (19 November 2009).

[86]   Article 12 of Kyoto Protocol, Decision 17/CP.7 (2001), 2/cmp.4 (2008).

[87]   Birnie (2009), supra, 364–366.

[88]   Sands (2003), supra, 372–374.

[89]   Directive 2003/87/EC of the European Parliament and of the Council of 13

improvement in the economic performance of renewable energy options, especially within the electricity generation sector.[90] In addition, around 45 per cent of the projects under the JI are for renewable energy,[91] and the first large wind farm installed in Estonia was a JI project.[92] Though the number of JI is still limited, the JI projects can have a leading role in introducing innovative projects on renewable energy.

While the target countries under ET and JI are the developed countries, CDM targets projects in the developing countries. The CDM establishes a mechanism under which an Annex B party to the Protocol may receive carbon credits (CERs) for an investment in an emission reducing project in a developing country.[93] A private company can be part of a CDM project and private entities can sell and acquire CERs from projects in developing countries.[94] Developed countries can buy the CERs from international financial institutions, private financial institutions, bilateral purchase agreements with host countries and they can participate in various projects under the carbon funds (such as the Prototype Carbon Fund).[95]

Renewable energy projects are common under the CDM. The CDM benefits both the investing country and the receiving country. It provides an incentive to companies to use clean technology in order to produce sustainable energy and reduce GHG emissions. Examples of renewable energy under the CDM include wind, solar, geothermal, hydro and biomass energy.[96] While the developing country participating in the CDM

October 2003 establishing a scheme for greenhouse gas emission allowance trading within the Community and amending Council Directive 96/61/EC, OJ L275/32, 25 October 2003.

[90] Christensen, J., F. Denton, A. Garg, S. Kamel, R. Pacudan and E. Usher (2006), *Changing Climates: The role of renewable energy in a carbon constrained world*, Nairobi: UNEP, 25–26. Available at: www.ren21.net/pdf/REN21_CC_report.pdf (accessed 15 January 2010).

[91] Cited in REN21 (2007), Renewable Energy and the Climate Change Regime: Considerations from REN21 Ahead of Bali COP13. Available at www.ren21.net/pdf/UNFCCC_and_RE.pdf (accessed 15 January 2010).

[92] Ibid., 3.

[93] In order to have a smooth running of CDM, each project has to be supervised by a designated national authority (DNA) in the host country. This DNA evaluates and approves CDM projects and serves as point of contact to the government. The DNA needs to be notified to the UNFCCC secretariat.

[94] UNDP (2005), *The Clean Development Mechanism: A User's Guide*, New York: Energy and Environment Group, Bureau for Development Policy, 11–12.

[95] Ibid., 76–79.

[96] Report of the GEF to the 15th Session of the Conference of the Parties to the UN Framework Convention on Climate Change, FCCC/CP/2009/9, 27 October 2009.

project has no reduction target under the Kyoto Protocol, it can still use the project to reduce its overall GHG emissions. It is, however, crucial to note that a CDM project needs to demonstrate that its envisaged emissions reductions are real, measurable and additional to any which would have occurred in the absence of the project, and some renewable projects may fail to fulfil this criterion.[97]

5.3. Transfer of Technologies

The Convention highlights the importance of 'transfer of technologies' and transfer of, and access to, environmentally sound technologies.[98] This implies that Annex I parties are required to undertake research and development on new technologies to produce clean energy and transfer such technology to developing countries. In the Delhi Declaration, parties were urged to transfer affordable and cost effective renewable energy technologies to developing countries on concessional terms.[99] In the Copenhagen Accord, parties were asked to adopt domestic actions which increase public–private research with a significant shift in emphasis towards safe and sustainable low GHG emitting technologies, especially renewable energy.[100] With the assistance from developed countries, large emitting developing countries can decrease their carbon intensity and increase reliance on renewable energy technology. The Poznan Strategic Programme on Technology Transfer encourages investment in the transfer of environmentally sound technologies to developing countries.[101] Projects on renewable energy initiated under the Poznan Programme are diverse and include technologies on renewable energy (solar, biomass,

---

[97]   Birnie (2009), supra, 365. For example, the CDM Board rejected ten wind farm proposals by China as the projects did not pass the 'additionality' criterion. Szabo, M. (2009), 'U.N. panel rejects China windfarms, lifts suspension', Reuters, 4 December 2009.

[98]   Article 4(1), 4(5) of the UNFCCC. Article 11 of the Kyoto Protocol. Performance indicators to monitor and evaluate the effectiveness of the implementation of the technology transfer framework, Final Report by the Chair of the Expert Group on Technology Transfer. FCCCC/SB/2009/9, 11 November 2009.

[99]   Delhi Ministerial Declaration on Climate Change and Sustainable Development. Decision 1/CP.8 (2002), para. k.

[100]   Para. 4(e), Enhanced action on technology development and transfer, Draft Decisions, Report of the Ad Hoc Working Group on Long-term Cooperative Action under the Convention on its eighth session, held in Copenhagen from 7 to 15 December 2009, FCCC/AWGLCA/2009/17, 5 February 2010.

[101]   UNFCCC, Development and Transfer of Technologies, Decision 2/CP.14, FCCC/CP/2008/7/Add.1, 18 March 2009.

wind, hydrogen storage of renewable energy and wave) and energy efficiency.[102] Transfer of technology supports adaptation activities, promotes a low-carbon energy pathway in terms of energy infrastructure and lowers the level of GHG emissions in developing countries.

5.4. Financial Mechanisms

Under the UNFCCC and the Kyoto Protocol, developed countries (Annex I parties) should provide additional financial resources to assist developing countries to implement the Convention.[103] This assistance can be provided either through bilateral or multilateral aid or by applying the financial mechanism established by the Convention.[104] The Global Environment Facility (GEF) is entrusted with the operation of the financial mechanism.[105] The GEF puts in place four initiatives supporting measures for adaptation to climate change, and the projects funded under these initiatives relate to the development sectors including energy.[106] These funds can be used to initiate projects on renewable energy.[107] For example, the GEF Trust Fund finances small-scale hydro-power development and biomass energy development projects.[108] These funding mechanisms promote sustainable development with emphasis on the introduction and use of clean and resource-efficient technologies, social and environmental sustainability and improved social equity.

---

[102] This Programme funds renewable energy projects from 16 countries in Africa, East Asia and the Pacific, South Asia, Latin America and the Caribbean, and Europe and Central Asia. Global Environment Facility, Implementation of the Poznan Strategic Programme on Technology Transfer: Second interim report of the Global Environment Facility on the progress made in carrying out the Poznan Strategic Programme on Technology Transfer. Note by the secretariat, FCCC/SBI/2009/14, 23 November 2009.

[103] Article 4 of the UNFCCC.

[104] Article 11 of UNFCCC. Article 11 of the Kyoto Protocol.

[105] Article 21(3) UNFCCC. In a Memorandum of Understanding endorsed by Decision 12/CP.2 (29 October 1996), the role of the GEF became permanent but subject to review every four years.

[106] These four funds include: GEF Trust Fund targeting climate change mitigation and adaptation activities, Least Developed Countries Fund, Special Climate Change Fund and Adaptation Funds.

[107] Global Environment Facility, Report of the GEF to the 15th Session of the Conference of the Parties to the UN Framework Convention on Climate Change (December 2009). Available at: www.gefweb.org/uploadedFiles/Focal_Areas/Climate_Change/GEF%20report%20to%20COP15_body_en.pdf (accessed 15 January 2010).

[108] Ibid., 10–18, Tables 1 and 2.

FOR DISCUSSION

- How are the various carbon trading schemes dealing with renewable energy?
- What are the advantages and disadvantages of renewable energy projects within the CDM? What steps, if any, are being taken to reduce these barriers?
- Are the financial mechanisms under the climate change regime sufficient to meet the need of renewable energy in the developing countries?

---

6.   THE ENERGY CHARTER TREATY

The Energy Charter Treaty (ECT), a European regional convention, establishes a multilateral legal framework for cross-border energy cooperation. It covers energy trade, investment and transit in a comprehensive manner.[109] Energy materials and products under the ECT cover nuclear energy, coal, natural gas, petroleum and petroleum products, and electrical energy.[110] Electrical energy includes all the renewable sources of energy such as solar, wind, biomass, tidal, wave and hydropower.[111] The ECT also defines 'Economic Activity in the Energy Sector' as 'economic activity concerning the exploration, extraction, refining, production, storage, land transport, transmission, distribution, trade, marketing or sale of Energy Materials or Products'.[112] According to the Final Act, economic activity in the energy sector includes 'construction and operation of power generation facilities, including those powered by wind and other renewable energy sources'.[113] By 2008, 46 parties had ratified the treaty including the European Union. Australia and the Russian Federation are signatories, and China and the

---

[109]   This multilateral treaty was signed in 1994 and came into force in 1998. Karl, J., T. Constantinescu, A. Lakatos, A. Parfitt and K.P. Waern (2002), *The Energy Charter Treaty: A Reader's Guide*, Brussels: Energy Charter Secretariat, 9.

[110]   Article 1(4) of and Annex EM to the ECT.

[111]   Sussman, E. (2008), 'The Energy Charter Treaty's Investor Protection Provisions: Potential to Foster Solutions to Global Warming and Promote Sustainable Development', ILSA Journal of International and Comparative Law, 14(2), 403.

[112]   Article 1(5) of the ECT.

[113]   Para. IV.2. Final Act of the European Energy Charter Conference (1994), 25.

US have observer status.[114] The Charter reaffirms the sovereignty of states over their energy resources[115] and aims:[116]

- to provide open energy markets, and to secure and diversify energy supply;
- to stimulate cross-border investment and trade in the energy sector;
- to assist countries in economic transition in the development of their energy strategies and of an appropriate institutional and legal framework for energy, and in the improvement and modernisation of their energy industries.

Article 19 (Environmental Aspects) of the ECT states:

(1) In pursuit of *sustainable development* and taking into account its obligations under those international agreements concerning the environment to which it is party, each Contracting Party shall strive to minimize in an *economically efficient manner* harmful Environmental Impacts occurring either within or outside its Area from all operations within the Energy Cycle in its Area, taking proper account of safety. In doing so each Contracting Party shall act in a Cost-Effective manner. In its policies and actions each Contracting Party shall strive to take *precautionary measures* to prevent or minimize environmental degradation. The Contracting Parties agree that the *polluter* in the Areas of Contracting Parties, should, in principle, *bear the cost of pollution*, including transboundary pollution, with due regard to the public interest and without distorting Investment in the Energy Cycle or international trade. Contracting Parties shall accordingly:

. . .

(d) have particular regard to Improving Energy Efficiency, to developing and using *renewable energy sources*, to promoting the use of cleaner fuels and to employing technologies and technological means that reduce pollution;

This is the only provision in the ECT which mentions renewable energy. This provision includes several principles of international environmental law such as sustainable development, the precautionary principle and the polluter pays principle. The Energy Efficiency Protocol of the ECT deals with the

. . . entire energy chain, including activities related to prospecting for, exploration, production, conversion, storage, transport, distribution and consumption of the various forms of energy, and the treatment and disposal of wastes, as

---

[114] Energy Charter Secretariat. List updated in October 2009.
[115] Article 18 of the ECT.
[116] Karl et al. (2002), supra, 9.

well as the decommissioning, cessation or closure of these activities, minimizing harmful environmental impacts.[117]

While the Protocol does not specifically mention renewable energy, the parties are urged to develop national policies on energy efficiency using environmentally sound technologies and reduce adverse environmental impacts of energy systems.[118]

The cross-border element of the ECT links it to the rules of the World Trade Organization (WTO), and parties cannot discriminate between member states.[119] Parties are asked to take necessary measures to facilitate the transit of energy materials and products 'consistent with the principle of freedom of transit and without distinction as to the origin, destination or ownership of such Energy Materials and Products or discrimination as to pricing on the basis of such distinctions, and without imposing any unreasonable delays, restrictions or charges'.[120] There are also certain specific rules relating to transit of energy: freedom of transit, access to energy transmission networks and transit tariffs.[121] These issues are relevant to renewable energy when one country is exporting grid bound renewable energy to another country (e.g. hydro-electricity, solar power).

7.   INTERNATIONAL INSTITUTIONS AND RENEWABLE ENERGY

This section examines the trade and financial bodies that are engaged in promoting access to and use of renewable energy. The international institutions include the multilateral banks (e.g. World Bank) and the funding bodies (e.g. Global Environment Facility) and trade organisations (e.g. WTO).[122]

---

[117]   Article 2(4) and (7) of the Energy Charter Protocol on Energy Efficiency and Related Environmental Aspects. Annex 3 to the Final Act of the European Energy Charter Conference. Environmental impact means any effect caused by a given activity on the environment, including human health and safety, cultural heritage or socio-economic conditions.

[118]   Article 8 of the Energy Charter Protocol on Energy Efficiency and Related Environmental Aspects deals with the issue of energy efficiency.

[119]   Article 5(1) deals with trade related investment measures.

[120]   Article 7(1) of the Energy Charter Treaty.

[121]   Article 7 of ibid. Issues relating to transit are being negotiated under the Transit Protocol. Energy Charter Secretariat, Final Act of the Energy Charter Conference with respect to the Energy Charter Protocol on Transit, Draft, 31 October 2003.

[122]   Discussed in chapter 4.

7.1. World Bank

In order to promote renewable energy projects, the World Bank is working with other multilateral banks, export credit agencies and private sector financiers to generate a long-term investment framework for low-carbon economic growth, specifically, for finance for energy efficiency, clean energy, and adaptation to climate change and variability.[123] Since 1990, the World Bank has committed more than US$11 billion for renewable energy and energy efficiency.[124] The renewable energy sector includes wind, solar, biomass, geothermal, and hydropower (of all sizes) and includes other energy efficiency projects. For example, the World Bank's China Renewable Energy Development project was completed in mid-2008 with solar PV systems for more than 400,000 households in north-western provinces.[125]

The World Bank has established several funds which finance projects on renewable energy.[126] The Prototype Carbon Fund was established in 1999 with financial support from governments and private companies to develop the CDM. Structured as a public–private partnership, this fund has projects on renewable energy in both developing countries and EIT countries.[127] The Community Development Carbon Fund finances small CDM projects implemented in the poorest countries and combines local development and investment in clean energy.[128] Since 2004, some 110,000 biogas plants have been installed in Nepal under this fund. This biogas project has improved waste management, reduced air pollution and reduced the workload of women who would otherwise spend a significant time collecting firewood for their household activities.[129] The World Bank has also established the Carbon Partnership Facility to catalyse large-scale, long-term investments in clean technology programmes which will assist developing countries to pursue low-carbon growth beyond 2012.[130]

---

[123]   Miller et al. (eds) (2007), supra. The World Bank group includes the World Bank (International Bank for Reconstruction and Development, International Development Association), Multilateral Investment Guarantee Agency, International Finance Corporation.

[124]   Ibid., xii.

[125]   REN21 (2009), supra, 22.

[126]   World Bank (2009), *Annual Report 2008: Carbon Finance for Sustainable Development*, Washington, DC: World Bank.

[127]   Ibid., 24–25.

[128]   Ibid., 26–29.

[129]   Ibid., 17.

[130]   Noting the shortcomings of a project by project approach of the CDM and JI, and with the regulatory period of the Kyoto Protocol ending in 2012, the World

The Facility will finance country-wide renewable energy, energy efficiency, waste management and urban transport programmes.

7.2. Global Environment Facility

The GEF is an independent financial organisation which provides grants to developing countries and EIT countries for projects related to bio-diversity, climate change, international waters, land degradation, the ozone layer, and persistent organic pollutants.[131] GEF encourages market approaches for the supply of and demand for renewable electricity and promotes sustainable energy production.[132] Up to 2009, the GEF had sup-ported 208 renewable energy projects, and most of the renewable energy investments have taken place in Asia, Africa, and Latin America and the Caribbean.[133] The GEF has identified several barriers to renewable energy in developing countries: lack of supportive policy frameworks, inadequate financing for installations or supporting businesses, lack of technical capacity, and lack of awareness and trust in the technologies by users and utility companies.[134] The renewable energy projects funded by the GEF include small hydropower in Indonesia, solar water heating in Tunisia, off-grid PV in India, wind power in Mexico, geothermal power in the Philippines, and biomass cogeneration in Thailand.[135] As the financial mechanism of the UNFCCC, the GEF allocates and disburses about $250 million dollars per year in projects in energy efficiency, renewable energy, sustainable urban transport and sustainable management of land use, land use change, and forestry.[136] These projects promote new technology and facilitate access to renewable energy.

Bank launched this programme during COP15 of the UNFCCC, Copenhagen, December 2009.

[131] Established in 1991, GEF works in partnership with 179 member govern-ments, international institutions, non-governmental organisations and the private sector.

[132] Global Environment Facility (2009), *Investing in Renewable Energy: The GEF Experience*, Washington, DC: GEF, 5.

[133] Ibid., 7.

[134] Fleming, C. (2005), *The GEF and Renewable Energy*, Washington DC: GEF, 1.

[135] Ibid., 10–27.

[136] Global Environment Facility (2009), *GEF 2008: Annual Report*, Washington, DC: GEF, 52–53.

7.3. World Trade Organization

A number of WTO agreements are dealing with or likely to deal with renewable energy.[137] For example, renewable energy subsidies including biofuels subsidies may raise issues of application and interpretation under the Agreement on Agriculture or the Agreement on Subsidies and Countervailing Measures. Renewable energy issues are relevant to the WTO regime in several ways. First, under the flexibility mechanisms of the UNFCCC, the emission reduction units or certified emission reduction (e.g. CERs from CDM projects) can be considered as goods or services and fall under the WTO regime. Second, national subsidies to promote and meet renewable energy targets can conflict with the WTO rules. For example, a minimum price scheme for domestic renewable sourced energy to address environmental goals and promote the domestic renewable energy industry can be less favourable and discriminatory to foreign producers. Third, energy taxes can conflict with the non-discrimination provisions of the WTO. Energy taxes will not be allowed if applied in a discriminatory manner. Fourth, international standards defining renewable energy sources and reporting and verification requirements to ensure that the energy is from a renewable energy source would be relevant under the WTO regime to ensure that these technical measures are not trade restrictive.

The two fundamental principles of the WTO are national treatment[138] and the most favoured nation.[139] These principles prohibit the parties to the WTO from having any rule or standard which is discriminatory or a disguised restriction on trade. Thus, the WTO agreements curtail the capacity of countries to adopt national legislation that may become a

---

[137] See the discussion on the WTO in chapter 4. For example, Trade Related Investment Measures Agreement, General Agreement on Trade in Services (GATS), General Agreement on Tariffs and Trade (GATT), Agreement on Agriculture, Agreement on Subsidies and Countervailing Measures, Agreement on Technical Barriers to Trade, Agreement on the Application of Sanitary and Phytosanitary Measures, Trade-related Intellectual Property Rights. Howse, R. (2006), 'World Trade Law and Renewable Energy: The Case of Non-Tariff Measures', in L. Parker, J. Ronk, B. Gentry, M. Wilder and J. Cameron (eds), supra.

[138] Article III of GATT, Article XVII of GATS. The principle of national treatment requires that the goods and services of other countries be treated in the same way as those of the host country.

[139] Article I of GATT, Article II of GATS. The most-favoured nation principle requires that if special treatment is given to the goods and services of one country, it must be given to all WTO member countries. No one country should receive favours which distort trade.

'unilateral restriction' or barriers to trade. There are exceptions, albeit limited. For example, the GATT allows national measures restricting trade if these measures are 'necessary to protect human, animal or plant life or health' or 'relating to the conservation of exhaustible natural resources'.[140] Such measures, however, cannot be 'applied in a manner which would constitute a means of arbitrary or unjustifiable discrimination between countries where the same conditions prevail, or a disguised restriction on international trade'.[141] If an environmental measure conforms to Article XX(b) or (g) and the chapeau of Article XX (i.e. no arbitrary or unjustifiable discrimination and not a disguised restriction), the measure may be allowed.[142] The measure should not be arbitrary or an unjustified discrimination, and multilateral (or bilateral, plurilateral) rather than unilateral restrictions or measures are encouraged.

Parties are able to impose environmental measures (or trade barriers) to promote renewable energy if the conditions set out in Article XX of GATT are met. To apply Article XX(b) of GATT, it is necessary to prove that there is a real health risk from the non-renewable energy, and

> . . . that measures to promote renewable are either an indispensable means of addressing the risk or 1) that there is a close connection between the renewable measures and solving the health risk and 2) the trade restrictive impact is not disproportionate of the measure to addressing risk.[143]

To apply the Article XX(g) exception, there must be a 'real' connection between the GATT inconsistent measures to conserve the exhaustible natural resources and its aim, and the measure must not be disproportionately wide in scope.[144]

In order to promote renewable energy, if the domestic measure imposes different taxes for products originated using polluting and cleaner technology – would that be discriminatory? The principle of non-discrimination suggests that there can be no discrimination between 'like

---

[140]   Article XX (b) and (g) of GATT. General Agreement on Tariffs and Trade, Article XX, 1947, 55 U.N.T.S. 194.

[141]   Article XX, Chapeau or preambular para.

[142]   A similar exception is found in GATS: Article XIV (a) 'necessary to protect public morals or to maintain public order' and (b) 'necessary to protect human, animal or plant life or health'. This exception does not include any provision to conserve natural resources.

[143]   Howse (2006), supra, 508 (applying *EC – Measures Affecting Asbestos and Asbestos-containing Products*, WT/DS135/AB/R, 12 March 2001).

[144]   Howse (2006), supra, 508 (applying *United States – Import Prohibition of Certain Shrimp and Shrimp Products*, WT/DS58/R, 12 October 1998).

products'.[145] The likeness of products is not defined in GATT and is determined on a case-by-case basis based on a range of relevant criteria and related facts.[146] The GATT dispute panels used four criteria to determine whether products were like: physical characteristics, end uses, consumer habits and tariff classification.[147] In the *Asbestos* case, the Appellate Body stressed that these criteria are not treaty mandated, not a closed list[148] and the health and environmental risks associated with a product must be evaluated.[149] When such risks arise from one product's physical characteristics, but not from the other product, this is a relevant factor in determining like products. If the final product has different qualities which would cause it to be treated differently in its use, handling or disposal, then different levels of taxation will not be discriminatory.[150]

Thus, for electricity generated using coal and electricity generated from solar power – if they both possess identical physical characteristics and have the same end use – they are 'like' products. It is, however, possible to argue that factors such as energy from renewable sources is clean, health risks from renewable energy sources are minimal and consumers prefer clean energy should be taken into consideration while deciding likeness of products.[151] This issue of likeness of products was discussed in several GATT/WTO cases.[152] For example, in the *Tax on Automobiles* case,[153] the

---

[145]   References to 'like' products are found in Articles I:1, II:2(a), III:2, III:4, VI, IX:1, XI:2(c), XIII:1, XVI:4, XIX:1 of GATT 1994.

[146]   Report of the Working Party on Border Tax Adjustment, BISD 18S/97, para. 18. Appellate Body Report, *Japan – Alcoholic Beverages II*, WT/DS8/AB/R, WT/DS10/AB/R, WT/DS11/AB/R, 4 October 1996, 113–114.

[147]   IISD and UNEP (2005), *Environment and Trade: A Handbook*, Manitoba: IISD, 35. Appellate Body Report, *EC – Asbestos*, supra, para. 101.

[148]   Ibid., para. 102.

[149]   Ibid., para. 113. The AB considered the textual difference between Article III:2 and III:4 of GATT and noted that the definition of 'like' products under Article III:2 should be construed narrowly. Paras 95–96.

[150]   IISD and UNEP (2005), supra, 31. Even if the products are not physically or chemically identical, they can still be considered like products if, e.g., the products have the same end use, are seen by consumers as substitutes, perform to the same standards or require nothing different for handling or disposal.

[151]   Howse (2006), supra, 506.

[152]   Cases relevant to the renewable energy issue are: *US – Standards for Reformulated and Conventional Gasoline*, 35 I.L.M. (1996) 603. *US – Tax on Automobiles*, GATT Panel Report, 11 October 1994, not adopted. *US – Restrictions on Import of Tuna*, GATT BISD 39S/155, 3 September 1991, not adopted. *US – Taxes on Petroleum and Certain Imported Substances*, GATT Panel Report, 34S/136, 17 June 1987.

[153]   The US imposed a tax on imported automobiles that are not fuel efficient as an incentive to buy more fuel efficient automobiles. The EU argued that the

---

FOR DISCUSSION

- In what way would the exceptions under GATT be applicable to products originated from using the renewable energy sources?
- Should the subsidy for renewable energy sources be allowed? What are the criteria for a renewable energy subsidy to be compatible with the WTO regime?
- Is there any role for Agreement on Technical Barriers to Trade in the regulation of renewable energy sources?

GATT Panel held that as fuel inefficient imported automobiles were not 'like' fuel efficient domestic automobiles for the purposes of Article III:2 of GATT, different and less favourable treatment could be accorded to them.

8. THE EUROPEAN UNION AND RENEWABLE ENERGY

The EU has adopted a common policy to reduce GHG emissions and dependence on fossil fuel.[154] The aim is to create a secure, competitive and sustainable energy policy with the support of market-based instruments (e.g. taxes, CO_2 emissions trading scheme).[155] This policy offers three objectives:

- *Sustainability* – actively to combat climate change by promoting renewable energy sources and energy efficiency
- *Competitiveness* – to improve the efficiency of the European energy grid by creating a truly competitive internal energy market
- *Security of supply* – better to coordinate between the Member States and other relevant players the EU's supply of, and demand for, energy.[156]

---

tax violated Article III:2 of the GATT since most cars affected by the tax were imported from the EU.

[154] Commission of the European Communities, Communication from the Commission to the European Council and the European Parliament: An Energy Policy for Europe, COM(2007)1 final, 10 January 2007.

[155] Ibid., 6.

[156] Commission Green Paper on a European Strategy for Sustainable, Competitive and Secure Energy, COM(2006)105 final, 3 August 2006.

The sources of renewable energy, as identified in the energy policy, are: wind power, solar and PV energy, biomass, hydropower and geothermal energy.[157] In the Renewable Energy Road Map, the EU pointed out that 'failure to systematically include external costs in market prices gives an economically unjustified advantage to fossil fuels compared with renewables'.[158] According to the Road Map, the 20 per cent target for the overall share of energy from renewable sources would reduce annual CO_2 emissions in the range of 600–900Mt in 2020.[159]

Within the EU, there are three main sectors where renewable energies are promoted:

- Electricity: Directive 2001/77/EC sets separate indicative targets for each Member State with a 22.1 per cent indicative share of electricity produced from renewable energy sources in total Community electricity consumption by 2010.[160]
- Transport: Directive 2003/30/EC sets a target of 5.75 per cent of biofuels of all petrol and diesel for transport placed on the market by 2010.[161] Under Directive 2009/28/EC, the share of renewable energy use including biofuel in the transport sector should rise to a minimum 10 per cent in every Member State by 2020.[162]
- Modifying or developing new heating and cooling systems which

---

[157] EU Energy Policy (2007), supra, 25–26.

[158] Commission of the European Communities, Communication from the Commission to the Council and the European Parliament: Renewable Energy Road Map – Renewable Energies in the 21st Century: Building a More Sustainable Future, COM(2006)848 final, 1 October 2007, 4.

[159] Ibid., 14.

[160] Article 3, Annex with EU-15 indicative targets. Directive 2001/77/EC of the European Parliament and of the Council of 27 September 2001 on the promotion of electricity produced from renewable energy sources in the internal electricity market 2001, OJ L283/33 (2001) (EC). This Directive will be repealed from 1 January 2012 by Directive 2009/28/EC EC of the European Parliament and of the Council of 23 April 2009 on the promotion of the use of energy from renewable sources and amending and subsequently repealing Directives 2001/77/EC and 2003/30/EC, OJ L140/16, (2009).

[161] Directive 2003/30/EC of the European Parliament and of the Council of 8 May 2003 on the promotion of the use of biofuels or other renewable fuels for transport 2003, OJ L123/42 (2003) (EC). This Directive will be repealed from 1 January 2012 by Directive 2009/28/EC, OJ L140/16, 5 June 2009.

[162] Preamble, para. 9, Directive 2009/28/EC, supra.

can run on renewable fuels. Directive 2009/28/EC deals with heating and cooling from renewable energy sources.[163]

The objectives of the Renewables Directive (2009)[164] are to achieve a 20 per cent share of energy from renewable sources in the Community's gross final consumption of energy and a 10 per cent share of energy from renewable sources in each Member State's transport energy consumption by 2020.[165] Non-road transport is excluded from the 10 per cent target for the purposes of calculating the total amount of energy consumed in transport. However, any renewable energy used for these forms (i.e. aviation, trains) still counts towards meeting the overall target.[166] The sources of renewable energy include

> . . . non-fossil sources, namely wind, solar, aerothermal, geothermal, hydro-thermal and ocean energy, hydropower, biomass, landfill gas, sewage treatment plant gas and biogases.[167]

Individual targets for each Member State vary widely,[168] with Finland (38 per cent), Austria (34 per cent), Latvia (40 per cent) and Sweden (49 per cent) being set the highest targets. A high proportion of the energy consumed in these countries already comes from renewable sources. On the other hand, countries such as the UK (15 per cent), Malta (10 per cent) and Luxembourg (11 per cent), which have traditionally relied more heavily on conventional fuels, will have to multiply the share of energy from renewable sources to meet the 2020 target.

Member States can make statistical transfers between themselves of quantities of renewable energy, i.e. if one country expects to exceed its target, it can sell some of its overspill to another country to go towards that country's target.[169] Member States can transfer renewable energy from their country only if it will not be to the detriment of meeting their own targets. Member States can cooperate on joint projects for renewable electricity, heating or cooling and have to inform the Commission

---

[163]   Articles 2(g) and (h), 4(1), 5(1)(b), 5(4), 13(3), 13(4), 13(6), 14(5), 15, 16(11), 22(1)(a) & (d), 22(3)(c).

[164]   Directive 2009/28/EC, supra. The deadline for implementation is 5 December 2010.

[165]   Articles 1, 3, 5, Annex I.

[166]   Article 3(4).

[167]   Article 2(a) of the Directive. The Directive also defines aerothermal energy, geothermal energy, hydrothermal energy, biomass, biofuels and bioliquids.

[168]   Annex 1 to the Directive.

[169]   Articles 6–11.

of the proportion of the renewable electricity which each Member State will count towards its target. Each Member State is to adopt a national renewable energy action plan.[170] These plans will set out Member States' national targets for the share of energy from renewable sources consumed in transport, electricity and heating and cooling in 2020.[171]

The 2009 Directive establishes sustainability criteria for biofuels and bioliquids.[172] According to the Directive, biofuels[173] produced from 'wastes, residues, non-food cellulosic material, and lignocellulosic material' shall count twice for national obligations and the 2020 transport target.[174] This provision encourages the use of second generation fuels, i.e. those produced from waste products. The minimum GHG saving from the use of biofuels and bioliquids relative to fossil fuels should be 35 per cent. This saving rises to 50 per cent from 2017.[175] Biofuels and bioliquids must not be made from land

- with high biodiversity value such as primary forest, highly biodiverse natural grassland and other designated habitats,[176]
- which had high carbon stock in January 2008 but no longer has that status, e.g. wetlands, continuously forested areas, peatland.[177]

While the sustainability criteria do not include any social aspects, the Commission will report, every two years, on the social impacts of the EU's biofuel policy including food security (especially in developing countries), land-use rights and wider development issues.[178]

There are, however, concerns about the use of biofuel as a sustainable form of renewable energy source. First, if the whole life cycle and the

---

[170] Article 4.
[171] Commission Decision of 30 June 2009 establishing a template for National Renewable Energy Action Plans under Directive 2009/28/EC of the European Parliament and of the Council. OJ L182/33 (2009).
[172] Articles 1 and 17 of the Directive.
[173] 'Biofuels' means liquid or gaseous fuel for transport produced from biomass (Article 2(i)). Article 2(e) defines biomass.
[174] Article 3. This only applies to transport biofuels and not bioliquids for heat or electricity (Article 21(2)).
[175] Article 17(2). Also see: communication from the Commission on voluntary schemes and default values in the EU biofuels and bioliquids sustainability scheme (2010/C 160/01, 19 June 2010). Communication from the Commission on the practical implementation of the EU biofuels and bioliquids sustainability scheme and on counting rules for biofuels (2010/C 160/02, 19 June 2010).
[176] Article 17(3).
[177] Article 17(4).
[178] Article 17(7).

FOR DISCUSSION

- What are the strengths and weaknesses of the sustainability criteria set out in the Renewable Energy Directive?
- Considering the human rights and environmental debates, what are the justifications for biofuel?
- What are the ways to improve the verification, auditing and reporting mechanisms of the Renewable Energy Directive?

---

direct and indirect effects are taken into account, some biofuel sources may in fact increase GHG emissions compared to fossil fuel.[179] Second, verification processes are crucial to ensure that the standards have an impact on the sustainability of the biofuels marketplace.[180] The verification requirements in the Directive are flexible and weak. Whether or not the sustainability criteria are complied with will be assessed on the basis of company information, or through voluntary certification schemes, or through the existence of bilateral and multilateral agreements.[181] Economic operators will be responsible for ensuring adequate independent auditing of the information they submit and the evidence they provide.[182] For the sustainability criteria to be a success, the auditing process must ensure that systems used are 'accurate, reliable and protected against fraud'.[183] Third, Member States can set up simplified planning procedures for all renewable energy projects.[184] This could make it considerably more difficult for people to oppose planning applications linked to renewable energy installations.

9.   CONCLUSION

The issues of energy security and access to energy are certainly pushing the agenda for renewable energy, and this is evident through various

---

[179]   Eide (2008), supra, 21.
[180]   Bowyer, C. (2008), 'Biofuels Provisions in the Renewable Energy Directive – A Summary', EU Environmental Policy Briefing, Brussels: IEEP.
[181]   Article 18. Also see: the communications from the Commission (2010/C 160/01, 19 June 2010) and (2010/C 160/02, 19 June 2010), supra.
[182]   Article 18(3).
[183]   Ibid.
[184]   Article 22(3)(b).

non-binding declarations and policy documents. Various funds from the World Bank and the climate change flexible mechanisms show that there is an increasing demand and market for renewable energy. The energy industries are facing a range of political, regulatory, environmental and market developments at the global, regional and domestic level. The legal development within the EU shows that renewable energy can play an important role in reducing carbon emissions and promoting diversity in energy sources. Apart from the EU Renewable Energy Directive and national level renewable energy measures,[185] the global community is yet to agree on a binding treaty on renewable energy.

With the rapid growth of the renewable energy market, the issue of sustainability of renewable energy sources becomes more important, especially with biofuel and hydropower. In addition, quality and access, including affordability and availability of renewable energy, will require strong commitments, effective monitoring mechanisms, financial incentives, government and private sector investment, participation of people, and a legal framework to regulate energy markets and pricing.

FURTHER READING

Boyle, G. (ed.) (2004), *Renewable Energy: Power for a Sustainable Future*, Oxford: Oxford University Press.

Bradbrook, A. (2008), 'The Development of Renewable Energy Through Public International Law', in D. Zillman, C. Redgwell, Y. Omorogbe and L.K. Barrera-Hernandez (eds), *Beyond the Carbon Economy: Energy Law in Transition*, Oxford: Oxford University Press.

Flavin, C. and M.H. Aeck (2005), *Energy for Development: The Potential Role of Renewable Energy in Meeting the Millennium Development Goals*, Washington, DC: Worldwatch Institute.

Ottinger, R.L. and R. Williams (2002), 'Renewable Energy Sources for Development', Environmental Law, 32, 331–368.

Parker, L., J. Ronk, B. Gentry, M. Wilder and J. Cameron (eds) (2006–2007), *From Barriers to Opportunities: Renewable Energy Issues in Law and Policy*, A Report on the Work of the Renewable Energy and International Law (REIL) Project, 2006–2007, New Haven, CT: Yale School of Forestry and Environmental Studies.

Redgwell, C. (2006), 'International Soft Law and Globalisation', in B. Barton, A. Lucas, A. Ronne and D. Zillman (eds), *Alternatives to Regulation in Energy and Natural Resources Law*, Oxford: Oxford University Press.

Roggenkamp, M., C. Redgwell, A. Ronne and I. del Guayo (eds) (2007), *Energy*

---

[185] REN21 (2009), supra, 17–21.

Law in Europe: National, EU and International Regulation, Oxford: Oxford University Press.

Scheer, H. (2007), *Energy Autonomy: The Economic, Social and Technological Case for Renewable Energy*, London: Earthscan.

9. Biological resources

1. INTRODUCTION

Globalisation offers both opportunities and challenges for biodiversity management. The legal instruments regulating biodiversity at the international level create opportunities including capacity building and technology transfer from developed countries to the developing countries. At the same time, there remain serious challenges, including over-exploitation, bioprospecting, unsustainable resource consumption, poverty, exclusion and inequality within and among states. One challenge of particular importance is where multinational companies are accessing genetic resources found in the biodiversity-rich developing countries and disseminating the product for commercial gain. A number of developing countries have inadequate law or environmental standards or standards lower than the parent country of the multinational company to protect and conserve their biological resources.

Biological resources have characteristics of both private and public goods. They are private goods as these resources are generally situated within the boundary of countries which control the use and conservation of these resources. Biodiversity or the diversity of living species is also a public good as the inherent value of and information on these resources are available to all, and everyone has an interest in contributing to their protection.[1] This public good aspect of biological resources can be found in the Millennium Development Goal (MDG) on ensuring environmental sustainability which explicitly deals with the wise use of biological resources.[2] Other MDGs can be linked to biological resources: e.g. MDG 1 on eradicating hunger requires sustainable agriculture, and MDGs 4, 5, and 6 on improving health and sanitation depend on healthy freshwater ecosystems.[3] In the WSSD Johannesburg Declaration (2002), the

---

[1] Guruswamy, L.D. and J.A. McNeely (1998), *Protection of Global Biodiversity: Converging Strategies*, Durham, NC: Duke University Press, 118.

[2] Goal 7, Millennium Development Goals (2000), UN GA Doc. A/Res/55/2, 18 September 2000, available at www.un.org/millenniumgoals/bkgd.shtml (accessed 15 January 2010).

[3] Ibid.

international community agreed to stop biodiversity loss by promoting sustainable use of natural resources for the benefit of all.[4]

> 44.　Biodiversity, which plays a critical role in overall sustainable development and poverty eradication, is essential to our planet, human well-being and to the livelihood and cultural integrity of people. However, biodiversity is currently being lost at unprecedented rates due to human activities; this trend can only be reversed if the local people benefit from the conservation and sustainable use of biological diversity, in particular in countries of origin of genetic resources, in accordance with article 15 of the Convention on Biological Diversity. The Convention is the key instrument for the conservation and sustainable use of biological diversity and the fair and equitable sharing of benefits arising from use of genetic resources. A more efficient and coherent implementation of the three objectives of the Convention and the achievement by 2010 of a significant reduction in the current rate of loss of biological diversity will require the provision of new and additional financial and technical resources to developing countries.

This chapter discusses the role of globalisation in accessing and sharing biological resources. It examines the international legal mechanisms regulating biodiversity (section 2), the Convention on Biological Diversity (hereafter Biodiversity Convention) and the effect of globalisation on benefit sharing and traditional knowledge (section 3). Section 4 considers the issue of traditional knowledge and human rights.

2.　INTERNATIONAL LEGAL MECHANISMS REGULATING BIODIVERSITY

Several international treaties regulate the conservation of biodiversity.[5] There are treaties applicable to all species and habitats,[6] to all species and habitats within a particular region, and to protect a particular habitat or species, such as wetlands, marine living resources and migratory

---

[4]　Para. 44, Part IV: Protecting and managing the natural resource base of economic and social development, Johannesburg Plan of Implementation, available at　www.un.org/esa/sustdev/documents/WSSD_POI_PD/English/POIChapter4.htm (accessed 15 January 2010).

[5]　Sands, P. (2003), *Principles of International Environmental Law*, Cambridge: Cambridge University Press, 502.

[6]　For example: the Convention on International Trade in Endangered Species of Wild Fauna and Flora, adopted on 3 March 1973 in Washington DC, 12 I.L.M. (1973) 1085, 1992 Convention on Biological Diversity, 31 I.L.M. (1992) 818.

species.[7] The discussion in this chapter concentrates on the Biodiversity Convention and the role it plays in conserving biological diversity as a natural resource.

The Biodiversity Convention promotes conservation of three types of diversity: ecosystem, species and genetic. Biological diversity is defined in the Convention as

> . . . the variability among living organisms from all sources including, inter alia, terrestrial, marine and other aquatic ecosystems and the ecological complexes of which they are a part, this includes diversity within species, between species and of ecosystems.[8]

The concept of the ecosystem connects biodiversity to nature as a whole, not just to living nature. *Ecosystem diversity* encompasses the variety of habitats which occur within a region. According to the Biodiversity Convention, an ecosystem means 'a dynamic complex of plant, animal, and micro-organism communities and their non-living environment interacting as a functional unit'.[9] *Species diversity* is the variety of different types of species which inhabit a region.[10] *Genetic diversity* is the combination of different genes found within a population of a single species, and the pattern of variation found within different populations of the same species.[11] The Biodiversity Convention promotes conservation of diversity at these three levels and they are interdependent. Sustainable management of ecosystem diversity improves both the species and genetic diversity.

The Biodiversity Convention stresses that the conservation of biological

---

[7] For example, the Convention on the Conservation of Migratory Species of Wild Animals, adopted on 23 June 1979 in Bonn, 19 I.L.M. (1980) 15; the Convention on Wetlands of International Importance Especially as Waterfowl Habitat, adopted on 2 February 1971 in Ramsar, 11 I.L.M. (1972) 963; the Convention for the Protection of the World Cultural and Natural Heritage, adopted on 23 November 1972 in Paris, 11 I.L.M. (1972) 1358; the Convention on the Conservation of Antarctic Marine Living Resources, adopted on 20 March 1980 in Canberra, 19 I.L.M. (1980) 837.

[8] Article 2.

[9] Article 2. Also CBD, The Ecosystem Approach, Decision VII/11, COP-7 (2004).

[10] World Resources Institute, World Conservation Union, and United Nations Environment Programme (1992), *Global Biodiversity Strategy: Guidelines for action to save, study and use Earth's biotic wealth sustainably and equitably*, Washington DC: WRI, available at www.wri.org/publication/global-biodiversity-strategy-guidelines-action-save-study-and-use-earths-biotic-wea (accessed 15 January 2010).

[11] Ibid.

diversity is a 'common concern of humankind'.[12] This principle implies the common interest and responsibility of the international community in the conservation of biological diversity. Noting the educational, scientific and cultural value which is shared by all, biodiversity is a public good. At the same time, the Biodiversity Convention recognises that nations have sovereign rights over their own biological resources.[13] The Biodiversity Convention highlights the general principle that states have

> the sovereign right to exploit their own resources pursuant to their own environmental policies, and the responsibility to ensure that activities within their jurisdiction or control do not cause damage to the environment of other states or of areas beyond the limits of national jurisdiction.[14]

This reflects the principle of permanent sovereignty over natural resources and the private good dimension of biological resources.[15] The 'common concern' and 'permanent sovereignty' principles require the member states to address and balance the economic, environmental and social values of biological resources.[16] When applying the sovereign rights, states parties have to recognise that the conservation of biological diversity is a 'common concern of humankind' and the obligation of each party is to endeavour

> . . . to create conditions to facilitate access to genetic resources . . . by other Contracting Parties . . . and not to impose restrictions that run counter to the objectives of this Convention.[17]

The sovereign rights of states over their biological resources are limited by the recognition that these resources are a 'common concern of humankind'. The 'common concern of humankind' may imply that multinational companies, community groups or the private sector can use the biological resources in *any* way possible including the development, exploitation and conservation of biological resources.[18] However, 'common concern' also

---

[12]   Preamble. See discussion in chapter 2.
[13]   Articles 3 and 15(1), United Nations Framework Convention on Biological Diversity, 5 June 1992, 31 I.L.M. (1992) 818.
[14]   Article 3.
[15]   Discussed in chapters 1 and 3 of this book.
[16]   Smagadi, A. (2006), 'Analysis of the Objectives of the Convention on Biological Diversity: Their Interrelation and Implementation Guidance for Access and Benefit Sharing', Columbia Journal of Environmental Law, 31, 243.
[17]   Preamble to and Article 15(2) of the Biodiversity Convention.
[18]   Dutfield, G. (2001), 'TRIPS Related Aspects of Traditional Knowledge', Case Western Journal of International Law, 33, 233.

refers to a common responsibility of the international community to share the burden and costs fairly and equitably to protect biodiversity.[19]

The objectives of the Biodiversity Convention are 'the conservation of biological diversity, the sustainable use of its components, and the fair and equitable sharing of the benefits arising out of the utilisation of genetic resources'.[20] In the Biodiversity Convention, these three objectives are translated into binding commitments in Articles 6 to 20. These objectives are discussed below in section 2.1 (objectives 1 and 2) and section 2.2 (objective 3).

2.1. The Conservation and Sustainable Use of Biological Diversity

The provisions on the conservation and sustainable use of biological diversity, the first two objectives of the Biodiversity Convention, are contained principally in Articles 6 to 11. As a framework document, the Biodiversity Convention provides qualified commitments, and their implementation depends on particular national circumstances and priorities of individual parties and resources available to them. The states parties are only obliged to take action 'as far as possible and as appropriate', leaving a broad level of discretion to parties to implement the Convention at the national level.[21] Sustainable use is defined in Article 2 of the Convention as

> . . . using the components of biodiversity in a way and at a rate that does not lead to the long-term decline of biological diversity, thereby maintaining its potential to meet the needs and aspirations of present and future generations.

The basic features of sustainable use include:

> . . . monitoring of use; management on a fexible basis atuned to the goals of observing biological unity, adopting a holistic ecosystem approach; restoring areas of depleted biodiversity; adoption of both an integrated and a

---

[19] Birnie, P., A. Boyle and C. Redgwell (2009), *International Law and the Environment*, Oxford: Oxford University Press, pp. 128–130. Attard, D. (ed.) (1991), *Proceedings of the Meeting of the Group of Legal Experts to Examine the Concept of the Common Concern of Mankind in relation to Global Environmental Issues*, Nairobi, Kenya: UNEP.

[20] Article 1. 'Genetic resources' means genetic material of actual or potential value. 'Genetic material' means any material of plant, animal, microbial or other origin containing functional units of heredity. Article 2. The full text of the Biodiversity Convention is available from www.biodiv.org.

[21] Articles 5 and 6(b).

precautionary approach; ensuring inter-generational equity; basing measures on scientific research.[22]

The meaning of conservation is not just to protect genetic resources, but also to 'conserve and enhance the ability of ecosystems to develop and regenerate themselves as living systems'.[23] At the same time, the Biodiversity Convention encourages parties to '[e]ndeavour to provide the conditions needed for compatibility between present uses and conservation of biological diversity and the sustainable use of its components'.[24]

The Biodiversity Convention requires parties to develop national strategies, plans or programmes for the conservation and sustainable use of biodiversity, or to adapt existing plans or programmes for this purpose.[25] Parties are to identify for themselves the components of biodiversity important for conservation and sustainable use.[26] Whilst it contains no lists, the Biodiversity Convention does indicate, in Annex I, the types of species and ecosystems which parties may consider for particular attention. It addresses both *in situ* and *ex situ* conservation.[27] *Ex situ* conservation means 'the conservation of components of biological diversity outside of their natural habitats'. Such conservation is necessary to protect some species from degeneration or extinction.[28] *In situ* conservation is

> . . . the conservation of ecosystems and natural habitats and the maintenance and recovery of viable populations of species in their natural surroundings and, in the case of domesticated or cultivated species, in the surroundings where they have developed their distinctive properties.[29]

The emphasis of *in situ* conservation is on the sustainable use and management of biological resources. Human intervention is necessary for the conservation of biological resources and Article 8 sets out a comprehensive framework for *in situ* conservation. A member state's national biodiversity planning process should include consideration of the following issues:[30]

---

[22]   Birnie et al. (2009), supra, 622. Addis Ababa Principles and Guidelines for the Sustainable Use of Biodiversity, Decision VII/12, Annex II, COP-7 (2004).
[23]   Smagdi (2006), supra, 253.
[24]   Article 8.
[25]   Article 6(a).
[26]   Article 7.
[27]   Article 2.
[28]   Smagdi (2006), supra, 253.
[29]   Article 2.
[30]   Articles 7, 8 and 10 of the Biodiversity Convention. Birnie et al. (2009), supra, 623.

- Establish a system of protected areas
- Regulation and management of biological resources
- Adopt an ecosystem approach
- Rehabilitation and restoration of degraded ecosystems
- Manage risks associated with the use and release of living modified organisms
- Prevent the introduction of alien species
- Respect, preserve and maintain traditional knowledge and practices
- Regulation and management of activities negatively affecting biodiversity

To ensure the sustainable use of biological resources, parties are encouraged to consider *ex situ* and *in situ* measures together, ensure collaboration between biodiversity users, develop supportive incentive measures and cooperate with other parties in case of transboundary resources.[31]

2.2. Fair and Equitable Sharing of Benefits

The benefit-sharing provisions are contained principally in Articles 15, 16 and 19. According to the Convention, where a country provides genetic resources, it should receive a share of any benefits derived from the use of those resources.[32] The Convention does not spell out the meaning of 'fair and equitable'[33] and there is a wide margin of discretion for the member states to apply this objective at the national level. This objective is to be achieved by appropriate access to genetic resources, appropriate transfer of relevant technologies and funding.[34] Genetic materials extracted from plants and animals provide the basis of research by, for example, pharmaceutical, chemical and agricultural seed companies. Products generated from this research are often protected by patents and marketed worldwide. The Biodiversity Convention allows the developing country to share the benefits accrued from the use of biological resources. Therefore, the Convention recognises that states parties have sovereign rights over

---

[31] Addis Ababa Principles, supra.
[32] Glowka, L., F. Burhenne-Guilmin, H. Synge, J.A. McNeely and L. Gundling (1994), *A Guide to the Convention on Biological Diversity: A contribution to the Global Biodiversity Strategy*, Gland, Switzerland and Cambridge, UK: IUCN, Environmental Policy and Law Paper No. 30.
[33] Article 15(7).
[34] Article 16 of the Biodiversity Convention deals with the transfer of technology. Articles 20 and 21 deal with financial resources.

their natural resources and 'the authority to determine access to genetic resources rests with the national governments and is subject to national legislation'.[35] In order for the sharing of benefits to be fair and equitable, the providers of the genetic resources must have prior informed consent and such consent to access genetic resources shall 'be on mutually agreed terms'.[36] The source country providing access to genetic resources must know in advance what will be done with the resource, and what benefits will be shared. Where a party provides genetic resources to another party, the receiving party 'shall endeavour to develop and carry out scientific research based on [those] genetic resources . . . with the full participation of, and where possible in, [the providing party]'.[37]

States parties are asked to take appropriate measures to provide for effective participation in biotechnological research by parties, especially developing countries which provide the genetic resources for such research.[38] In general, each party shall take measures 'with the aim of sharing in a fair and equitable way the results of research and development and the benefits arising from the commercial and other utilisation of genetic resources with the [party] providing such resources'.[39] Parties are required to 'take all practicable measures to promote and advance priority access on a fair and equitable basis' for parties providing genetic resources, especially developing countries, 'to the results and benefits arising from biotechnologies based upon genetic resources . . . on mutually agreed terms'.[40] The Convention also provides a broad framework for member states' policies concerning access, development and transfer of technologies.[41] Each party shall take measures 'with the aim that Contracting Parties, in particular those that are developing countries, which provide genetic resources are given access to and transfer of technology which makes use of those resources, on mutually agreed terms including technology protected by patents and other intellectual property rights'.[42]

The underlying philosophy of the Biodiversity Convention is that sovereign rights are restricted by providing access to genetic resources in exchange for a share of the benefits. Resource user states need to share the results of research and development as well as the benefits arising from

---

35   Article 15(1).
36   Article 15(4) and 15(5).
37   Article 15(6).
38   Article 19(1).
39   Article 15(7).
40   Article 19(2).
41   Article 16.
42   Article 16(3).

FOR DISCUSSION

- Is it possible to reconcile the issue of the sovereign rights of states over their biological resources and biodiversity as a 'common concern of humankind'?
- What does equitable sharing of benefits mean to a biodiversity-rich developing country?
- What problems might arise in the implementation of prior informed consent procedures by countries providing access to genetic resources? How might some of these problems be addressed by supportive legislation in user and provider countries?

---

commercial and other uses of the resources with the provider country upon mutually agreed terms.[43] Resource provider countries are required to facilitate access to such use of genetic resources and minimise restrictions on access. Provider countries can benefit from the participation in scientific research, access to technology and other forms of benefit sharing.[44]

3. GLOBALISATION, BENEFIT SHARING AND TRADITIONAL KNOWLEDGE

Loss of biodiversity is largely driven by the destruction of the habitats of species, the growth of the human population and climate change. In addition, economic globalisation including expansion of trade and capital movement has increased pressure on the biodiversity-rich countries. The definition of globalisation implies that there should be a movement of biological resources and traditional knowledge from the South to the North and the transfer of technology and funding from the North to the South.[45] Therefore, with globalisation arrive new markets and competing claims. For example, the local communities' right to protect their traditional knowledge competes with the patent rights of multinational companies.

---

[43] Birnie et al. (2009), supra, 630.
[44] Articles 15(7), 16(3), 19(1) and (2). Birnie et al. (2009), supra, 631–632.
[45] Warner, J. (2006), 'Using Global Themes to Reframe Bioprospecting Debate', Indiana Journal of Global Legal Studies, 13, 645. Bender, E.K. (2003), 'North and South: WTO, TRIPS and the Scourge of Biopiracy', Tulsa Journal of Comparative and International Law, 11, 281.

The effect of globalisation is apparent in the reduction of global genetic diversity.[46]

> Since 1970, pharmaceutical, petrochemical and other transnational corporations have purchased more than 1,000 once-independent seed companies. . . . Loss of germplasm occurs as transnationals drop all but the most profitable seed varieties from their inventories. For example, the fifth edition of the *Garden Seed Inventory* . . . a list of all commercially available, non-hybrid vegetable varieties in the United States and Canada, shows that sugar beets, broccoli, cabbage, cauliflower, onions and garden peas lost an average of 41 per cent of named varieties between 1981 and 1998. New commercial varieties also appeared during this time, but these were mostly introduced by tiny, independent seed companies, some of them non-profit, and typically represent the commercialisation of preexisting private varieties, not the result of new breeding efforts. It is likely that losses of non-commercial varieties maintained by individual farmers, especially in Third World countries, are even greater, as representatives of giant seed corporations reach more and more agricultural areas that have been hitherto isolated from global trade. When this happens, local farmers drop a wealth of existing varieties in favour of the new, commercial, 'high-yielding' seeds . . .
>
> The impacts of globalisation are being experienced not only by domesticated varieties but by wild relatives of food plants. The wild relatives of cereals, vegetables, fruits, nuts and other crops constitute a critical resource for genes affecting disease resistance, pest resistance, yield, vigour, environmental adaptations, high starch content, soluble solids, vitamins, cytoplasmic male sterility, petaloid male sterility and harvest and transport adaptations. Many of these wild relatives are highly endemic, and their ranges are decreasing sharply because of development, overgrazing, increased herbicide use, logging and conversion of marginal lands to production and export agriculture – all of them related at least in part to globalisation . . .

While globalisation and international trade allow the pharmaceutical or seed companies to benefit from the biological resources of the developing countries, they can also empower the communities to be aware of their identities and rights through strategic alliances between groups in the North and the South and through participation in international negotiations.[47] The language used by the Biodiversity Convention provides an interesting balance. For example, Article 15 lays down standards for access to

---

[46]   Ehrenfeld, D. (2003), 'Globalisation: Effects on Biodiversity, Environment and Society', Conservation and Society, 1, 100–101. Footnotes omitted.

[47]   Coombe, R.J. (2001), 'The Recognition of Indigenous Peoples' and Community Traditional Knowledge in International Law', St Thomas Law Review, 14, 278. Gupta, J. (2007), 'Globalization, Environmental Challenges and North–South Issues', in K.V. Thai, D. Rahm and J.D. Coggburn (eds), *Handbook of Globalization and the Environment*, Boca Raton, FL: CRC Press, 449–472.

biological resources signifying a flow from the biodiversity-rich developing countries. Article 8(j) of the Biodiversity Convention deals with traditional knowledge and recognises that indigenous and local communities should share the benefits arising from the use of their knowledge. As a balance, Article 16 deals with technology transfer including biotechnology, with an emphasis on the obligations of technology rich developed countries.[48]

Globalisation, as has been pointed out before, necessitates a recalibration of national sovereignty. In respect of biodiversity, the issue of sovereign right and effective control of biological resources is criticised on the ground that the rights to the biological resources should remain with the communities and knowledge holders and not with the state or government.[49] State sovereignty over biological and genetic resources within national borders means that the indigenous peoples' right to own, use, control and manage their lands, territories and natural resources can be restricted. The parameter of sovereign rights is also narrowed by the access and benefit-sharing regime, as benefit sharing with developed countries restricts the right of the source country over their natural resources. As the sovereign rights of states are not absolute, states are required to take effective action to manage biodiversity.[50] The effective control of the biological resources depends on the national protection of biodiversity evidenced by the nature of the access and benefit-sharing regime and the level of protection of traditional knowledge.

3.1. Access and Benefit Sharing (ABS)

The ABS regime created by the Biodiversity Convention recognises that uncontrolled access to genetic resources can negatively impact not only on the people who depend upon such resources for their sustained livelihood, but also on the natural environment including biodiversity. An adequate ABS mechanism influences and facilitates the development of a number of policy areas including public health, biotechnology and food security. The provision of traditional knowledge under Article 8(j) is closely linked to the provision on access and benefit sharing under Article 15.[51] For many

---

[48]   Article 16 (dealing with the transfer of technology) recognises that patents and other intellectual property rights may have an influence on the implementation of the Biodiversity Convention.

[49]   Discussed in the Introduction and chapter 3.

[50]   Birnie et al. (2009), supra, 130.

[51]   This link was addressed in the ad hoc open-ended inter-sessional Working Group on the implementation of Article 8(j) and related provisions, COP-4 (1998). COP-6 (2002) established an ad hoc Working Group on ABS with the aim of

indigenous communities over the world, the use of or access to genetic resources has come at a high price without sufficient compensation or benefits derived from such use of or access to biological resources.

Apart from the Biodiversity Convention, some of the international treaties include ABS mechanisms such as the International Labour Organization's Convention Concerning Indigenous and Tribal Peoples in Independent Countries (ILO Convention 169),[52] the International Convention on the Protection of New Varieties of Plants[53] and the Food and Agriculture Organization's International Treaty on Plant Genetic Resources for Food and Agriculture (ITPGRFA).[54] For example, the ITPGRFA aims at

> . . . the conservation and sustainable use of plant genetic resources for food and agriculture and the fair and equitable sharing of the benefits arising out of their use, in harmony with the Convention on Biological Diversity, for sustainable agriculture and food security.[55]

Regional agreements in Africa, Southeast Asia and Central America provide guidance on developing ABS regimes.[56] Some of the non-binding international instruments that promote ABS include the Bonn Guidelines,[57] the UN Declaration on Indigenous Rights,[58] and the FAO

---

adopting an instrument to implement effectively the provisions of Articles 15 and 8(j) of the Biodiversity Convention.

[52]   ILO Convention No. 169, Articles. 6, 15(2), 27 June 1989, 28 I.L.M. (1989) 1382 (entered into force 5 September 1991).

[53]   International Convention for the Protection of New Varieties of Plants, opened for signature 2 December 1961, 815 U.N.T.S. 90 (1961).

[54]   International Treaty on Plant Genetic Resources for Food and Agriculture (2001), entered into force 29 June 2004. Available at: www.fao.org/legal/treaties/033s-e.htm (accessed on 20 August 2010).

[55]   Article 1.1. McManis, C.R. (2003), 'Intellectual Property, Genetic Resources and Traditional Knowledge Protection: Thinking Globally, Acting Locally', Cardozo Journal of International and Comparative Law, 11, 554–556.

[56]   The Andean Pact Decision 391 on the Common Regime on Access to Genetic Resources (1996). The Association of South-East Asian Nations Framework Agreement on Access to Biological and Genetic Resources (2000, draft). The Central American Agreement on Access to Genetic Resources and Bio-chemicals and Related Traditional Knowledge (2001, draft). The African Model Law for the Protection of the Rights of Local Communities, Farmers and Breeders, and for the Regulation of Access to Biological Resources (2000) developed by the Organization of African Unity.

[57]   Bonn Guidelines on Access to Genetic Resources and Fair and Equitable Sharing of the Benefits Arising out of their Utilisation, Decision VI/24, COP-6 (2002).

[58]   UN Declaration on the Rights of Indigenous Peoples (2007), Articles 28 and

International Code of Conduct for Plant Germplasm Collecting and Transfer,[59] among others.

When a micro-organism, plant or animal is used for a commercial application, the providers and the users/collectors of genetic resources need to enter into a benefit-sharing arrangement.[60] These arrangements are generally subject to the conditions set in the national law. Multinational pharmaceutical companies using biological resources in the developing countries for medicine, cosmetics, agricultural and horticultural products rarely show any evidence of a benefit-sharing arrangement.[61] According to the WSSD Johannesburg Declaration (2002), the states are to:[62]

(j)   Subject to national legislation, recognize the rights of local and indigenous communities who are holders of traditional knowledge, innovations and practices, and, with the approval and involvement of the holders of such knowledge, innovations and practices, develop and implement benefit-sharing mechanisms on mutually agreed terms for the use of such knowledge, innovations and practices;
(l)   Promote the effective participation of indigenous and local communities in decision and policy-making concerning the use of their traditional knowledge;
(n)   Promote the wide implementation of and continued work on the Bonn Guidelines on Access to Genetic Resources and Fair and Equitable Sharing of Benefits arising out of their Utilization, as an input to assist the Parties when developing and drafting legislative, administrative or policy measures on access and benefit-sharing as well as contract and other arrangements under mutually agreed terms for access and benefit-sharing;

Arrangements for the sharing of benefits may include advance payments for samples, royalty provisions, non-monetary benefits such as

---

32, UN GA Doc. 61/295, 13 September 2007. The Declaration mandates 'just, fair and equitable compensation' for the use of resources traditionally owned by indigenous people. Parties are to consult the indigenous people on any 'development, utilization, or exploitation' of natural resources held by them.

[59]   Food and Agriculture Organization, The International Code of Conduct for Plant Germplasm Collecting and Transfer (1993), available at: www.fao.org/WAICENT/FaoInfo/Agricult/AGP/AGPS/pgr/icc/icce.htm (accessed 15 January 2010).

[60]   Article 15 of the Biodiversity Convention. Guideline 16, Bonn Guidelines, supra.

[61]   McGowan, J. (2006), 'Out of Africa: Mysteries of Access and Benefit Sharing', available at: www.edmonds-institute.org/outofafrica.pdf (accessed 15 January 2010).

[62]   Para. 44. Chapter IV, Protecting and managing the natural resource base of economic and social development, Johannesburg Plan of Implementation, World Summit on Sustainable Development (2002).

capacity-building, and access to technology.[63] It is crucial to have national laws on access and benefit sharing which include rules relating to species conservation, minimise the negative impacts of the use of genetic resources upon species, obtain prior informed consent from the communities affected by the use of genetic resources and control the use of genetic resources through the creation of mutually agreed terms.[64] The Bonn Guidelines suggest that

> . . . 'mutually agreed terms should be set out in a written agreement' with 'guiding parameters in contractual agreements' and provide 'an indicative list of typical mutually agreed terms' which may be applicable in contracts regarding access to genetic resources. They provide basic requirements in the development of MATs [Mutually Agreed Terms] for ABS, including legal certainty, awareness, institutional mechanisms, and an indicative list of elements that could be included as MATs. These elements range from resources that can be accessed to issues of ownership over the final product, terms to use and transfer the material and benefit sharing. A separate section on benefit sharing highlights what could be covered under the terms including type (monetary types and non-monetary types of benefits), timing (short-term, medium or long-term benefits) and distribution mechanisms among the different stakeholders (including government, indigenous and local communities, industry, etc.) to ensure that the sharing process is fair and equitable.[65]

Provisions on access to genetic resources at the national level are generally contained in the environmental, nature conservation or bio-diversity laws, in the existing laws through amendment or there may be specific access and benefit-sharing laws.[66] There are some weaknesses in these access related national laws.[67] These laws do not always ensure equitable sharing of benefits, thus limiting the ability of the poorer community to access genetic resources. All stakeholders may not be included in the process of determining access and use rights to genetic resources. Moreover, the national seed laws may not offer adequate protection to indigenous varieties and may not ensure distribution or access rights of

---

[63] Appendix II, Bonn Guidelines, supra.

[64] Bonn Guidelines, supra.

[65] UNU/IAS and UNEP, *Benefit Sharing in ABS: Options and Elaborations*, Japan: United Nations University, 10, available at: www.cbd.int/abs/doc/unu-abs-report-2009-en.pdf (accessed 15 January 2010).

[66] Ibid. CBD, International Regime on Access and Benefit-Sharing, Proposals for an International Regime on Access and Benefit-Sharing, UNEP/CBD/MYPOW/6 (7 January 2003).

[67] Tvedt, M.W. and T. Young (2007), *Beyond Access: Exploring Implementation of the Fair and Equitable Sharing Commitment in the CBD*, Gland, Switzerland: IUCN.

the indigenous and local communities.[68] These national rules relating to ABS need to provide sufficient information to the community regarding the aims, risks and implications of using the biological resources[69] and a mechanism for compensation to communities for the impact of the use of a resource upon the community.

3.2. Traditional Knowledge (TK)

Traditional knowledge is a broad term referring to knowledge systems, encompassing a wide variety of areas, held by traditional groups or communities or to knowledge acquired in a non-systemic way.[70] These knowledge systems have significance and relevance to their holders and to the global ecosystem.[71] There is no universal definition of traditional knowledge approved or agreed to by international organisations. The term traditional knowledge refers to

> . . . tradition-based literary, artistic or scientific works; performances; inventions; scientific discoveries; designs; marks, names and symbols; undisclosed information; and all other tradition-based innovations and creations resulting from intellectual activity in the industrial, scientific, literary or artistic fields.[72]

The relationship between access to and use of genetic resources and associated or non-associated traditional knowledge is dealt with under Articles 15 and 8(j) of the Biodiversity Convention. The link between genetic resources and traditional knowledge is inextricable in the sense that any access to genetic resources may involve access to traditional knowledge. Traditional knowledge associated with genetic resources is of particular relevance in the context of Article 15 and the Bonn Guidelines.[73]

There are ongoing discussions regarding the nature of the relationship between intellectual property rights and the knowledge and innovations of

---

[68]   Aoki, K. (2003), 'Weeds, Seeds and Deeds: Recent Skirmishes in the Seed War', Cordozo Journal of International and Comparative Law, 11, 247.

[69]   Guideline 36, Bonn Guidelines, supra.

[70]   Traditional Knowledge Online, Franklin Pierce Law Center, available at: www.traditionalknowledge.info/ (accessed 15 January 2010).

[71]   Ibid.

[72]   WIPO (2001), Intellectual Property Needs and Expectations of Traditional Knowledge Holders: WIPO Report on Fact-finding Missions on Intellectual Property and Traditional Knowledge (1998-1999), WIPO, Geneva, 25. Available at: www.wipo.int/tk/en/tk/ffm/report/index.html (accessed 15 January 2010).

[73]   Guideline 9, Bonn Guidelines, supra.

local and indigenous communities within the terms of Article 8(j).[74] Article 8(j) requires each party as far as possible, as appropriate, and subject to its national legislation, to

> . . . respect, preserve and maintain knowledge, innovations and practices of indigenous and local communities embodying traditional lifestyles relevant for the conservation and sustainable use of biological diversity and promote their wider application with the approval and involvement of the holders of such knowledge, innovations and practices and encourage the equitable sharing of the benefits arising from the utilization of such knowledge, innovations and practices.

Traditional knowledge is 'developed from experience and gained over the centuries and adapted to the local culture and environment, traditional knowledge is transmitted orally from generation to generation'.[75] Moreover, '[traditional knowledge] tends to be collectively owned and takes the form of stories, songs, folklore, proverbs, cultural values, beliefs, rituals, community laws, local language, and agricultural practices, including the development of plant species and animal breeds'.[76] Examples of traditional knowledge include the use of *plao-noi* by Thai traditional healers to treat ulcers, and the use of *argyapaachya* by the Kani people in South India to suppress fatigue and reduce stress.

A number of models are available to protect traditional knowledge. For example, the public domain model, the trust model, the commercial use model and the ownership model.[77]

> . . . (1) a 'public' domain model, where certain basic biological, genetic or other information is treated as unowned but appropriable; (2) a 'trust' model where certain basic biological, genetic or other knowledge is treated as a sort of communal 'res' by 'trustees' for the benefit of designated 'beneficiaries'; (3) a 'commercial use' model, where ownership rights in certain basic biological, genetic

---

[74] For example, in the WTO, both the TRIPs Council and the Committee on Trade and Environment, in the CBD, Ad hoc open-ended inter-sessional Working Group on Article 8(j), and in the WIPO, Intergovernmental Committee on Intellectual Property and Genetic Resources, Traditional Knowledge and Folklore are examining the relevant provisions of the TRIPs Agreement and TK.

[75] CBD, Traditional Knowledge and the Convention on Biological Diversity, Available at www.cbd.int/doc/publications/8j-brochure-en.pdf (accessed 15 January 2010).

[76] Ibid. Intergovernmental Committee on Intellectual Property and Genetic Resources, Traditional Knowledge and Folklore, Traditional Knowledge: Operational Terms and Definitions. WIPO/GRTKF/IC/3/9, 20 May 2002.

[77] Aoki (2003), supra, 251. Ghosh, S. (2003), 'Globalization, Patents and Traditional Knowledge', Columbia Journal of Asian Law, 17(1), 112.

or other information are assigned to the first party to reduce such knowledge to a commercially marketable product; and (4) a 'private property' model, where rights in certain biological, genetic or other information are assigned by the geographically superordinate sovereign within which such resources are located and treated as the assignee's 'private property'.

At one end of the spectrum would be the public domain model which is about keeping traditional knowledge accessible by everyone. The other end of the spectrum is about individual or group ownership of traditional knowledge. The commercial model allows 'the first entity to make use of the traditional knowledge' and does not provide adequate protection for traditional knowledge.[78] The trust model, on the other hand, allows any provider state or non-state actors to 'act as a trustee for the benefit of the traditional knowledge holder'.[79]

A number of international treaties and declarations support the development of TK legislation and procedures, including prior informed consent and principles of equitable sharing of benefits. International organisations, such as the UN,[80] WTO,[81] WIPO[82] and UNCTAD[83] have produced a number of non-binding instruments which link intellectual property rights to TK. Beyond the intellectual property rights regime, the TK issues are relevant to other international conventions. For example, the ITPGRFA requires measures to protect TK 'relevant to plant genetic resources for food and agriculture'.[84] The Desertification Convention provides for the protection of traditional knowledge as well as the sharing of benefits arising from the utilisation of the TK.[85]

---

[78] Ibid., 114–116.

[79] Ibid., 117–118.

[80] United Nations Declaration on the Rights of Indigenous Peoples (2007), Article 31 (Indigenous peoples have the 'right to maintain, control, protect and develop their intellectual property over such cultural heritage, traditional knowledge, and traditional cultural expressions').

[81] World Trade Organization (WTO), Agreement on Trade-Related Aspects of Intellectual Property Rights, 15 April 1994, 33 I.L.M. (1994) 1197.

[82] WIPO (2001), supra.

[83] United Nations Conference on Trade and Development (2000), Expert Meeting on Systems and National Experiences for Protecting Traditional Knowledge, Innovations and Practices, Geneva: UNCTAD.

[84] Food and Agriculture Organization (FAO), International Treaty on Plant Genetic Resources for Food and Agriculture, FAO Conf., 31st Sess., FAO, adopted on 3 November 2001.

[85] Articles 16(g) and 17(1)(c), UN Convention to Combat Desertification in Countries Experiencing Serious Drought and/or Desertification, particularly in Africa, adopted in 14 October 1994, 1954 U.N.T.S. 3 (1994), entered into force 14 October 1994.

Countries such as Brazil, Ethiopia, India and the Philippines have national laws to protect the TK rights of indigenous peoples.[86] At the national level, traditional knowledge can be protected through conventional intellectual property laws,[87] and through *sui generis* laws, such as laws for the protection of TK associated with genetic resources. Effective national legislation is crucial because of the role TK has on the economic and social life of these communities (see box 9.1). These national laws need to reflect the expectations of the knowledge holder, provide adequate protection against piracy associated with the TK, promote respect for indigenous and customary practices, contain the principle of prior informed consent and ensure effective participation of the TK holder in safeguarding their right to the TK.[88]

3.3.   Intellectual Property Rights and Traditional Knowledge

Intellectual property rights to protect traditional knowledge are discussed in several international organisations including the WIPO and WTO. The focus of this section is the TRIPs Agreement of the WTO[89] and its complex relationship with the Biodiversity Convention. According to the Biodiversity Convention, the traditional knowledge holder, as a custodian of genetic resources, has the right to have control over and receive a share of the benefits from biodiversity related traditional knowledge. This right is linked to the right of access and sharing of genetic resources, and the right to access technology that is based on these resources.[90]. However, the TRIPs Agreement allows patent rights over genetic resources such as micro-organisms, plants and animals.[91]

---

[86]   Biodiversity Rights Legislation (BRL) available at: www.grain.org/brl/ (accessed 15 January 2010).

[87]   For example, patents, designs, trademarks and geographical indications. Abbott, F., T. Cottier and F. Gurry (1999), *International Intellectual Property System: Commentary and Materials*, The Hague: Kluwer, 25.

[88]   WIPO, Consolidated Survey of Intellectual Property Protection of Traditional Knowledge, Document WIPO/GRTKF/IC/5/7, 4 April 2003. CBD, Decision IX/13 (2008) on Article 8(j) and related provisions.

[89]   Agreement on Trade Related Aspects of Intellectual Property Rights, Including Trade in Counterfeit Goods, Annex 1C, Legal Instruments – Results of the Uruguay Round, Vol. 31, 33 I.L.M. (1994) 81. The TRIPs Agreement was concluded in the package of agreements in the WTO in 1993 and entered into force in 1995. The TRIPs Agreement sets minimum standards for patents and other intellectual property rights and all WTO members are obliged to provide comprehensive protection of intellectual property rights.

[90]   Articles 8(j), 15 and 16 of the Biodiversity Convention.

[91]   Article 27(3) of the TRIPs Agreement. Article 27(3)(b) deals with

BOX 9.1.   EFFORTS IN THE PHILIPPINES
            TOWARDS TK PROTECTION AND
            AWARENESS[1]

Plant variety protection was introduced in the Philippines in 2002 with the Plant Variety Protection Act (PVP Act) as a *sui generis* system in compliance with the TRIPs Agreement. Many small-scale farmers engaged in participatory plant breeding feared that their innovations could be misappropriated by breeding companies. As a collective response to the Act, the Campagao Farmers' Production and Research Association (CFPRA) of Bilar on the island of Bohol decided to establish a community registry, as the community's way of asserting control over and access to seeds and propagating material. This was done in collaboration with the Philippines-based Southeast Asia Regional Initiatives for Community Empowerment (SEARICE). Following a series of group meetings and discussions, a community affidavit was formulated declaring that all rice varieties maintained in the community should not be included in the PVP Act, and that seeds of these varieties should remain freely accessible to farmers wishing to use, sell, save or exchange them with other farmers. The affidavit included a list of names and characteristics of rice varieties which the community had been using and developing since its participatory plant breeding (PPB) efforts started. It was supplemented by a resolution detailing the process of how entries in the registry should be updated every cropping season. After successful lobbying by the CFPRA, the local village council expressed its full support for the farmers' efforts and the community affidavit. By registering their varieties in this way, and continually updating the list, the farmers are protecting these varieties from misappropriation by commercial actors.

Note:
1. Farmers' Rights, 'Best Practices: Community Registry in the Philippines', available at: www.farmersrights.org/bestpractices/success_tk_3.html (accessed 15 January 2010).

patentability or non-patentability of plant and animal inventions, and the protection of plant varieties. Para. 19 of the 2001 Doha Ministerial Declaration adds that the TRIPs Council should also look at the relationship between the TRIPs Agreement and the Biodiversity Convention.

Article 27 (Patentable Subject Matter)

1.   Subject to the provisions of paragraphs 2 and 3, patents shall be available for any inventions, whether products or processes, in all fields of technology, provided that they are new, involve an inventive step and are capable of industrial application.

. . .

2.   Members may exclude from patentability inventions, the prevention within their territory of the commercial exploitation of which is necessary to protect *ordre public* or morality, including to protect human, animal or plant life or health or to avoid serious prejudice to the environment, provided that such exclusion is not made merely because the exploitation is prohibited by their law.

3.   Members may also exclude from patentability:

. . .

(b)   plants and animals other than micro-organisms, and essentially biological processes for the production of plants or animals other than non-biological and microbiological processes. However, Members shall provide for the protection of plant varieties either by patents or by an effective *sui generis* system or by any combination thereof. The provisions of this subparagraph shall be reviewed four years after the date of entry into force of the WTO Agreement.

The emphasis of Article 8(j) of the Biodiversity Convention on knowledge and innovations makes it relevant to intellectual property rights.[92] Parties to the Biodiversity Convention recognise that 'patents and other intellectual property rights may have an influence on the implementation of the convention' and must endeavour to ensure that the protection of private intellectual property rights is 'supportive of and do[es] not run counter' to the objectives of the CBD.[93] Therefore, patenting or other intellectual property protection of genetic material under the TRIPs Agreement must ensure that the provisions of the Biodiversity Convention, including those relating to prior informed consent and benefit sharing, are respected. The Bonn Guidelines suggest that parties encourage the disclosure of the country of origin of relevant traditional knowledge, innovations and practices in intellectual property rights applications in order to help track compliance with requirements relating to PIC and MAT.[94]

---

[92]   A number of other provisions such as Articles 12(c), 17, and 18, involving technology, research and sharing of benefits could also relate to intellectual property rights.

[93]   Article 16(5) of the Biodiversity Convention.

[94]   Guidelines 16(d) and 31 of the Bonn Guidelines (2002).

3.3.1. International arrangements

A number of discussions are ongoing within the WTO (TRIPs Council and Committee on Trade and Environment) and outside the WTO (e.g. Biodiversity Convention) to determine the nature of the relationship between traditional knowledge and intellectual property rights. The web of international treaties, international (e.g. ITPGRFA, International Convention for the Protection of New Varieties of Plants) and regional initiatives in Africa (e.g. Model Law), and bilateral trade agreements add another layer of complexity to the already strained relationship between the Biodiversity Convention and the TRIPs Agreement. This situation is not helped by the fact that several international agencies and institutions (e.g. WIPO, FAO) overlap on these issues and are pursuing different agendas and priorities with varying levels of coordination among them.

The TRIPs Agreement requires parties to provide patent protection for inventions in all fields of technology.[95] Article 27 allows companies and researchers from industrialised countries to obtain patents on inventions based on genetic resources from the developing countries without having to fulfil some of the basic principles of the Biodiversity Convention, such as benefit sharing, prior informed consent and the protection of the traditional knowledge associated with genetic resources. Article 27 extends patent protection to pharmaceutical and agricultural chemical products and microbiological products and processes. Several intellectual property mechanisms, such as copyright, patent, trademarks and geographical indications, can be used for this purpose.[96]

The TRIPs Agreement, however, allows some exceptions to the patenting requirement, specifically plants, animals, and processes for their production.[97] It requires parties to protect plant varieties by means of patents or an effective *sui generis* system of production or any combination of the two.[98] Using the *sui generis* system, parties can enact laws compatible with their national requirements in order to protect their plant varieties.[99] A *sui generis* system may consist of some standard forms of intellectual property protection combined with other forms of protection for genetic

---

[95] Article 27 of the TRIPs Agreement.
[96] Council for Trade-Related Aspects of Intellectual Property Rights, The Protection of Traditional Knowledge and Folklore: Summary of Issues Raised and Points Made, IP/C/W/370/Rev.1, 9 March 2006, 13.
[97] Article 27(3) (b) of the TRIPs Agreement.
[98] Ibid.
[99] The International Union for the Protection of New Varieties of Plants (UPOV) convention provides a *sui generis* system of plant variety protection.

resources.[100] For example, the Costa Rican Biodiversity Law recognises and protects, under the community intellectual rights, the knowledge, practices and innovations of indigenous peoples and communities relating to the use of components of biodiversity and associated knowledge. This right exists and is legally recognised by the mere existence of the cultural practice or knowledge related to genetic resources and biochemicals. It does not require prior declaration, explicit recognition or official registration.[101]

3.3.2. Impact of intellectual property rights on traditional knowledge

Countries such as the USA strongly assert that there is no apparent conflict between the TRIPs Agreement and the Biodiversity Convention as 'criteria for patentability will ensure the grant of valid patents over inventions that use genetic material'.[102] Some biodiversity-rich countries, however, are of the view that there is an inherent conflict between the two agreements: the TRIPs Agreement accommodates private rights which could potentially overrule the sovereign rights recognised by the Biodiversity Convention.[103] Their concern is related to the impacts of patent protection on genetic resources and associated traditional knowledge. Patents over plant varieties require these to be genetically uniform, which favours the commercial production of seeds on a global scale rather than locally adapted varieties. The cultivation of uniform varieties is linked both to the loss of agro-biodiversity and to the increase of genetic erosion, making crops more vulnerable to diseases.

Providers of traditional knowledge are encouraged to make benefit-sharing arrangements with users such as companies and governments. These arrangements could open up new sources of income for local communities or other entities in developing countries. For example, the traditional healers of Samoa were acknowledged in a benefit-sharing agreement concerning the development of prostratin, an anti-AIDS compound derived from the Samoan native *mamala* tree (*Homalanthus nutans*). It proposes that revenues from the development of prostratin will be shared

---

[100] WIPO, Elements of a *sui generis* system for the protection of traditional knowledge, WIPO/GRTKF/IC/4/8, 30 September 2002.

[101] National Legislation of Costa Rica, Biodiversity Law, Article 82 (Sui generis Community intellectual rights), Law No. 7788, 23 April 1998.

[102] Council for Trade-Related Aspects of Intellectual Property Rights, The Relationship Between the TRIPs Agreement and the Convention on Biological Diversity: Summary of Issues Raised and Points Made, IP/C/W/368/Rev.1, 8 February 2006, 4–6.

[103] Ibid., 8.

with the village where the compound was found and with the families of the healers who helped discover it.[104]

One concern is that the level of access and benefit sharing of traditional knowledge depends on the model followed at the national level to protect traditional knowledge, culture and indigenous practice. The impacts of intellectual property rights laws in developing countries can be very negative for small farmers. For example, patents can make seeds more expensive for small farmers due to royalty payments, restrictive contracts and increased commercialisation. According to ActionAid,[105] only a handful of multinational corporations hold the vast majority of the 918 patents on rice, maize, wheat, soybean and sorghum, with 633 patents, or nearly 69 per cent, on the staples.

In addition, the intellectual property right, as a private property right, does not adequately protect the rights of communities over their traditional knowledge.[106] Vandana Shiva considers biodiversity as a 'local common resource' which combines a sense of 'utilization and conservation'.[107] The developing countries fear that arrangements under the intellectual property rights regime do not provide protection to the countries and communities which supply the genetic material and traditional knowledge.[108] However, it is possible for the developing countries to adopt higher standards of laws (e.g. *sui generis* laws) than required by the TRIPs Agreement and to include provisions on benefit sharing.[109]

Another concern relates to the displacement of traditional varieties and depletion of biodiversity. Traditional knowledge may pass from generation to generation and one or more families or tribes may share the same knowledge. This characteristic makes it difficult to meet the 'novelty'

---

[104] WIPO, *Intellectual Property and Traditional Knowledge*, WIPO Publication 920(E), Geneva: WIPO, available at www.wipo.int/freepublications/en/tk/920/wipo_pub_920.pdf (accessed 15 January 2010).

[105] Madeley, J. (2001), *Crops and Robbers*, London: Action Aid, available at: www.actionaid.org.uk/doc_lib/crops_robbers.pdf (accessed 15 January 2010).

[106] Khor, M. (2002), *Intellectual Property, Biodiversity and Sustainable Development: Resolving the Difficult Issues*, London: Zed Books and Penang: Third World Network, chapter 2.

[107] Shiva, V. (1997), *Bio-piracy: The Plunder of Nature and Knowledge*, Cambridge MA: South End Press, 65.

[108] Council for Trade-Related Aspects of Intellectual Property Rights, The Relationship Between the TRIPs Agreement and the Convention on Biological Diversity: Summary of Issues Raised and Points Made, IP/C/W/368/Rev.1, 8 February 2006, 8.

[109] UNEP/IISD (2005), *Trade and Environment: A Handbook*, Canada: International Institute for Sustainable Development, 73–74.

required by the patent. Traditional knowledge may lack documented evidence and may not fulfil the requirement of 'non-obviousness'.[110] Moreover, the grant of excessively broad patents does not fully meet the tests of patentability. Therefore, on the one hand, knowledge holders are unable to protect their knowledge as they may not meet the patent requirements. On the other hand, even if the traditional knowledge directly contributed to the development of a product, it may not be recognised during the patent procedure. These issues give rise to the consequent problems of 'bio-piracy' in respect of traditional knowledge.

3.3.3. Biopiracy and genetic resources

Control and use of genetic resources remains a crucial issue both for public and private industries and for communities dependent on these resources. Through patents, the biotechnology industries can claim ownership of genetic resources and, in effect, own the knowledge developed by indigenous farmers or resources which were developed by nature. Granting private property rights over traditional knowledge raises serious questions in respect to 'prior art',[111] and can also be viewed as 'bio-piracy'. Biopiracy is defined as 'the illegal appropriation of life – micro-organisms, plants, and animals – and the traditional cultural knowledge that accompanies it'.[112] Many academics have termed this as 'biocolonialism' or 'bioprospecting',whereby companies or institutions from the industrialised countries appropriate the genetic resources and traditional knowledge in the biodiversity-rich countries and become the new owners of these resources.[113]

According to Graham Dutfield, '[b]iopiracy generally refers either to the unauthorised commercial use of biological resources and/or associated

---

[110] Council for Trade-Related Aspects of Intellectual Property Rights, The Relationship between the TRIPs Agreement and the Convention on Biological Diversity: Summary of Issues Raised and Points Made, Note by the Secretariat, IP/C/W/368/Rev.1, 8 February 2006, 10–13.

[111] The 'prior art' is the body of knowledge that exists prior to the invention. It helps to determine whether or not the invention is 'new' and 'non-obvious'.

[112] DeGeer, M.E. (2002), 'Biopiracy: The Appropriation of Indigenous Peoples' Cultural Knowledge', New England Journal of International & Comparative Law, 9(1), 179.

[113] Sarma, L. (1999), 'Biopiracy: Twentieth Century Imperialism in the Form of International Agreements', Temple International and Comparative Law Journal, 13, 107. Shiva (1997), supra. Coombe, R.J. (1998), 'Intellectual Property, Human Rights and Sovereignty: New Dilemmas in International Law Posed by the Recognition of Indigenous Knowledge and the Conservation of Biodiversity', Indiana Journal of Global Legal Studies, 6, 59.

TK from developing countries, or to the patenting of spurious inventions based on such knowledge or resources without compensation'.[114] In his view,

> ... 'biopirates' are those individuals and companies accused of one or both of the following acts: (i) the theft, misappropriation of, or unfair free-riding on, genetic resources and/or traditional knowledge through the patent system; and (ii) the unauthorised and uncompensated collection for commercial ends of genetic resources and/or traditional knowledge.[115]

Biopiracy 'refers to the privatisation of genetic resources ... from those people who hold, maintain, embody, develop, breed, or otherwise create, foster or nurture those resources'.[116] These biopirates can be individuals or institutions who impose exclusive control over the resources or knowledge. There are a number of ways in which biopiracy can take place: unauthorised use of traditional knowledge and technologies, unauthorised use of biological resources and lack of benefit sharing with the resource providers such as the community and tribes.[117] Biopiracy allegations arose in several cases:[118] a US patent granted for the healing properties of turmeric, known for centuries in India; a US patent on the 'ayahuasca' plant, considered sacred and used for medicinal purposes by Amazon's indigenous peoples. The example in Box 9.2 relates to Hoodia, an appetite suppressant which capitalised on the traditional knowledge of the San people.

---

[114] Dutfield, G. (2001), 'TRIPS-related Aspects of Traditional Knowledge', *Case Western Reserve Journal of International Law*, 33, 237 (cited in footnote 16).

[115] Dutfield, G. (2005), 'Identification of Outstanding ABS Issues: Access to GR and IPR. What Is Biopiracy?', International Expert Workshop on Access to Genetic Resources and Benefit Sharing, 2005, available at: www.canmexworkshop.com/documents/papers/I.3.pdf (accessed 15 January 2010).

[116] ETC Group, From Global Enclosure to Self Enclosure: Ten Years After – A Critique of the CBD and the 'Bonn Guidelines' on Access and Benefit Sharing (ABS), Communiqué, January–February 2004, 2. (cited in footnote 14 of Ho, C.M. (2005), 'Biopiracy and Beyond: A Consideration of Socio-Cultural Conflicts with Global Patent Policies', *University of Michigan Journal of Law Reform*, 39(3), 433).

[117] G. Dutfield (2005), supra.

[118] Kothari, A. and R.V. Anuradha (1999), 'Biodiversity and Intellectual Property Rights: Can the Two Co-Exist?', *Journal of International Wildlife Law and Policy*, 2(2), 204–223. Commission on Intellectual Property Rights (2002), *Integrating Intellectual Property Rights and Development Policy*, London: Commission on Intellectual Property Rights, chapter 4 (Traditional Knowledge and Geographical Indications), available at: www.iprcommission.org/papers/pdfs/final_report/Ch4final.pdf (accessed 15 January 2010).

BOX 9.2.   BIODIVERSITY, TRADITIONAL KNOWL-
EDGE AND IPRS IN SOUTHERN AFRICA:
THE CASE OF THE HOODIA PLANT[1]

The San, the indigenous inhabitants of Southern Africa, have traditionally eaten the Hoodia cactus to stave off hunger and thirst on
long hunting trips. The active ingredient in Hoodia and its possible
use as a slimming drug have attracted the attention of pharmaceutical companies. The hunger suppressing chemical component (P57) of the Hoodia cactus was identified and patented by
the Council for Scientific and Industrial Research in South Africa
(CSIR). CSIR licensed the British company Phytopharm to further
develop and commercialise P57. However, CSIR retained the
patent. In 1998, Phytopharm then sold the exclusive global licence
to commercialise the drug to Pfizer, for US$21 million.

In 2001, the South African San Council opened talks with the
CSIR demanding recognition of their knowledge and a share
of the benefits across borders. In 2003, the South African San
Council and the CSIR signed an agreement recognising and
rewarding the San people as traditional knowledge-holders, with a
reported share of up to 8 per cent of profits from the drug derived
from the Hoodia plant. In the same year, Phytopharm announced
that Pfizer had decided to discontinue the clinical development of
P57, returning the right to Phytopharm.

The San agreement has been criticised because of the meagre
profit received by the San people from CSIR compared to the profit
received by the companies. The companies, Pfizer and Phytopharm,
are exempt from sharing their benefits and protected by the agreement from any further financial demands by the San. In addition, the
agreement prevents the San from using their knowledge of *Hoodia*
in any other commercial application. The wider implications and
concerns raised by this agreement relate to the patenting and privatisation of knowledge in communities where the sharing of knowledge is part of their culture and central to their way of life.

Note:
1.   Source: Wynberg, R. (2004), 'Rhetoric, Realism and Benefit Sharing: Use of
Traditional Knowledge of Hoodia Species in the Development of an Appetite
Suppressant'. Journal of World Intellectual Property, 7(6), 851–876, avail-
able at: www.biowatch.org.za/main.asp?include=pubs/wjip.html (accessed 15
January 2010).

FOR DISCUSSION

- Would you agree that the ABS regime has restricted the sovereign rights of the country over their biological resources?
- In order to be fair and equitable, what components must a benefit-sharing arrangement contain?
- Does the *sui generis* model adequately protect the traditional knowledge of the communities?

With modern ways of life and poverty, traditional knowledge holders require adequate incentives to maintain traditional knowledge and intellectual property rights may offer them financial benefits.[119] However, creating private property rights[120] will not solve the problem of biodiversity or knowledge loss. As Brush suggests,

> . . . [t]urning public good into private property is now heavily promoted for conservation purposes. Unfortunately, this is also a high-risk method for societies and cultures that have long been subordinated. Privatisation of biological resources could result in greater poverty and exploitation without achieving conservation or equity.[121]

4. INTELLECTUAL PROPERTY, TRADITIONAL KNOWLEDGE AND HUMAN RIGHTS

The discussion in section 3 shows that international platforms dealing with the conservation of biodiversity have their own set of priorities and targets. Within the WTO and WIPO, discussion on the protection of traditional knowledge is based on private property models, granting rights to individual innovators over innovations with commercial or industrial applications. Another set of discussions revolves round conservation and access and benefit sharing in the Biodiversity Convention and

---

119 Coombe (1998), supra, 91–92.
120 TRIPs Agreement, Preamble (recognising that intellectual property rights are private rights).
121 Brush, S.B. (1996), 'Whose Knowledge, Whose Genes, Whose Rights?', in S.B. Brush and D. Stabinsky (eds), *Valuing Local Knowledge: Indigenous People and Intellectual Property Rights*, Washington DC: Island Press, 18 (cited in Coombe (1998), supra, 95).

FAO. These require equitable sharing of benefits from the use of genetic resources between user and provider states, in return for access to genetic resources.

The third set of discussions revolves round the status of intellectual property rights and traditional knowledge as a human right. Some intellectual property mechanisms, as discussed above, are used to protect genetic resources, and it is crucial to assess whether all or some attributes of intellectual property rights are compatible with human rights. Some favour the coexistence approach whereby intellectual property rights can be balanced within the human rights standards.[122] Others argue that these two regimes are not compatible and there are inherent conflicts between the two.[123] Resolution 2000/7 on Intellectual Property Rights and Human Rights emphasises that 'actual or potential conflicts exist between the implementation of the TRIPs Agreement and the realization of economic, social and cultural rights'.[124]

Resolution 2000/7 identifies the conflicts between TRIPs and 'the right of everyone to enjoy the benefits of scientific progress and its applications, the right to health, the right to food and the right to self-determination'.[125] The conflicts between human rights and intellectual property rights are evident in the consequences for the right to food of patenting genetically modified organisms, biopiracy, control of indigenous communities' natural resources and culture, and the impact on the right to health from restrictions on access to patented pharmaceuticals. The Resolution adds that the TRIPs Agreement could infringe the rights of the world's poorest to access their genetic resources and pharmaceuticals.[126] It recognises that there is a conflict between the 'private' interests of intellectual property right holders and the 'social' or 'public' concerns embodied in international human rights law, and requests governments to

> . . . integrate into their national and local legislations and policies, provisions, in accordance with international human rights obligations and principles, that protect the social function of intellectual property.[127]

---

[122]   Yu, P.K. (2006), 'Reconceptualizing Intellectual Property Interests in a Human Rights Framework', UC Davis Law Review, 40, 1076–1078.

[123]   Ibid., 1076–1078. Helfer, L.R. (2006), 'Towards a Human Rights Framework for Intellectual Property', UC Davis Law Review, 40, 971.

[124]   Resolution 2000/7 on Intellectual Property Rights and Human Rights, UN Subcommission on the Promotion and Protection of Human Rights, 52nd session, UN Doc. E/CN.4/Sub.2/RES/2000/7, Preamble.

[125]   Ibid., para. 2.

[126]   Ibid., Preamble.

[127]   Ibid., para. 5.

Many states parties include development of intellectual property rights in their report to the ICESCR. This, according to Rosemary Coombe, may indicate that an intellectual property right is a cultural right under international human rights law.[128] If an intellectual property right were a right under the ICESCR, all parties would have to ensure that 'the IPRs recognised in their jurisdiction are established, granted, exercised, licensed, and otherwise used in a fashion that does not infringe upon the human rights . . .'.[129] States are required to ensure compliance of such human rights and can be held accountable for the actions of private actors.[130] However, the intellectual property rights are not expressly recognised as a social, economic and cultural right. From the protection of investments and corporate interests, the focus of the intellectual property right regime needs to broaden to take into account human rights obligations.[131] The intellectual property regime must contribute to the full realisation of human rights and human rights obligations should be taken into account in interpreting intellectual property law.[132] According to CESCR:[133]

> . . . intellectual property is a social product and has a social function. The end which intellectual property protection should serve is the objective of human well-being, to which international human rights instruments give legal expression.

The discussion on the status of traditional knowledge as a human right addresses the social, economic and cultural rights of indigenous peoples, including the rights to own and control access to traditional resources and territories, and the right to decide their own priorities and participate fully in decisions which affect them.[134] The basis for this discussion is found in the UN Declaration on Indigenous Peoples and Human Rights,[135] the International Labour Organization (ILO) Convention 169[136] and

---

[128] Coombe (1998), supra, 64.

[129] Ibid., 70.

[130] Ibid., 69–70.

[131] CESCR, Human Rights and Intellectual Property; Statement of the Committee on Economic, Social and Cultural Rights, E/C.12/2001/15, 14 December 2001, paras 6, 11.

[132] Ibid., para. 18.

[133] Ibid., para. 4.

[134] IIED (2005), 'Protecting Community Rights over Traditional Knowledge: Implications of Customary Laws and Practices', Research Planning Workshop, Cusco, Peru.

[135] Declaration on the Rights of Indigenous Peoples. UN GA Doc. 61/295, 13 September 2007.

[136] Convention concerning Indigenous and Tribal Peoples in Independent

the World Health Organization's (WHO) Constitution.[137] According to Razzaque and Ssenyonjo,[138]

> The discussion relating to traditional knowledge within the human rights platforms may be approached from several perspectives. The first is the right of everyone to benefit from the protection of the moral and material interests resulting from 'any scientific, literary or artistic production' of which one is the author . . . The second one is the right to the highest attainable state of physical and mental health (. . . the 'right to health')[139] particularly the availability of, and accessibility to, traditional medicine . . . The third perspective is the right to education (which includes access to traditional knowledge).[140] The fourth dimension is the right to self-determination and the right to sovereignty over natural resources.[141] The final perspective is the right of the individuals or the population (including indigenous peoples) to participate in the conduct of public affairs.[142] This includes participation in 'all aspects of public administration, and the formulation and implementation of policy at international, national, regional and local levels'.[143]

Countries (ILO No. 169), 72 ILO Official Bull. 59, entered into force 5 September 1991.

[137]   Constitution of the WHO as adopted by the International Health Conference, New York, 19–22 June 1946, signed on 22 July 1946 by the representatives of 61 states (Official Records of the WHO, No. 2, p. 100), entered into force on 7 April 1948.

[138]   Razzaque, J. and M. Ssenyonjo (2007), 'Protection of Traditional Knowledge and Human Rights Obligations: The Status of Discussion in International Organisations', Netherlands Quarterly of Human Rights, 25(3), 404–405. Footnotes included.

[139]   The term 'right to health' in used as a shorthand to refer to the right of everyone to the enjoyment of the highest attainable standard of physical and mental health.

[140]   Committee on Economic, Social and Cultural Rights (CESCR), General Comment 13, The Right to Education (Twenty-first session, 1999), UN Doc. E/C.12/1999/10 (1999), para. 6(d) states that: 'education has to be flexible so it can adapt to the needs of changing societies and communities and respond to the needs of students within their diverse social and cultural settings'.

[141]   See the International Covenant on Civil and Political Rights (ICCPR), GA Res. 2200A (XXI), 21 U.N. GAOR Supp. (No. 16) at 52, UN Doc. A/6316 (1966), 999 U.N.T.S. 171, Article 1(1) and the International Covenant on Economic, Social and Cultural Rights (ICESCR), GA Res. 2200A (XXI), 21 U.N.GAOR Supp. (No. 16) at 49, UN Doc. A/6316 (1966), 993 U.N.T.S. 3, Article 1(1): 'All peoples have the right of self-determination. By virtue of that right they freely determine their political status and freely pursue their economic, social and cultural development'.

[142]   Article 25 ICCPR provides: 'Every citizen shall have the right and the opportunity . . . to take part in the conduct of public affairs'.

[143]   Human Rights Committee (HRC), General Comment 25 (57), UN Doc. CCPR/C/21/Rev.1/Add.7 (1996), para. 5.

The ICESCR recognises that there is a right of everyone 'to benefit from the protection of the *moral and material interests* resulting from any *scientific, literary or artistic production* of which he is the author'.[144] This right is recognised in several international[145] and regional[146] human rights instruments. The interpretation of this provision suggests that this right extends to the protection of all types of knowledge including traditional knowledge.[147]

The fact that traditional knowledge is being subjected to biopiracy or patented without any compensation to knowledge holders and without their prior consent raises questions for both health and cultural rights.[148] The right to health is available to 'everyone' including the indigenous groups as the ICESCR recognises 'the right of *everyone* to the enjoyment of the highest attainable standard of physical and mental health'[149] and the states are obliged to respect, protect and fulfil the right to health. Specifically, states parties should protect '[t]he vital medicinal plants, animals and minerals necessary to the full enjoyment of health of indigenous peoples'.[150] Protection of traditional knowledge needs to be supported by the individual and collective human rights of the knowledge holder and the indigenous community.

The UN Declaration on the Rights of Indigenous Peoples provides further support for the protection of traditional knowledge of the indigenous communities.[151] The Declaration affirms that indigenous peoples have the right to maintain authority over their lands, territories and

---

[144] Article 15(1)(c) of the ICESCR, 993 U.N.T.S. 3. General Comment 17, E/C.12/GC/17 (12 January 2006), para. 1. Emphasis added.

[145] Article 27(2), of the Universal Declaration of Human Rights, GA Res. 217A (III), UN Doc. A/810 at 71 (1948).

[146] Article 13(2), of the American Declaration of the Rights and Duties of Man of 1948, reprinted in Basic Documents Pertaining to Human Rights in the Inter-American System, OEA/Ser.L.V/II.82 doc.6 rev.1 at 17 (1992). Article 14(1(c), of the Additional Protocol to the American Convention on Human Rights in the Area of Economic, Social and Cultural Rights of 1988, O.A.S. Treaty Series No. 69 (1988), entered into force 16 November 1999.

[147] General Comment 17, para. 9 states that ' "any scientific, literary or artistic production", within the meaning of article 15, paragraph 1(c), refers to creations of the human mind, that is to "scientific productions", such as scientific publications and innovations, including knowledge, innovations and practices of indigenous and local communities . . .'.

[148] Razzaque et al. (2007), supra, 406.

[149] Article 12(1).

[150] CESCR, General Comment 14, UN Doc. E/C.12/2000/4, 11 August 2000, para. 27.

[151] Declaration of the Rights of Indigenous Peoples (2007), supra.

resources, as well as their decision-making powers on the use and development of those resources.[152]

Article 24
1. Indigenous peoples have the right to their traditional medicines and to maintain their health practices, including the conservation of their vital medicinal plants, animals and minerals. Indigenous individuals also have the right to access, without any discrimination, to all social and health services.

Article 26
1. Indigenous peoples have the right to the lands, territories and resources which they have traditionally owned, occupied or otherwise used or acquired.
2. Indigenous peoples have the right to own, use, develop and control the lands, territories and resources that they possess by reason of traditional ownership or other traditional occupation or use, as well as those which they have otherwise acquired.
3. States shall give legal recognition and protection to these lands, territories and resources. Such recognition shall be conducted with due respect to the customs, traditions and land tenure systems of the indigenous peoples concerned.

Article 27
States shall establish and implement, in conjunction with indigenous peoples concerned, a fair, independent, impartial, open and transparent process, giving due recognition to indigenous peoples' laws, traditions, customs and land tenure systems, to recognize and adjudicate the rights of indigenous peoples pertaining to their lands, territories and resources, including those which were traditionally owned or otherwise occupied or used. Indigenous peoples shall have the right to participate in this process.

Article 28
1. Indigenous peoples have the right to redress, by means that can include restitution or, when this is not possible, just, fair and equitable compensation, for the lands, territories and resources which they have traditionally owned or otherwise occupied or used, and which have been confiscated, taken, occupied, used or damaged without their free, prior and informed consent.

Article 31
1. Indigenous peoples have the right to maintain, control, protect and develop their cultural heritage, traditional knowledge and traditional cultural expressions, as well as the manifestations of their sciences, technologies and cultures, including human and genetic resources, seeds, medicines, knowledge of the properties of fauna and flora, oral traditions, literatures, designs, sports and traditional games and visual and performing arts. They also have the right to maintain, control, protect and develop their intellectual property over such cultural heritage, traditional knowledge, and traditional cultural expressions.

---

[152] Article 26.

2. In conjunction with indigenous peoples, states shall take effective measures to recognize and protect the exercise of these rights.

The recognition of the rights of indigenous peoples over their resources protects their rights to genetic resources and traditional knowledge. This Declaration affirms indigenous peoples' human rights, including cultural rights and rights to lands, waters, territories and natural resources, genetic resources and traditional knowledge. This Declaration acknowledges the collective right of indigenous peoples to genetic resources and associated traditional knowledge as well as a right to participate in the development of national laws on access and benefit-sharing and traditional knowledge.[153] They have the right to redress or compensation if there is no free, prior informed consent.[154] The Declaration suggests that indigenous peoples hold rights to natural resources and traditional knowledge within their territories and the states should respect those rights.[155]

There is no doubt that human rights are intrinsically linked to the protection of traditional knowledge. However, human rights standards alone will not protect traditional knowledge and genetic resources. States and non-state actors, such as WTO and WIPO, should take into account and prioritise human rights obligations to protect genetic resources and traditional knowledge.

5. CONCLUSION

The sovereign rights of the state to biological resources are not absolute as the scope of these rights is guided by a number of international and regional treaties. States, as part of this international regime, are under the obligation to develop national strategies and plans to protect and conserve their biological resources. International actors including the WTO, WIPO and FAO influence the management of biological diversity at the domestic level. With effective collaboration between resource user and provider countries, it is possible to minimise the adverse effects of unsustainable practices.

At the domestic level, there is a tension between the state and resource holder regarding access to and use of biological resources. The issue of biopiracy, a direct effect of the globalisation process, shows the tension

---

[153] Article 27.
[154] Article 28.
[155] Article 31.

between the private and public good aspects of biological resources. Privatisation of biological resources can lead to restricted access, greater poverty and unsustainable exploitation of biological resources. The state, as a trustee of biological resources, needs to provide adequate legal protection to the biological resources including traditional knowledge. Strong national laws with effective benefit-sharing arrangements, compensation mechanisms and participatory tools will empower the resource holders to protect their rights.

FURTHER READING

Aoki, K. (2003), 'Weeds, Seeds and Deeds: Recent Skirmishes in the Seed War', Cordozo Journal of International and Comparative Law, 11, 247–331.

Birnie, P., A. Boyle and C. Redgwell (2009), *International Law and the Environment*, Oxford: Oxford University Press, 612–648.

Coombe, R.J. (1998), 'Intellectual Property, Human Rights and Sovereignty: New Dilemmas in International Law Posed by the Recognition of Indigenous Knowledge and the Conservation of Biological Diversity', Indiana Journal of Global Legal Studies, 6, 59–115.

Coombe, R.J. (2001), 'The Recognition of Indigenous Peoples' and Community Traditional Knowledge in International Law', St Thomas Law Review, 14, 275–286.

Dutfield, G. (2001), 'TRIPS Related Aspects of Traditional Knowledge', Case Western Reserve Journal of International Law, 33, 233–276.

Ghosh, S. (2003), 'Globalization, Patents and Traditional Knowledge', Columbia Journal of Asian Law, 17(1), 73–120.

Ho, C.M. (2005), 'Biopiracy and Beyond: A Consideration of Socio-Cultural Conflicts with Global Patent Policies', University of Michigan Journal of Law Reform, 39(3), 433–542.

Roht-Arriaza, N. (1996), 'Of Seeds and Shamans: The Appropriation of the Scientific and Technical Knowledge of Indigenous and Local Communities', Michigan Journal of International Law, 17, 919–966.

Sands, P. (2003), *Principles of International Environmental Law*, Cambridge: Cambridge University Press, chapter 11.

Shiva, V. (1997), *Bio-Piracy: The Plunder of Nature and Knowledge*, Cambridge, MA: South End Press.

Smagadi, A. (2006), 'Analysis of the Objectives of the Convention on Biological Diversity: Their Interrelation and Implementation Guidance for Access and Benefit Sharing', Columbia Journal of Environmental Law, 31, 243–284.

Yu, P.K. (2006), 'Reconceptualizing Intellectual Property Interests in a Human Rights Framework', UC Davis Law Review, 40, 1039–1150.

Index

Abbott, F. 382
Addo, M. 224, 227
Adger, W. 22
Aeck, M. 329
Africa
  FDI, land acquisition and food
    security 63–4
  and GMO 101
  governance and democratic
    structures, weak 42–3
  MNCs' development role and
    poverty alleviation 231
  see also individual countries
Ago, R. 99, 100
Alexander, G. 330
Allee, T. 259
Alston, P. 227
Amnesty International 115
Amoco 70, 71
Anderson, K. 254
Anderson, M. 133, 270
Anghie, A. 13, 15
Angola 63, 114, 115, 124, 127
Antarctic Treaty 88, 182–3
Anuradha, R. 389
Aoki, K. 379, 380
Appleton, A. 121
Arenas, L. 248
Argentina 149
  Aguas v. Argentina cases 156, 324
  *Pulp Mills on the River Uruguay
    (Argentina v. Uruguay)* 88, 101
Arnstein, S. 151
ASEAN 98, 142–3, 156, 203–4, 206–9,
  243
Asia
  irrigation projects, community-
    managed 24–5
  land acquisition and food security
    63–4
  see also individual countries

Attard, D. 369
Australia 95, 208–9
  Australia – Salmon 155
  forum non conveniens principle 280
  legal aid 166
  *Nuclear Tests Case (Australia v.
    France)* 87, 99
Austria 162, 302, 360
Ayes, I. 55

Baker, J. 260
Banisar, D. 162
Bannon, I. 124, 125, 128
Barnes, R. 9, 67
Barnet, R. 218
Barton, B. 104, 106, 324
Bates, B. 303
Baughen, S. 206
Baxi, U. 164, 227, 279
Bayer 225
Bayliss, K. 322, 323
Bedjadoui, M. 48, 49
Belize, *Maya Indigenous Community v.
    Belize* 15–16, 145
Bender, E. 373
Bhagwati, J. 36
Bigge, D. 225
biological resources 365–98
  access and benefit sharing (ABS)
    375–9
  biopiracy and genetic resources
    388–91, 395
  and Bonn Guidelines 378, 379, 384
  conservation and sustainable use
    369–71
  global genetic diversity, reduced 374
  and globalisation 373–91
  intellectual property rights and
    traditional knowledge 379–91
  international arrangements and
    IPRs 385–6